Lecture Notes
in Business Information Processing

283

More information about this series at http://www.springer.com/series/7911

Hubert Baumeister · Horst Lichter
Matthias Riebisch (Eds.)

Agile Processes
in Software Engineering
and Extreme Programming

18th International Conference, XP 2017
Cologne, Germany, May 22–26, 2017
Proceedings

 Springer Open

Editors
Hubert Baumeister
Technical University of Denmark
Kongens Lyngby
Denmark

Horst Lichter
RWTH Aachen University
Aachen
Germany

Matthias Riebisch
University of Hamburg
Hamburg
Germany

ISSN 1865-1348   ISSN 1865-1356   (electronic)
Lecture Notes in Business Information Processing
ISBN 978-3-319-57632-9   ISBN 978-3-319-57633-6   (eBook)
DOI 10.1007/978-3-319-57633-6

Library of Congress Control Number: 2017937714

Printed on acid-free paper

This Springer imprint is published by Springer Nature
The registered company is Springer International Publishing AG
The registered company address is: Gewerbestrasse 11, 6330 Cham, Switzerland

Preface

The 18th XP conference was held 2017 in the wonderful city of Cologne, Germany. In the spirit of past XP conferences, XP 2017 was a place where researchers and practitioners met to exchange new ideas and present their work. These proceedings contain the full research papers, short research papers, and doctoral symposium papers presented at the conference.

In all, 46 research papers were submitted (39 full and seven short papers). All submitted papers went through a thorough review process, with each paper receiving at least three reviews. Finally, the Program Committee accepted 14 papers as full research papers (an acceptance rate of 35%). Moreover, six papers — submitted as short or full research papers — were accepted as short research papers. The selected papers cover a wide range of agile techniques and approaches. Many of them present results of empirical studies aiming to systematically evaluate successful agile practices, others are technology studies that are relevant to both researchers and practitioners.

In the tradition of former XP conferences, the XP 2017 conference program offered many different session topics. Besides the scientific program, i.e., the research track, doctoral symposium, and scientific workshops, the conference featured an industry and practice track, experience reports, and Open Space sessions. Materials from all of these sessions are available on the conference website at www.xp2017.org.

Moreover, three keynotes were given by highly renowned speakers. Andrea Goulet from Corgibytes presented a talk on "Makers and Menders: Putting the Right Developers on the Right Projects" focusing on a group of developers called "menders" – people who love taking an existing project and making it better over time. In his keynote "End-to-End Agility at GitHub" Alain Hélaïli talked about the organization and the efficient workflows at GitHub. Finally, Claes Wohlin from Blekinge Institute of Technology answered the question "Evidence-Driven Change in Software Development: Is It Feasible?"

Many people contributed to the success of the XP 2017 conference. We would like to thank everyone, especially the authors and presenters of all papers, the Program Committee members, the volunteers, and sponsors. Furthermore, we want to express our gratitude to the XP 2017 organizers; they did a great job.

March 2017

Hubert Baumeister
Horst Lichter
Matthias Riebisch

Organization

Organizing Committee

General Chair

Jutta Eckstein   IT communication, Germany

Conference Chairs

Marc Clemens   codecentric AG, Germany
Nils Wloka   codecentric AG, Germany

Academic Program Committee

Academic Program Chairs

Hubert Baumeister   Technical University of Denmark
Horst Lichter   RWTH Aachen University, Germany
Matthias Riebisch   University of Hamburg, Germany

Scientific Workshops

Roberto Tonelli   University of Cagliari, Italy

Poster Chair

Ademar Aguiar   University of Porto, Portugal

PhD Symposium Chair

Stefan Wagner   University of Stuttgart, Germany

Industrial Program Committee

Tutorials/Workshops

Nancy Van Schooenderwoert   Lean-Agile Partners, USA

Working Software

Aslak Hellesøy   Cucumber, UK

Individuals and Interaction

Diana Larsen   FutureWorks Consulting, USA

Customer Collaboration

Ken Power   Cisco Systems, Ireland

Responding to Change

Jan Coupette   codecentric AG, Germany

Experience Reports

Rebecca Wirfs-Brock   Wirfs-Brock Associates, USA
Avraham Poupko   Cisco Systems, Israel

Open Space

Alexander Kylburg   Paragraph Eins, Germany

Program Committee (Research Papers)

Ademar Aguiar   University of Porto, Portugal
Mikio Aoyama   Nanzan University, Japan
Leonor Barroca   The Open University, UK
Hubert Baumeister   Technical University of Denmark, Denmark
Jan Bosch   Chalmers University of Technology, Sweden
Steve Counsell   Brunel University, UK
Torgeir Dingsøyr   SINTEF, Norway
Christof Ebert   Vector Consulting Services, Germany
Hakan Erdogmus   Carnegie Mellon University, USA
Juan Garbajosa   Technical University of Madrid, Spain
Alfredo Goldman   University of São Paulo, Brazil
Des Greer   Queen's University Belfast, UK
Peggy Gregory   University of Central Lancashire, UK
Rashina Hoda   The University of Auckland, New Zealand
Helena Holmström Olsson   Malmö University, Sweden
Casper Lassenius   MIT, USA
Horst Lichter   RWTH Aachen University, Germany
Lech Madeyski   Wroclaw University of Science and Technology, Poland
Michele Marchesi   University of Cagliari, Italy
Sabrina Marczak   Pontifícia Universidade Católica do Rio Grande do Sul,
                                 Brazil
Tommi Mikkonen   University of Helsinki, Finland
Alok Mishra   Atilim University, Turkey
Nils Brede Moe   SINTEF, Norway
Juergen Muench   Reutlingen University and University of Helsinki,
                                 Germany/Finland
Sridhar Nerur   University of Texas at Arlington, USA
Maria Paasivaara   Helsinki University of Technology, Finland
Kai Petersen   Blekinge Institute of Technology/Ericsson AB, Sweden

Matthias Riebisch	University of Hamburg, Germany
Pilar Rodríquez	University of Oulu, Finland
Knut H. Rolland	Westerdals Oslo School of Arts, Communication and Technology, Norway
Bernhard Rumpe	RWTH Aachen University, Germany
Kurt Schneider	Leibniz Universität Hannover, Germany
Helen Sharp	The Open University, UK
Darja Smite	Blekinge Institute of Technology, Sweden
Roberto Tonelli	University of Cagliari, Italy
Rini Van Solingen	Delft University of Technology, The Netherlands
Stefan Wagner	University of Stuttgart, Germany
Xiaofeng Wang	Free University of Bozen-Bolzano, Italy
Hironori Washizaki	Waseda University, Japan
Agustin Yague	Universidad Politecnica de Madrid, Spain

Reviewers (Industry and Practice)

Giovanni Asproni	Asprotunity, UK
Emily Bache	Bache Consulting, Sweden
Filipe Correia	Uphold, Portugal
Aino Corry	Metadeveloper, Denmark
Lisa Crispin	Pivotal, USA
Jutta Eckstein	IT communication, Germany
Sallyann Freudenberg	Sallyann Freudenberg Consulting, UK
Steve Holyer	Steve Holyer and Associates, Switzerland
Lise Hvatum	Schlumberger, USA
Allan Rennebo Jepsen	Core Agile, Denmark
Jason Kerney	Hunter Industries, USA
David Kramer	Agile New England, USA
Casper Lassenius	Aalto University, Finland
Olaf Lewitz	trustartist.com, Germany
Ralph Miarka	sinnvollFÜHREN, Austria
Maria Paasivaara	Alto University, Finland
Dana Pylayeva	Hudson's Bay Company, USA
Seb Rose	Cucumber, UK
Johanna Rothman	Rothman Consulting Group, USA
Aki Salmi	Ambientia, Finland
Andreas Schliep	Das ScrumTeam, Switzerland
Irina Tsyganok	Yoox Net-A-Porter Group
Nils Wloka	codecentric AG, Germany
Joseph Yoder	The Refactory, USA
Joe Wright	Arnold Clark Automobiles, UK

Additional Reviewers

Adam, Kai
Bjørnson, Finn Olav
Britto, Ricardo
Butting, Arvid
Da Silva, Tiago Silva
Díaz, Jessica
Edison, Henry
Fernández-Sánchez, Carlos
Fögen, Konrad

Kautz, Oliver
Kusmenko, Evgeny
Raco, Deni
Santana, Célio
Santos, Viviane
Stray, Viktoria
Vestues, Kathrine
Wang, Yang

Sponsors

"Cologne Cathedral" Sponsor

REWE digital

"Albertus Magnus" Sponsor

Accenture Interactive

"River Rhine" Sponsors

DATEV
EPLAN Software & Service
OPITZ CONSULTING
XebiaLabs

"Kölsch" Sponsor

Hänneschen and Bärbelchen

Organizer

codecentric

Contents

XII   Contents

Improving Agile Processes

Reflection in Agile Retrospectives

Yanti Andriyani[1(✉)], Rashina Hoda[1], and Robert Amor[2]

[1] SEPTA Research, Department of Electrical and Computer Engineering,
The University of Auckland, Building 903, 386 Khyber Pass, New Market,
1023 Auckland, New Zealand
yand610@aucklanduni.ac.nz, r.hoda@auckland.ac.nz
[2] Department of Computer Science, The University of Auckland, Auckland, New Zealand
trebor@cs.auckland.ac.nz

Abstract. A retrospective is a standard agile meeting practice designed for agile software teams to reflect and tune their process. Despite its integral importance, we know little about what aspects are focused upon during retrospectives and how reflection occurs in this practice. We conducted Case Study research involving data collected from interviews of sixteen software practitioners from four agile teams and observations of their retrospective meetings. We found that the important aspects focused on during the retrospective meeting include identifying and discussing obstacles, discussing feelings, analyzing previous action points, identifying background reasons, identifying future action points and generating a plan. Reflection occurs when the agile teams embody these aspects within three levels of reflection: reporting and responding, relating and reasoning, and reconstructing. Critically, we show that agile teams may not achieve all levels of reflection simply by performing retrospective meetings. One of the key contributions of our work is to present a reflection framework for agile retrospective meetings that explains and embeds three levels of reflection within the five steps of a standard agile retrospective. Agile teams can use this framework to achieve better focus and higher levels of reflection in their retrospective meetings.

Keywords: Agile retrospective meeting · Reflection · Levels of reflection · Teams · Agile software development · Reflective practice

1 Introduction

Retrospective meetings embody the 'inspect and adapt' principle of Agile Software Development (ASD) [1, 2]. They are designed to enable agile teams to frequently evaluate and find ways to adjust their process [3]. There are several purposes for retrospective meetings, such as to evaluate the previous work cycle or sprint; to determine the aspects that need to be focused on as areas of improvement; and to develop a team action plan [4]. The purpose and the techniques of the retrospective meeting have been stated and described clearly as a guide for agile teams [2, 5, 6].

Much of the existing research focuses on the techniques of performing retrospective meetings and provides lesser detail about the reflection process involved [5–9]. The Reflective Agile Learning Model (REALM) [7] classified reflection in ASD practices

© The Author(s) 2017
H. Baumeister et al. (Eds.): XP 2017, LNBIP 283, pp. 3–19, 2017.
DOI: 10.1007/978-3-319-57633-6_1

into *reflection-in-action* or reflection that occurs during a practice, and *reflection-on-action* or reflection that occurs post a practice based on definitions of the same by Argyris and Schön [10]. A retrospective meeting was seen to embody reflection-on-action where the agile teams reflect post finishing their sprint [7]. However, what is focused on during retrospectives and how reflection occurs in this practice is not well understood.

To address this gap, we conducted Case Study research by observing four agile teams and interviewing 16 of their members guided by the following research questions:

RQ 1: What aspects are focused on during the retrospective meeting?
RQ 2: How does reflection occur in the retrospective meeting?

2 Related Work

2.1 Agile Retrospective Meeting

There is a standard format commonly used to conduct an agile retrospective meeting which involves *setting the stage, gathering data, generating insight, deciding what to do and closing the retrospective meeting* [2]. *Setting the stage* involves welcoming and explaining the aim of the retrospective meeting. *Gathering data* involves agile teams sharing their review and feedback, reporting on what happened during the previous sprint and briefly discussing with other team members. In *generating insight*, agile teams participate in a further discussion and making agreements about what issues to focus on, and then on how to solve those issues and what areas that need to improve in the *deciding what to do stage. Closing the retrospective* involves summarizing the retrospective meeting and appreciating all team members' efforts.

There are several recommendations for embedding reflective practice within standard agile practices as it is related to team performance improvement [7–9]. Cockburn [8] introduced a reflection workshop which involves collecting issues and generating tasks and decisions. This workshop is performed regularly during or after the post-iteration workshop. Babb et al. [7] investigated reflection in agile practices based on Argyris and Schön's [10] classification and introduced the Reflective Agile Learning Model (REALM). REALM describes how some agile practices embody reflection-in-action and reflection-on-action. Retrospective meetings were seen to embody reflection-on-action where the agile teams reflect post finishing their sprint [7].

Most of the existing research focuses on the techniques of performing a retrospective or identifying a broad classification of the type of reflection that occurs, e.g. reflection-on-action [7]. What actual topics or aspects are discussed during a retrospective and how reflection occurs, however, is not well understood. We build upon these works by investigating the retrospective meeting in depth.

2.2 Reflective Practice

Reflective practice according to Osterman and Kottkamp [11], is defined as *"a means by which practitioners can develop a greater level of self-awareness about the nature*

*and impact of their performance, an awareness that creates opportunities for profes-
sional growth and development".*

Bain et al. [12] classified reflection into five levels: reporting, responding, relating,
reasoning and reconstructing. Level 1 and 2 are *reporting and responding* and enable
learners to share brief descriptions of their experience, their feelings about events, facts
or problems that they encountered. Level 3 is *relating* and involves connecting experience with personal meaning. Understanding at this level occurs when learners try to
highlight good points (e.g. their ability, successful work) and negative points (e.g.
mistakes, failure) to learn and identify areas of improvement. Level 4 is *reasoning* where
learners explore the information shared as well as background knowledge related to the
occurrences. Level 5 is *reconstructing* which signifies a high level of learning where
learners generate the general framework of thinking, which is specified in a plan or action
for responding to similar obstacles in the future.

Our study refers to levels of reflection proposed by Bain et al. [12] and adjusts the
levels into three main levels, i.e. *reporting and responding, relating and reasoning and
reconstructing*, based on our observations of the agile retrospectives in practice.
Reporting and responding are grouped together as the first level as these levels closely
related to reviews sharing and discussions at the beginning of the retrospective meeting.
Relating and responding are grouped as the second level as agile teams participate in a
further discussion after they reported and responded to the reviews. The third level, the
reconstructing level is embodied when agile teams discuss to formulate a plan as an
improvement for the next sprint.

3   Research Method

The aim of this study is to investigate how reflection occurs in retrospective meetings.
Understanding this is particularly important as agile teams are reported to focus more
on their technical progress and tend to pay less attention to how reflection is performed
thereby compromising their potential for improvement [7, 13].

This research is conducted by implementing the Case Study research method [14].
First, existing studies related to reflection in retrospective meetings were reviewed, as
summarized in Sect. 2. The research gaps identified provided guidance on formulating
the interview questions. To gain rich data from interviews, we developed semi-structured questions consisting of main questions and follow-up questions. The data collection method is described in Sect. 3.1 and participant demographics summarized in
Table 1. All interviews and observation data were collected by the first author in person.
The raw data and emerging findings from the analysis were discussed in detail with the
supervisory team (co-authors) who provided feedback and guidance.

3.1   Data Collection

Participants. We wanted to include software practitioners with a minimum of 2 years'
industrial agile experience to participate in our research. During one of the Auckland
Agile meetups, we received interest in participation from an agile team lead working at

Table 1. Team and team members demographics (RMD: Retrospective meeting duration in minutes; P#: Individual participant number; FAP: first agile project)

Team Name	Interviewed/total members	Agile method	RMD and the frequencies	P#	Role	Agile experience (Year)	Agile projects (Total)
Jupiter	5 out of 10	Scrum	65 min (every two weeks)	P1	UI Designer	1	6–8
				P2	Developer	0.5	1
				P3	Developer	7+	6–7
				P4	Business analyst	7+	20+
				P9	Tester	3+	10+
Saturn	6 out of 10	Scrum	55 min (every two weeks)	P4	Business analyst	7+	20+
				P5	Developer	3	10+
				P6	Designer	1 month	FP
				P7	Designer	0.5	FAP
				P8	Tester	3+	6
				P9	Tester	3+	10+
Uranus	2 out of 3	Kanban	45 min (every two weeks)	P10	Tester, Developer	1	2
				P11	Scrum Master, Business Analyst, Product Owner	6	6
Neptune	4 out of 6	Scrum	15 min (when needed)	P12	Tester	2	1
				P13	Developer	1.5	FAP
				P14	Developer	1	FAP
				P15	Tester	<1 year	FAP
Working across all four teams				P16	Test chapter lead	7	10+

the largest online auction company in New Zealand, Trade Me. Trade Me had been practicing agile software development for over three years and provided access to four teams. Its headquarters are located in Wellington and the regional offices are in Auckland and Christchurch.

For confidentiality purposes, the teams are named Jupiter, Saturn, Uranus, and Neptune. The team names and team members' details can be seen in Table 1. Each team consisted of between 3 and 10 members. All members were invited and those willing were interviewed. All teams held retrospective meetings, which lasted for between 15 and 65 min. Sixteen individual practitioners from the four teams participated in the interviews and the observations. All team members had a dedicated role in their team and there were three participants that committed across different teams: P4 was not only fully committed as a Business Analyst in Team Jupiter but also supported Team Saturn. Similarly, P9 was a tester in Team Saturn and a half tester in Team Jupiter. P16 worked as a test lead across all four teams.

Interviews and Observations. Face-to-face individual and one group interview (of six team members) were conducted to gain comprehensive explanations, which would help derive the real concerns from both individual and team perspectives. We conducted one-on-one interviews with all participants (P1–P16), where the duration of individual interviews varied from 35 to 50 min. We asked some semi-structured questions about their experiences and perspectives related to reflection in a retrospective meeting. Some sample questions include: *"Based on the three main points discussed in a retrospective (i.e. what went well, what went wrong, what can you improve), which one(s) do you think are most helpful for your team's reflection?"*, *"How does your team use those points to find solutions and ways to improve? Could you give some real examples?"* and *"What is the outcome of your retrospective meeting? Does your team/scrum master preserve points from the meeting?"*. A sample question of the group interview includes: *"I noticed that your team exhibited some different ways of sharing knowledge, (e.g. post-it notes, verbal communication, drawing). Did it help your team to perform reflection? How?"*

The group interview was conducted immediately after the retrospective meeting of Team Jupiter with six of its team members. Given the variable meeting times, work commitments and deadlines for different teams, it was not possible to gain further team availability for group interviews with the remaining three teams over and above the individual interviews and team observations.

Observations were conducted during the retrospective meetings of all the teams and of their general workplace. The observations aimed to capture the details of the retrospective meeting (i.e. time spent, attendees, and discussion involved) and to help validate the findings from the interviews. Photographs were taken during the observations in order to document the actual situations in the meetings and the report presented by the agile team members. Notes were taken to highlight the important aspects being shared. The information collected (e.g. photographs and notes) from the observations were used to support individual interviews by including the photographs and describing the activities in the retrospective meetings as observed first hand. The duration of each observation depended on how long the team conducted the retrospective meeting. Three out of four teams conducted the meeting for around 40–60 min each and one team, Neptune, had a shorter 15 min' retrospective. Observational data (e.g. photographs and notes) were found to support the findings from the interview data analysis thereby strengthening them.

3.2 Data Analysis

This research involved sixteen individual interviews, one group interview (of six team members), and notes taken from retrospective meeting observations which were analyzed by conducting a thematic analysis. Thematic analysis is a method that aims to recognize, analyze, evaluate and report patterns in data [15], which enables researchers to search across a data set of interviews. Braun and Clarke [15] classify the analysis into six phases: transcribing data, generating initial codes, searching for themes, reviewing themes, defining and naming themes and making a report.

Sixteen interviews were transcribed and imported into NVivo software to facilitate coding and thematic analysis. Generating initial codes involved code identification by analyzing interesting features of a sentence, which were highlighted and added as a node in NVivo representing a new code, such as *identifying and discussing obstacles* and *discussing feelings*. Searching for themes involved comparing data with different codes to see whether they have similar meanings or aspects. Parent themes were classified based on five (grouped into three) levels of reflection, where each code was classified based on the definition of each level.

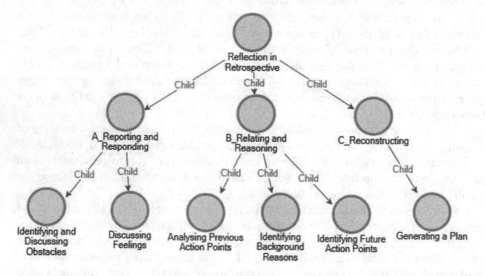

Fig. 1. Levels of reflection in retrospective meetings: a thematic map (using levels of reflection from Bain et al. [12])

Reviewing themes involved generating a thematic model to define the links and the relationships between the themes (see Fig. 1). Defining and naming themes involved the generation of several themes that emerged from the analysis, representing the aspects discussed during retrospective meetings, which was formulated and explained in this paper.

4   Findings

Following the thematic data analysis process, we identified seven themes that represent important topics or aspects discussed in the retrospective meeting, which were then mapped to the five (grouped into three) levels of reflection [12] (see Sect. 2.2).

Table 2 summarizes these themes along with their mapping to the reflection levels. These themes and levels are described below along with pertinent quotes and photographs from observations. The figures below (see Figs. 2 and 3) were captured during the observation and show a glimpse of Team Jupiter and Team Saturn's retrospective meeting.

Table 2. Themes representing topics discussed during retrospectives, their description, examples, and mapping to levels of reflection based on [12].

Levels of reflection	Themes/topics discussed	Description of themes	Examples
Reporting and Responding	Identifying and discussing obstacles	Problems, issues and concern causing blockages	Unfinished tasks and dependencies (e.g. expertise, activity, resource or entity and technical.)
	Discussing feelings	The Subjective response that reflects the situation, fact or events from the previous sprint	Negative and positive feelings
Relating and Reasoning	Analyzing previous action points	Evaluate the process improvement based on previous action points	Some improvement achieved or persisting obstacles
	Identifying background reasons	Analyzing some causes and aspects related to issues on team improvement	Testing environment issue related to external person in different location, who is difficult to contact
	Identifying future action points	Evaluating what areas need to be focused on more to be defined as future action points	Evaluate successful stories and failures
Reconstructing	Generating a plan	Define some action points for the next plan	Action points

Fig. 2. Team Jupiter's retrospective

Fig. 3. Team Saturn's retrospective

4.1 Reporting and Responding

Reporting and responding can be realized when an agile team shares some aspects (e.g. identifying and discussing obstacles and discussing feelings) while providing reviews and feedback of the previous sprint. Each team had different techniques of performing their reviews.

All teams were seen to engage in the reporting level of reflection by actively identified and discussed obstacles and feelings. Similarly, all four teams were seen to be actively involved in responding to their retrospective meeting discussions by providing brief comments on the obstacles and feelings being shared. Teams were seen to report on obstacles such as dependencies and unfinished tasks and respond with negative and positive feelings based on the previous sprint, described below.

Identifying and Discussing Obstacles. Obstacles reported in the retrospective meetings related to the aspects that hindered the team from making progress. During the retrospective meeting, agile teams gathered all the problems that occurred in the previous sprint, which would be useful for the teams to highlight areas of improvement. There were two specific obstacles reported: *dependencies and unfinished tasks*.

Dependencies. Most of the participant (11 out of 16) mentioned dependencies as the specific type of obstacle most commonly reported in the retrospective meeting.

> *"If it's delayed at the first point, if something is wrong at the first point the next person feels it. So, if one brings it up [in the retrospective] and if it's a true concern you will have support because it does affect people." P16 – Test Chapter Lead (Across All Teams)*

By sharing problems about dependencies team members became aware of the other team members' tasks and how they related to their own tasks. By being aware of this issue the team could think about ways to solve the dependency problems.

Unfinished tasks. Unfinished tasks were mentioned by three participants as an obstacle reported in retrospective meetings. An unfinished task was a problem where team members could not accomplish the tasks they had planned or considered the team to be making slow progress.

> *"We were not achieving that daily goal and it is a kind of demotivating... let's say you plan 10 stories for the sprint and you achieve just two or three. The rest we couldn't complete for whatever reason. So, we say that is one thing which didn't go well." P12 – Tester, Team Neptune*

Surfacing this obstacle was helpful for teams to understand how much more effort was required to finish the tasks, what tasks were challenging and why the tasks were difficult to finish. For example, when Team Neptune faced a problem with a requirement that delayed finishing tasks, they asked for clarifications from the product manager. It was evident that dependencies led to unfinished tasks in some cases.

Discussing Feelings. Besides obstacles, agile teams also shared their feelings which were visualized in several forms, e.g. as drawings or journey lines. The feelings shared by team members represented the sense of facts and occurrences from the previous sprint, such as when they were feeling down or happy.

There was an example of positive feelings shared, which had a positive impact on the team's productivity, where their work can be distributed well. Team Neptune recruited an additional tester after they had a problem with tester resource. They felt happy because their team was complete and balanced between developers and testers.

"We do put down smiley. When we got a new tester on board, a new person we had a happy smiley saying that our squad is complete." P12 – Tester, Team Neptune

These obstacles and feelings identified and discussed during the retrospective meeting were supported by our observations of the retrospective meetings of Teams Jupiter, Saturn, and Uranus. It was observed that Team Jupiter reported their review by defining some words on sticky notes (see Fig. 4(a)).

(a) Team Jupiter   (b) Team Saturn   (c) Team Uranus

Fig. 4. (a) Words to describe obstacles and feelings in the Retrospective meeting; (b) and (c) Journey lines visualizing emotions during a sprint in Retrospective meetings

For example, 'muddy' was used to describe a difficult situation where team members had difficulty in understanding the detailed description of specific user stories in the project. Upon asking a team member about what was the meaning of 'muddy', a participant explained:

"So, I think, he and I came up with the term of 'muddy'; from observation - they were really struggling to get the right data and really had to analyse the data for this project. I observed that and for me, I would pick out a description which would explain what I've observed; as a general team.", P1 – User Interface Designer, Team Jupiter.

4.2   Relating and Reasoning

Relating and reasoning can be seen when agile teams compile the obstacles and the feelings shared (from the previous *reporting and responding level*) and investigate the relationship between those aspects. These levels consisted of activities such *as analyzing previous action points, identifying background reasons, identifying future action points.* The explanations below present the results from the individual interviews, which supported by group interview and observations.

Analyzing Previous Action Points. An 'action point' refers to a specific item selected by the team to focus on for improvement. In analyzing previous action points, agile teams referred to the action points agreed upon by the team in the previous retrospective and evaluated the actual effort made by the team on that specific point.

"..that's how you define if you made any changes, we measure yourself based on your action points and that you've actually made changes for. You could make 200 action points of your 20 weeks, but not a single one of those was followed up on, you really haven't done anything." P4 – Business Analyst, Team Jupiter and Saturn

From the example above, it was seen that agile teams reflected on the previous action points by measuring the outcomes achieved by the teams (i.e. good or slow progress). This statement was further supported by the observations where during the retrospective meetings, agile teams shared the process improvement or the failures of the previous sprint.

Identifying Background Reasons. The background reasons of the existing issues were identified when teams were not actively progressing, they would explore the reasons why and what blockers were related to this problem. By identifying the background reasons, teams would understand what aspects needed to be improved.

This point is supported by Team Jupiter's group interview, which a team member tried to identify the reason of the major problem during the retrospective meeting.

"I think we addressed like the major issues are causing the squad stuck at the moment and things like test environment and [..] dealing with an external dependency like platform team in [city name]" P4 – Business Analyst, Team Jupiter and Saturn

During the retrospective meeting observation of Team Saturn, it was seen that there was a cause analysis discussion. For example, when team members shared their sad feelings experienced during the first week sprint, team members shared the reasons, such as unclear user stories or the user story was considered as a big task. The scrum master guided the team to identify the causes by asking why they used the sad feeling notation for the first week. Several reasons were shared, such as too many tasks, the previous estimation and the actual effort were different, the unclear scope of work restricted their progress. Discussing those reasons led to the point where the team realized the main background reason was about inaccurate estimation, i.e. the team had created high achievement expectations for the big tasks without considering the actual effort required.

Identifying Future Action Points. Identifying future action points happened when the teams analyzed previous action points and identified the background issues, which followed by identifying areas of improvement and asking ideas and agreement from the teams. From the discussion, the teams gained the understanding of the existing issues which lead to the thoughts of what areas need to improve and how to improve. Identifying future action points, the teams discussed areas of improvement, which were focused on the process improvement. For example, in the retrospective meeting, most agile teams stressed testing environment issues that delayed the team progress.

"we list down what didn't go well or problems or whatever, we usually derive action points on those things, which is a good way to improve maybe something immediately like getting a test environment set up so we can test something....like a more immediate thing... but there are also action points that are related to the squad as well; determine a team chart or something like that." P2 – Developer, Team Jupiter

From the example above, it was seen that by knowing the existing issues the team to will understand several areas of the process that need to be focused on. To determine future action points the teams also discussed by asking each other's opinions.

"when we discussed it [a plan], we asked other people what they think about it, do they agree or don't they? If everyone says they think they agree with what you are saying, then we say so what the action for that?" P12 – Tester, Team Neptune

During the retrospective observations of Team Saturn, an example of how the team identified their future action points was noted. Team Saturn had identified that the main reason for their slow progress was inaccurate estimation. Some ideas for addressing this included elaborating the stories into small tasks, providing the clear 'definition of done' for specific tasks, and asking for clarifications from the product manager about the scope of work. The team members were asked their opinions and perspectives about these ideas. Most team members agreed on asking for clarifications from the product manager and elaborating the stories into small tasks. Consequently, the Scrum master of Team Saturn made these ideas as official action points for the next sprint.

4.3 Reconstructing

The *Reconstructing* level of reflection seems to happen when a team constructs an agreement on a specific plan based on the team members' perspectives. There were three out of the four teams (Jupiter, Saturn, Uranus) that seemed to engage in the reconstructing level as they performed further discussions and finalized by generating action points.

Generating a Plan. In reconstructing, teams generated plans decided from their discussion in the retrospective meeting. Action points are an explicit outcome of the retrospective meeting. It is useful to remind all team members about the goal for the next sprint, who will responsible, and what are the associated deadlines.

"So, when they go up on their board and they are doing their sprint work, they can see, "Right, let's not forget what came out of this retro" and it is getting ticked off." P11 – Scrum Master, Business Analyst and Product Owner, Team Uranus

This point was brought up in a group interview (of Team Jupiter) where most of the team members agreed that action points were used as a reference for evaluating improvement in the next retrospective meeting.

"umm we pulled out action points on the board. So, over the next two weeks, we will make sure that everything talked about we follow through on." P4 – Business Analyst, Team Jupiter and Saturn

It was observed that Team Jupiter preserved their concrete action points on their Scrum board (see Fig. 5). Another evidence from the observations was Teams Saturn and Uranus did not have action points but their Scrum master made some notes during the meetings and shared verbally the points that needed to be focused on at the end of the retrospective meeting.

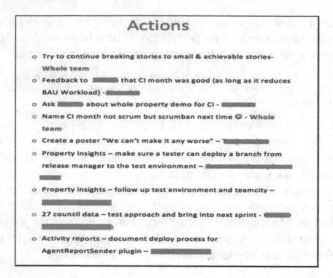

Fig. 5. Action points generated by team Jupiter posted on their Scrum Board (Photo taken during on-site observations)

5 Discussion

We now discuss the findings related to a reflection framework for agile retrospectives including the levels of reflection achieved by the teams studied, implications for practice and limitations of the study.

In response to the RQ1: *What aspects are focused on during the retrospective meeting?* We found that there are six important aspects discussed in the retrospective meetings: *identifying and discussing obstacles, discussing feelings, analyzing previous action points, identifying background reasons, identifying future action points and generating a plan.* In response to the RQ 2: *How does reflection occur in the retrospective meeting?* We found that the reflection that occurs in retrospective meetings can be classified into three levels of reflection [12], *reporting and responding, relating and reasoning, and reconstructing.*

5.1 A Framework of Reflection in Agile Retrospective Meeting

Based on these findings, we present a reflection framework for agile retrospectives (Fig. 6) that combines the five steps of the standard agile retrospective – *set the stage, gather data, generate insight and decide what to do, close the retrospective* – and the levels of reflection – *reporting and responding, relating and reasoning, and reconstructing* [12] within those steps.

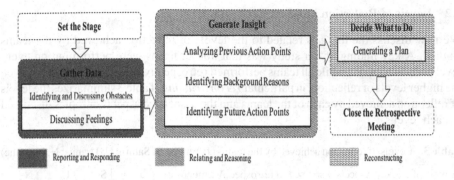

Fig. 6. Reflection in agile retrospective meeting (levels of reflection depicted in shaded areas based on [12])

Setting the stage involves welcoming and explaining the aim of the retrospective meeting. *Gathering data* step embodies the *reporting and responding* level of reflection as agile teams share their reviews (e.g. *identifying and discussing obstacles and discussing feelings*). Identifying and discussing obstacles and feelings in retrospective meetings was seen to correspond to 'descriptive reflection' [16] – a reflection which attempts to answer questions such as: *What is happening? What is this working, and for whom? For whom is it not working? How do I know? How am I feeling? What am I pleased and/or concerned about? What do I not understand?* The obstacles and feelings shared by all team members answer these questions. From the obstacles and feelings reported, the teams would be able to record and collect important points of the previous sprint. By having reviews (e.g. obstacles and feelings) of the previous sprint, team members can be prepared to deal with other similar experiences.

Generating insight step embodies the *relating and reasoning* level, where agile teams are involved in *analyzing previous action points*, *identifying* the *background reasons* behind identified issues and *identifying future action points*. Discussing these aspects was seen to be related to 'descriptive reflection', which attempts to answer questions: *does this relate to any of my stated goals and to what extent are they being met?* [16] and *why the issues happen in the previous sprint?* The answers to these questions support the reflection in the form of comparative analysis and looking back to the background issues, which help agile teams to *determine what areas needed to be focused on*. Agile teams move to deep analysis on ideas or perspective shared to identify future action points for the next sprint. It can be perceived that there is a transformation in the discussion from answering *what is happening?* in the previous sprint; to *what are the alternative views of what is happening?* and *what are the implications of the matter when viewed from these alternative perspectives?* [16]. These questions are answered when all team members provide their accounts about solutions of the obstacles or ways to improve.

In the *deciding what to do* step, agile teams have an explicit formulation which is generated in the form of action points (generating plans). The action points will be used as a reference for agile teams to act upon and improve the process. *Close the retrospective* step involves summarizing the outcomes of the retrospective meeting.

5.2   Levels of Reflection Build on Each Other

We now discuss the findings related to the levels of reflection achieved by the teams studied. A key finding of our study was that not all teams were performing on every level of reflection. So, while all teams performed retrospective meetings, not all achieved the higher levels of reflection, in particular *reconstructing*. Table 3 summarizes the levels of reflection achieved by each of the teams and the associated aspects or topics discussed in each level.

Table 3. Levels of reflection achieved by the teams (J: Jupiter; S: Saturn; U: Uranus; N: Neptune)

Levels of reflection	Aspects discussed in retrospective meeting	J	S	U	N
Reporting and responding	Identifying and discussing obstacles	✓	✓	✓	✓
	Discussing feelings	✓	✓	✓	X
Relating and reasoning	Analyzing previous action points	✓	✓	✓	✓
	Identifying background reasons	✓	✓	✓	✓
	Identifying future action points	✓	✓	✓	X
Reconstructing	Generating a plan	✓	✓	✓	X

Three teams were found to be fully engaged in all levels of reflection and one of the teams, Team Neptune, performed partially on the first two levels and did not achieve the final level of reflection, i.e. reconstructing. Based on the observation of their retrospective meeting, it was seen that they did not discuss their *feelings* explicitly and only discussed briefly the *obstacles* related to changing of task priorities needing confirmation with the product manager. They did not discuss it further as once they agreed on that obstacle then the product manager directly proceeded to the Scrum Board, discussed the issue and wrapped up the meeting. They did not record any outcomes, such as a plan or action points, from the meeting. There was little evidence of analyzing previous action points, identifying background reasons and identifying future action points. Besides, the duration of the meeting was also short, around 15 min, and they reported performing retrospective meetings only when it was necessary. Another interesting observation was that they had adapted the retrospective practice, which seemed too repetitive for them and people often seemed to have forgotten about what happened during the last two weeks' sprint. As result, they were used to placing all the individual reviews written up on sticky notes in a "retro box" – a box especially allocated to collect individual reflection. If there were no sticky notes during a two weeks' sprint, they would not perform a retrospective meeting.

The case of Team Neptune is likely related to the fact that three out of six members of Team Neptune were new to agile projects. They had in effect introduced a new reflective practice, that of using a retro box, as a way to identify the need for conducting a standard retrospective. However, a lack of reaching the reconstruction level suggests that they were not able to generate a plan for improvement as several aspects of the retrospective meeting were missing. Our findings confirm that the levels of reflection are related and build on each other [12]. Furthermore, we show that the highest level of reflection, *reconstructing*, may not be reached at all or not reached effectively until the prior levels are accomplished effectively.

5.3 Implications for Research and Practice

For the researchers in the area of reflective practice and agile teams, our findings present a new perspective for exploring reflective practice in agile teams. Using the framework presented in the previous section, researchers can study agile teams' reflective practice in terms of levels of reflection both in retrospective meetings and other practices that involve reflection (e.g. daily standup, pair programming [7]). Future studies can explore new aspects or topics covered in each level and further explore how the levels build upon each other in different team contexts.

For agile practitioners, our findings show that not all agile teams reach all levels of reflection by simply performing retrospectives. By being aware of the different levels of reflection meant to be achieved in each retrospective step, teams can consciously strive to achieve the most out of their retrospective meetings. In particular, they can see that only *reporting and responding* and *relating and reasoning* levels are not enough rather *reconstructing* to generate action points and following up on those points in future meetings is critical to harnessing retrospective meetings to achieve continuous improvement. Thus, in order to maximize the benefits of their retrospective meetings, we recommend agile teams use our reflection framework (Fig. 6) to self-assess their level as a whole based on their personal understanding of their team context and track it in practice to achieve higher levels of reflection.

5.4 Limitations

A key limitation of this study lies in the fact that observations of a single retrospective meeting per team is not strong enough to establish and confirm a particular team's overall level of reflection. For example, it may be that in other retrospective meetings Team Neptune reached higher levels of reflection. However, the findings were arrived at by combining the data from interviews as well as the observations, which provides multiple perspectives that support the findings. Another related limitation is that the findings are limited to the contexts studied in this research, which in turn are dictated by the availability of participants. Further studies can confirm, adapt, or extend our framework to include different team contexts and reflective practices.

6 Conclusion

Previous studies have focused on specifying the techniques of conducting a retrospective meeting, with little focus on how the reflection in the retrospective meeting actually occurs. One of the key contributions of our work is to present a reflection framework for agile retrospective meetings that explains and embeds five (grouped into three) levels of reflection within the five steps of a standard agile retrospective meeting. Critically, we show that agile teams may not achieve all levels of reflection simply by performing retrospective meetings. As the levels of reflection build upon each other, teams need to effectively identify and discuss their obstacles and feelings in the reporting and responding level, followed by analyzing previous action points, identifying background reasons, and identifying future action points in the relating and reasoning level and generating a plan in the reconstructing level. Embedding these levels of reflection into the retrospective meeting will help agile teams achieve better focus and higher levels of reflection from performing retrospective meetings. Another implication is an increase in their awareness of the main aspects that need to be discussed in the retrospective meeting and how to formulate these aspects to generate a plan for improvement.

Acknowledgement. This research is supported by The University of Auckland and the Indonesia Endowment Fund for Education (LPDP) S-669/LPDP/2013 as scholarship provider from the Ministry of Finance, Indonesia.

References

1. Deemer, P., Benefield, G., Larman, C., Vodde, B.: A Lightweight Guide to the Theory and Practice of Scrum Version 2.0, vol. 2015 (2012)
2. Derby, E., Larsen, D., Schwaber, K.: Agile Retrospectives: Making Good Teams Great. Pragmatic Bookshelf, Raleigh (2006). 0977616649
3. Fowler, M., Highsmith, J.: The agile manifesto. Softw. Dev. **9**, 29 (2001)
4. Sutherland, J., Schwaber, K.: The Scrum Guide. The Definitive Guide to Scrum: The Rules of the Game (2011)
5. Salo, O.: Systematical validation of learning in agile software development environment. In: Althoff, K.-D., Dengel, A., Bergmann, R., Nick, M., Roth-Berghofer, T. (eds.) WM 2005. LNCS (LNAI), vol. 3782, pp. 106–110. Springer, Heidelberg (2005). doi: 10.1007/11590019_13
6. Salo, O., Kolehmainen, K., Kyllönen, P., Löthman, J., Salmijärvi, S., Abrahamsson, P.: Self-adaptability of agile software processes: a case study on post-iteration workshops. In: Eckstein, J., Baumeister, H. (eds.) XP 2004. LNCS, vol. 3092, pp. 184–193. Springer, Heidelberg (2004). doi:10.1007/978-3-540-24853-8_21
7. Babb, J., Hoda, R., Nørbjerg, J.: Embedding reflection and learning into agile software development. IEEE Softw. **31**, 51–57 (2014). doi:10.1109/MS.2014.54
8. Cockburn, A., Highsmith, J.: Agile software development: the people factor. Computer **34**, 131–133 (2001)
9. Dingsøyr, T., Hanssen, G.K.: Extending agile methods: postmortem reviews as extended feedback. In: Henninger, S., Maurer, F. (eds.) LSO 2002. LNCS, vol. 2640, pp. 4–12. Springer, Heidelberg (2003). doi:10.1007/978-3-540-40052-3_2
10. Argyris, C., Schon, D.A.: Organisational Learning II: Theory, Method and Practice. Organisation Development Series. Adisson Wesley, Reading (1996)
11. Osterman, K., Kottkamp, R.: ReflectivePractice for Educators: Improving Schooling through Professional Development. Corwin Press, Newbury Park (1993)
12. Bain, J.D., Ballantyne, R., Packer, J., Mills, C.: Using journal writing to enhance student teachers' reflectivity during field experience placements. Teachers Teach. Theor. Pract. **5**, 51–73 (1999). doi:10.1080/1354060990050104
13. Hoda, R., Babb, J., Nørbjerg, J.: Toward learning teams. IEEE Softw. **30**, 95–98 (2013). doi: 10.1109/MS.2013.90

14. Yin, R.K.: Case Study Research: Design and Methods. Sage Publications, Inc. (2003)
15. Braun, V., Clarke, V.: Using thematic analysis in psychology. Qual. Res. Psychol. **3**, 77–101 (2006)
16. Jay, J.K., Johnson, K.L.: Capturing complexity: a typology of reflective practice for teacher education. Teach. Teacher Educ. **18**, 73–85 (2002)

What Influences the Speed of Prototyping? An Empirical Investigation of Twenty Software Startups

Anh Nguyen-Duc[1(✉)], Xiaofeng Wang[2], and Pekka Abrahamsson[1]

[1] Department of Computer and Information Science (IDI), NTNU, 7491 Trondheim, Norway
{anhn,pekkaa}@ntnu.no
[2] Free University of Bozen-Bolzano, Piazza Domenicani 3, 39100 Bolzano, Italy
xiaofeng.wang@unibz.it

Abstract. It is essential for startups to quickly experiment business ideas by building tangible prototypes and collecting user feedback on them. As prototyping is an inevitable part of learning for early stage software startups, how fast startups can learn depends on how fast they can prototype. Despite of the importance, there is a lack of research about prototyping in software startups. In this study, we aimed at understanding what are factors influencing different types of prototyping activities. We conducted a multiple case study on twenty European software startups. The results are two folds; firstly we propose a prototype-centric learning model in early stage software startups. Secondly, we identify factors occur as barriers but also facilitators for prototyping in early stage software startups. The factors are grouped into (1) artifacts, (2) team competence, (3) collaboration, (4) customer and (5) process dimensions. To speed up a startup's progress at the early stage, it is important to incorporate the learning objective into a well-defined collaborative approach of prototyping.

Keywords: Prototype · MVP · Prototyping-learning loop · Validated learning · Speed · Software startups

1 Introduction

With the startup movement, software industry is witnessing a paradigm shift from serving customer requirements to creating customer value. The challenge for software companies is no longer primarily on implementing customer requirements, but rather on finding customer demands and providing a solution that delivers customer value [2]. Addressing uncertainty in both solution and problem domains has often been ad-hoc and based on guesswork, which becomes one of the main reasons for failing startup companies [3]. A demand on systematic approaches to manage the uncertainty has led to an increased research interest on Lean Startup [4], New Product Development (NPD) [5], software startups [6] and continuous experimentation [7].

In a competitive environment such as software industry, time-to-market is becoming more and more critical as a success factor for startup companies. Business ideas under development once revealed can be easily threatened by high speed copycats [9]. Moreover, competitors can also follow an on-going journey of validating product-market fit

H. Baumeister et al. (Eds.): XP 2017, LNBIP 283, pp. 20–36, 2017.
DOI: 10.1007/978-3-319-57633-6_2

and arrive faster in the destination. Regardless of company sizes and application domains, the knowledge of influencing factors for a quick learning loop is important for software startups to form best-fit strategy in developing business experimentation [10].

A 'Build-Measure-Learn' loop, as a central concept of the Lean Startup methodology, aims at speeding up the new product development cycle [4]. The central part of the loop is to build a representation of the business, a so-called Minimum viable product (MVP), to collect feedback from customers and to learn from that. Steve Blank emphasizes the goal of MVPs is *"to maximize learning through incremental and iterative engineering"* [2]. In the startup context, developers quickly and iteratively develop a software application to validate business ideas [12]. As such, the study of validated learning can be beneficial from Software Engineering (SE) concepts and practices, such as rapid prototypes and evolutionary prototypes [13–15]. Consequently, the time-to-release of prototypes is essential to determine the total time in the validated learning loop.

Software startup research is increasingly recognized by researcher's community, with many practical aspects, such as User Experience, Software practices, competences and startup ecosystem [6]. Despite of the importance, there is a lack of research about prototyping in software startups. In a multi-influenced context with funding, human resource and market concerns, it is crucial to understand how the speed of learning can be supported by prototyping activities and what are the influencing factors. In a previous study, we investigated how a prototype is built in software startups [12]. We found that prototyping activities as a core value of startup experimentation needed to be seen as a multifaceted phenomenon [12]. In this work, we are particularly interested in the factors that slow down the learning process and those that speed it up. The research question (RQ) is:

What factors influence the speed of prototyping in software startups?

The paper is organized as follows. Firstly, we present the background about business-driven experimentation in software projects, software prototype and a proposal of an analytical model of startup prototyping (Sect. 2). Then, we describe our research approach and the cases studied (Sect. 3). After that, the qualitative findings are presented (Sect. 4). Finally, we reflect on the findings, the threats to validity (Sect. 5), and draw the conclusion and future work (Sect. 6).

2   Background

2.1   Business Driven Experimentation

From SE perspective, validated learning means the focus on integrating business value in defining software development processes and practices. Even though experiment systems are recognized as beneficial to software projects, there are barriers in adopting them, such as integration of customer feedback, synchronizing vendors in short cycles and lack of reasoning about customer requirements [16, 17]. Bosch et al. [18] advocate for adjusting the Lean startup methodology to accommodate the development of multiple ideas and to integrate them when time for their testing and validation is too long. Bosch suggested using 2-to-4-week experimentation iterations followed by exposing the product to customers in order to collect feedbacks. Fagerholm et al. present a model for continuous experimentation for start up companies [7], in which a key element is the ability to release a prototype with suitable instrumentation, to manage experiment plans, link experiment results with a product roadmap, and to manage a flexible business strategy. Olsson et al. present a Hypothesis Experiment Data-Driven Development model that integrates feature experiments with customer feedback in Agile projects [19]. While these work characterize a process-like approach in developing startups' software products, Paternoster et al. grounded a model from 13 software startups which describes a pattern that software startups often build evolutionary prototypes [20]. This study focuses on how startups are prototyping in reality and the influencing factors of the speed of learning by prototyping.

2.2 Prototype and Prototyping Activities

Brook mentioned "*In software engineering, at least, the concept of rapid prototyping has a name and a recognized value, whereas it does not always have the same status in computer design and in building architecture*" [21]. Prototyping implies a quick and economic approach that serves to achieve understanding of what final products should be [15]. From a technical perspective, prototypes can be differentiated according to its relation to later product development. Throwaway prototypes are used mainly for specification purposes; and they are not used as actual building blocks [15]. They are mostly used in exploratory and experimental prototyping. Evolutionary prototypes provide a basis for a real system, which is evolved out of the prototypes; they are used in evolutionary prototyping but can also be found in experimental prototyping (if it shows that they provide a good basis for a system) [15].

From a business perspective, startups can create a representation of product ideas, a so-called MVP, without actual product implementation. Eric Ries describes a classification of different types of MVPs [4], which are commonly used in the startup communities. For instance, a MVP can be a short animation that explains what a product does and why users should buy it. It can also be a user interface that looks like a real working product, but the actual business process is manually carried out (Wizard of Oz MVP). A concierge MVP is a manual service that consists of exactly the same steps users would go through with the product.

A few research paid attention on improving prototyping activities, such as the speed and effectiveness [28, 29]. Janssen et al. suggested code reuse to speed up writing code to prototype [28]. Grevet et al. described a 6-stage prototyping approach to speed up throw-away prototyping for new social computing systems using existing online systems [29]. In our work, we address the speed of prototyping from a socio-technical perspective, considering prototyping activities under human, market, finance and team factors.

2.3   A Prototype-Centric Learning Model in Software Startups

The Build-Measure-Learn loop is a key concept in Lean Startup [4]. The loop is used to manage and to operate software startups in finding a sustainable business model. A key idea is to minimize waste and to focus only on the elements, which will be tested. Lynn et al. describe another cycle, Probe and Learn, that is applicable to manage uncertainties about market, technology and time-to-market [25]. The authors suggest that startups should go to customers with an early version of a product to learn about the market, different applications and segments. Nguyen-Duc et al. propose a hunter-gather double loop to capture the evolution of startup activities from idea to achieving a product market fit [26]. The model visualizes the portion of product development vs. customer development activities across the startup stages. While these studies provide an emphasis on organization and evolution, they are well landed in an abstract space, not straightforward to apply from the SE perspective.

In the SE literature, Gordon et al. propose a rapid prototyping system approach to understand the prototype development of a system [27]. In the model, both low-fidelity and high-fidelity prototypes are essential parts of developing a system [27]. Preliminary product design activities create a throwaway prototype from the problem domain. A series of throwaway low-fidelity prototypes can be created to capture the ideas of what to built. Similarly, high-fidelity prototypes can also be evolved several times before reaching the product launch.

A literature survey of software development shows that startups often build a prototype in an evolutionary fashion and quickly learn from users' feedback [20]. We argue that both throwaway prototypes and evolutionary prototypes are important parts of startups' journey to a launched product. From the Lean startup perspective [4], learning is an input and also an outcome for a prototype. We tailored the double loop model in the previous work [26] by adapting Gordon's system prototyping elements [27] to capture the prototyping processes in the startup context, as shown in Fig. 1. The model focus on prototyping as the core concept and compose four loops:

- Idea-prototype loop: iterations of refining business idea through throwaway prototyping
- Throwaway prototype loop: iterations of constructing and learning from throwaway prototypes
- Evolutionary prototype loop: iteration of constructing and learning from evolutionary prototypes
- Pivot loop: starting a new cycle from the current product to a pivoted idea

Considering the model as a state-based system, it is possible to travel from a state to any other one. However, the typical flow would happen within two loops. It can also happen that a startup starts the loop from any state, for example, by doing a throwaway prototype before getting to a stated problem. In the scope of this work, we did not go in-depth about how these loops happen in our cases. The work will explore factors that occur during the startup progress and influence throw-away and evolutionary prototyping.

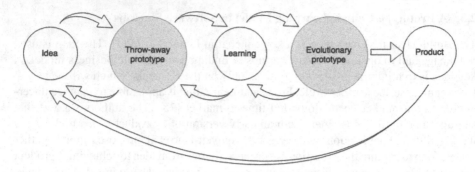

Fig. 1. A prototype-centric learning model in software startups

3   Research Approach

3.1   Multiple Case Study Design

This study is one part of a larger research activity that investigates the role of engineering activities in software startups. The objective is to explore commonalities, challenges and engineering patterns in software startups, from the business idea to a launched product. This study reports the findings from empirical data regarding prototyping activities. We conducted multiple case studies for a robust result in typical software startup population [11]. The unit of analysis is a startup company. We aimed at collecting as many startups as possible for a variety of the sample. As the aim is to reflect the state-of-practice rather than finding a secret recipe of success, we included startups in different stages and with different revenue statuses.

There is often a difficulty in identifying a real startup case among other similar phenomenon, such as freelancers, SMEs or part-time startups. We defined five criteria for our case selection: (1) a startup that operates for at least six months, so their experience can be relevant, (2) a startup that has at least a first running prototype, (3) a startup that has at least an initial customer set, i.e. first customer payments or a group of users, (4) a startup that has an intention to scale their business model, (5) a startup that has software as a main part of business core value.

The process of identifying and collecting data was done in 11 months, from March 2015 to February 2016. Cases were searched from four channels, (1) startups within the professional networks of the authors, (2) startups in the same town with the authors, (3) startups listed in Startup Norway and (4) Crunchbase database. The contact list includes 219 startups from Norway, Finland, Italy, Germany, Netherlands, Singapore, India, China, Pakistan and Vietnam. After sending out invitation emails, we received 41 feedbacks, approximately 18.7% response rate. Excluding startups that are not interested in the research, or startups that do not pass our selection criteria, the final set of cases are 20 startups, aliased as S1 to S20.

3.2 Data Collection and Analysis

Semi-structured individual interviews were used to collect data, since they enable the focus on pre-defined research topics and flexible structures to discover unforeseen information [28]. Methodological triangulation in data collection is also implemented by using evidence from documents and observations (in S01-S05, S09). Business documents, such as business model canvases and business plans were exposed to the research team as a preliminary step prepared for interviews. Observations were useful to understand how prototypes were implemented and used in the working environment.

The interviewees were asked questions about (1) business background (2) idea visualization and prototyping (3) product development (4) challenges and lessons learnt. The stories about startup ideas, prototypes and product development is organized into the schema as described in Fig. 1. Most of the interviews were conducted by the first author, with the attendance of a second researcher (the third author or sometimes external researchers in our network). This researcher has a long experience conducting interviews in software companies. Each interview lasted from 55 min to 70 min and the interviewees were informed about the audio recording and its importance to the study.

We used a thematic analysis – a technique for identifying, analyzing, and reporting standards (or themes) found in qualitative data [22]. We started by reading all interview transcripts and relevant documents, and coded them according to open coding [22]. A set of pre-determined categories were used to guide the coding process, as we have some interests in topics of (1) business original, (2) prototyping practices (3) pivoting (4) testing (5) challenges and (6) key performance indicators (KPIs). We attempted to label all meaningful text segments with appropriate codes. To feed data to this study, we filtered the codes that are related to prototyping, technical implementation, and testing activities prior to product launching. According to Sect. 2.2, throwaway prototypes were low-fidelity artifacts, such as mockup, wireframe, or simple code. Evolutionary prototypes were perceived as product building blocks, such as heavy code activities, i.e. feasibility testing of functionality, building new feature, etc. The relationship of the factors to the speed of prototyping or production was identified via text about challenges, or text specifying consequence on time-to-market or time to collect user feedback. We noted and reported evidence on prototyping as follows (1) factors that relate to prototyping activities in generals, (2) factors that slow down the prototyping activities and (3) factors that speed up the prototyping activities.

3.3 Case Description

The characteristics of our cases are given in Table 1. It is noticeable that a large number of the studied cases deliver peer-to-peer services as marketplaces or platforms (S01, S02, S03, S07, S08, S11, S13, S16, S20). There are also cases that deliver value in Business-to-Business model (B2B) (S04, S06, S10, S12, S15, S17). The cases are dominantly characterized by web-based and mobile-based software product with client-server architecture. We also identified the product focuses in early and later phases of the software startups [23]. Among them, there are some startups with annual revenue of one million euro or more (S06, S09).

Regarding the development strategy, interestingly, there are seven cases (35%) that have (parts of) product developed outside company boundary.

Table 1. Startup cases characteristics

Code	Product type	Early focus	Later focus	Dev. strategy	No. of prot.	Dev. method.
S01	Photo marketplace	Feature		Insource	2	Agile
S02	News generator	UX	New feature	Outsource	4	Agile
S03	Homemade food market	UX		Insource	2	Adhoc
S04	Construction management	Simple feature	New feature	Outsource	5	Distributed agile
S05	Underwater camera	Feasible technology		Outsourcing, subcontracting	7	Informal agile
S06	Sale visualization tool	UX	Flexible, scalable	Insource	3	Informal scrum
S07	Location recommendation	Feature, UX		Insource	3	Informal agile
S08	Ticket platform	Intuitiveness, friendliness	Scalable and new features	Outsource	2	Agile
S09	Educational quiz system	User friendliness	Scalable, Stable	Insource	5	From adhoc to distributed agile
S10	IoT OS platform	Ecosystem	Functionality	Insource	4	NO INFO.
S11	Ticket platform	User friendly, simple	More features, complexity	Insource	2	Adhoc
S12	Elearning platform	Feature		Insource	3	Agile
S13	Shipping services	NO INFO.	NO INFO.	Outsource	3	NO INFO.
S14	News services	Feature provider	Platform as a service	Insource	2+	Continuous development
S15	Smart grid application	NO INFO.	NO INFO.	Insource	NO INFO.	NO INFO.
S16	Secondhand marketplace	innovative feature	Product line	Insource	3	NO INFO.
S17	Simulation based training	UX, feature	Flexibility, Scalability	Insource	2 +	NO INFO.
S18	Open source messenger	Community	Feature	Open source	4	Adhoc
S19	Location based alert system	UX	Feature and enhanced UX	Insource	5	Agile
S20	Elearning system	User friendliness	Standardization	Insource	2	Agile

Notation: NO INFO. means missing information

The major reported development methodology is Agile, with iterative deliveries and frequent customer feedback: *"… Scrum based development, sprints of two weeks, standup, wrap-up meeting, we like to work in this way."* (S06). In some cases, the company reports a type of informal Agile process: *"… fully informal but truly agile process with working release maintained, … iterative development of functionality and refactoring"* (S05)

One specific question asked to interviewees is how many prototypes have been made before product launching. The answers vary from two to seven prototypes, either throw-away or evolutionary ones, before a launch. In many cases, we considered prototypes as a tangible artifact that is experimented with (potential) users, customers and internal/external stakeholders.

4 Result

Figure 2 describes the influencing elements on throw-away prototyping (detail on Sect. 4.1) and evolutionary prototyping (detail on Sect. 4.2). It should be noticed that the direction of impact is not given. Some elements specifically show the positive/negative influences while other elements remain as general observations.

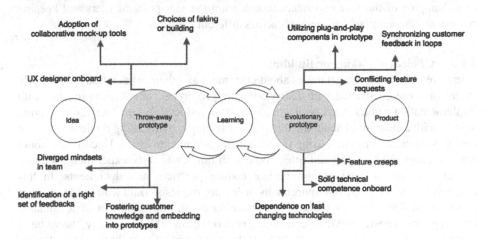

Fig. 2. Factors influencing the prototype-centric learning loops

4.1 Elements Influencing Throwaway Prototyping

4.1.1 Adoption of Collaborative Mock-up Tools

By adopting various tools, i.e. paper sketch, GUI mockups and wireframe tools, startups achieve a fast and an economic prototype without any technical expertise, as described in (S02, S09, S11, S13). In these cases, startups conducted very short iterations, from a few days (S02, S11, S13) to a few weeks (S09), from a product or a service idea to having the first user feedback. In S04, printing GUI layout in papers is reported as a good practice for teamwork, especially improving the customer involvement: "*normally we draw in the piece of paper first and then we make mock-ups... and then the customer joins us on that journey, then we click on the paper, we go to another one ...*" (S04). It is also common that startups build mockups by using cloud-based software services. For such an online tool, the teamwork mode is reported as an important feature that facilitates collaborative design efforts among distributed team members (S02).

4.1.2   UX Designer Onboard

Business side of a startup (often CEOs) is always in a need of expressing and visualizing their ideas into more tangible artifacts. By doing that, sitting next to a designer is highly desirable for CEOs in early stages. In S02, the CEO expresses the need for a close collaboration with a designer in team: *"In this case, I would really like a designer that sits here together with us ..."* (S2). The role of a design in mobile application is highlighted in another discussion with S2: *"You might think of user interface as a make-up for a person. But I think UI is the capacity that an app needs to interact with people."* It happens similarly in S12, when the CEO mentions about the process of designing the graphical part of their prototypes: *"The alternative is to create a specification ... and just developing that document and all the process around it is typically very resource intensive. We talk about a future, ... we make a prototype at a first phase implementation and then we adjust from there based on dialogues in between us."* (S12). For frontend-rich applications, a designer is a champion of the user experience, considering the viewpoint of users and keeping consistency among graphical elements across different platforms.

4.1.3   Choices of Faking or Building

There are often many uncertainties about customers and their expectations in the early stages of startups. Starting with a single-feature prototypes, or other approaches with implementation come always with a risk of wasting effort. It is considered time-saving to start with a clear mind about the throw-away strategy, by focusing on demonstrating business value rather than reusing the technical components (S02). Uncertainty about what to build and how to build often come with quick and dirty experiments without proper architectural designs, appropriate coding practices and documents. In this manner, frequent change of requirements or feature requests could lead to the increase of technical debts in later phase. Experimenting by the development of a runnable prototype was a costly and time-consuming experience in S09. In this way, the value of a prototype should exceed its cost. In S03, the development team has a clear plan for experimenting without *"making the product"* until they get the right product design. S11 applies the concept of *"fake it until you make it"*, to simulate a final product without primary quality, both with functionalities and user experience. However, the focus on the speed has also led to the minimum part of viability. In S11, customer demonstration was done in a wizard of oz manner [4], customer interacting with an actual user interface, but business logics and backend functionality were done by manual work. Even though it is inefficient, the approach is easy and fast to build.

4.1.4   Collaboration Across Diverged Mindsets

We observed that in most of the cases, the ideas came from the CEOs, who are often business people or serial entrepreneurs. While the decisions about what the products should do come from a business mindset, they are implemented by developers with a technical mindset. In some cases (S01, S04, S05), there are challenges in communicating the product ideas and convincing the developers about the product value. In S04, it took as much time to discuss on the value proposition as to sketch a mockup. Vice versa, the communication of technical difficulties is also a time-consuming task, as mentioned by a developer in S05: *"She [the CEO] is very sharp about business and finance stuffs, but it takes a long discussion to explain her about the importance of having flexible product design ..." (S05).* The communication challenge might also happen between startups and customers, when no concrete prototypes are provided: *"We work with a customer organization, learn how they have worked with the current solutions and describe our proposal via the prototype. It is hard for them to realize the benefit without concrete examples..." (S04).* It also appears that a prototype is late released due to the wrong estimation of the CEO, who has no technical background. For example, in S1, the CEO insisted on a customer feedback having a new field in a frontend form, which caused the change of both business logic layer and data table structure.

4.1.5   Identification of a Right Set of Feedbacks

Steve Blank emphasizes the importance of early involvement of end users in product development [2]. Particularly, in startups developing products for mass market (or B2C business model), the feedback from the representative users of a market segment is essential. Nevertheless, not all users' input is equally valuable to product development. It was difficult to find the customer feedback that is useful for validating hypotheses in S02: *"I have attended a various types of events like that. To be honest, there are not so many interesting things there ..."* (S02). The CEO wandered in town and talked to different people about the product idea. However, the approach is quickly found inefficient, as the users' feedbacks are often shallow. After that, the CEO targeted a group of innovative users from startups and research community and documented many interesting ideas for the product features. The integration of such lead users, *"whose strong needs will become general in a market-place months or years in the future"* [24], appears to be an important factor to accelerate the speed of startup learning. Lead users are also able to contribute via suggestions, testing and feedback, or even participate in the development and co-creation of new products or services, as observed in S14: *"We always do that in a close relation to our actual client stakeholders. Once we decide to narrow it on a new product area, the first thing we do is to get a partnership with a customer so that we can work together on a daily basis as stakeholders and product developers..."* (S14).

4.1.6   Fostering Customer Knowledge and Embedding into Prototypes

Prototypes can be seen from three different perspectives, function, look-and-feel and role, in which role is the representation of usability of the prototype [2]. In order to maximize lessons learned from a prototype, the vision on how end-users adopt a final product need to be visualized and captured in the prototype. As the actual end users are often not well known in the early phases, the integration of the user's role into the prototype design is a fuzzy task. The time pressure on prototyping makes startups skip a detailed analysis of users' behaviors. It seems that the adoption of customer/ market analysis tools are not so common in our startup sample. In S02, the CEO emphasized the role of mapping tools, such as a customer journey map to describe the customer's experience: *"I have been told by my friends about the tool [a customer journey map]. We used it to describe how customer interact with the system and where could be the gap" (S02).*

4.2 Elements Influencing Evolutionary Prototyping

4.2.1 Utilizing Plug-and-Play Components in Prototype

Utilizing ready-made components, such as Open source software (OSS) libraries and frameworks unlocks the capacity of experimenting functional as well as non-functional features. The adoption of OSS components was mentioned in all of the cases, from using tools (S19), integration of OSS code (S02, S03, S05, S20), to participation in OSS community (S18). The main benefits include reduced development cost and faster time-to-release, which were mentioned by the CTOs of (S19) and (S20): *"...we might not even come to the idea of making it happen if we do not have OSS as an experiment. Without OSS it would take a lot of time and very costly"* (S19). It is an even more obvious choice in open source type of platforms: *"It is very hard nowadays not to use OSS artifacts, especially when with Android development ..."* (S20). It also appears that many advanced technologies were adopted via using OSS: *"A core part of our product includes a machine learning algorithm. We are lucky enough to find ml library in C++, entirely OSS, super cool"* (S02). By taking ready-made components, startups also reduce prototyping time by simplifying architectural aspects to some existing patterns.

4.2.2 Synchronizing Customer Feedback in Loops

Communication among team members or between a startup company and its external stakeholders is found as a significant factor delaying an iteration release. Insufficient communication due to misunderstanding, cultural difference, language barrier, lack of supporting tools happens often in outsourcing and remote partnership scenarios (S01, S09): *"Basically, we found some limitations that made it difficult to be efficient in the way to communicate. And since we're teams in different places it's really important that information flow works and also to make sure that all people—don't have to be involved in everything, and be able to group efficiently and create like projects, and store documents, and all these things, and have video-share links, and articles, and all these things."* (S09). The misunderstanding and reworking also happens when customers are distant to developers and the customer feedbacks are not fully perceived. In S13, the CEO and sales people interacted with customers and collected insightful feedback from them. However, the feedback is not communicated efficiently to the development team in other locations. This leads to unnecessary re-work with communication and implementation effort and hence slows down the time to release.

4.2.3 Conflicting Feature Requests

It is a typical situation that evolutionary prototypes are built based on feature requests from the first customers. Gradually, when having more customers, new feature requests might vary from the business direction or even conflict with the previous functionalities. S14 describes how they handled such situation: *"either we solve them by providing them different products or we do ignore parts of the market... We make a very clear statement to what we think the future of journalism is, then we pursue that and the cost of that is neglecting parts of our market"* (S14). Similarly, S15 expresses how their product evolved through different iterations: *"There will always be requirements arriving... Sometimes the new requirements disrupt the old requirements. At the moment, we are working to disrupt the old products"* (S15). Considering what to develop and which features to include adds complexity to future releases. Additionally, requests coming in the middle of the development sprint from large customers might influence the feature priority and delay the release further: *"We're in that situation all the time, it's very difficult to say no because giant customers telling you we need that functionality. If you're going to have us as customers you're going to have to make it, we need it in the contract that you have to make it. We also build it, we built it bigger and bigger"* (S11).

4.2.4   Feature Creeps

Many startups add new features to fit the prototype to a changing group of early customers. This leads to two possible challenges of satisfying customer demands, so-called (1) feature creep and (2) product portfolio. Feature creep refers to the addition of features to a product in a continuous manner: *"We are adding features all the time. This is not a product that will ever stop evolving. We will always have a strong engineering team to develop the product forward. We are not talking about maintenance here. We are talking about this being the core of the company's competence"* (S13). Startups rarely have a requirement management process to manage product complexity. Consequently, feature creeps are considered harmful to the production and enhancement of core features.

Moreover, this can be an unwanted expansion that requires changes also in the product architecture and even in the strategic direction. In S04, after the first two releases addressing a construction manager's requirements, the third release was developed for a construction operator's demands. Consequently, S04's product scope has grown from a single feature MVP to a supply-chain management system: *"So then we had a small one just for easy communication between users of the building and the maintenance guys... So the second feature was to manage document flow. And the third was to have a 3D model of the building. And all these things here we spent a lot of time and we were building in parallel with different prospects"* (S04).

In a larger scale, the expansion could lead to deriving a product portfolio. Startups face with challenges of keeping both the focus to increase the quality of core delivered values and satisfaction of important customers. While not all good ideas can be turned into features, some ideas are selected to develop further and might become the core value providers for startups.

4.2.5   Solid Technical Competence Onboard

In several cases (S09, S01, S03, S06) the technical competence determines the speed of feature releasing. Startups' technical members are required to possess good technical skills and they also need to be productive in an ambiguous development environment: *"We don't hire people basically for them being cheap because we don't have time. Our challenge is time and to be more productive other kind of competing companies ... it's much better to have people that can—within a short time, could produce good code*" (S09). It is also important to write code in a clean and structured manner, to be quality-aware in the early phases: "*The back end was pretty good because he had hired my boss at my current company ... there was some friction there in how to develop systems between the professional programmer, my boss, and the copy paste programmers. I think that also contributed to it not working.*" (S11). The combination of technical competence and customer understanding is emphasized in another case: "*... It is very hard to find people both good at technology and have a good sense of commercial edge...*" (S08).

4.2.6 Dependence on Fast Changing Technologies

Startups often struggle with thriving in a technical uncertainty, whether under market pull or technology push impacts [20]. Due to different reasons, e.g., specific devices, platforms or protocols becoming popular in market, or new technology gaining momentum, there are needs for changing the current product's features to accommodate new technology (S01, S09, S11). In a small scale, for instance, the adoption of new animation effects, a different type of map, etc. leads to an extension of the current or coming iterations. In S02, the development of an IOS application is delayed after the codebase and all dependent libraries were forced to be upgraded to a newer version of Swift. The team took time to resolve all the changes so the next release can be done in Swift 3.0. The technology uncertainty is expected with mobile applications, as stated by the CEO of S11: "*...at the moment we are changing the technology platform. This perhaps has been the biggest challenge we have decided where to stand and make a new platform on development technology... So next generation which will be out in the market place around summer next year will be quite heavily rearranged.*" (S11). In a large scale, the technical change can lead to a change of business directions.

5   Discussion

5.1   Reflections on the Results

We captured what happened during the early phases of the studied twenty software startups. We identified the factors that are found to influence the speed of prototyping across different types of prototypes. They can be grouped into (1) Artifacts, (2) Team competence, (3) Collaboration, (4) Customer and (5) Process dimensions. **Artifacts** include collaborative tools and reusable components. The practices of adopting artifacts are important for saving time of prototyping user interfaces and functionalities. The issue here is to select the suitable tools and components to match the prototyping's purposes. The requirement of **team competence** might vary due to the type of prototyping and the type of products. For instance, UI-rich application would require a designer onboard at the early stage while a good developer in the later stage. **Collaboration**, including efficient communication of visions and tasks among startup teams and interaction with external stakeholders, is important for shorten the learning loops. Besides, how **customers** are involved in the prototyping loops has an impact on the duration of the prototyping. While inappropriate customer feedback delays the learning and creates more prototyping loops, too many requests from customers delay the time-to-release and introduce complexity to product management. Last but not least, prototyping is performed under many uncertainty and dependencies. Defining practices and **processes** to support decision-making under uncertainties would help in prototyping.

5.2 Threats to Validity

There are several threats to validity worth discussing [1]. One internal threat to validity is the bias in the data collection, as the data might not represent the comprehensive case. This is worth discussing as most of the cases are represented by one interview. In order to mitigate this threat, we selected CTO and CEO as interviewees, who have the best understanding about their startups. We also use other types of data sources, such as documents and observations to increase our understanding about the cases (S01 – S05, S09). The participative observations in S01 and S02 enabled deeper insights that go beyond cross-sectional interviews. A construct validity threat is the possible inadequate descriptions of constructs. We tried at our best to collect contextual information about the startups, from social media and personal contacts. When analyzing data, the coding process of interview transcripts was assisted by the authors' prior knowledge about prototyping and validated learning. This helped to focus on the investigated phenomenon without losing relevant details.

The external validity is normally not addressed by case study research. Our result is grounded on twenty cases, with diversity in company size, application domain, financial model, and growth stage and organization structure, which adds the robustness to our findings. Many themes, such as Sect. 4.1.1, Sect. 4.2.1, Sect. 4.2.5, Sect. 4.2.6 are observed in more than half of the cases. Our sample is characterized by Norwegian software startups, with a small team and bootstrap financing model. We do not consider other types of startups, for example, internal cooperate startups, venture capital invested startups, and American startups. Hence, the results cannot be directly applied to other contexts, though analytical generalization may be possible in similar contexts.

6 Conclusions

To the best of our knowledge, this is the largest multiple case study research about software startups. Grounded on twenty European startups, we adopted an analytical framework to reveal different factors that influence the prototyping activities in early stages of software startups. We found that both throw-away and evolutionary prototypes were influenced by artifacts adoption approach, available team competence, collaboration and customer involvement. Even though there is certain limitation in our case sample, there are still valuable lessons learnt for practitioners. For startups that follow the Lean Startup approach, it is important to align the learning objective with a collaborative and well-defined approach of prototyping. Moreover, startups need to find a systematic approach to integrate relevant external feedback in all phases of prototyping.

This work does not address the evolution of startups according to the learning loops, i.e. what are lessons from idea to throw-away prototype, what are lessons from switching from throw-away prototypes to evolutionary ones. Besides, future work can investigate different types of learning brought by different types of prototypes. This work addressed validated learning through an important angle, which is the speed of prototyping loops. In the future work, we will explore another equally important aspect, which is the quality of learning. Further studies might also identify the effective prototyping and development patterns among software startups.

References

1. Runeson, P., Höst, M.: Guidelines for conducting and reporting case study research in software engineering. Empirical Softw. Eng. **14**(2), 131–164 (2009)
2. Blank, S.: The Four Steps to the Epiphany: Successful Strategies for Products that Win, 2nd edn. K & S Ranch Press (2013)
3. Giardino, C., Wang, X., Abrahamsson, P.: Why early-stage software startups fail: a behavioral framework. In: Lassenius, C., Smolander, K. (eds.) ICSOB 2014. LNBIP, vol. 182, pp. 27–41. Springer, Cham (2014). doi:10.1007/978-3-319-08738-2_3
4. Ries, E.: The Lean Startup: How Today's Entrepreneurs Use Continuous Innovation to Create Radically Successful Businesses. Crown Business, New York (2011)
5. Cooper, R.G.: Stage-gate systems: a new tool for managing new products. Bus. Horiz. **33**(3), 44–54 (1990)
6. Unterkalmsteiner, M., Abrahamsson, P., Wang, X., Nguyen-Duc, A., Shah, S., Bajwa, S.S., Yagüe, A.: Software startups: a research agenda. e-informatica. Softw. Eng. J. **10**(1), 89–123 (2016)
7. Fagerholm, F., Guinea, A.S., Mäenpää, H., Münch, J.: The RIGHT model for continuous experimentation. J. Syst. Softw. (2016)
8. Houde, S., Hill, C.: What do prototypes prototype. In: Helander, M., Landauer, T., Prabhu, P. (eds.) Handbook of Human-Computer Interaction, 2nd edn. Elsevier Science (1997)
9. Accessed 1 Dec 2016. http://qz.com/771727/chinas-factories-in-shenzhen-can-copy-products-at-breakneck-speed-and-its-time-for-the-rest-of-the-world-to-get-over-it/
10. Cohen, M.A., Eliasberg, J., Ho, T.H.: New product development: the performance and time-to-market tradeoff. Manage. Sci. **42**, 173–186 (1996)
11. Yin, R.K.: Case Study Research: Design and Methods, 4th edn. Sage Publications Inc, Thousand Oaks (2008)
12. Duc, A.N., Abrahamsson, P.: Minimum viable product or multiple facet product? The role of MVP in software startups. In: Sharp, H., Hall, T. (eds.) XP 2016. LNBIP, vol. 251, pp. 118–130. Springer, Cham (2016). doi:10.1007/978-3-319-33515-5_10
13. Lichter, H., Schneider-Hufschmidt, M., Züllighoven, H.: Prototyping in industrial software projects-bridging the gap between theory and practice. IEEE Trans. Softw. Eng. **20**(11), 825–832 (1994)
14. Floyd, C.: A systematic look at prototyping. In: Budde, R., Kuhlenkamp, K., Mathiassen, L., Zullighoven, H. (eds.) Approaches to Prototyping, pp. 1–18 (1984)
15. Beaudouin-Lafon, M., Mackay, W.E.: Prototyping development and tools. In: Jacko, J.A., Sears, A. (eds.) Handbook of Human-Computer Interaction, Revisited edn, pp. 1006–1031. Lawrence Erlbaum Associates, New York (2007)

16. Karvonen, T., Lwakatare, L.E., Sauvola, T., Bosch, J., Olsson, H.H., Kuvaja, P., Oivo, M.: Hitting the target: practices for moving toward innovation experiment systems. In: Fernandes, J.M., Machado, R.J., Wnuk, K. (eds.) ICSOB 2015. LNBIP, vol. 210, pp. 117–131. Springer, Cham (2015). doi:10.1007/978-3-319-19593-3_10

17. Sauvola, T., Lwakatare, L.E., Karvonen, T., Kuvaja, P., Olsson, H.H., Bosch, J., Oivo, M.: Towards customer-centric software development: a multiple-case study. In: 41st Euromicro Conference on Software Engineering and Advanced Applications (2015)

18. Bosch, J., Holmström Olsson, H., Björk, J., Ljungblad, J.: The early stage software startup development model: a framework for operationalizing lean principles in software startups. In: Fitzgerald, B., Conboy, K., Power, K., Valerdi, R., Morgan, L., Stol, K.-J. (eds.) LESS 2013. LNBIP, vol. 167, pp. 1–15. Springer, Heidelberg (2013). doi:10.1007/978-3-642-44930-7_1

19. Olsson, H.H., Alahyari, H., Bosch, J.: Climbing the "stairway to heaven": a multiple-case study exploring barriers in the transition from agile development towards continuous deployment of software. In: 38th Euromicro Conference on Software Engineering and Advanced Applications (2012)

20. Paternoster, N., Giardino, C., Unterkalmsteiner, M., Gorschek, T., Abrahamsson, P.: Software development in startup companies: a systematic mapping study. Inf. Softw. Technol. 56(10), 1200–1218 (2014)

21. Brooks, F.P.: The Design of Design: Essays From a Computer Scientist. Addison-Wesley Professional, Boston (2010)

22. Boyatzis, R.E.: Transforming Qualitative Information: Thematic Analysis and Code Development. Sage Publications, Thousand Oaks (1998)

23. Nguyen-Duc, A., Shah, S., Abrahamsson, P.: Towards an early stage software startups evolution model. In: 42nd Euromicro Conference on Software Engineering and Advanced Applications (2016)

24. Von Hippel, E.: Lead users: a source of novel product concepts. Manage. Sci. 32(7), 791–805 (1986)

25. Lynn, G.S., Morone, J.G.: Marketing and discontinuous: the probe and learn process. Calif. Manage. Rev. 38(3) (1996)

26. Nguyen-Duc, A., Seppnen, P., Abrahamsson, P.: Hunter-gatherer cycle: a conceptual model of the evolution of startup innovation and engineering. In: 1st Workshop on Open Innovation on Software Engineering, ICSSP (2015)

27. Luqi, F.K.: An introduction to rapid system prototyping. IEEE Trans. Softw. Eng. 28(9), 817–821 (2002)

28. Jansen, S., Brinkkemper, S., Hunink, I., Demir, C.: Pragmatic and opportunistic reuse in innovative start-up companies. IEEE Softw. 25(6), 42–49 (2008)

29. Grevet, C., Gilbert, E.: Piggyback prototyping: using existing, large-scale social computing systems to prototype new ones. In: 33rd Annual ACM Conference on Human Factors in Computing Systems; Seoul, Republic of Korea, pp. 4047–4056 (2015)

Key Challenges in Agile Requirements Engineering

Eva-Maria Schön[1,2(✉)], Dominique Winter[3], María José Escalona[1],
and Jörg Thomaschewski[3]

[1] University of Seville, Seville, Spain
`eva.schoen@iwt2.org, mjescalona@us.es`
[2] CGI Deutschland Ltd. & Co. KG, Hamburg, Germany
[3] University of Applied Sciences Emden/Leer, Emden, Germany
`dominique.winter@designik.de,`
`joerg.thomaschewski@hs-emden-leer.de`

Abstract. Agile Software Development (ASD) is becoming more popular in all fields of industry. For an agile transformation, organizations need to continuously improve their established approaches to Requirements Engineering (RE) as well as their approaches to software development. This is accompanied by some challenges in terms of agile RE. The main objective of this paper is to identify the most important challenges in agile RE industry has to face today. Therefore, we conducted an iterative expert judgement process with 26 experts in the field of ASD, comprising three complementary rounds.

In sum, we identified 20 challenges in three rounds. Six of these challenges are defined as key challenges. Based on the results, we provide options for dealing with those key challenges by means of agile techniques and tools. The results show that the identified challenges are often not limited to ASD, but they rather refer to software development in general. Therefore, we can conclude that organizations still struggle with agile transition and understanding agile values, in particular, in terms of stakeholder and user involvement.

Keywords: Agile Software Development · Requirements Engineering · Challenges · Agile RE · Stakeholder and user involvement · Human-Centered Design

1 Introduction

Agile Software development (ASD) gains in popularity in today's business world due to enabling immediately changes in the direction of product development. These short-term changes in direction require a flexible approach to Requirements Engineering (RE) as well. In addition, agile methodologies (such as Scrum [1], Kanban [2] or Extreme Programming [3]) are often combined with Human-Centered Design (HCD) [4] activities in order to emphasize a value-driven approach to product development [5, 6]. To this end, the field of agile RE has emerged during the last decade.

Focusing on user needs and value delivery becomes an important aspect in product development due to the increasing competition in all areas. With regard to ASD, plan-driven organizations moved away to value-driven organizations. On the one hand,

© The Author(s) 2017
H. Baumeister et al. (Eds.): XP 2017, LNBIP 283, pp. 37–51, 2017.
DOI: 10.1007/978-3-319-57633-6_3

people in plan-driven organizations often negotiate about project plans, pricing models and the amount of features they can develop with the available resources. They are emphasizing the generated outputs such as number of created features during a time period. On the other hand, people in value-driven organizations discuss visions, experiences and human values as well as the way to address them through the product. They focus on the outcomes that the delivered outputs entail.

Compared to sequential approaches to RE, which comprise a requirement analysis phase before the development can even begin, agile RE is carried out along with the development itself. Therefore, continuous management of requirements is a crucial attribute. Requirements are regularly described from a user perspective in the form of epics and user stories [7] instead of creating a requirements document [8]. Recent research is showing that there are several ways of running RE in an agile environment while involving users and stakeholders [5, 9–12].

Performing agile RE can lead to challenges organizations have to deal with. In literature, there can be found some studies investigating challenges in agile RE (see [11–15]). However, the related work still lacks in giving a general overview of the challenges in current industry.

This study pursues the main objective of identifying the most important challenges in agile RE industry has to address today. We aim to build a shared understanding concerning these challenges among voices that matter by means of experts in the field of agile RE. Thus, the research questions we pose are listed below:

- RQ1: What are the key challenges in Agile Requirements Engineering?
- RQ2: How can we deal with the identified key challenges?

The paper is structured as follows: Sect. 2 briefly summarizes the related work and points out the research gap. Section 3 presents the applied research method and describes the iterative expert judgement process. Then, Sect. 4 identifies the findings and discusses both on their meaning and on the limitations of this study. Finally, Sect. 5 provides the conclusions as well as an outlook on future research.

2   Related Work

There are related studies in the literature that investigate challenges in agile RE by means of different research methods. Table 1 shows an overview of the reported challenges and used research methods.

Analyzing the related work, we can state that the authors use two different kinds of research approaches in general. On the one hand, Ramesh et al. [13] and Bjarnason et al. [14] utilize case studies to investigate the challenges in the field. On the other hand, Inayat et al. [11], Heikkila et al. [15] and Soares et al. [12] report challenges in agile RE by analyzing primary studies with the aim to identify available evidence in existing research.

Table 1. Challenges in agile RE reported by related work

Authors	Research method	Reported challenges
Ramesh, Cao, Baskerville [13]	Multi-case study (16 companies)	Problems with cost and schedule estimation; inadequate or inappropriate architecture; neglect of non-functional requirements; customer access and participation; prioritization on a single dimension; inadequate requirements verification; minimal documentation
Bjarnason, Wnuk, Regnell [14]	Case study	Planning for agility; weak requirements prioritization; weak effort estimates; quality issues; system completed late; capturing innovation; lack of documented requirements; customer-proxy role; ensuring competence (RE, VV); motivating teams for requirements work; weak requirements at start
Inayat, Salim, Marczak, Daneva, Shamshirband [11]	Systematic literature review	Minimal documentation; customer availability; inappropriate architecture; budget and time estimation; neglecting non-functional requirements (NFRs); customer inability and agreement; contractual limitations; requirements change and its evaluation
Heikkila, Damian, Lassenius, Paasivaara [15]	Mapping study	Problems with client or customer representatives; insufficiency of user story format; difficulties in prioritization of requirements; growing technical debt; reliance on tacit requirements knowledge; imprecise effort estimates
Soares, Alves, Mendes, Mendonca, Spinola [12]	Systematic literature review	Requirement prioritization; non-functional requirements identification; lack of information; volatility of requirements; requirements definition; dependence among requirements; prediction of impacts of changes; user dependence; communication and collaboration with users; requirements validation

Ramesh et al. [13] results were published in 2010. However, as ASD is a rapidly changing research area and the body of knowledge has evolved over the last years, we need to clarify whether the reported challenges are still relevant today. For instance, NFRs may not be longer a challenge for industry since the concept of the Definition of Done and the usage of acceptance criteria are widely spread. Bjarnason et al. [14] carry out a case study in only one company, therefore the results may not be applicable to other companies and may not be representative in general. In comparison, Inayat et al. [11], Heikkila et al. [15] and Soares et al. [12] review primary studies by analyzing existing literature, which is a good approach to get an impression of relevant aspects from a theoretical viewpoint. Nevertheless, one could argue that this is not an appropriate approach to investigate the existing challenges in practice.

To this end, the aim of this study is to identify the most important challenges in agile RE industry has to face up today by getting insights from 26 experts in the field. To the best of our knowledge there is no existing study investigating these challenges by means of a qualitative study with practicing experts in ASD working for many different companies.

3   Research Method

We used an iterative expert judgement process rooted in a Delphi study [16–18] in order to respond to our RQs. We applied a modified Delphi study where measuring consensus and stability at group level among several iterations was not the most crucial part. On the contrary, we shifted the focus to applying the valuable features of Delphi for conducting our iterative expert judgement process [19]:

- Anonymity among experts to avoid influence of dominant individuals
- Iterative approach
- Controlled feedback with statistical group response

The main benefit of our modified approach was utilizing the learnings from a previous iteration for carrying out the following ones.

3.1   General Study Design

The study was performed in three complementary rounds. Figure 1 gives a general overview of the process. At the beginning of each round, we started designing the questionnaire, optimized by a pretest. Once finished, the invitation was sent to the experts via email. In the second and third round, we attached the results of the previous rounds to the invitation in order to share the outcomes among the panel. The experts had two weeks to fill in the questionnaire. During the following two weeks we evaluated the results, created the report, specified the criteria for dropping items for the following round and designed the questionnaire for the next round.

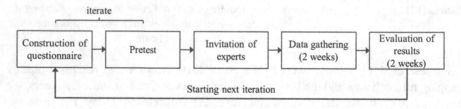

Fig. 1.   General process of study

We conducted the study in German since most of the experts are native speaker. Since we are aware that the term agile RE is not very accepted in the agile community and some experts understand this as a contradiction in itself, we decided not to ask for challenges in agile RE directly. On the contrary, we phrased our questions differently and described the context of our study within the introduction part of each questionnaire.

We used google forms for the first and second round, whereas limesurvey was used for the third round due to the complexity of the questionnaire. In general, we decided to use 7-point Likert items since this has been proven to be the best choice in terms of avoiding interpolations within related research fields [20]. Besides, we adapted the quality criteria proposed by Diamond et al. [17] so as to ensure the quality of our study.

3.2 Panel of Experts

We selected our panelists specifically for their knowledge or position regarding the issue under study. As shown in previous work, the research field of agile RE is very close to existing work practices in industry [5]. To this end, we defined the reproducible criteria for selecting participants as follows:

- Many years of experience as professional in the field of ASD
- Working experience in one or more of the following roles: Product Owner, Scrum Master, Agile Coach, Consultant for Agile Transition, Kanban Expert or Lean Startup Expert

The panel consisted of 26 experts who are working in 19 different companies located in Germany and Switzerland. In general, they had 2–10 years of experience working in ASD (average = 6.14 years). In comparison, experts have about 0–16 years of experience with RE (average = 6.65 years). Even though one expert stated that he had no experience with RE at all, we decided to include his answers into the study, since he has long experience in ASD and in general there do not exist a specific role of a requirements engineer.

Figure 2 shows the kind of process models experts have been working with. It is worth mentioning that most of the experts have experience both with sequential approaches and with agile approaches.

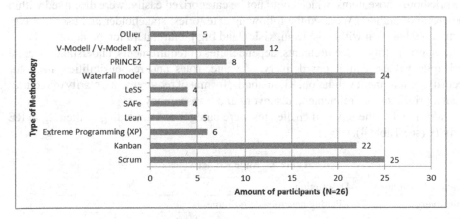

Fig. 2. Process models used by experts

In addition, Table 2 displays the know-how level in terms of ASD rated by experts themselves.

Table 2. Know-how of panel in terms of ASD

know-how very poor	1	2	3	4	5	know-how very high
	0.0%	0.0%	15.4%	69.2%	15.4%	

3.3   Round 1

The questionnaire of the first round comprised two open questions, repeated 15 times. On the one hand, the experts were asked what the most important challenges with requirements in terms of ASD were. On the other hand, they should give a statement for each challenge to clarify why they considered this challenge as important. The minimum number of required answers was 3, whereas the maximum was 15. In sum, we received 107 answers (items) from 26 experts. Table 3 shows an example of an item consisting of a challenge and a statement concerning importance. The full results can be found in [21].

Table 3. Exemplary item in round 1

Question round 1	Answer given by expert
What challenge do you perceive with requirements in terms of Agile Software Development?	Stakeholders affected by requirements or changing the system are not involved
Why do you consider this challenge as important?	In one of my projects, representatives of end users did not really knew the pain of end users. Even the early UI prototypes were tested by incorrect stakeholders, which led to risks of conflicts and failure

With respect to data analysis, each challenge was categorized by the authors during a workshop. Those items, which could not be categorized easily, were discussed within the group of authors. We used the following categories: stakeholder and user involvement, collaboration within the team, vision and big picture, iteration planning and estimation, granularity of requirements, dependencies of requirements, understanding agile and agile values, continuous delivery of value, roles and responsibilities, need for security, requirement validation, RE methods, format of requirements, clarity of requirements, prioritization, refinement, discovery and transparency.

Additionally, the reported challenges were categorized according to their agile RE activity (see Table 4).

Table 4. Agile RE activities

Agile RE activity	Description
Discovery	Eliciting new ideas/requirements
Refinement	Clarifying and analyzing new ideas/requirements
Prioritization	Measuring the value that the development will add to the product
Review	Checking if requirement is implemented in the manner to deliver value
Documentation	Capturing discussion and decisions around the requirement

3.4   Round 2

We checked each item of round one critically, whether or not it was appropriate for answering our RQs and being queried in the next round. Thus, items of round 1 were consolidated or excluded. In the end, we identified 34 items as relevant for assessing them in round 2. Based on those items, we created the questionnaire for the second round.

The resulting questionnaire assessed 34 items related to the following topics: stakeholder and user involvement (6 items), understanding agile and agile values (6 items), RE methods (10 items), iteration planning and estimation (6 items) and format of requirements (6 items).

The experts rated each item using 7-point Likert items (see Fig. 3). Moreover, they could choose giving no statement. To sum up, we received responses from 23 experts. For each item we calculated mean, variance and standard deviation. Additionally, we created a diagram showing the distribution of experts' opinion (see Fig. 3) and discussed on the meaning of findings. The results of round two can be found in [22].

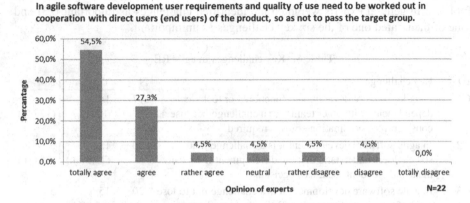

Fig. 3. Exemplary item of round 2

3.5   Round 3

We reduced the number of items when designing the questionnaire for the third round. Considering items from round 2, we assessed each item according to (a) its relevance in terms of our RQs, (b) the importance in terms of the attributes of agile RE, (c) the opinion of the experts and the comprehensibility of the items.

The final questionnaire comprised two parts. The first part queried in sum 20 potential key challenges of agile RE (see Appendix). The experts were asked to rate each item, whether or not it is a challenge in agile RE. Moreover, they had the option to choose giving no statement. Then, the second part evaluated those items that experts identified as challenge in terms of importance, following 7-point Likert items (totally important, important, rather important, neutral, rather unimportant, unimportant, totally unimportant, no statement). In addition, experts optionally had the chance to provide a solution for solving the challenge.

In sum, 22 experts filled in the questionnaire. We classified each of the 20 items as challenge in Agile RE since we derived all items from the results of the previous rounds. Besides, we calculated the number of experts who rated each item as a challenge. Then, we defined challenges as key in those cases where 2/3 of the experts' answers were: "Yes, it is a challenge". Finally, we calculated the importance for those items. The results of round 3 can be found in [23].

4   Results and Discussion

Summarizing the results of the three complementary rounds, we derived 20 challenges that companies have to cope with in terms of agile RE (see Appendix). We categorized such challenges into stakeholder and user (3 items), requirements management (7 items), methods and artifacts (5 items) and format of requirements (5 items).

4.1   (RQ1) What Are the Key Challenges in Agile Requirements Engineering?

We identified six key challenges industry has to face today in terms of agile RE (see Table 5). In general experts weighted the identified challenges as important [23] and none of them rated one of the six key challenges as unimportant.

Table 5.   Key challenges in agile RE

ID	Key challenge	N	Yes	No
C1	In agile software development functional or technical dependencies with other teams are a challenge because a considerable coordination effort is required	17	14 (82.4%)	3 (17.6%)
C2	In agile software development it is a challenge that stakeholders understand that the development team can make independent (detailed) decisions	20	15 (75.0%)	5 (25.0%)
C3	In agile software development it is a challenge not to lose sight of the big picture during the implementation of complex requirements	20	15 (75.0%)	5 (25.0%)
C4	In agile software development continuous management of requirements is a challenge since not all of them are fixed at the beginning and they may change over the course of the project	22	16 (72.7%)	6 (27.3%)
C5	In agile software development it is a challenge to work out user requirements and quality of use in cooperation with direct users (end users) of the product	18	13 (72.2%)	5 (27.8%)
C6	In agile software development it is a challenge to involve stakeholders throughout the whole development process in regular iterations, so that product development will succeed	20	14 (70.0%)	6 (30.0%)

All challenges related to the category stakeholder and user are classified as key challenges (C2, C5, C6). Therefore, we can conclude that organizations still struggle to the agile transition. Evolving an agile mindset within a whole organization even in parts that are not close to development is still a challenge companies have to address.

Typically, agile transformation starts in development-oriented parts of an organization. Transforming an organization to become more agile implies a change within the whole organization. The results show that there is a gap between knowledge and understanding agile values [24] within organizations. Development-oriented techniques evolve rapidly. In comparison, there are still challenges involving stakeholders and users into the agile processes (C2, C5, C6).

Two challenges (C1, C4), related to category requirements management, are key in agile RE. On the one hand, companies have an issue with the continuous management of requirements. On the other hand, they have a problem with technical or functional dependencies due to raising effort in coordination. Besides, one challenge of methods and artifacts (C3) is a key challenge.

ASD is commonly used in environments where people have to solve complex adaptive problems [25]. Concerning C1, C3, and C4 we can state that there are still challenges to be solved, due to the complexity of problems, which are not addressed by agile techniques properly. To this end, existing techniques and methods must be adapted or new techniques need to be found.

Figure 4 offers an overview of the categorized key challenges.

Stakeholder and user	• understanding of agile values of the stakeholders (C2) • refine requirements in collaboration with users (C5) • involve stakeholder iteravely (C6)
Requirements management	• technical or functional dependencies to other teams (C1) • continuous requirements management (C4)
Methods and artifacts	• staying focused on the big picture (C3)

Fig. 4. Categorized key challenges in agile RE

4.2 (RQ2) How Can We Deal with the Identified Key Challenges?

Experts recommend techniques, methods and tools in order to deal with the challenges in agile RE. Below, we will list the techniques and methods proposed by the panel for each key challenge.

C1: In agile software development functional or technical dependencies with other teams are a challenge because a considerable coordination effort is required.
More than three experts recommended using scaled frameworks such as LeSS, SAFe or Scrum of Scrum. Moreover, they proposed the use of the following techniques: creating a common understanding among all, enhancing continuous communication and collaboration, training the ability to solve dependencies, holding weekly coordination meetings, organizing teams in matrix management, building communities of practices for transcending topics, release planning (SAFe), team-transcending availability of product und sprint backlogs, involving temporary representatives in other teams, enforcing continuous integration, improving API-driven development and microservices.

C2: In agile software development it is a challenge that stakeholders understand that the development team can make independent (detailed) decisions.

The following techniques were suggested: continuous coordination and presenting possible solutions to stakeholder, providing transparency about rationales of the decisions, strengthening product owner with competency in decision making and helping stakeholders become aware of the consequences of interfering into detailed decisions.

More than three experts recommended providing alternative solutions for one requirement. In addition, it is useful to demonstrate that the recommended solution of a stakeholder is an alternative out of many. In previous rounds, more than one expert stated that product owner and stakeholder altogether decide what to be developed. In contrast, the development team decides how the requirement should be developed.

C3: In agile software development it is a challenge not to lose sight of the big picture during the implementation of complex requirements.

The following techniques were recommended: creating a shared understanding regarding the meaning of the big picture by means of a product vision, defining epics or subgoals in the beginning, managing the big picture as a responsibility of the product owner, providing transparency concerning changes among all, understanding connections among user stories by means of story mapping, visualizing customer journey in the beginning, involving users continuously in order to focus on the problem to be solved and identifying central contact person for related topics to enable rapid coordination. Moreover, the experts advised to use visualization by means of roadmaps, sketches of the system and processes, and value streams.

C4: In agile software development continuous management of requirements is a challenge since not all of them are fixed at the beginning and they may change over the course of the project.

The experts proposed the following techniques, methods and tools: collaborating closely with the requesting stakeholder, communicating regularly within the team, refining and prioritizing continuously the product backlog, grooming on demand (Kanban), describing in detail the requirements in the sprint backlog, reviewing the results regularly, discussing the maturity level of a requirement with the team, grouping user stories to epics, using Kano analysis, screening and scoring the theme, weighting relatively, utilizing spike stories to evaluate uncertainty in requirements and using ticketing tools (e.g. JIRA).

C5: In agile software development it is a challenge to work out user requirements and quality of use in cooperation with direct users (end users) of the product.

The experts recommended utilizing the following techniques: prototypes, interviews, observing users by the think aloud method, A/B testing, UX labs, analyzing usage behavior, friendly user tests, alpha/beta/silent launches, improving continuously a released version, utilizing a UX-board for play back user insights and testing hypotheses with real users. In addition, one expert suggested adapting user research to ASD by reducing the methods to the minimal, evaluate within the team without report creation, reduce financial restrictions for user involvement as well as problems of accessing real user by means of panels or a prior recruitment.

C6: In agile software development it is a challenge to involve stakeholders throughout the whole development process in regular iterations so that product development will succeed.
The following techniques were proposed: defining stakeholders and their involvement in regular iterations, proposing goals instead of prescribing solutions, involving all possible stakeholders in the beginning and reducing the amount of people over time.

More than eight experts suggested involving stakeholders by regular planning and review meetings to gather feedback and useful information. In light of this, they recommended clarifying the purpose of the meetings and the importance of the outcomes to be discussed beforehand.

4.3 Meaning of Findings

Comparing our findings to the identified challenges of the related work (see Table 1), we can conclude that 16 out of our challenges are not reported by the related studies.

Our key challenge C5 (user involvement) is reported by all related studies. In addition, three studies [11–13] report issues with non-functional requirements, which is comparable to our challenge C13. There is also a relation between the key challenge C4 (continuous requirements management) and the challenge "requirements change and its evaluation" reported by [11]. Moreover, the key challenge C1 (technical or functional dependencies to other teams) is reported by [12] in a slightly different manner since they phrase it like "dependence between requirements".

Moreover, the results show that the identified challenges are often not limited to ASD, but they rather refer to software development in general. Therefore, we can conclude that organizations still struggle with agile transition and understanding agile values, in particular, in terms of stakeholder and user involvement.

4.4 Limitations

We are aware that the design of a questionnaire is important for the process of data gathering. To this end, we made several pretests of each questionnaire we used with participants matching our criteria of expert selection. Nevertheless, we observed two experts struggling with the user experience of the questionnaire tool (Google Forms) used in round 1. Therefore, we decided to use another tool (LimeSurvey) for the questionnaire in round 3, which was more complex than the previous two.

To carry out the study, the group of authors created summaries of the results and made decisions concerning the kind of items they had to query in the following rounds. That may lead to bias in the opinion building process of the panel. We tried to prevent this point by being very accurate in terms of data analysis and by creating the reports. In addition, we selected items for the following rounds through the selection criteria defined earlier.

5   Conclusions and Future Work

This paper has addressed the identification of the most important challenges in agile RE industry has to face up today. Moreover, we examined how to deal with those challenges. For that purpose, we carried out an iterative expert judgement process comprising three complementary rounds. The learnings from previous iterations were used for carrying out the following ones. Our panel consisted of 26 experts in the field of ASD working for 19 different companies.

We have contributed to the body of knowledge of software development by identifying 20 challenges industry has to address at present in terms of agile RE. Six of these challenges have been defined as key challenges. In addition, we have analyzed options to deal with those key challenges by means of agile techniques recommended by the experts.

Future research may specifically identify challenges in agile RE by means of an international panel of experts, for instance with experts from Scandinavian countries. Our aim is to conduct a comparative analysis among the statements of German-speaking experts with the viewpoint of international experts. In addition, we are creating a tool that supports practitioners solving the identified challenges using agile techniques. Therefore, we are working on agile RE patterns. Some experts stated that the queried challenges are not limited to ASD. To this end, future studies may analyze whether the challenges appear in terms of RE in general.

Acknowledgements.   First of all, we would like to thank all experts for their participation and sharing their valuable knowledge. Moreover, we would like to thank all participants in our pretests for their collaboration. This research has been supported by the MeGUS project (TIN2013-46928-C3-3-R), Pololas project (TIN2016-76956-C3-2-R) and by SoftPLM Network (TIN2015-71938-REDT) of the Spanish Ministry of Economy and Competitiveness.

Appendix

See Table 6.

Table 6. Challenges in agile Requirements Engineering

ID	Challenge in agile RE	N	Yes	No
C1	In agile software development functional or technical dependencies with other teams are a challenge because a considerable coordination effort is required	17	14 (82.4%)	3 (17.6%)
C2	In agile software development it is a challenge that stakeholders understand that the development team can make independent (detailed) decisions	20	15 (75.0%)	5 (25.0%)
C3	In agile software development it is a challenge not to lose sight of the big picture during the implementation of complex requirements	20	15 (75.0%)	5 (25.0%)
C4	In agile software development continuous management of requirements is a challenge since not all of them are fixed at the beginning and they may change over the course of the project	22	16 (72.7%)	6 (27.3%)
C5	In agile software development it is a challenge to work out user requirements and quality of use in cooperation with direct users (end users) of the product	18	13 (72.2%)	5 (27.8%)
C6	In agile software development it is a challenge to involve stakeholders throughout the whole development process in regular iterations so that product development will succeed	20	14 (70.0%)	6 (30.0%)
C7	In agile software development it is a challenge that the requirements to be implemented are clearly defined from the development start since the priorities often change in the short term	21	13 (61.9%)	8 (38.1%)
C8	In agile software development it is a challenge to analyze requirements with regard to the past development in order to avoid side effects	15	9 (60.0%)	6 (40.0%)
C9	In agile software development it is a challenge to formulate requirements as objectives that describe the problem area so that the creativity in solution finding is not restricted	22	13 (59.0%)	9 (41.0%)
C10	In agile software development it is a challenge to slice requirements in such a way that they offer added value for the product	20	11 (55.0%)	9 (45.0%)
C11	In agile software development it is a challenge to justify the benefits of the requirements in order to make the added value of the implementation clear as well as decisions for a specific requirement comprehensible	21	11 (52.4%)	10 (47.6%)
C12	In agile software development it is a challenge to document changes to the requirements comprehensibly	18	9 (50.0%)	9 (50.0%)
C13	In agile software development it is a challenge to establish non-functional requirements	19	9 (47.4%)	10 (52.6%)
C14	In agile software development it is a challenge to focus only on the refinement of the requirements for the short-term iterations	22	10 (45.5%)	12 (54.5%)
C15	In agile software development it is a challenge to develop an outlook on the next iterations without making it a binding one	21	9 (42.9%)	12 (57.1%)
C16	In agile software development it is a challenge to design requirement documents in such a way that they can be adapted to changing surrounding factors at reasonable effort	21	9 (42.9%)	12 (57.1%)
C17	In agile software development it is a challenge to use methods for elicitation and evaluation of requirements in which the findings are shared with the development team	20	8 (40.0%)	12 (60.0%)
C18	In agile software development it is a challenge to capture requirements in such a way that detailed test cases can be derived from them for quality assurance	21	8 (38.1%)	13 (61.9%)
C19	In agile software development it is a challenge to formulate clear and comprehensible requirements in order to avoid uncertainties in the development	22	7 (31.8%)	15 (68.2%)
C20	In agile software development it is a challenge that elicitation and evaluation of requirements are not fast enough in the project context	17	5 (29.4%)	12 (70.6%)

References

1. Schwaber, K.: Agile Project Management with Scrum. Microsoft, Redmond (2004)
2. Anderson, D.J.: Kanban - Successful Evolutionary Change for your Technology Business. Blue Hole Press, Sequim (2010)
3. Beck, K.: Extreme Programming Explained: Embrace Change. Addison-Wesley, Reading (2000)
4. International Organization for Standardization: ISO 9241-210:2010 - Ergonomics of human-system interaction - Part 210: Human-centred design for interactive systems (2010)
5. Schön, E.-M., Thomaschewski, J., Escalona, M.J.: Agile requirements engineering: a systematic literature review. Comput. Stand. Interfaces **49**, 79–91 (2017)
6. Schön, E., Winter, D., Uhlenbrok, J., Escalona, M.J., Thomaschewski, J.: Enterprise experience into the integration of human-centered design and Kanban. In: Proceedings of the 11th International Joint Conference on Software Technologies (ICSOFT 2016), Lisbon, Portugal, pp. 133–140 (2016)
7. Cohn, M.: User Stories Applied: For Agile Software Development (2004)
8. Sommerville, I., Sawyer, P.: Requirements Engineering: A Good Practice Guide. Wiley, New York (1997)
9. Silva da Silva, T., Martin, A., Maurer, F., Silveira, M.: User-centered design and agile methods: a systematic review. In: 2011 AGILE Conference, pp. 77–86. IEEE (2011)
10. Brhel, M., Meth, H., Maedche, A., Werder, K.: Exploring principles of user-centered agile software development: a literature review. Inf. Softw. Technol. **61**, 163–181 (2015)
11. Inayat, I., Salim, S.S., Marczak, S., Daneva, M., Shamshirband, S.: A systematic literature review on agile requirements engineering practices and challenges. Comput. Hum. Behav. **51**, 915–929 (2015)
12. Soares, H.F., Alves, N.S.R., Mendes, T.S., Mendonca, M., Spinola, R.O.: Investigating the link between user stories and documentation debt on software projects. In: 2015 Proceedings of the 12th International Conference on Information Technology - New Generations, pp. 385–390. IEEE (2015)
13. Ramesh, B., Cao, L., Baskerville, R.: Agile requirements engineering practices and challenges: an empirical study. Inf. Syst. J. **20**, 449–480 (2010)
14. Bjarnason, E., Wnuk, K., Regnell, B.: A case study on benefits and side-effects of agile practices in large-scale requirements engineering. In: Proceedings of the 1st Workshop on Agile Requirements Engineering - AREW 2011, pp. 1–5. ACM Press, New York (2011)
15. Heikkila, V.T., Damian, D., Lassenius, C., Paasivaara, M.: A mapping study on requirements engineering in agile software development. In: 2015 Proceedings of the 41st Euromicro Conference on Software Engineering and Advanced Applications, pp. 199–207 (2015)
16. Dalkey, N., Helmer, O.: An experimental application of the DELPHI method to the use of experts. Manage. Sci. **9**, 458–467 (1963)
17. Diamond, I.R., Grant, R.C., Feldman, B.M., Pencharz, P.B., Ling, S.C., Moore, A.M., Wales, P.W.: Defining consensus: a systematic review recommends methodologic criteria for reporting of Delphi studies. J. Clin. Epidemiol. **67**, 401–409 (2014)
18. Linstone, H.A., Turoff, M.: The Delphi Method - Techniques and Applications (2002)
19. Dalkey, N.: An experimental study of group opinion. Futures **1**, 408–426 (1969)
20. Finstad, K.: Response interpolation and scale sensitivity: evidence against 5-point scales. J. Usability Stud. **5**, 104–110 (2010)
21. Schön, E.-M., Winter, D., Thomaschewski, J., Escalona, M.J.: Results of "Challenges in Agile Requirements Engineering" (Round 1) (2017). doi:10.13140/RG.2.2.34571.28961

22. Schön, E.-M., Winter, D., Thomaschewski, J., Escalona, M.J.: Results of "Challenges in Agile Requirements Engineering" (Round 2) (2017). doi:10.13140/RG.2.2.32893.56802
23. Schön, E.-M., Winter, D., Thomaschewski, J., Escalona, M.J.: Results of "Challenges in Agile Requirements Engineering" (Round 3) (2017). doi:10.13140/RG.2.2.16116.35201
24. Beck, K., Beedle, M., van Bennekum, A., Cockburn, A., Cunningham, W., Fowler, M., Grenning, J., Highsmith, J., Hunt, A., Jeffries, R., Kern, J., Marick, B., Martin, R., Mellor, S., Schwaber, K., Sutherland, J., Thomas, D.: Manifesto for Agile Software Development. http://www.agilemanifesto.org/
25. Schwaber, K., Sutherland, J.: Scrum Guide. http://www.scrumguides.org/scrum-guide.html

Eeny, Meeny, Miny, Mo...
A Multiple Case Study on Selecting a Technique for User-Interaction Data Collecting

Sampo Suonsyrjä$^{(\boxtimes)}$

Tampere University of Technology, P.O. Box 553, 33101 Tampere, Finland
sampo.suonsyrja@tut.fi

Abstract. Today, software teams can deploy new software versions to users at an increasing speed – even continuously. Although this has enabled faster responding to changing customer needs than ever before, the speed of automated customer feedback gathering has not yet blossomed out at the same level. For these purposes, the automated collecting of quantitative data about how users interact with systems can provide software teams with an interesting alternative. When starting such a process, however, teams are faced immediately with difficult decision making: What kind of technique should be used for collecting user-interaction data? In this paper, we describe the reasons for choosing specific collecting techniques in three cases and refine a previously designed selection framework based on their data. The study is a part of on-going design science research and was conducted using case study methods. A few distinct criteria which practitioners valued the most arose from the results.

Keywords: Agile software development · User-interaction data · Multiple case study · Software data collecting

1 Introduction

In the last few years, the world has witnessed a tremendous progress in the ways software is developed with. On one hand, this has already benefited both customers and vendors by improving productivity, product quality, and customer satisfaction [1]. On the other hand, the acceleration of release velocity has been such a strong focus point, that the evolution of the means of understanding user wants and needs could not have kept up the pace. For example, Mäkinen et al. [2] describe that customer data analytics are still used sparingly. Similarly, research related to the techniques of automatic collecting of post-deployment data and its use to support decisions still seems to be in its infancy [3]. This feels partly unfortunate, because agile software development has always had the intention of faster responding to changing customer requirements – and to achieve this, both rapid releasing and rapid understanding of customers are needed.

Addressing this, one of the promising solutions is to track users in the user-interface level, then analyze that data to understand how they use the software,

© The Author(s) 2017
H. Baumeister et al. (Eds.): XP 2017, LNBIP 283, pp. 52–67, 2017.
DOI: 10.1007/978-3-319-57633-6_4

and finally make decisions based on the analysis [4]. To start such a process, the first thing to do is to select a collecting technique that is suitable for the case. There are many restrictions to this, however, and these make the selecting a rather problematic task. Therefore, guidelines for evaluating and selecting a suitable collecting technique are needed. In our previous work [5], we have designed such a selection framework, which should serve as a guideline and help practitioners in these tasks. The objective of this study is to evaluate and refine that selection framework.

In this paper, we describe the reasons for choosing specific collecting techniques in three different case contexts and evaluate and refine the previously presented selection framework based on their data. The study is a part of ongoing design science research in which we have already designed the selection framework. This part uses the case study method to evaluate and refine the previous design and explore its contexts. Specifically, we address the research question:

- **What reasons software teams have for selecting a specific technique for user-interaction data collecting?**

To answer this overarching research question, we have derived two sub-questions. Firstly, the process of choosing a collecting technology will be explained. Secondly, we try to find out if some of the criteria we presented in our previous work are more significant than others or if there are completely other and more relevant reasons for choosing the technologies. The sub-questions for the study are declared as follows:

1. **How were the collecting techniques selected in each case?**
2. **What kind of criteria for choosing a certain technique were the most significant in each case?**

The rest of the paper is structured as follows. In Sect. 2, we present the background of the study, namely the selection framework which consists of selection criteria and a process. In Sect. 3, we explain how and why we used case study methods and describe the cases involved. In Sect. 4, we describe the process and criteria for choosing a specific technique for user-interaction data collecting in each case. In Sect. 5, we discuss those results to evaluate and refine the selection framework and in Sect. 6 we present the final conclusions of the study.

2   Background

To the best of our knowledge, related work for selecting techniques for user-interaction data is very limited. For example, a recently published systematic mapping study by Rodriguez et al. [6] identified the analysis of why certain technologies for monitoring post-deployment user behavior are selected over other similar existing solutions as a concrete opportunity for future work. However as a background for this study, we revisit the basics of the previously designed selection framework for user-interaction data collecting techniques.

The selection framework forms the basis for this study, as our goal is to evaluate the framework and refine it where necessary. It consists of a set of selection criteria and a process for the selecting. In addition, we introduce different techniques for user-interaction data collecting. These techniques and their evaluations are presented in a more detailed manner in [5]. They are mentioned nonetheless here for an overlook to the different alternatives that software teams have when they start collecting user-interaction data and for demonstrating the criteria part of the selection framework.

2.1 Selection Framework for a Collecting Technique

Criteria. The selection framework guides software teams to evaluate user-interaction data collecting techniques in terms of the technique's *timeliness, targets, effort level, overhead, sources, configurability, security, and reuse*. In the following list, each criterion is described by demonstrative questions which could be asked as a team evaluates collecting techniques.

- *Timeliness*. When can the data be available? Does it have a support for real-time?
- *Targets*. Who should benefit from the data? What is the intended use? Does it support many targets? Does it produce different types of data?
- *Effort level*. What kind of a work effort is needed from the developers to implement the technique?
- *Overhead*. How does it affect performance, e.g. system response time to user-interactions?
- *Sources*. Does it support many source platforms?
- *Configurability*. Can the collecting be switched on and off easily? Can it change between different types of data to collect?
- *Security*. Can the organization who developed the collecting technology be trusted with the collected data? Is the data automatically stored by the same organization?
- *Reuse*. Is the collecting always a one-time solution or can it be reused easily?

Process. The first thing to do when selecting a technique for user-interaction data collecting, is to rapidly **explore the case** to get a grasp of the most critical technical limitations. These include things such as the size of the code base, availability of automated tools and AOP libraries for the target application's language and platform, and access to the UI libraries and execution environments.

If any critical limitations are faced, the next step is to **reject the unsuitable techniques** accordingly. For example, if there are many security issues related to the data being collected or if data needs to be sent in real-time, collecting techniques using 3rd party tools might have critical limitations that cannot be avoided resulting in the rejection of the technique.

The following step is to **prioritize the evaluation criteria**. In addition to the explored case information, one should find out the goals different stakeholders

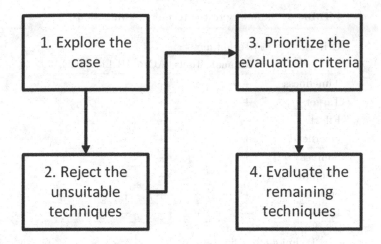

Fig. 1. Selection framework for user-interaction data collecting techniques.

have for the usage data collecting as these can have a major impact on the approach selection. If the goals are clearly stated, and the aim is e.g. to simply find out which of two buttons is used the most, manual instrumentation can work sufficiently. However, if the goal is stated anything like "to get an overall view of how the system is used" or if the goal is not stated at all, the more automated and more configurable approaches most likely become more appealing. Therefore, one of the most crucial things to find out in this step is to understand what different stakeholders want to accomplish with the collected data.

After this, the final step is to **evaluate the remaining approaches**. The plus and minus signs used in Table 1 work as guidelines in this, but their emphasis obviously varies on a case to case basis. To summarize, the selection framework is illustrated in Fig. 1.

2.2 Techniques for User-Interaction Data Collecting

Firstly, in **manual instrumentation** (Manual) developer adds extra statements to the relevant locations of the software. On one hand, this highlights the flexibility of the technique but on the other, adoption to new targets and sources would require significant rework making reuse practically impossible.

Secondly, there are multiple **tools for automated instrumentation** (Tools) of the code, e.g. GEMS [7], for various data logging, quality assurance and performance monitoring purposes. This technique frees the programmers from the manual work and reduces the probability for errors lowering the effort significantly.

Thirdly in between of the above techniques, **aspect-oriented programming approach** (AOP) is something of a mixture from the two. The research presented e.g. in [8,9] use aspect-oriented programming as a tool for code instrumentation. Aspect-based instrumentation allows the instrumentation to be

Table 1. Summary of the technique evaluations.

Criteria	Techniques				
	Manual	Tools	AOP	UI Lib.	E.E.
Timeliness	+	−	+	+	−
Targets	+	−	+	−	−
Effort	−	+	+	+	+
Overhead	+	−	+	−	−
Sources	+	−	−	−	−
Configurability	+	−	+	+	−
Security	+	−	+	+	−
Reuse	−	+	−	−	+

+ = Supports selecting
− = Technique has limitations

system and application specific, which focuses the collecting better on the relevant targets.

Fourthly, **an alternative implementation of a user-interface library** (UI Lib.) can be set to automatically collect user-interaction data. Because user-interaction is usually implemented with standard UI libraries, their components can be altered so that they include the collection of user-interaction data within them. Finally, the data collection can also be integrated into the environment without modifications to the original application. For languages like Java and JavaScript the virtual machine is an **execution environment** (E.E.) where method and function calls can be monitored by instrumenting critical places.

We have summarized the evaluations of different collecting techniques for the basis of the selection framework, i.e. Table 1, giving each technique either a plus if it has a positive impact or if it does not have restrictions in terms of the criterion. A technique is marked with a minus sign if it limits the selection or the use of a data collecting implementation according to a criterion.

3   Research Approach

The study was conducted using case study methodology. It allowed us to explore and describe the case specific situations and their circumstances related to the selection framework from deeper and more insightful viewpoints than if a research method with set variables had been used. Case study investigates contemporary phenomena in their real-life context [10], and this suited the purposes of the study well. The study is a part of on-going research effort, where we design, evaluate, and diffuse the selection framework by design science guidelines presented in [11] and with the process presented in [12]. The design science method of the underlying research effort affected this study as well especially in how actively the researchers had to take part in the cases. This participation was obviously required because the automated collecting of user-interaction data and its use for software development was still an unknown area for each of the case organizations. Moreover, the researchers had a substantial expertise considering the designed selection framework.

3.1 Explanatory Case Study

The selection framework, as presented in [5], includes predetermined criteria for evaluating the collecting technologies. These criteria could have been used straightforwardly as variables of a study with more experimental setting. However, the criteria have been derived from a literature survey and from only one case study. Therefore, we acknowledge that there can be other criteria that affect the selection as well, and perhaps with a greater impact. To allow the inclusion of these other possible factors into the selection framework, we have chosen to use specifically *multiple* case study method and gather data from three different cases.

This study uses *explanatory* case study methodology because its aim is at finding the reasons why software teams choose a specific collecting technology. The results of this explanatory case study are used for evaluating and refining the designed selection framework where necessary. Runeson & Höst [13] have categorized case studies by their purposes into exploratory, descriptive, explanatory, and improving. Since explanatory case studies are "...seeking an explanation of a situation or a problem, mostly but not necessary in the form of a causal relationship", their aims are well-suited for the study.

Case Selection. Given the purpose of the studied selection framework, its potential users are mainly software teams that are only beginning to collect user-interaction data. This limited the potential cases for this study to software teams that had not yet selected a technique for user-interaction data collecting but were still willing to try such collecting out. Clearly, the selected cases had to be open enough that publishing the results reliably was possible and also accessible in the first place for the first author to do the research with them.

Similarly, the number of the cases selected for the study was affected by the fact that the first author had to spend considerable effort in each case. As suitable software teams for this study had not tried out user-interaction data collecting or explored its techniques, the first author had to have access to a potential software team to tell about the possibilities of such data collecting and initiate these tasks. All of these limited the number of selectable cases to few, and finally three software teams were selected for the study.

Data Collection. The data was gathered from February to December 2016. Main parts of the data consist of meeting notes written down by the first author of this paper. Workshop type of meetings were held in each of the cases. Since collecting user-interaction data was a novelty for each participating software team, simple interviewing would not have worked. Rather, the meetings were organized as workshops where the first author motivated the software team to try out user-interaction data collecting and described the different possible techniques for doing so. In addition to the data gathered in meetings, the first author had designated work desks in the same rooms where the software teams were working in cases A and B. Therefore, data was also gathered by observation and by participating in informal meetings. However, these data were only used for verifying some of the previously collected meeting note data, such as how many standup meetings a team have in a week. Although these observational data were not collected in a formal fashion, for the first author it improves the reliability of the results in terms of data triangulation.

Validity and Reliability Considerations. Although this study tries to investigate what kind of things have an effect on the decisions of software teams, the aim is not to find definitive proofs or certain amounts of statistical significance in these relations – rather to broaden the scope of possible causes. Therefore, the internal validity needs especially careful considering. Firstly, selections in earlier cases can have had effects on later ones. This was obviously not intentional but still surely possible because the same researcher explained the different options for the teams in each case. However, the author of this paper separated himself from the decision making in each of the cases and the decisions were made only by the software teams.

Secondly, the criteria presented with the selection framework can have guided the author of this paper to identify only those as the reasons for selection. Consequently, there can have been reasons that have not been mentioned aloud in the meetings but which still have had an effect on the decision. For example, a technology might have been seen as an unsuitable option in such an indisputable manner that the software team has not even mentioned it. This risk was mitigated in cases A and B by not only gathering data from meetings, but also by observing the working of the teams in the their offices and participating in their informal meetings.

The results of this study will not be generalizable for any software team. However, they provide a detailed look on the reasons these three software teams had for choosing a user-interaction data collecting technique. The three case organizations are different from each other in many ways, and therefore the results can give interesting insights to a wide audience. Although only one researcher gathered the data in each case, the meeting notes were shown to and accepted by team members in each case.

3.2 Case Organizations

Case A. Organization A is a large international telecommunications company. The software team that was involved in this case consisted of around eight members. The border of one team in this organization is quite flexible as employees work for many products. The team members had titles of software architect, UX designer, software developer, and line manager. Their products consist primarily of software in the field of network management, and these range from Java software to web based systems. The software development method used in their team has some properties from agile development methods such as Scrum. They, for example, have bi-daily standup meetings and they use Kanban boards to organize their work. New versions of their product are released usually a few times a year.

Case B. Organization B is a privately held software company in Finland. At the time of the study, they had around 300 employees and offices in three major cities in Finland and they primarily develop software in projects for their customers as ordered. The software team involved in this case, however, develops their own software-as-a-service solution. As in case A, the software team in case B also uses things such as daily standup meetings, Kanban boards and retrospective sessions familiar from some of the agile development practices. On the contrary however, they are releasing new versions of their product to the end-users far more often – usually biweekly. Their software team consists of seven members with titles such as product owner, UX specialist, software architect, and software developer.

Case C. Organization C is a research and education center of around 10000 students and 2000 employees. The case C software team is part of a research group who have specialized in embedded systems design. They have developed Kactus2, which is an "open source IP-XACT-based tool for ASIC, FPGA and embedded systems design"[1]. The software has created traction from users world wide. It has been downloaded around 5500 times during the last year requests coming mainly from the USA and from middle Europe. The development team consists of four employees with the titles of software developer, software architect and business architect. The developed tool itself is an installable software system and installer packages for Windows and Linux tar-packages of its new versions are released three to four times a year.

4   Results

The results of the study are twofold. Firstly, we describe the processes with which the techniques were selected in each case. Secondly, we dive into the reasons the software teams had for their selection.

4.1   The Processes of Choosing a Collecting Technology

Case A. In February 2016, members of the software team of Case A explained to the researcher that they had an overall interest in trying out the use of user-interaction data for the further development of their software products. The researcher had presented the different technological approaches for collecting such data in a previous informal meeting. These were the same approaches as described in [5]. Two of the software team's products had been then analyzed by

---

[1] http://funbase.cs.tut.fi/.

the Organization A in terms of the suitability of the products in experimenting with user-interaction data collecting. The first of the two was Tool X written in Java, and the second one a JavaScript based Web-system Y. The team decided to carry on the collecting efforts with the System Y.

After this decision, the team had a meeting with the researcher to give a short presentation about the code base of the System Y and its software architecture. The meeting was arranged as a workshop to find out what kind of user-interaction data the team wanted to have collected. In addition, the team described what is important for the collecting technology and its implementation.

From this point on, the job of the researcher in the eyes of the software team was to develop a demonstrative collecting tool for their product. The researcher then used the criteria from the selection framework and was left with only one suitable technology approach – developing a new tool for **monitoring the execution environment**. After developing a prototype of such a collecting tool, the researcher presented it in a demo show for the team in March and got a thumbs up from the team to go on with experimenting with the actual System Y. A testing day with eight users from within the Organization A was held in December 2016 to try out an improved version of the collecting tool implemented in a lab version of the System Y. The developed collecting tool is available in GitHub[2].

Case B. In case B, a similar workshop meeting as in Case A was held by the researcher with the software team in March 2016. The team explained the method they use for developing their software and what kind of a software the product is architecturally. It turned out, however, that this team had more experiences with collecting use related data even at that point. For example, they had tried out Google Analytics with some default settings for their product already. After explaining that the data was mainly collected for debugging, two of the team members and the researcher worked out also new targets in their software development process which could be improved with user-interaction data. These ideas ranged from prioritizing their product backlog to improvements in the user interface of the product.

The team was well motivated to try out user-interaction data collecting. However, as its return on investment was still unclear the first few tasks for data collecting were agreed upon to be completed with as little work effort and changes to the software architecture as possible. Therefore, three very specifically described places in the UI of the product were selected to be improved with the help of user-interaction data collecting. As the team had already tried out Google Analytics on the same product, it was a straightforward choice for the storing and analyzing the data of the tasks at hand as well.

At that point, the researcher described the same technological approaches to the team as in Case A. Also similar to Case A, the selecting of the collecting technology was an obvious pick since the three tasks were specified so explicitly. The team members and the researcher made an unanimous decision to use **manual implementation** for instrumenting the required places of the source code.

[2] https://github.com/ssuonsyrja/Usage-Data-Collector.

The researcher was then given rights to change the source code. After applying the collecting code to six places in it, the version was sent to end-users for a two week collecting period in April 2016.

Case C. In case C, an initial meeting was held with two members of the software team and the researcher in September 2016. Similar to the previous cases, the team members described the environment for which they develop software and the architecture of their product. The meeting then continued as a workshop, where each participant tried to figure out ways for how user-interaction data collecting could be used for their software development. Such targets were plenty, and no specific tasks were selected at that point. The researcher then explained the same technological approaches for user-interaction data collecting to the team members. The option of monitoring execution environment was rejected at this point, but the rest still remained possible for selecting.

The evaluation criteria from the selection framework were then used for the analysis of the product and its environment. Since the aspect-oriented approach raised the most interest among the software team, it was decided that the availability of AOP libraries and their suitability to the product were to be examined. An alternative implementation of a UI library was considered as a second choice, but the rest of the alternatives were rejected at this point. During the fall of 2016, the **aspect-oriented approach** was implemented technically successfully to the product. The first data collecting period is planned to be held during the spring of 2017 with a student group as experimental end-users.

4.2   Reasons for Choosing a Collecting Technique

Case A. The first decision made by the Organization A was that they selected to try out user-interaction data collecting with System Y. This decision was based on **the sources and the reuse possibilities** of the collecting effort, because the motivation was to specifically try out this kind of data collecting as a technical concept rather than immediately produce actionable insights from exact places of a product. Had the collecting effort been carried out with the Tool X, the reuse would have been practically impossible since its environment was not as common as with the System Y.

Although the overall motivation was to test user-interaction data collecting conceptually, the team wanted to focus the requirements of the data collecting after the selection of the specific **source**, i.e. product. Finding a technology that could be easily reused with as little implementation **effort** as possible became a goal. This made the option of manual instrumentation heavily unfavorable. The team also emphasized how **the security and configurability** were important for the collecting technology. For example, the environment of their product was such that the collecting should be easy to be left out of the whole product when necessary. Consequently, the unobtrusiveness of the technology was highly valued.

Although the need for low configuring effort increased the attractiveness of using an automated tool for instrumentation, the security concerns were so heavy that the use of a tool developed outside the organization was not recommended. Therefore, the option of finding and using 3rd party tools was quickly rejected. In addition, the availability and effects of AOP libraries to things such as the **overhead** were unknown in the environment of System Y. Possibly the most significant of all, there was no motivation to make as big **a change to the software architecture** as needed by the aspect-oriented approach. The same reason applied for rejecting the option of an alternative UI library, because having different versions of the libraries was not acceptable for the delivery pipeline.

Case B. Similar to case A, the motivation for the team of case B in user-interaction data collecting was to try it out as a concept. On the contrary however, this resulted in this case in a faster and a narrower scoped experiment. In other words, the **targets** and the **source** of their data collecting were very clearly defined in the first place. At the same time, this resulted in the lack of significance of the implementation **effort** because it would be so low even with the manual approach. Similarly, **reuse** was not considered as a significant reason, since there were no guarantees that the data collecting mechanism would be ever reused. All this resulted in a very straightforward choice of the manual approach. It was by far the easiest approach to implement on a small scale and it allowed the team to try out if user-interaction data collecting in a fast and low-effort way.

Case C. Being a new thing for the case C software team, the user-interaction data collecting was again designed as a demonstrative experiment similar to the case A. Likewise, the interests of the team in this case were technical in the sense that they firstly wanted to find out a suitable technique for user-interaction data collecting. In the best case scenario, this technique could be then used with their actual product and actual end-users after the initial experiment. Because there was no simple access to experiment the collecting with real users, in the manner of case B, and the **security** requirements were weighted a lot heavier, the technical design of the collecting was the primary focus. Although the possible user-interaction data types and collection places, i.e. **sources**, were plenty, they were to be considered only secondly after validating the technical setup for the collecting.

This affected the evaluation of the collecting techniques in terms of prioritizing the criteria from the selection framework. Not limiting the **sources and targets** became important, because the collecting technique would not be selected and designed for just a one time try out. Although not mentioned out loud by the team, this could hint towards them valuing the **reuse** possibilities. All of these resulted in the attractiveness of the techniques enabling lower work **effort** spend on each distinct collecting place. Further on, the whole collecting was required to be able to be switched off as easily as possible. In other words, the **configurability** of the collecting technique was valued high.

5   Discussion

In each case, the process of choosing a collecting technology for user-interaction data was more or less the same. Members of the software team and the researcher had a meeting, where the researcher described the different technologies overall. After finding out what was the underlying goal for the team in the user-interaction data collecting, the most important criteria for the selecting became quite clear for both the researcher and the team members.

Comparing those criteria with the ones in the selecting framework, it is safe to say that most of the evaluation criteria from the selection framework were used without the researcher pushing the team towards those specific points. However, **timeliness** was never mentioned by the teams, which could signal either its insignificance or that its need is self-evident. On the contrary, **overhead** rose up in each case as a conversation topic but similar to the timeliness it did not seem to have any effect on the selecting in any case.

For both of these, it is worth mentioning that none of the techniques had a known disadvantage nor a limitation in terms of these criteria (timeliness and overhead) that would have been significant enough to get the whole technique rejected. However, in the original selection framework they were marked with minus signs for the monitoring execution environment technique. Therefore, the summary table with the evaluation criteria from the original selection framework, i.e. Table 1, requires some refining.

Firstly, the evaluations should consist of a wider scale than a plain plus or a minus sign. In these cases, some of the criteria affected the selection clearly a lot more than others. For example, the timeliness and overhead criteria did not seem to have an effect on the selection but on the other hand, the effort level of the manual technique had it rejected. Therefore, we propose an additional exclamation mark to the evaluations in case the criterion is a possible ground for a rejection. We have gone through the rest of the summary evaluations and added an exclamation mark where necessary based on the cases.

Secondly, some of the evaluations are not clearly pluses nor minuses. Therefore, we have added an option of $+/-$ marking for the evaluation, if the technique does not definitely support nor limit the selection in terms of the specific criterion. Adding this option has had effects especially on the evaluations of the techniques that are heavily intertwined with specific tools. For example, the minus signs in the execution environment column of timeliness and overhead rows can be then replaced with this option. We have reviewed the evaluations and changed the original signs into $+/-$ markings where necessary.

Thirdly, the *effort* criterion should be divided into two and renamed to *scalability*. The intention of the criterion is to depict the work effort that is required from the software developers to implement collecting snippets to the different places of the source code. Finally, however, there was a clear need for an evaluation criterion of how great an effort is needed from the software developers to change the software architecture and/or environment of the moment to support the collecting technique. This criterion could be named as the *change* that is

Table 2. Refined summary of the technique evaluations.

Criteria	Techniques				
	Manual	Tools	AOP	UI Lib.	E.E.
Timeliness	+	+/−	+	+	+/−
Targets	+	−	+!	−	+/−
Scalability	−!	+	+!	+	+!
Overhead	+	−	+/−	−	−
Sources	+	−	−	−	−
Configurability	+	−	+	+	+/−!
Security	+	+/−!	+/−	+	+/−
Reuse	−	+	−	−	+!
Change	+!	+	−!	−!	+

+ = Supports selecting
− = Technique has limitations
+/− = No clear support nor limitations
! = A possible ground the rejection

required. With these refinements to the criteria and evaluations, the summary table of the evaluations is as listed in Table 2.

In addition to the changes in the evaluations, the original selection framework requires some refinements based on the cases as well. First of all, in these cases the underlying goal of the whole collecting effort was the most important driver in the selection process. In cases A and C the delivery pipelines did not allow fast and flexible releases of new software versions with user-interaction data collecting capabilities, and so the software teams decided to develop their environment so that the collecting would be possible in the future. This became their real target, where as the team in case B did not have to develop their environment. On the contrary, they had the luxury of aiming straightforwardly at just testing out the collecting and the resulting user-interaction data with a minimum effort.

Therefore, the first step of the selection framework, *exploring the case*, should be clarified and replaced by a step of *defining a main goal* for the collecting effort. Based on these cases, it would be easy to then *remove the irrelevant evaluation criteria* after defining such a goal. For example, in case B the *scalability* of the collecting technique was seen unnecessary after the collecting was designed to be implemented as a one time solution.

Exploring the case still included important things that should be part of the selecting framework. Thus, the next thing of the process should be to *find out the critical limitations*. The rest of the original selection framework worked out as it was in these cases, and so no other changes were required to the final refined version of the selection framework. This framework is illustrated in Fig. 2.

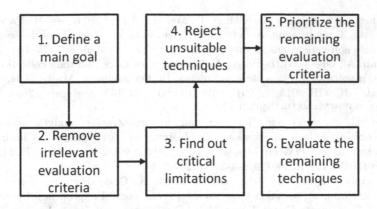

Fig. 2. Refined selection framework for user-interaction collecting techniques.

6   Conclusions

In this paper, we studied three cases where software teams selected techniques for user-interaction data collecting. More specifically, we examined the reasons the software teams had for the selection. To complement this, we evaluated our previously designed selection framework and refined it based on the data gathered from the cases.

In these cases, two of the most valued criteria for the selection were the scalability of the technique and the lack of changes required to the software architecture and deployment pipeline of the moment. Additionally, teams appreciated the reuse, security, and configurability of the techniques as well as the support for a wide range of monitoring targets. On the other hand, the rest of the criteria presented with the original selection framework, i.e. timeliness, overhead, and support for different source applications, did not seem to have a significant effect on the selections.

The original evaluations of the different user-interaction data collecting techniques were refined to include markings for the different levels of significance. In addition, the original selection framework was fixed to better support these more detailed evaluations. With these changes, we think the selection framework and its complementary technique evaluations can help practitioners greatly to the beginning of their journey of user-interaction data collecting.

Acknowledgments. The authors wish to thank DIMECC's Need4Speed program (http://www.n4s.fi/) funded by the Finnish Funding Agency for Innovation Tekes (http://www.tekes.fi/en/tekes/) for its support for this research.

References

1. Leppänen, M., Mäkinen, S., Pagels, M., Eloranta, V.P., Itkonen, J., Mäntylä, M.V., Männistö, T.: The highways and country roads to continuous deployment. IEEE Softw. **32**(2), 64–72 (2015)

2. Mäkinen, S., Leppänen, M., Kilamo, T., Mattila, A.L., Laukkanen, E., Pagels, M., Männistö, T.: Improving the delivery cycle: a multiple-case study of the toolchains in finnish software intensive enterprises. Inf. Softw. Technol. **80**, 175–194 (2016)
3. Fabijan, A., Olsson, H.H., Bosch, J.: Customer feedback and data collection techniques in software R&D: a literature review. In: Fernandes, J., Machado, R., Wnuk, K. (eds.) ICSOB 2015. LNBIP, vol. 210, pp. 139–153. Springer, Cham (2015). doi:10.1007/978-3-319-19593-3_12
4. Suonsyrjä, S., Mikkonen, T.: Designing an unobtrusive analytics framework for monitoring Java applications. In: Kobyliński, A., Czarnacka-Chrobot, B., Świerczek, J. (eds.) IWSM/Mensura -2015. LNBIP, vol. 230, pp. 160–175. Springer, Cham (2015). doi:10.1007/978-3-319-24285-9_11
5. Suonsyrjä, S., Systä, K., Mikkonen, T., Terho, H.: Collecting usage data for software development: selection framework for technological approaches. In: Proceedings of The Twenty-Eighth International Conference on Software Engineering and Knowledge Engineering (SEKE 2016) (2016)
6. Rodriguez, P., Haghighatkhah, A., Lwakatare, L.E., Teppola, S., Suomalainen, T., Eskeli, J., Karvonen, T., Kuvaja, P., Verner, J.M., Oivo, M.: Continuous deployment of software intensive products and services: a systematic mapping study. J. Syst. Softw. **123**, 263–291 (2017)
7. Chittimalli, P.K., Shah, V.: GEMS: a generic model based source code instrumentation framework. In: Proceedings of the Fifth IEEE International Conference on Software Testing, Verification and Validation, pp. 909–914. IEEE Computer Society (2012)
8. Chen, W., Wassyng, A., Maibaum, T.: Combining static and dynamic impact analysis for large-scale enterprise systems. In: Jedlitschka, A., Kuvaja, P., Kuhrmann, M., Männistö, T., Münch, J., Raatikainen, M. (eds.) PROFES 2014. LNCS, vol. 8892, pp. 224–238. Springer, Cham (2014). doi:10.1007/978-3-319-13835-0_16
9. Chawla, A., Orso, A.: A generic instrumentation framework for collecting dynamic information. SIGSOFT Softw. Eng. Notes **29**(5), 1–4 (2004)
10. Yin, R.K.: Case Study Research: Design and Methods. Sage Publications, Thousand Oaks (2013)
11. Von Alan, R.H., March, S.T., Park, J., Ram, S.: Design science in information systems research. MIS Q. **28**(1), 75–105 (2004)
12. Peffers, K., Tuunanen, T., Rothenberger, M.A., Chatterjee, S.: A design science research methodology for information systems research. J. Manage. Inf. Syst. **24**(3), 45–77 (2007)
13. Runeson, P., Höst, M.: Guidelines for conducting and reporting case study research in software engineering. Empirical Softw. Eng. **14**(2), 131 (2008)

Comparing Requirements Decomposition Within the Scrum, Scrum with Kanban, XP, and Banana Development Processes

Davide Taibi[1]([✉])[iD], Valentina Lenarduzzi[1][iD], Andrea Janes[1][iD], Kari Liukkunen[2][iD], and Muhammad Ovais Ahmad[2][iD]

[1] Free University of Bolzano/Bozen, Bolzano, Italy
{davide.taibi,valentina.lenarduzzi,andrea.janes}@unibz.it
[2] University of Oulu, Oulu, Finland
{kari.liukkunen,muhammad.ahmad}@oulu.fi

Abstract. **Context:** Eliciting requirements from customers is a complex task. In Agile processes, the customer talks directly with the development team and often reports requirements in an unstructured way. The requirements elicitation process is up to the developers, who split it into user stories by means of different techniques. **Objective:** We aim to compare the requirements decomposition process of an unstructured process and three Agile processes, namely XP, Scrum, and Scrum with Kanban. **Method:** We conducted a multiple case study with a replication design, based on the project idea of an entrepreneur, a designer with no experience in software development. Four teams developed the project independently, using four different development processes. The requirements were elicited by the teams from the entrepreneur, who acted as product owner and was available to talk with the four groups during the project. **Results:** The teams decomposed the requirements using different techniques, based on the selected development process. **Conclusion:** Scrum with Kanban and XP resulted in the most effective processes from different points of view. Unexpectedly, decomposition techniques commonly adopted in traditional processes are still used in Agile processes, which may reduce project agility and performance. Therefore, we believe that decomposition techniques need to be addressed to a greater extent, both from the practitioners' and the research points of view.

1 Introduction

Eliciting requirements from customers is a complex task. In Agile processes, the introduction of the product owner usually facilitates the process, suggesting that the customer talk directly with the development team and thus reducing the number of intermediaries. However, the product owner, especially when he or she is not an expert in the project domain, reports requirements in natural language, in their own words, and often in an unstructured way.

The requirements elicitation process is up to the developers, who usually split it up into user stories in the case of Agile processes.

© The Author(s) 2017
H. Baumeister et al. (Eds.): XP 2017, LNBIP 283, pp. 68–83, 2017.
DOI: 10.1007/978-3-319-57633-6_5

To the best of our knowledge, there are no studies that have attempted to understand how requirements are decomposed in Agile processes and, moreover, no studies that compare requirements decomposition among different Agile processes or other processes.

To bridge this gap, we designed and conducted the first such empirical study, with the aim of comparing the requirements decomposition process of an unstructured process and three Agile processes, namely XP, Scrum, and Scrum with Kanban [21]. We conducted the study as a multiple case study with a replication design [1] since it was not possible to execute a controlled experiment because of the unavailability of developers for the major effort required. We selected four groups of second-year master students as participants, which constitute a good sample of the next generation of developers entering the job market. They were perfectly suited for this task since the project did not require the use of new technologies unknown to the students, and they can thus be viewed as the next generation of professionals [10–13]. Students are perfectly suitable when the study does not require a steep learning curve for using new technology [13, 17].

We selected a project idea to be developed by means of an idea contest for entrepreneurs, selecting an idea from a designer with no experience in software development. This project idea was then developed by four teams using four different development processes. The requirements were elicited by the teams from the same entrepreneur who acted as product owner with all four groups.

The results show interesting differences regarding requirements decomposition. The team that developed in XP decomposed a lot more stories, followed by the one using Scrum with Kanban, then the one using Scrum, and finally the team using the unstructured process. Another interesting result is related to the development effort, which was perfectly inversely proportional to the number of user stories decomposed, resulting in the highest effort for the unstructured process and the lowest for the XP one.

This paper is structured as follows. Section 2 introduces the background and related work. Section 3 presents the multiple case study and Sect. 4 the results obtained. Section 5 describes the threats to validity and Sect. 6 draws conclusions and future work.

2 Background and Related Work

The term "user story decomposition" describes the act of breaking a user story down into smaller parts [8]. User stories are typically decomposed into parts that have a scope that is large enough to provide value to the customer but small enough so that the effort for implementing the story can be estimated with a low risk of being wrong. A story with a smaller scope is likely to be less complex than a story with a large scope. Moreover, if the scope is large, more things can go wrong, e.g., unknown details might emerge, the architecture may be inadequate, and so on [4]. Altogether, the expectation is that it should be easier to estimate the effort for developing a small story than that for a large one. As a consequence, sprint planning, i.e., defining which stories the team should be able to complete during a sprint, is more likely to be accurate with small user stories.

Additionally, developing stories with a smaller scope allows the team to complete a user story more often than if it were to develop only a few large user stories. This allows it to regularly deliver business value to the customer, with the consequence that the customer can provide feedback earlier, allowing the team to learn faster which requirements the system being developed should fulfill.

A popular technique for decomposing user stories is "User Story Mapping" [9], which decomposes the stories from the user's point of view, i.e., it decomposes the flow of user activities "into a workflow that can be further decomposed into a set of detailed tasks" [8]. User Story Mapping uses the terms "activity", "task", and "subtask" to describe high-level activities (e.g., "buy a product"), tasks (e.g., "manage shopping cart"), and subtasks, i.e., the decomposed user stories, which are the ones assigned to developers (e.g., "add product to shopping cart"). Rubin uses the terms "epic", "theme", and "sprintable story" to apply it within Scrum [8].

Outside of an Agile context, the decomposition of requirements into different parts has been discussed to prepare their technical implementation: for example, [14] describes techniques used in service-based applications to decompose complex requirements in order to reuse relatively simple services; in [15], the authors develop a technique for matching parts of the requirements to COTS components; in [16], the authors discuss how to decompose architectural requirements to support software deployment in the cloud; in [17, 20], the authors study conflicting requirements; in [18], the authors propose an extension to UML to allow decomposing use case models into models at several levels of abstraction; and in [19], the authors decompose requirements to identify security-centric requirements.

All these examples rather describe decomposition as an activity to devise a specification that describes the system to be built. Within an Agile context, decomposition is used to reduce the risk of providing a constant flow of value; therefore, user stories are typically decomposed following the principle that each one should deliver value to the customer. To the best of our knowledge, no peer-reviewed works exist that describe decomposition techniques used within an Agile context. However, various other techniques worth mentioning have been developed by practitioners, who describe them on their blogs. In the following, we will describe the approaches they propose.

As a general approach, Lawrence [3] suggests two general rules of thumb: choosing a decomposition strategy that allows deprioritizing or throwing away parts of a story, thus isolating and removing unnecessary smaller parts of a larger user story, and then choosing a strategy that results in equally sized small stories. Verwijs [5] distinguishes between two ways to break down user stories: horizontal and vertical. Horizontal breakdown means dividing user stories by the type of work that is needed or the layers or components that are involved, e.g. separating a large user story into smaller user stories for the UI, the database, the server, etc. He suggests avoiding this type of break-down as user stories will no longer represent units of "working, demonstrable software", as it will be hard to ship them separately to the user, as it increases bottlenecks since developers will tend to specialize in types of user stories, e.g., the "database guy", and as it is hard to prioritize horizontally divided stories. Verwijs suggests breaking down user stories "vertically", i.e., "in such a way that smaller items still result in working, demonstrable, software [5]." Recent works also support Verwijs proposal, suggesting to decompose the user stories incrementally, starting from the minimum viable product [16] and decomposing each functionality vertically, so as to also improve the user stories effort estimation accuracy [7, 15] and the testing easiness [20]. However, this process is more suitable for projects started from scratch with SCRUM instead of project where SCRUM has been introduced later [14].

As these are specific techniques for decomposing a large user story into smaller ones in an Agile context, we integrated their proposals into the following list:

1. Input options/platform [5]: decompose user stories based on the different UI possibilities, e.g., command line input or a graphical user interface;
2. Study conjunctions and connecting words (like "and") to separate stories [4];
3. Data types or parameters [3, 5]: user stories are split based on the datatypes they return or the parameters they are supposed to handle; for example, during a search process, one could define different user stories for the different search parameters the user is allowed to define;
4. Operations, e.g. CRUD [3, 5]: whenever user stories involve a set of operations, such as CRUD (create, read, update, delete), they are separated into smaller versions implementing each operation separately;
5. Simple/Complex [3, 5]: a complex user story is decomposed into a simple, default variation and additional variations that describe special cases or additional aspects;
6. Major effort [3, 5]: a complex user story is decomposed into smaller ones isolating the difficulty in one user story;
7. Workflow steps [3–5, 8]: the temporal development of the user story is studied by imagining the process that the typical user has to follow to accomplish the user story in order to develop (smaller) step-by-step user stories;
8. Test scenarios/test case [4, 5]: user stories are divided based on the way they will be tested. If they will be tested by first executing a sequence of steps and then executing another sequence of steps, these two groups of steps will be implemented as two separate user stories;
9. Roles [5]: one functionality is formulated as separate user stories describing the same story for different user roles (personas) in each user story;
10. Business rules [3, 5]: user stories are extended by "business rules", i.e., constraints or rules that are defined by the context in which the system has to be developed, e.g., a specific law that has to be fulfilled, and the single constraints and rules are used to formulate more fine-grained user stories;
11. Happy/unhappy flow [5]: separate user stories are created for successful variations and unsuccessful variations of the user story;
12. Browser compatibility [5]: if there is a large effort connected to particular technologies, e.g., a text-based browser, [5] recommends splitting user stories according to browser compatibility. Having separate user stories for different browsers allows the product owner to prioritize the work;
13. Identified acceptance criteria [4, 5]: acceptance criteria are defined for user stories that can be used to develop a refined set of (smaller) user stories;
14. External dependencies [5]: user stories can be separated based on the external systems to which they have access;
15. Usability requirements [5]: user stories are separated based on particular usability requirements, e.g., particular implementations for color-blind users;

16. SEO requirements [5]: user stories are separated based on search-engine-optimization requirements, e.g., separate landing pages for specific keywords;
17. Break out a Spike [3]: a user story that is not well understood is divided into one that develops a prototype, a so-called "spike", and one that implements the actual functionality; and
18. Refinement of generic words (like "manage") into more concrete user stories [4].

3   The Multiple Case Study

As stated in the introduction, the objective of this research is to compare the requirements gathering processes and user story decomposition in Agile and unstructured development processes. Therefore, we designed this study as a multiple case study with a replication design [1].

As depicted in Fig. 1, we first identified the research questions, then selected the case studies and their design.

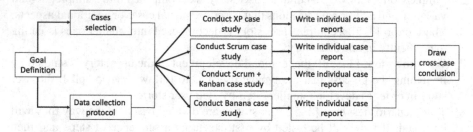

Fig. 1. Study design (adapted from [1])

In this section, we present the study process we adopted, the goal, the research questions, and the metrics for the case study. This is followed by a description of the designs used for the case study, the measurement instruments, and the results obtained.

3.1   Study Goal

According to our research objective, we formulated the goal of the case study following the GQM approach [2] as follows:

Analyze requirements decomposition in user stories (or tasks)
For the purpose of comparison
With respect to the granularity
From the point of view of software developers
In the context of Scrum, Scrum with Kanban, XP, and an ad-hoc development process

Note that in the case of Agile processes, we refer to user stories, whereas in the case of the ad-hoc development process, we refer to tasks. This leads to the following research question:

RQ1: How does the requirements decomposition of user stories differ between the four considered development processes?

For this research question, we defined six metrics:

M1: Number of requirements: the number of requirements provided by the product owner;

M2: Number of user stories: the number of decomposed user stories;

M3: Number of tasks/user stories per requirement: describes how each requirement was decomposed in each team for each requirement;

M4: Total effort (actual development time): time spent (hours) to develop the whole application;

M5: Total effort for each requirement: time spent (hours) to implement requirements among the different teams;

M6: Total effort per task/user story: time spent (hours) to implement each task/user story; and

M7: Strategy used to decompose requirements into tasks or user stories: strategy described in the literature used to decompose each requirement, assigned to two researchers of this paper studying the names of the decomposed requirements.

3.2 Study Design

We designed our study as a multiple-case replication design [1]. We asked four development teams to develop the same application. The four sub-case studies are sufficient as replications since the teams have similar backgrounds. All the teams received the same requirements provided by the same entrepreneur, who acted as product owner and within the same timeframe.

One team was required to develop the project in Scrum, one in Scrum with Kanban, another one using XP, and the last one was free to develop using an ad-hoc process, as shown in Fig. 2. We call the ad-hoc development process the "Banana" process, since this term is used among practitioners to describe processes that produce immature products, which have to "ripen" after being shipped to the customer, like bananas.

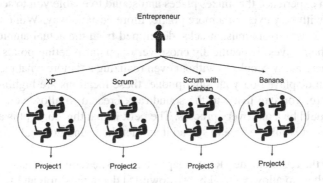

Fig. 2. Study design

As the population of our study, we selected four groups of master students in computer science from two universities involved in the Software Factory Network [6]. One group was from the Master in Computer Science curriculum of the University of Bolzano-Bozen (Italy) and the other four groups were from the Master in Information Processing Science curriculum of the University of Oulu (Finland). The groups had very similar backgrounds since they were all master students in computer science and both universities have similar programs due to their participation in the European Master in Software Engineering (EMSE, http://em-se.eu/) program and having taken classes on agile software development and software engineering. International students took part in this project, originating from Finland, India, Nepal, China, Russia, Bangladesh, Germany, Italy, and Ghana.

The students were randomly assigned to each group taking into account that each team needed to have at least one experienced developer.

The groups were asked to develop the same application. The application requirements were proposed by the product owner, a designer from Bolzano with no experience in software development who described the requirements to the groups with the same schedule and using the same terminology.

The developers elicited the requirements, translating them from the "designer language", a non-technical language, to a more technical one. The groups working with Scrum (with and without Kanban) and XP decomposed the requirements into user stories, while the group using "Banana" decomposed them into tasks.

The developed project. The teams were required to develop an Android application called Serendipity. The idea was selected in a contest for entrepreneurs, where entrepreneurs were asked to submit the minimum viable product [16] description of their project ideas that could be implemented in the software factory lab (http://ideas.inf.unibz.it/). Serendipity is an Android application and a web application intended to share a set of sounds in a specific location, so as to have the user recall special moments by listening to the sounds.

The entrepreneur, a designer from Bolzano, initially defined the project idea as: "Serendipity means "fortunate happenstance" or "pleasant surprise". This project is meant to be an experience that mixes places and sound to enable you to see places you usually go to with new eyes, in a more poetic, more ecstatic way. While taking walk, you will have access to six music tracks, developed from the actual ambient sound of those places themselves. I specifically chose very popular meeting points in my town (Bolzano), where many people go without even realizing anymore what the place looks like. On a map displayed on your smartphone, these locations are highlighted. When you arrive there, you can listen to the soundtrack created to allow you to enjoy the moment. It should be a discovery process. The perk is that this concept is applicable to any city/place – it would be nice to spread it and let the sound go local".

The entrepreneur acted as product owner and described the project to the groups, which elicited the requirements (Req) independently. The requirements were intentionally stated such as to allow vertical break-down [5] decomposition and were proposed to the groups within this timeframe:

Week #0:

Req 1: Minimal Viable Product, with all pages with fake content. The parts of the product comprised: Sign-in/Login; Maps; Listen to sound; Record sound; Rules; and About.

Req 2: Show the list of available sounds on a map.

Req 3: Allow only registered users to record tracks.

Req 4: The main sound can only be played when the user is exactly in the correct location.

Week #3:

Req 5: No more than three sounds allowed within a radius of 300 m.

Req 6: Sounds cannot be downloaded but only played.

Req 7: Any user (registered or not) can listen to sounds.

Req 8: Users are allowed to listen to an ambient sound within a radius of 300 m from the main sound.

Week #5:

Req 9: Play a notification when entering the notification area, so as to alert the user to a sound in the neighborhood.

Req 10: Due to the lack of accuracy of GPS signals in smartphones, the main sound must to be playable within a radius of 10 m instead of only at the exact point, as previously required in Req 6.

Week #7:

Req 11: Create a "liking" system for each sound, allowing users to "like" a maximum of one sound per spot. In this way, sounds with a lower number of likes can be replaced by new sounds after three weeks.

Req 12: Create a web application to allow users to login to their profile with the only purpose of uploading sounds, especially for professional users who would like to upload high-quality or edited sounds.

Req 13: Allow users to register with their Facebook account.

The teams in Oulu that started the development in February were asked to develop the same tool with the same requirements proposed with the same schedule. To ensure the correct succession of requirements and to prevent the development of the previous project in Bolzano to influence the entrepreneur's perception of her project, we recorded every requirement elicited in Bolzano so as to ask her to request the same things without revealing any details to the other teams.

3.3 Study Execution

The web application was developed at the Software Factory Lab of the two participating universities. The participants were initially informed about the study and about the usage of the collected data. The development took place at the University of Bolzano-Bozen (Italy) from October 2015 until the end of January 2016 and at the University of Oulu from February 2016 to the end of April 2016. The groups were required to spend a minimum effort of 250 h on their work.

Three groups were composed of second-year master students in computer science at the University of Oulu (Finland), while one group was composed of second-year master students in computer science from the University of Bolzano-Bozen. The selected students represent typical developers entering the market. It is therefore interesting not only to understand how they break down requirements but also to observe their work processes. All of the teams had iterations lasting two weeks. The Banana team also met the entrepreneur every two weeks in order to be updated on the requirements.

The first group (Kanban, https://github.com/Belka1000867/Serendipity) was composed of five master students who developed in Scrum with Kanban. The second group (Scrum, https://github.com/samukarjalainen/serendipity-app and https://github.com/-samukarjalainen/serendipity-web) was composed of five master students who developed in Scrum with 2-week sprints, while the third group (XP, https://github.com/davidetaibi/unibz-serendipity) was composed of four master students who developed in Extreme Programming (XP). The fourth group (Banana, https://github.com/Silvergrail/Serendipity/releases) was composed of six master students who developed in an unstructured process, which we defined as "Banana" process.

3.4 Data Collection and Analysis

The measures were collected during meetings with the developers. They also used the collected data to draw burn-down charts and track results. We defined a set of measures to be collected as follows:

- number of sprints;
- opening and closing date for each user story;
- user story description;
- responsible developer for each user story; and
- the actual effort for each user story.

The requirements were elicited from the entrepreneur. However, to avoid interference with the development process, two researchers attended the requirements elicitation meetings and reported the requirements independently.

Three sets of decisions were used to measure pairwise interrater reliability in order to get a fair/good agreement on the first process iteration. In order to resolve any differences, where necessary, we discussed any incongruity to get 100% coverage among the authors.

We associated user stories/tasks with each requirement defined by the entrepreneur. Then we calculated sums, medians, and averages.

4   Study Results

The teams developed the project according to the assigned development process. The XP team developed with a test-first approach, while the two Scrum teams (Scrum and

Scrum with Kanban) developed test cases during the process. The Banana team developed a limited set of test cases at the end of the process. All four teams delivered a final product with the same set of features, with no requirement missing.

The three Agile teams delivered the first version of the product with a limited set of features that could be evaluated by the customer after two sprints, while the Banana team delivered the application, with nearly all the features implemented, only three weeks before the end of the development and then started to implement tests. This result was expected because of the structure of the process, since they decomposed the requirements by means of a horizontal break-down. For example, they developed the whole server-side application first, starting from the design of the database schema, and then the Android application connecting the frontend with the server-side functionalities.

The three Agile teams decomposed the requirements by means of a vertical breakdown [5], so as to deliver to the entrepreneur a working product with the required features as soon as possible. For example, Req 2 (Show the list of available sounds on a map) was decomposed by the XP team into: "Show a Google map centered on the user location in the Android app" and "Show existing sounds as map placeholders", while the Scrum team and the Scrum with Kanban team decomposed this into: "Show a Google map", "Centered on the user location in the Android app," and "Show existing sounds as map placeholders."

As expected, the groups decomposed the 13 requirements into different subsets of user stories/tasks. As reported in Table 1 and Fig. 3, the team working in XP is the one that decomposed the requirements with the lowest granularity (46 user stories), followed by the team using Scrum with Kanban (40 user stories) and the team using Scrum (27 stories). However, the team using the Banana approach decomposed the requirements into only 13 tasks. Moreover, they merged two requirements into one single task. Considering the number of decomposed user stories or tasks per requirement, the results are obviously similar to the total number of user stories and tasks reported.

Table 1. Summary of metrics results

Metrics	XP	Scrum	Scrum+Kanban	Banana
M1 (# of requirements)	13	13	13	13
M2 (# of user stories/tasks)	46	27	40	19
M3 (user stories per requirements)	3.54	2.08	3.08	1.46
M5 (effort per requirement)	23.04	36.77	24.46	48.85
M6 (effort per user story/task)	6.51	17.70	7.95	33.42
Total effort all user stories/tasks	299.5	478	318	635
Other effort	92	10	0	481
M4 (total effort entire project)	391.5	488	318	1116

Taking into account the required effort, the team developing with Scrum with Kanban was the most efficient one, spending a total of 318 h on development. The XP and Scrum teams followed with an effort of 391 h for XP and 478 h for Scrum. The Banana team, unexpectedly, spent dramatically higher effort (1116 h), nearly 3.5 times more than the teams developing with Scrum and Kanban. Considering the effort spent on other tasks not related to user stories, such as database design, server setup, and such, the team using Scrum with Kanban was also the most efficient one, spending no effort on these tasks.

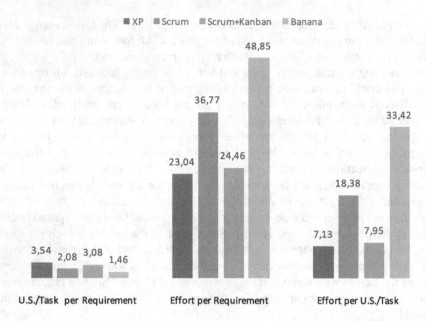

Fig. 3. Comparison of user stories and task decomposition and effort (hours)

The Scrum team only spent 10 h on other activities (2%), the XP team spent 92 h (23%), and the Banana team 481 h (43%).

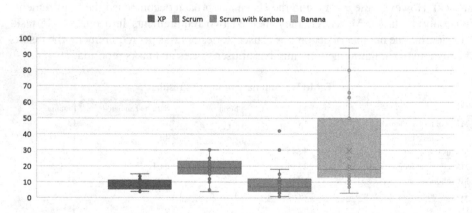

Fig. 4. Boxplot of the effort spent per user story/task

When analyzing the average effort spent to implement each requirement, the teams developing with XP and Scrum with Kanban obtained similar results, while the Scrum and the Banana teams spent similar amounts of effort per requirement, nearly 2.5 times more than the XP and Scrum with Kanban teams. Taking into account the distribution of effort depicted in Fig. 4, there is a similar distribution of effort spent on user stories between the Agile teams, while, as expected, the Banana team had the highest variability of effort. Looking at the decomposition for each task (Table 2), other differences among the groups emerge. Req 6 was not implemented by all the teams since it was related to "not implementing" the download sound feature. The Banana team also considered zero effort for Req 7 since they merged the tasks with the activities related to Req 4.

Table 2. Effort and user stories/tasks per requirement

Requir ement	XP			Scrum			Scrum with Kanban			Banana		
	Effort	# of user stories	Effort/ user story	Effort	# of user stories	Effort/ user story	Effort	# of user stories	Effort/ user story	Effort	# of tasks	Effort/ task
R1	40.5	6	6.8	81	3	27.0	77	5	15.4	140	5	28
R2	20.5	2	10.3	47	3	15.7	17	3	5.7	50	1	50
R3	94	11	8.5	57	3	19.0	112	9	12.4	150	3	50
R4	66.5	7	9.5	46	2	23.0	27	4	6.8	94	1	94
R5	9	2	4.5	16	1	16.0	5	1	5.0	19	1	19
R6												
R7	4	1	4.0	6	1	6.0	5	1	5.0			
R8	13	1	13.0	10	1	10.0	1	1	1.0	18	1	18
R9	17	2	8.5	12	2	6.0	15	1	15.0	25	1	25
R10	10.5	1	10.5	2	1	2.0	1	1	1.0	13	1	13
R11	10	1	10.0	21	1	21.0	2	4	0.5	21	2	10.5
R12	7	1	7.0	165	8	20.6	44	9	4.9	87	2	43.5
R13	7.5	1	7.5	15	2	7.5	12	1	12.0	18	1	18

Table 3 illustrates the various methods applied by the various teams to break down the requirements into user stories (or tasks for the Banana approach), i.e., the results of collecting metric M7. To obtain this table, two researchers studied the user stories and tasks provided by the teams and compared the approach adopted to break down the requirements with the approaches described in the literature. All disagreements in the classification were discussed and clarified based on the description of the broken-down user stories or tasks as well as the description of the approaches found in the literature.

To also be able to classify approaches not recommended in an Agile project, we added the three horizontal break-down strategies described by Verwijs [5]: divide user stories by (1) the type of work that is needed, (2) the layers that are involved, or (3) the components that are involved.

All teams used the approaches "Input options/platform" and "Conjunctions and connecting words". All Agile teams used the approaches "Data types or parameters", "Operations", and "Simple/Complex". Only the Banana team adopted the "Workflow steps" approach and only the XP team adopted the approaches "Test scenarios/test case" and "Roles". The approach "Major effort" was used by the teams XP, Scrum with Kanban, and Banana.

Unexpectedly, the Banana team was not the only one that adopted horizontal break-down approaches such as dividing user stories or tasks based on the layers of the solution, types of work, or components. Typically, Agile teams avoid such types of break-down since this contradicts with the principle that a user story should provide value to the user. We conjecture that the frequent application of horizontal break-down approaches by the

Scrum team was the reason for their bad performance in terms of total effort, compared to the other Agile teams. This also shows that the experiment was conducted with university students with little experience in the field. Nevertheless, their behavior is comparable to professionals at the beginning of their careers. We did not involve freshmen students in the study, as recommended by [10].

Table 3. Requirement decomposition strategies adopted by the studied teams

Strategy	XP	Scrum	Scrum with Kanban	Banana
Vertical decomposition strategies				
Input options/platform [5]	×	×	×	×
Conjunctions and connecting words [4]	×	×	×	×
Data types or parameters [3, 5]	×	×	×	
Operations e.g. CRUD [3, 5]	×	×	×	
Simple/Complex [3, 5]	×	×	×	
Major effort [3, 5]	×		×	×
Workflow steps [3–5, 8]				×
Test scenarios/test case [4, 5]	×			
Roles [5]	×			
Business rules [3, 5]				
Happy/unhappy flow [5]				
Browser compatibility [5]				
Identified acceptance criteria [4, 5]				
External dependencies [5]				
Usability requirements [5]				
SEO requirements [5]				
Break out a Spike [3]				
Refinement of generic words [4]				
Horizontal decomposition strategies				
Layers, e.g. database, GUI [5]	×	×		×
Type of work, e.g. testing, coding [5]		×		×
Components, e.g. server, client [5]		×		×

5   Threats to Validity

Concerning the internal validity of the study, even though we did our best to select developers with a similar background, the results could be partially dependent on the subjects. A replication study could confirm or reject our findings. Concerning the external validity of the study, the use of students to investigate aspects of practitioners is still being debated but considered very close to the results of real practitioners in the case of master students [9] and when one is interested in evaluating the use of a technique by novices or non-expert software engineers [10–13, 17].

6   Conclusion and Future Work

In this work, we conducted a preliminary multiple case study with a replication design with the aim of comparing the requirements decomposition process of an ad-hoc process and Extreme Programming, Scrum, and Scrum with Kanban.

With this study, we contribute to the body of knowledge by providing the first empirical study on requirements decomposition in the Agile domain.

To achieve this purpose, we first provided an overview of the different requirements decomposition techniques and then a description of the study we executed.

Although some results might depend on the participants' skills, we observed the usage of different decomposition techniques in our groups, which often adopted traditional decomposition techniques, which are more suitable for waterfall processes, in combination with other Agile techniques.

The teams developing with Scrum with Kanban and with XP decomposed the requirements into the highest number of user stories, while the team working with an unstructured process, as expected, decomposed the requirements into a very limited number of tasks. Two decomposition approaches were adopted by all processes, namely "Input options/platform" and "Conjunctions and connecting words". All Agile teams used the "Data types or parameters", "Operations", and "Simple/Complex" approaches, while, as expected, only the Banana team adopted the "Workflow steps" approach and only the XP team adopted the approaches "Test scenarios/test case" and "Roles".

Unexpectedly, the Banana team was not the only one that adopted horizontal breakdown approaches such as dividing user stories or tasks based on the layers of the solution, types of work, or components. We suppose that the bad performance in terms of total effort of the Scrum team compared to the other Agile teams was probably due to the application of horizontal break-down approaches.

The main result of this work is that requirements decomposition is not only team-dependent but also process-dependent, and that therefore decomposition techniques need to be addressed to a greater extent in order to improve the efficiency of the development process.

Therefore, we recommend that developers investigate requirement break-down approaches more thoroughly and that researchers study the impact of different approaches, so as to identify the most effective ones in different contexts.

In the future, we plan to validate the results obtained with studies involving more students and practitioners and using larger projects.

References

1. Yin, R.K.: Case Study Research: Design and Methods, 4th edn. Sage, Thousand Oaks (2009)
2. Basili, V.R., Caldiera, G., Rombach, H.D.: The goal question metric approach. In: Encyclopedia of Software Engineering (1994)

3. Lawrence, R.: Patterns for splitting user stories. Agile For All Blog, 28 October 2009. http://Agileforall.com/patterns-for-splitting-user-stories/. Accessed 8 Dec 2016
4. Irwin, B.: Boulders to gravel: techniques for decomposing user stories. VersionOne Blog, 9 May 2014. https://blog.versionone.com/boulders-to-gravel-techniques-for-decomposing-user-stories/. Accessed 8 Dec 2016
5. Verwijs, C.: 10 useful strategies for breaking down large User Stories (and a cheatsheet). Agilistic Blog. n.d. http://blog.agilistic.nl/10-useful-strategies-for-breaking-down-large-user-stories-and-a-cheatsheet/. Accessed 8 Dec 2016
6. Taibi, D., Lenarduzzi, V., Ahmad, O.M., Liukkunen, K., Lunesu, I., Matta, M., Fagerholm, F., Münch, J., Pietinen, S., Tukiainen, M., Fernández-Sánchez, C., Garbajosa, J., Systä, K.: Free innovation environments: lessons learned from the software factory initiatives. In: The Tenth International Conference on Software Engineering Advances, ICSEA 2015 (2015)
7. Lenarduzzi, V., Lunesu, I., Matta, M., Taibi, D.: Functional size measures and effort estimation in agile development: a replicated study. In: 16th International Conference on Agile Processes in Software Engineering and Extreme Programming, XP2015 (2015)
8. Rubin, K.S.: Essential Scrum: A Practical Guide to the Most Popular Agile Process, 1st edn. Addison-Wesley Professional, Boston (2012)
9. Patton, J., Economy, P.: User Story Mapping: Discover the Whole Story, Build the Right Product, 1st edn. O'Reilly Media, Inc., Sebastopol (2014)
10. Runeson, P.: Using students as experiment subjects – an analysis on graduate and freshmen student data. In: Proceedings 7th International Conference on Empirical Assessment & Evaluation in Software Engineering (2003)
11. Kitchenham, B.A., Pfleeger, S.L., Pickard, L.M., Jones, P.W., Hoaglin, D.C., El Emam, K., Rosenberg, J.: Preliminary guidelines for empirical research in software engineering. IEEE Trans. Softw. Eng. 28(8), 721–734 (2002)
12. Tichy, W.F.: Hints for reviewing empirical work in software engineering. Empirical Softw. Eng. 5(4), 309–312 (2000)
13. Salman, I., Misirli, A.T., Juristo, N.: Are students representatives of professionals in software engineering experiments? In: 2015 IEEE/ACM 37th IEEE International Conference on Software Engineering, Florence (2015)
14. Lavazza, L., Morasca, S., Taibi, D., Tosi, D.: Applying SCRUM in an OSS development process: an empirical evaluation. In: 11th International Conference on Agile Processes in Software Engineering and Extreme Programming, XP 2010, pp. 147–159 (2010)
15. Diebold, P., Dieudonné, L., Taibi, D.: Process configuration framework tool. In: 39th Euromicro Conference on Software Engineering and Advanced Applications (2014)
16. Taibi, D., Lenarduzzi, V.: MVP explained: a systematic mapping on the definition of minimum viable product. In: 42th Euromicro Conference on Software Engineering and Advanced Applications 2016, Cyprus (2016)
17. Basili, V.R., Shull, F., Lanubile, F.: Building knowledge through families of experiments. IEEE Trans. Softw. Eng. 25(4), 456–473 (1999)
18. Wang, H., Zhou, S., Yu, Q.: Discovering web services to improve requirements decomposition. In: 2015 IEEE International Conference on Web Services, New York, NY (2015)
19. Abbasipour, M., Sackmann, M., Khendek, F., Toeroe, M.: Ontology-based user requirements decomposition for component selection for highly available systems. In: Proceedings of the 2014 International Conference on Information Reuse and Integration (2014)

20. Morasca, S., Taibi, D., Tosi, D.: OSS-TMM guidelines for improving the testing process of open source software. Int. J. Open Source Softw. Process. **3**(2), 1–22 (2011)
21. Ahmad, M.O., Markkula, J., Oivo, M.: Kanban in software development: a systematic literature review. In: 39th EUROMICRO Conference on Software Engineering and Advanced Applications (SEAA), pp. 9–16, September 2013

Effects of Technical Debt Awareness: A Classroom Study

Graziela Simone Tonin[1(✉)], Alfredo Goldman[1], Carolyn Seaman[2], and Diogo Pina[1]

[1] Institute of Mathematics, Statistics and Computer Science, University of Sao Paulo,
São Paulo, Brazil
{grazzi,gold,diogojp}@ime.usp.br
[2] Department of Information Systems, University of Maryland Baltimore County,
Baltimore, USA
cseaman@umbc.edu

Abstract. Technical Debt is a metaphor that has, in recent years, helped developers to think about and to monitor software quality. The metaphor refers to flaws in software (usually caused by shortcuts to save time) that may affect future maintenance and evolution. We conducted an empirical study in an academic environment, with nine teams of graduate and undergraduate students during two offerings of a laboratory course on Extreme Programming (XP Lab). The teams had a comprehensive lecture about several alternative ways to identify and manage Technical Debt. We monitored the teams, performed interviews, did close observations and collected feedback. The results show that the awareness of Technical Debt influences team behavior. Team members report thinking and discussing more about software quality after becoming aware of Technical Debt in their projects.

Keywords: Technical debt · Technical debt awareness · Technical debt impact · Extreme programming

1 Introduction

Several studies have shown that agile methods have provided significant gains in software projects [19]. However, it is also known that when prioritizing delivery speed, as may happen in agile projects, Technical Debt may be incurred. Much of this debt is not even identified, monitored or managed. Technical Debt that is not well managed runs the risk of high maintenance costs.

The term Technical Debt was introduced by Cunningham, who explained it in the following way [4], "...Although the immature code may work fine and be completely acceptable to the customer, excess quantities will make a program unmasterable, leading to extreme specialization of programmers and finally an inflexible product. Shipping first time code is like going into debt. A little debt speeds development so long as it is paid back promptly with a rewrite [...]. The danger occurs when the debt is not repaid. Every minute spent on not-quite-right code counts as interest on that debt...". Technical Debt is recognized as a critical problem for software companies [2] and has received a lot of attention in the recent years from both practitioners and researchers [16, 17].

© The Author(s) 2017
H. Baumeister et al. (Eds.): XP 2017, LNBIP 283, pp. 84–100, 2017.
DOI: 10.1007/978-3-319-57633-6_6

Lim et al. [18] emphasize that: "...most project teams now recognize that Technical Debt is unavoidable and necessary within business realities. So managing Technical Debt involves finding the best compromise for the project team...", but a project team cannot do this if they are not aware of Technical Debt. Also, Lim et al. highlighted that when the development team is not aware of Technical Debt, it will probably result in challenges for maintenance and evolution tasks. Given this scenario, our motivation was to observe the effects of Technical Debt awareness in teams in an academic setting.

The Extreme Programming Laboratory (XP Lab) is a course that has Undergraduate and Graduate students at the University of São Paulo since 2001. The aim of this course is to provide the experience of a real software development scenario using the Extreme Programming values and practices [1].

Extreme Programming emphasizes teamwork; managers, customers and developers are all equal partners in a collaborative team. The main values of Extreme Programming are communication, simplicity, feedback, respect and courage [3].

The objective of our research is to characterize the impact on the team when Technical Debt items are visible, based on team members' perceptions. This study aims to answer the following research question (RQ):

- **What is the impact on the team when Technical Debt is explicitly considered?**

The study was applied in two editions of XP Lab. Four teams were followed in the 2013 edition and five teams in the 2014 edition. We conducted the study and collected data through questionnaires and interviews, and analyzed the source code of the projects with Sonar Qube and Code Climate tools to identify the impact on the teams that explicitly considered Technical Debt (TD).

In the next section, related work is described. In Sect. 3, we describe the context of the Extreme Programming Laboratory. After, in Sect. 4, we provide a description of the research steps, data collection and analysis. Section 5 describes the results. In Sect. 6, we discuss the findings and present the threats to validity. Finally, in Sect. 7, we present the final considerations and future work.

2 Related Work

Few studies deal directly with the technical debt awareness. The study of Kruchten [22] showed that agile teams believe that they are immune to TD, because they use an interactive development process. Therefore, he explains that in these teams, TD items could be contracted rapidly and massively, because code is often developed and delivered very rapidly, without time to devote to good design or to think about longer term issues. This could result in contracting TD items such as a lack of rigor or systematic tests. To deal with TD and to avoid accumulating too much TD, he suggests: *"The first step is awareness: identifying debt and its causes. The next step is to manage this debt explicitly, which involves listing debt-related tasks in a common backlog during release and iteration planning, along with other "things to do."*. Bavani [21] shows that if teams are unaware of the context of meaning of the term TD, they can consider trivial issues or technical tasks as a TD. These teams have to improve the awareness of it, so he proposes a quadrant to help teams to better recognize and understand the TD concept. The study of Martini [23] listed some causes of architecture technical debt and one of the reasons he found was the lack of awareness about the dependencies between the specific architectural TD and the other parts of the software. Furthermore, there are many related studies on not managing TD and how this affects software quality, such as in the studies of Guo [20], Sterling [24], Li [16], Lim [18], and Curtis [25]. McConnell [26] emphasizes that when a team makes the decision to contract a debt or not, they are really deciding between two ways to complete the current development task, one faster and the other resulting in better quality. Bavani [21] talks about management of TD items in distributed agile teams, and he emphasizes that the management of TD items directly affects the economics of software maintenance and according to him, the key for success in the current global economy is building and maintaining software under optimal costs. Sterling [24] said that TD exists and is detrimental to the maintenance of software quality. Buschmann [27] suggests that teams doing a refactoring in the code should also pay the TD items and improve internal quality. A recent report showed that one of the consequences of incurring TD is the impact on quality [28].

3   Context: Extreme Programming Laboratory

The XP Lab is a regular course offered at the University of São Paulo, to graduate and undergraduate Computer Science students. The motivation is to provide them an opportunity to learn agile software development methods on real projects. In the 2013 offering, there were four teams, with five or six students each. In the 2014 offering, five teams with six students each attended the course. XP Lab students have the support of meta-coaches who are experts in agile methods. They provide agile mentoring for all the teams with the professor's help. Each team also has a coach, who is a student that has more experience in agile methods. The teams develop real projects with on-site customers. The teams have to follow some agile practices, for instance; pair programming, automated tests, continuous improvement, continuous integration, etc. In both studies, the teams worked in pairs and in threes, and the groupings changed many times during the course, sometimes according to the tasks they needed to develop. The course requires a minimum attendance of at least 8 h a week of dedication (four hours in the laboratory and four hours of extra classes), and there is a lunch once a week, to encourage the students' presence in the lab and to allow the students to share experiences. On some weeks, there are short presentations about some difficulties that the teams are facing, where a specialist explains and discusses specific topics. A complete description of the course settings can be found in [1].

3.1   Projects

In Table 1, we briefly describe each of the projects involved in our study:

Table 1. Extreme programming projects

Project	Description
Arquigrafia	Arquigrafia is a public digital collaborative environment, nonprofit, dedicated to the dissemination of architectural images, with particular attention to Brazilian architecture [6].
Games-VidaGeek	A platform for games that support the teaching of programming (with games for Scala, Java, Html, CSS, SQL and other languages being produced) [7].
TikTak	A project focused on collecting feedback data from users and display it in a web dashboard [5].
Mezuro	A framework for monitoring source code metrics [8].
Monitoring system	An online system where students can apply to be a teacher assistant of a regular courses [14].
System specialist in sport	An application to enable researchers working with physiological data to apply metabolic mathematical models [15].
Social networking startups	A social network for Startup, with the goal of creating a community of highly connected and committed entrepreneurs [5].
Family tree	A genealogy community where each individual can create a family tree and from time to time the system attempts to "link" the trees [5].
CoGroo	Portuguese grammar corrector used by LibreOffice [9].

3.2 The Informative Workspace

Each team had its private informative workspace[1] [10, 11], where they physically displayed TD items. In the XP Lab 2013 offering, all teams had a TD board (Figs. 1 and 2). In the XP Lab 2014 offering, each team decided by themselves how to manage the TD items in their informative workspaces. Some teams decided to have the TD board and other teams kept the TD items list on a Kanban board.

3.2.1 Boards

In the TD board (Fig. 1) a team placed the TD items that were incurred and/or identified. On the top of the board, there is a supply of blank cards called 'Fichas'. These cards were used to document the TD items.

Figure 2 shows another team's board where they kept the list of TD items that were incurred and identified. On the right side, they have a reserve of blank cards.

---

[1] The informative workspace is the place where the teams put all the physical boards and graphics, with the metrics they used to manage the project development also the list of the task they will develop in each sprint.

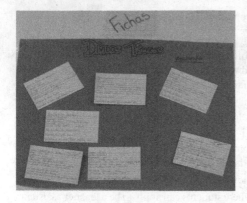

Fig. 1. Technical debt board   **Fig. 2.** Board of the technical debt list.

Figure 3 shows one TD item about *duplicated code*. Each card had nine categories to fill out. Below we transcribe the data contained in Fig. 3.

Fig. 3. Technical debt item

In this case the <u>Name</u> of TD item was *Duplicated code in the Mezuro plugin,* the <u>Date</u> (when the item was identified), was 05/16/2013, the <u>Responsible</u> (the person that incurred or found the TD item, in this case Alessandro), the <u>Type</u> was *duplication,* (could be test, documentation, design, etc.), the <u>Location</u> (which part of the code the items was related), was in *lib/mezuro-puglin-rb*. The <u>Description</u> (a brief description of the TD item), *the class control-panel-buttons* has duplicated code. The <u>Estimated Principal,</u> was *twenty minute*s (how much expected time they need to spend now if they implemented that task in the correct way, if they did not know how much time, then they could use a scale of *high* - if they probably will spend a large amount of time -, *medium* - if they probably will not spend much time - and *low* - if they probably will solve it quickly).

The <u>Estimated Interest Amount</u> should be filled out when they pay the TD item. The <u>Probability of being a future problem</u> (i.e. the interest probability) in this case was *low*. In this case, they also added in the card the Date when they paid the TD item, *05/23/2013* and how long it took them to pay off the item, also *twenty minutes*.

These boards represent some of the boards used in the team's informative workspace. Some teams used a specific board to manage TD, as shown in Figs. 1 and 2, other teams used the Kanban board and put the TD items together with the tasks of the sprint. Furthermore, some teams also placed the list of TD items in the tool used to manage the project.

3.2.2   Tools

The teams had two code quality analysis tools:

- Code Climate: a tool for quality analysis of code repositories (https://codecli-mate.com/).
- Sonar Qube: a code quality analysis platform that has a plugin that identifies TD (http://www.sonarqube.org/).

4   Research Methods

Data was collected and analyzed for this study through interviews and questionnaires. Before data collection, the teams spent some time identifying TD items in their projects. Below, we first describe how TD items were identified, and then we describe our data collection and analysis methods.

4.1   Technical Debt Identification

In the two offerings of the XP Lab, we followed slightly different steps to help the teams to identify TD.

4.1.1   XP Lab 2013

Four weeks after the students started working on their projects, we gave a presentation about TD, as some students were familiar with the term, but others were not. After the presentation, we had a discussion and we encouraged the students to talk about their views of TD. We also talked about some concrete examples they had in their projects. The discussion lasted for about one hour and after that, each team had to prepare a TD board, where they would have to document their TD items (Fig. 3 shows an example of a TD item). Each TD item was written on a card, and in this card they had to fill out a list of topics, after that it was then pinned to the board. The card structure was based on the template developed in [12]. Each team had a board with a set of cards representing TD items. Every team that identified or incurred a debt put the information on the board.

4.1.2   XP Lab 2014

In the XP Lab 2014 offering, we made a presentation about TD for all the students together for 30 min, about two months after the course began. After that, we discussed it for another 20 min, during this time the students could clarify their doubts about TD. The students already had the code quality analysis tools available, Sonar Qube and Code Climate, since the beginning of the course. We did not impose the use of either the boards or the tools to identify TD. We showed them the meanings of TD items and some examples in each project. We also presented examples of a TD board and of the categories they could use to identify TD items. Then each team decided whether they would monitor TD on their project or not.

4.2   Second Step – Interviews and Questionnaires

Data collection was done differently in the two XP Lab offerings. In both cases, similar data was collected both at the beginning and at the end of the course.

4.2.1   XP Lab 2013

Eight weeks after the teams started to identify TD items and fill the boards with cards, we carried out a face-to-face interview with the pairs in each team. The interview motivation was to verify the influence on the team of the TD visibility. The interview was composed of twenty questions, with open-ended and multiple-choice questions, separated into the following topics[2]:

- The concept of TD.
- Were there any changes in the software development process?
- Negotiation with clients.
- About the experience of identifying TD.
- What is the relevance of identifying TD?
- What is the impact on software quality?
- Do the teams pay off TD?
- Will the teams pay off some TD?

Four weeks after the first interview, at the end of the course, we did the last interview with an open format and we performed it for each team. In the last interview, each team was invited to talk about the experience of making TD explicit. Each interview took about twenty minutes.

4.2.2   XP Lab 2014

In this edition of the course, we decided to apply a questionnaire on what each team member thinks about TD (the questionnaire was answered by the students individually; this approach was taken to try decrease a possible bias). This questionnaire was applied

---

[2] It is possible to access all the questions in the following link https://www.dropbox.com/sh/gen3dr97xxofs21/AACo11oqbBsaCprOCQtSYv5Ja?dl=0.

one week before the class received a talk about TD. We sent a link to the questionnaire by email and then the students had one week to answer it.

The questionnaire was composed of seventeen open-ended and multiple-choice questions, separated into the following topics[3]:

- Software quality
  - What does the team do about quality?
- Familiarity with TD.
  - Do you know about and use the TD concept?
- How TD is used in the project.
  - Are you using the Sonar Qube or Code Climate report?
  - Are you using a TD list?
  - Have you paid any TD item?
  - Is there any evidence that having the TD items visible has an influence on the team?
- Did you identify any TD item that was not identified by the tools?
- Are you going to consider TD in future projects?
- Do you think the TD concept is relevant?

The same questionnaire was applied a second time at the end of the course. The aim was to see if there was any change in the team members' behavior.

4.3   Third Step – Data Analysis

For the data analysis, we used coding techniques from the grounded theory approach [13]. Grounded theory methods are aimed at building or discovering a theory. In this approach, the data analysis proceeds in three interdependent steps: open coding, axial coding, and selective coding. In the open coding step, the researcher interprets the data to identify patterns and define codes, "…event/action/interaction, are compared against others for similarities and differences; they are also conceptually labeled […] conceptually similar ones are grouped together to form categories and their subcategories…" [13]. In axial coding "…categories are related to their subcategories, and these relationships tested against the data…" [13]. Then in selective coding "…all categories are unified around a central 'core' category and categories that need further explanation are filled-in with descriptive details…" [13].

For data analysis, we used the NVivo[4] tool, which is widely used for analysis of qualitative data. In this case, the goal was not to use grounded theory to develop a new theory but only use its coding steps to answer our research questions.

We also analyzed the source code of the projects with the Sonar Qube and Code Climate tools, to try to identify relationships between team's beliefs and the reports from these tools.

---

[3] It is possible to access all the questions in the following link https://www.dropbox.com/sh/gen3dr97xxofs21/AACo11oqbBsaCprOCQtSYv5Ja?dl=0.

[4] http://www.qsrinternational.com/support/downloads/nvivo-9.

5   Results

In this section, we describe our findings organized by the coding steps. As the main question in the both editions of XP Lab was the same and the obtained results were similar, we analyzed the results of both editions together.

5.1   Open Coding

In this step, the data analysis was conducted by reading the transcripts of the interviews and also the answers from the questionnaires. We applied the coding process to this material, line by line. In this phase, we discovered the open codes. In Table 2, we list three code samples. It is possible to access the list of the open codes that emerged from this first codification in an appendix[5].

Table 2.   Example of codes resulting from open coding

Open codes	What they talked about
Changed attitude of the teams	The team discussed more the tasks they have to do before incurring a TD and they thought more before taking the decisions.
Communication	After the identification of TD items, the team had more discussions.
Maintainability	The identification of TD items helps the teams to know that there will be some changes in the software in the future.

5.2   Axial Coding

The open codes were reassembled in new ways during axial coding to form categories. The goal was to create a higher abstraction level. Thus, codes were grouped to form subcategories, and in turn, they were organized into categories. This process was highly iterative, with codes and categories forming and re-forming as more data were incorporated into the evolving understanding [13].

In Fig. 4, it is possible to observe the list of categories and subcategories resulting from axial coding analysis. The first level is the main category resulting, this category emerged from the subcategories of the second level, the subcategories are resulting from the codes emerged in the third and fourth level.

One of the most important influences when we make a list of TD items is the *attitude of the team (team behavior)*, "...registers by not forgetting, there was a change in the attitude of the team..." and "...increased people's concern regarding the Technical Debt...". The team had less 'untouchable' expert professionals and behaved more as a whole team. They *talked more about the TDs* "...we discussed these debts. Otherwise, the project would not have advanced..." and thought about the necessity of incurring it. *It helped* them to have the same understanding of the concept of TD because they discuss it (*TD concept*). In addition, if the team members were not sure whether to incur

---

5 It is possible to access all the codes in the following link https://www.dropbox.com/sh/gen3dr97xxofs21/AACo11oqbBsaCprOCQtSYv5Ja?dl=0.

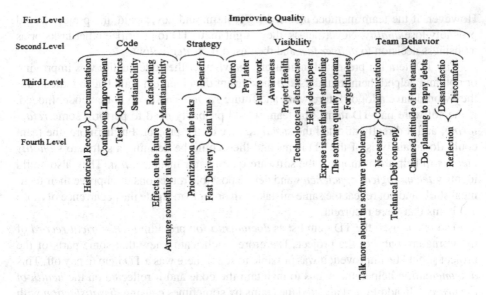

Fig. 4. Categories and subcategories of the XP Lab 2013 and 2014 edition

a TD item or not, the team member debated with another team member to help him to take this decision, thus improving the team's *communication*. Team members started *talking more* with each other and because of it, they knew what part of the project was being modified and the problems of the software, "…It was easier to remember that we have to fix things, debts…". Furthermore, if team *communication* was good, they were more comfortable to share with each other their difficulties. After the team began to identify TD, developers discussed their decisions rather than just doing something and moving on, now that all the software problems were more clear to the team members, "…usually only the person thought or knew about it (…), now with the TD it becomes clearer as well…". They began to argue among themselves, before incurring a debt, "… As evidenced here we even got everyone talking about the debts, instead of just looking to give a quick solution and move along…".

They started to *think more about* if it was *necessary* or not to incur some TDs. Several times they concluded that it was not required, a team member says: "[…] From the moment I started to think about that item, which was debt, I asked myself about what is the current cost, compared to the future cost. Because if the cost of doing now is less, then it's better to fix it now…", other student says: "…we think twice before making a TD…".

When TD items were visible, the team had more *control*, over whether they will pay off the TD item, whether they will incur more debts or not, or whether they will incur and *pay later*. Moreover, this facilitates planning to repay the TD items, "…we analyzed some of the debts, now we will plan, what we might kill, to kill some of those debts, then it becomes easier to make this analysis…". Therefore, if they incur a TD item, they would make it visible, would monitor it, and sometimes they would look back at this TD item. This way, they always thought about *continuous improvement*. Thus, the team could be defining a strategy to pay off or not some TD items to improve the *code* quality.

However, if the team member incurred a TD item, and never paid, the project would probably lose *quality*. Nevertheless, they might incur TD to prioritize other tasks or as a business decision to *deliver fast* and then used it *strategically*.

The TD item list presented indications on whether the code quality was improving or not, and helped them to understand the current development state It also indicated if they would have a lot of future work and future *refactoring* to do in that code. Indeed, if the software had TD items, the team would probably need to perform some *refactoring*, and it directly affected the *sustainability* of the project. Furthermore, the team could do an analysis of the TD items and they could be defining a software's *quality metrics* to help them monitor the software quality, for instance, *test*. They also could identify *technological deficiencies* and define possible directions to improve their technical skills and not repeat the same mistakes, in order to mitigate the occurrence of those TD items that were recurrent.

The teams used the TD item list as *documentation* providing a *historical record* of the immature parts of the project. Therefore, each team knew that some parts of the project should be improved; it was possible to see if there was a TD item to pay off. This *documentation* helped the teams to maintain the code and it reflected on the *health of the project*. In addition, it affected the teams by sometimes causing *dissatisfaction* with the *quality* of the software. Many team members saw that it was very *uncomfortable* to arrive at work and see that the *health of the project* was not so good. If the source code health of other teams was good, it was even more *uncomfortable*. Therefore, this process of the team having discussions, and having *dissatisfaction* impacted in the following *reflection:* when a team member decided to incur or not TD, thought and discussed it, he better understood the problem that he had to solve. This often resulted in the non-insertion of a TD item in the code, since it only lacked the understanding of what should be done.

Considering TD implied generating a culture focused on *quality*. It affected factors related to project continuity. It has an influence on the cost and the viability of *maintainability* and evolution of the project. A developer said that, if they did not have the TD items *visible* it was so difficult to identify *the software quality landscape,* "…it was difficult for you to identify the whole landscape…". Therefore, if in the *future* the team needed to make some changes in the legacy code, they already knew what they were and where the problems were located. It provided a general *awareness* to the team about the problems of the software. It also might help a new team member that did not know about the code to have a notion on the quality of the code and the location of the code problems.

5.3 Selective Coding

Selective coding constituted the third stage of data analysis, with the objective to refine and integrate categories, unveiling a category deemed as central, encompassing all the others. The full potential of abstraction was employed to incorporate the full scope of the data investigated and coded [13].

In our case, the objective was not to generate a theory, but rather to identify the main categories. The aim was to describe the impact of TD awareness.

The categories, *Strategy, Team Behavior, Code,* and *Visibility* represent the main influences on teams due to making TD items explicit. Each of these categories captures part of our results, although none of them describes the phenomenon entirely. For this reason, another abstract category is required, a conceptual idea on which all categories are included. As such, we concluded that the resulting core category might be a perceived notion on "*Improving Quality*".

All teams progressed towards creating a culture of *Quality* of the *code, team,* and *project*. This arose primarily because each team member started to think more about the need to incur TD items. Many times they decided that incurring TD was not necessary in a given situation. When a team member was not sure about the necessity or not to incur the debt, they spoke with other members to make a decision. Therefore, the team improved their communication and then it was clearer what each member was doing. So, it was easier to understand the objective of the project. Then, making TD explicit has a direct implication on the *Team Behavior*. Most of the team members said that after they started to identify TD, they talked more with each other, thought more about the real need to incur debt or not, discussed more about code quality, refactored more frequently some parts of the code, knew where the code problems were, and where each team member was working at any time on the project. In addition, when communication among the team was good, people felt more comfortable to expose and discuss their problems with the team. The team then became more a group that works together, rather than a group of experts on different parts of the system.

In some situations incurring some TD items was a *Strategy* to gain some time, due to the time to market. Moreover, if there was a list of TD items it might be possible in the future to correct them, by refactoring. The list of TD items was used as documentation, this enabled the historical record of the TD items list that the code contains. When the need to change a particular part of the system appeared, it was possible to verify if it had some TD item and if this debt would affect such functionality. Therefore, the team members had the option of paying it off or not. The documentation helped in the *Visibility* of the project's health. If the software had any TD, probably it would have more deficiencies.

Finally, when a team had the TD items list they automatically became *Aware* of the TDs of the project, consequently about the software quality. So, the team could think about it, before possibly incurring in another TD item. The team could decide when and where they would improve the software quality.

5.4   The Code Analysis with the Tools

In XP Lab 2013 edition, we analyzed one project with Code Climate tool (supported the language used in the project, in this case, Ruby). Further, we analyzed two projects with the Sonar Qube tool. In the XP Lab 2014 edition, we also analyzed two projects with Code Climate tool and four projects with the Sonar Qube. We considered the Code Climate metric, grade point average[6] (GPA) and in the Sonar Qube the following metrics: code smells, security, reliability, maintainability, duplications, documentation,

---

[6] https://docs.codeclimate.com/docs/code-climate-glossary#gpa.

issues, technical debt rating, complexity, size, duplicated blocks, bugs & vulnerability and duplications. The GPA of the Mezuro's code and the Monitoria project increase after the teams considered TD. Then the quality of project increased, it means that the remediation (the amount of effort required to improve a software issue), was 0 to 2 M (too short). In the analysis with Sonar Qube of the projects: Game VidaGeek, Tiktak, Arquigrafia, Family Tree, Social Networking Startups and Specialist in Sport we did not identify large variations in the measured metrics comparing the two different versions of each project (Before and after they consider TD). However, in 5 of the 6 projects, the rate of duplication and the duplicated blocks decreased after the team started to consider TD, indicating an improvement in code quality.

It is important to highlight that the students said that most of TD items were not identified by the tools, which explains the modest size of the changes in these metrics. For instance, one team was using Handsontable[7] for data entry, and they had a problem with the validation of the data. The presence of this type of TD item, nor the impact of paying it off, could not be identified with Sonar Qube or Code Climate reports. In general, many types of TD items (e.g. those related business rules) cannot be identified through static metrics.

6 Discussion of the Findings

The teams had some similar views on the importance and benefits of making TD explicit. A significant finding is that the teams considered it very helpful because they could see the whole landscape of the software quality (they knew which part of the software had immature code). They also emphasized that it was very useful to have a board where every day they could see the health of the code. Before becoming aware of TD, the team members reported that they sometimes incurred TD but never remembered to go back and correct it. But after considering TD, they thought about the necessity of incurring TD and often decided against it. Also, they could see the TD list and so they did not forget the TD items that needed to be addressed. They discussed more about how to implement the tasks, also they talked more about the problems of the software because they had the list of the TDs visible. This process of thinking about incurring or not TD, discussing about it and reviewing the TD during the project can create a culture focused on improving the software quality.

In addition, in this study we explored some ways of identifying and monitoring TD. Our subjects found some form of a TD board very useful for documenting TD, making it visible, and adjusting both the TD board and their behavior accordingly. By using the TD board, they always know the list of software deficiencies so have a constant reminder of how to organize their work and improve the software. As a complementary aid, they may use tools to help them to identify and monitor TD occurrence. However, it is important to highlight that tool reports provide a static analysis of the software quality and some TD item could not be identified using static metrics.

---

[7] https://handsontable.com/.

The results of this study could motivate teams to consider TD further, to help developers convince leaders and directors, the decision makers, to start considering TD. These approaches used by the XP Lab teams, such as boards, cards and tools can help teams in companies to deal with TD. In addition, they could define the list of TD items that are crucial to the project but hard to identify with the tools. As a result they can define a strategy to deal with the TD over time.

6.1 Threats to the Validity

In this study, we took some actions to mitigate possible biases, we describe these in the following points:

- *Construct validity (credibility):* We used multiple data collection approaches with the aim to reduce possible bias. When planning the interviews and the questionnaire we discussed the best way to formulate the questions. We did a first interview and questionnaire with one member of the group as a pilot test. Based on this test we reviewed the questions. We did not include these data in the final analysis. One thing that it is important to highlight is that the students might not have understood the main meaning of the questions correctly, in the interviews and questionnaires. Because of this, in the interviews, if the student did not understand the question the interviewer explained the question for them. The researcher was available throughout both studies if the students had any questions.
- *External Validity:* This study can be replicated in other academic courses, also in companies. In both cases, the study can be separated into two parts and can be applied in these situations: one in teams that do not consider technical debt yet, to verify if awareness of TD influences something in the team, such as communication. Furthermore, this study can be analyzed with teams that already consider technical debt, by identifying, monitoring and managing if it is possible to identify some changes in the team behavior and in the software quality. If they have a historical record, we could also measure the software quality with tools. Finally, to carry out this study is not necessary to make significant changes in the team's environment, which makes feasible to replicate in companies.
- *Internal Validity:* We analyzed the data separately, first the interview transcriptions, then the questionnaire responses, and then compared and merged the findings that were relevant and had a lot of evidence in the results of both studies. In the case of any doubt about a specific point, we went back to the data and re-analyzed them. After that, the advisor and co-advisor read the results and if they indicated some points to be re-analyzed, the researcher re-analyzed the data. We did analysis and re-analysis many times until we were sure of the conclusions.
- *Reliability:* To interpret the data we followed the coding techniques from the grounded theory steps. Also, the data analysis was made by a single researcher, however, the results of the analysis were discussed by the two researchers and with the advisor and co-advisor, every time a doubt arose the data were re-analyzed. Also, this paper is a result of an analysis of the data that lasted two years, where the researcher compared the data many times. Furthermore, the preliminary results were

presented and discussed at seminar[8] attended by top researchers in this field. It is important to observe that when we infer that awareness of TD could impact software quality, we are describing the perceived quality by the team.

- *Objectivity:* The results show the information derived from the data, the codes and categories emerged were related with the data quotes.

7   Final Considerations and Future Works

This work describes results about the influences of making TD explicit in an academic setting. Our results show the importance of making TD visible and how that influences teams. It is important to point out that no negative influences were identified. The team members were always very excited about the results of making TD items visible. As communication in the team was improved, all team members thought more about quality, not just specific members. The "agile" culture of the teams improved and in addition, the team believed that it was easier to show the impact of the TD level to clients, showing that it is possible to invest some time to improve the quality. The main results emphasize the Extreme Programming values and helped the teams to support values such as communication at all levels, courage to change and feedback to continuously improve the software.

In future work it is important to verify the influence on the team in the long term, especially concerning speed and code quality. It is also important to create ways to compare the perceptions of the developers with the results of the tool reports. For instance, in these studies the students believed that when they started considering TD, the project quality improved, but when we analyzed the code with the tools, we saw that the reports did not indicate significant changes in source code quality. Then, it is interesting to investigate why this happened, and possible future solutions.

Acknowledgments.   We are grateful to all the students and TAs of the XP Lab course (2013 and 2014 offerings) for providing valuable data for this research. We would like to thank IBM, CNPQ, CAPES and FAPESP, too, for funding this work.

References

1. Santos, V. et al.: Uncovering steady advances for an extreme programming course. CLEI Electron. J. **15**(1) (2012). paper 1
2. Edith, T., Aybuke, A., Richard, V.: An exploration of technical debt. J. Syst. Softw. **86**, 1498–1516 (2013)
3. Kent, B.: Extreme Programming Explained: Embrace Change. Person Education Inc, United States (2005)
4. Ward, C.: The WyCash portfolio management system. In: Addendum to the Proceedings on Object-Oriented Programming Systems, Languages, and Applications, pp. 29–30 (1992)
5. Extreme Programming Projects – CCSL. (http://www.ccsl.org.br/oldwiki/index.php)
6. Arquigrafia. http://www.arquigrafia.org.br/. Accessed May 2016

---

[8] http://www.dagstuhl.de/de/programm/kalender/semhp/?semnr=16162.

7. VidaGeek. http://aprenda.vidageek.net/. Accessed May 2016
8. Mezuro. http://mezuro.org/pt. Accessed May 2016
9. CoGroo. http://ccsl.ime.usp.br/cogroo/. Accessed May 2016
10. Oliveira, R.M., Goldman, A., Mello, C.: Designing and managing agile informative workspaces: discovering and exploring patterns. In: Proceedings of the 46th Hawaii International Conference on System Sciences (2013)
11. Oliveira, R., Goldman, A.: How to build an Informative workspace? an experience using data collection and feedback. In: Agile Conference (2011)
12. Seaman, C.: Technical Deb Minicourse. At the University of São Paulo (2013)
13. Corbin, J., Strauss, A.: Grounded theory research: procedures, canons and evaluative criteria. Zeitschrift fur Soziologie **19**(6), 418–427 (1990)
14. Monitoria. www.monitoria.ime.usp.br. Accessed May 2016
15. System Specialist in Sport. http://journals.plos.org/plosone/article?id=10.1371/journal.pone. 0145733. Accessed May 2016
16. Li, Z.G., Avgeriou, P., Liang, P.: A systematic mapping study on technical debt and its management. J. Syst. Softw. **101**, 193–220 (2014)
17. Poliakov, D.: A systematic mapping study on technical debt definition. Lappeenranta University of Technology School of Industrial Engineering and Management Degree Program in Computer Science (2015)
18. Lim, E., Taksande, N., Seaman, C.: A balancing act: what software practitioners have to say about technical debt. IEEE Comput. Soc. Softw. **29**(6), 22–27 (2012)
19. VersionOne.: State of Agile Report (2015). http://info.versionone.com/state-of-agile-report-thank-you.html
20. Guo, Y., Seaman, C.: A portfolio approach to technical debt management. In: Proceeding of the 2nd Workshop on Managing Technical Debt (2011)
21. Bavani, R.: Distributed agile, agile testing, and technical debt. IEEE Softw. **29**, 28–33 (2012)
22. Kruchten, P., Nord, R.L., Ozkaya, I.: Technical debt: from metaphor to theory and practice. IEEE Softw. **29**, 18–21 (2012)
23. Martini, A., Bosch, J., Chaudron, M.: Architecture technical debt: understanding causes and a qualitative model. In: Proceedings of the 40th Euromicro Conference on Software Engineering and Advanced Applications (2014)
24. Sterling, C.: Managing Software Debt: Building for Inevitable Change. Addison-Wesley Professional, Boston (2010)
25. Curtis, B., Sappidi, J., Szynkarsky, A.: Estimating the size, cost, and types of technical debt. In: Proceedings of the IEEE 3rd International Workshop on Managing Technical Debt (MTD 2012) (2012)
26. McConnel, S.: Managing Technical Debt. http://www.construx.com/File.ashx?cid=2797. Accessed April 2008
27. Buschmann, F.: To pay or not to pay technical debt. IEEE Softw. **28**(6), 29–31 (2011)
28. Avgeriou, P., Kruchten, P., Ozkaya, I., Seaman, C.: Managing technical debt in software engineering. Dagstuhl Rep. **6**, 110–138 (2016)

Agile in Organizations

Don't Forget to Breathe: A Controlled Trial of Mindfulness Practices in Agile Project Teams

Peter den Heijer[2(✉)], Wibo Koole[3], and Christoph J. Stettina[1,2]

[1] Centre for Innovation The Hague, Leiden University,
Schouwburgstraat 2, 2511 VA The Hague, The Netherlands
c.j.stettina@fgga.leidenuniv.nl
[2] Leiden Institute of Advanced Computer Science, Leiden University,
Niels Bohrweg 1, 2333 CA Leiden, The Netherlands
pdheijer@gmail.com
[3] Centrum voor Mindfulness,
Raadhuisstraat 15, 1016 DB Amsterdam, The Netherlands
wibokoole@cvm.nl

Abstract. While the effects of mindfulness are increasingly explored across different fields, little is known about the application of these practices in agile project teams. In this paper we report on a rigorous controlled trial executed to understand the impact of the three minute breathing exercise on the perceived effectiveness of stand-up meetings. We compare (1) an active group using a three minute breathing exercise, to (2) a placebo, and (3) a control group in 3 organizations and 8 teams with over 152 measurements. Our findings indicate an immediate positive impact on perceived effectiveness, decision-making and improved listening in the active groups compared to the placebo and natural history groups. We provide a preliminary agenda for future research based on our findings and previous evidence from other fields.

Keywords: Empirical study · Mindfulness · Scrum · Teamwork · Resilience · Agile software development

1 Introduction

In a world led by 'volatility, uncertainty, complexity and ambiguity', depending solely on automatic pilots can have disastrous effects on human life [1]. Present-day organizations are facing the same problem as they are operating in a highly unpredictable and stressful environment to which they daily need to respond adequately. It is difficult for organizations to adapt to changing circumstances and demands in a highly volatile world. Carefully crafted plans, that should work like business or project auto-pilots, are met by a stubborn reality that does not fit the envisioned strategy. Such an increase in speed and uncertainty leads to an increase in stress for teams and management [2,3]. As a consequence people fall back on autopilot behavior with suboptimal results.

© The Author(s) 2017
H. Baumeister et al. (Eds.): XP 2017, LNBIP 283, pp. 103–118, 2017.
DOI: 10.1007/978-3-319-57633-6_7

This is a problem because organizations that do not possess the agility to reply to the present and its changed demands, run a great risk of becoming obsolete or at least lose some of their striking power within the market that they operate. Big corporations like Atari, Kodak, DeLorean, Polaroid, Pan Am and Compaq, once cutting edge businesses, have failed to meet these changing demands and showed no signs of agility, which eventually led to their demise. Their business auto-pilot was focused on a fixed point and failed to prevent them from crashing into new competitors, new technologies, new demands and waning public interest at the next junction. Companies that cannot alter their course because they cannot recognize the changes in the market, will fail or decline. Their employees will likely have to deal with stress levels that keep on building up in their system with a great chance of burnout and demoralization.

Mindfulness, a concept increasingly popular in practice, promises relief to some of those symptoms. Mindfulness deals with a certain attitude towards reality in which the practitioner approaches the here-and-now in 'the fullest attention to whatever the moment presents' [4]. Mindfulness provides tools to increase attention and aims to create habits of mind that lead to stress reduction [5]. While there is a firm evidence base of mindfulness in clinical psychology, research on the application of these practices in the context of professional organizations such as agile teams, is still in its infancy.

In this report we present the first empirical perspective on the application of a very concrete mindfulness practice in agile teams: the three minute breathing exercise. While previous studies predominantly conducted in the field of clinical psychology only revealed results after several weeks, our findings point at an immediate effect of the exercise in a subsequent meeting. Based on our experiences we draw out an agenda for further research. Our findings provide a strong base for further exploration relevant for both research and practice.

2   Background and Related Work

While the debate on the definition of mindfulness is ongoing, it's roots can be traced to Buddhist psychology where it has been practiced for several millennia [6]. The concept has then been introduced in the field of contemporary psychology by Jon Kabat-Zinn in the mid-1980s, as 'paying attention in a particular way, on purpose, in the present moment, and nonjudgmentally' [7,8]. Since then mindfulness has been applied in many fields such as education [9], law [10], "prison programs" [11], "IT" [12], and "business" [13] to stimulate more positive responses and better-decision making. While there is a growing base of evidence that specific mindfulness practices can have a positive effect on human behaviour, little is known on its impact in professional organizations such as agile teams.

In the following subsections we will discuss existing evidence of mindfulness practices applied in clinical psychology, organizational psychology, information systems, management research, and lastly in agile teams.

Mindfulness in Clinical Psychology. Several therapies and trainings have been developed to execute mindfulness based interventions. Kabat-Zinn for example introduced Mindfulness-Based Stress Reduction (MBSR). This treatment was originally designed to "treat patients with chronic pain" [8]. Eighteen known studies have been undertaken toward fathoming the consequences of MBSR on different groups of participants [14]. All of the research indicates that there is a positive correlation between MBSR and psychological well-being. Shapiro, Schwarz and Bonner for example have conducted a study among medical students, wanting to find out if the students would be able to cope better with stress after they had gone through an official MBSR program [5]. The results indicate that participation in a mindfulness-based stress reduction intervention can effectively (1) reduce self-reports of overall psychological distress including depression, (2) reduce self-reported state and trait anxiety and (3) increase scores on overall empathy levels [5]. Studies have shown that mindfulness has a general positive impact on one's psychological health [7]. Mindfulness has been correlated to a myriad of positive effects on people with psychological issues. Good results have been shown in the areas of "self-esteem" [15], "self-efficacy" [16], "clarity" [17], "self-compassion and empathy" [18]. The correlation of mindfulness has also been associated with the reduction of "depression" [19] and "stress" [20].

Mindfulness in Organizational Psychology, Information Systems and Management Research. Several randomized controlled trials have been undertaken to prove the effectiveness of mindfulness in a business setting. In an integrative review Good et al. [21] integrate the impact of mindfulness into five areas of basic functioning (attention, cognition, emotion, behavior, and physiology) and into three clusters of workplace outcomes (performance, relationships, and well-being).

Reb et al. [22] for example examined the effect of "leader's mindfulness on employee well-being and performance". The study showed that the higher the supervisor's mindfulness: (1) the higher the employees' psychological need satisfaction, (2) the higher the job satisfaction of the employee, (3) the more favorable overall job performance ratings, (4) the higher the in-role performance, and (5) the higher the engagement with organizational citizenship behaviors. Other randomized controlled trials in this area have also shown a positive correlation between the trait mindfulness and psychological well-being, better decision-making and better handling of stress [23].

Hafenbrack et al. [23] discuss the association with a mindfulness condition towards (1) positive emotions, (2) focus on the present, and (3) better decision-making. Mindfulness practices are associated with an augmentation of a positive emotional state of being, since mindfulness "increases the willingness to tolerate uncomfortable emotions and sensations" [24] which indirectly increases the quality of decision making [25]. There is a significant direct correlation between the mindfulness state and decision making [23]. Lastly mindfulness has a focus on the present [8, 23] which indirectly increases the value of decision making.

Mindfulness, Agility and Agile Teams: Initial work on agile teams and well-being indicates that teams that feel more empowered experience less stress [26]. However, while the popularity of agile methods is continuously rising, establishing the right team atmosphere and leadership approach remains a challenge [27,28]. Especially in situations of increased speed and competition, agile teams are experimenting with practices to counter the loss of focus [29].

Mindfulness, while promising relief to some of the aforementioned symptoms, has so far received little attention in the context of agile methods. In existing literature the concept has been explored in two main directions in relation to agility: (1) Mindfulness as an organizational condition and a theoretical concept that supports agility through attention to detail and reliability of systems (compare [30]), and (2) Mindfulness practices as a set of tools to achieve it.

Mindfulness as a theoretical concept to support agility in organizations has been explored by McAvoy et al. [30] to compare *'Doing' Agile* vs. *'Being' Agile* - thus understanding the effectiveness of agile practices in organizational contexts. Nagle et al. [31] utilize a mindfulness measure to understand how an organization can achieve flexibility and reliability in the context of Global Software Development (GSD).

The interaction of concrete mindfulness practices and agile practices is far less well understood. Agile practices such as stand-up meetings for team coordination [32], Iteration Reviews for continuous customer feedback, or Retrospectives for teams to reflect and improve their ways of working, are concrete routines that help teams to deliver their products and improve. Mindfulness practices, similarly to agile practices, provide very specific patterns of action and reproducible protocols, routines that can help build mindful behaviour in organizations [33]. For example, Bernárdez et al. [12] conducted an experiment comparing groups of students conducting a mindfulness exercise to a control group practicing public speaking, with the former being more efficient in developing conceptual models.

Following evidence across various fields we know that mindfulness exercise can have a positive impact on decision-making, the ability to focus and psychological well-being. However, until now little is known on the impact of those exercises in business settings, especially in agile project teams. The three minute breathing space exercise [34], for example, is a concise mindfulness exercise that can be applied relatively easy in teams with little investment. The participant approaches the short exercise with an attitude of alertness and curiosity throughout its three stages of 'becoming aware', 'focusing attention on breathing' and 'extending the attention' [34]. Similarly to meeting routines in agile teams, such as stand-up meetings, it provides a concrete and convenient protocol. As such, the two practices, stand-up meeting and the breathing exercise, can be combined into an experiment.

Based on the literature reviewed above we thus pose the following question: *What is the effect of the three minute breathing space exercise on the quality of meetings in an agile project team?*

Table 1. Stand-up meeting protocol for the three trial groups

Step	Duration	Activity			Actor(s)
		Active	Placebo	Control	
1	5 min	Execute the three minute breathing space	Listen to Tango by Igor Stravinsky	-	Facilitator & Teams
2	15 min	Participate in Stand-up meeting			Teams
3	5 min	Fill out questionnaire			Teams
4	1 min	Collect questionnaires			Facilitator

3   Research Method and Conduct

Following the research question this paper aims to help understand the impact of a specific mindfulness practice, the three minute breathing space, applied in agile project teams. As the three minute breathing exercise as well as the Scrum stand-up meetings provides reproducible and comparable routines, we embedded our research question in an experiment following the design of a controlled trial as common in clinical settings [35,36]. As the trial is executed in a social context with many interconnected factors such as teamwork, process, culture and the perceptions of individuals, we applied a mixed methods approach using quantitative and qualitative sources to analyse the data [37].

Protocol: The trial was divided into three phases, a (1) preparatory phase from April until May 2016, three organizations were asked to join and facilitators were instructed, (2) collection of a baseline measurement in the beginning of June 2016, and (3) the actual trial period lasting from mid-June until mid-July 2016.

In order to reduce bias, we designed a controlled trial including a placebo as well as a natural history control group to compare the effect of the mindfulness exercise. To do so, we created a trial protocol including three groups, (1) an active group with teams executing the breathing exercise before their meetings, (2) a placebo group, which would listen to classical music by composer Igor Stravinsky, and (3) a control group. In order to distract attention from the actual mindfulness exercise, the study was strictly framed as an *"experiment to increase effectiveness in Scrum Meetings"* across participants and supporting facilitators. The placebo[1] group was added to compare the impact to a non-meditative form of relaxation, which could have an impact on the team, and

---

[1] We are aware that similarly to trials in social therapy, there is no placebo for an intervention in a social environment, as even a trivial interaction across individuals does have an impact [36]. For the sake of simplicity we still call the second trial group as "placebo" although it is technically not the case.

to further remove attention from the mindfulness exercise. All data collection was kept strictly anonymous and we repeatedly asked the teams to give honest opinions.

We chose stand-up meetings as the agile practice the trial was aligned to, also referred to as "Daily Scrum". We chose that specific meeting type due to frequency, commonly accepted format and contribution to decision-making within the team [32]. The meetings are short in nature and strictly time limited. The team members address the three questions *"What have I done? What will be done? What obstacles are in my way?"* and make operational decisions [32].

The interventions for the three trial groups were designed as depicted in Table 1. For the active and placebo groups a guided 5-minute exercise was given just before the start of the stand-up meeting, the natural history control group had no exercise whatsoever. The mindfulness breathing exercises (for a protocol compare [34]) as well as the Stravinsky[2] placebo exercise were both guided by experienced mindfulness instructors to give the best results. The breathing exercise was chosen due to its short nature, accessibility and prior exploration in the context of software teams [12].

The instructors were present 5 min before the meeting started and conducted the exercise type that was assigned to the team. After the exercise had taken place the team would start with its meeting. Shortly thereafter the team would fill out the forms. The natural history control group (nh) was not guided at all, but needed to fill out the forms at exactly the same moments as the other teams to follow their heartbeat. The procedure was repeated for the active and placebo groups four times until the end of the trial. Due to different iteration lengths, and to have sufficient time between the measurements to ensure that the interventions themselves would not influence each other because of too short an interval between exercises, the measurements took place once per week.

Organizations, Teams and Participants: Between April 2016 and May 2016 we reached out to organizations with software development departments in the Netherlands. The selection criteria was to find organizations with at least three software development teams applying Scrum for a period of at least three years.

Table 2. Distribution of the three trial groups (active, placebo, control) across the three participating organizations and involved teams

Organisation	Alpha			Beta			Gamma	
Team	T1	T2	T3	T4	T5	T6	T7	T8
Trial group	Active	Placebo	Control	Active	Placebo	Control	Active	Control
Team size	5	8	7	8	10	10	5	8
Measurements	4	4	1	4	4	4	4	2
Total responses	32	13	7	24	24	19	19	14

---

[2] "Igor Stravinsky - Tango (audio + sheet music)", URL to the video: https://www.youtube.com/watch?v=VcXTFRXenwI.

This ensures that these teams are working with short cyclical iterations in which working software is completed after each sprint, and applying stand-up meetings. Out of the 10 inquired organizations, three organizations and a total of 8 teams agreed to participate. After gaining the commitment of the teams, we assigned them to one of the three trial groups as depicted in Table 2. Organisation Gamma originally included a placebo team as well, however, the team dropped out due to internal deadlines before the trail execution. At last there were 8 teams included in the trial and respective analysis. Furthermore, seven facilitators were instructed to conduct the respective exercises and collect the data on-site.

Questionnaire Design and Data Collection: Following our literature study we compiled a questionnaire based on two dimensions: mindfulness and effectiveness. The questions can be found in Table 3. The questions addressing mindfulness (Q03, Q05, Q07, Q08, Q09, Q10) have been selected based on the dimensions mindfulness has been reported to have an impact on, such as: improved decision-making, better emotional responses, focus on the present [23]. In addition to that we added questions on effectiveness of the meeting (Q01, Q02, Q04, Q06). The questions have been administered with a 7-point Likert scale: *1 = Never, 2 = Rarely, 3 = Sometimes but infrequently, 4 = Neutral, 5 = Sometimes, 6 = Usually, 7 = Always*

Before the actual trial we conducted a baseline measurement which would later serve as a base for comparison. The baseline measurement was collected at the beginning of June 2016, the actual trial followed in mid-June 2016. During the trial team members were asked to fill out the questionnaire directly after the meeting and respective intervention (compare Table 1). In order to have sufficient time between the measurements, the exercises were conducted and data was collected once per week across the participating teams. After each allocated meeting, being three stand-up meetings per team, the stated items were graded by each team participant and were handed over to the facilitators. The time frame in which these measurements took place is from May 30th until July 25th of the year 2016. The facilitators made sure that the forms were then forwarded to the researcher.

At the end of the trial we asked the participants that took part in both the active and the placebo group to answer a number of open questions to get a more qualitative view on their perceptions. The questions were: *How valuable did you find this exercise? Would you continue this exercise without the trainers? What are the challenges you had? What worked well?*. For this qualitative view we used a deductive and exploratory approach in order to understand whether the personal perceptions of the participants would confirm or refute the quantitative analysis.

Data Analysis: The data generated was analyzed by question and by preparation type, i.e. the baseline of each question of each preparation type was aggregated and compared to the figures that were the result of the actual

Table 3. Questions Q01–Q10

• Q01 - Everyone is involved in the decision-making process.
• Q02 - The team vision was well defined.
• Q03 - The meeting atmosphere was constructive, calm and open
• Q04 - The meeting was effective
• Q05 - All meeting participants listened well to each other
• Q06 - The meeting objectives were met
• Q07 - The level of disagreement during the meeting was acceptable
• Q08 - The tension during the meeting was tolerable
• Q09 - The interaction in the meeting was good
• Q10 - The emotional responses within the meeting were healthy

measurements that were taken after the experiments had been conducted. With that aggregation level a t-test was executed on the difference between the baseline and the experiment per preparation type, finding the difference in average scores on all questions and the significance value (the p.value) of all these differences indicating if the difference could be explained through the intervention itself. The significance value we sought was a p-value $< 0{,}05$.

Besides the differences in average per question given the preparation type, we also took an average on the aggregated sum of the questions per team and tried to identify the maturity of the team. Furthermore the variance of all questions per team was measured to ensure the homogeneity of the given answers per team. To control for any unexpected influences T-values were measured.

4   Results

This section presents the results of the experiment. Table 2 depicts the participating teams, the respective team size, the number of measurement points, as well as the number of completed questionnaires. Every team consisted of approximately eight members. Each team, with the exception of the control groups, had four measurement moments. Those consisted of one baseline to measure the effectiveness and culture of the team before any intervention was provided and three guided measuring moments.

Table 4 summarizes the results for the ten questions (Q01–Q10) for the three trial groups. As depicted in the table teams that submitted themselves to the mindfulness exercise showed a slight but statistically significant ($p < 0.05$) increase in some key elements of effectiveness and cultural aspects of the team. Specifically our data indicates an improvement on the perception of (1) listening, (2) decision-making, (3) effectiveness of the meeting, (4) good interaction and (5) healthiness of emotional responses. Neither the placebo nor the natural history control groups showed statistically significant differences.

Table 4. Difference to baseline measurement for questions Q01–Q10 (Total $n = 152$)

Question/Trial group	Active ($n = 75$)	Placebo ($n = 37$)	Control ($n = 40$)
Q01 Decision-making	0.6659*	0.1666	0.1190
Q02 Team-vision well defined	0.2513	−0.4666	0.2857
Q03 Atmosphere constructive	0.3170	0.4	0.0238
Q04 Meeting effective	0.6139*	0.1333	0.2142
Q05 Listening	0.6299**	0.0666	0.4285
Q06 Objectives met	0.2905	0.2666	0.2857
Q07 Disagreement acceptable	0.3276	0.1000	−0.0238
Q08 Tension tolerable	0.3382	−0.0666	−0.1190
Q09 Interaction good	0.5673*	0.1333	0.0000
Q10 Emotional responses	0.4178*	0.2333	0.4333

* $p < 0.05$, ** $p < 0.01$

5   Discussion

The main query of this paper is whether a short mindfulness intervention has an impact on the effectiveness and culture in stand-up meetings of agile development teams. In the following subsections we will discuss (1) the perceptions of the teams with respect to our research question, (2) the embedding of the exercise in a broader organizational setting and barriers to its adoption, and (3) directions for future research.

5.1   Three Minute Breathing Exercise in Agile Teams, Does It Work?

The trial shows that even short mindfulness exercises, such as the here presented three minute exercise have a positive impact on the teams similarly to those reported in other domains (compare Table 4). The data indicates a self-reported improvement along five of the ten questionnaire items, particularly: (1) participants listened well to each other, (2) Everyone is involved in the decision-making process, (3) the meeting was effective, (4) the interaction in the meeting was good, and (5) the emotional responses within the meeting were healthy. The questions with the biggest difference to the baseline were *Q01 Everyone is involved in the decision-making process*, and *Q05 participants listened well to each other*. These perceptions were supported by the qualitative data ($n = 14$), e.g.: *"The 3 min of silence helped me rest and relax. It helped gather my senses back after a few hours of (usually) stressful work."* (Participant Team 4). We did not observe any statistically significant negative effects in our data. In the placebo group the question Q02 had a statistically not significant decrease compared to the baseline measurement. Here we could raise the question if the Stravinky song had a distracting effect on the team and its vision during the meeting. Looking back at our research question we will now lead the discussion in two ways: (1) how the exercise can support building emotional intelligence and leadership skills in the individual, and (2) how the exercise can help building mindful teams.

Taking the perspective of the individual our findings indicate that the breathing exercise could help agile team members and team leaders to build up their emotional leadership skills. As pointed out by Porthouse and Dulewicz [38] emotional leadership competencies (e.g., emotional resilience, sensitivity, self-awareness, conscientiousness) are of greater importance for leaders in agile projects compared to traditional projects. As the leadership skills and style of individual managers have a big impact on the culture of an organization, emotional leadership skills are important for the success of agile methods. A meta-analysis conducted by Giluk [39] on the relationship between mindfulness and the Big Five personality traits shows relationships with neuroticism, negative affect, and conscientiousness, but also with agreeableness.

Taking the perspective of the team our findings indicate that the practice could help building agile teams. Self-managing teams are considered to be one of the corner stones of agility, yet they are difficult to establish [28]. The five dimensions of agile teamwork, such as shared leadership, team orientation, redundancy, learning and autonomy [28,40] require shared decision making and the ability to listen to each other and understand each others opinions, as supported by the breathing exercise. Further, similarly to what McAvoy et al. [30] call *'Doing' Agile* vs. *'Being' Agile*, our experiences with the trial indicate that the exercise could help build up mindful behaviour, which helps the team understand agility and agile practices in context rather than blindly following them. The lack of focus can be an issue for agile and entrepreneurial teams [29]. Hafenbrack et al. [23] researched the positive influence of mindfulness on decision making and the sunk-cost bias, the tendency to continue investing in a project once time, money or effort was invested, although that project might not be a viable initiative after all. Stettina and Smit [29] researched agile teams working in entrepreneurial settings. The results reveal that when trying to handle many project requests due to customer pressure, mindfulness could help making better decisions on what projects to follow.

5.2   Mindfulness in Our Case Organisations: Barriers to Adoption

Our quantitative results show that mindfulness enhances qualities of effectiveness and team cooperation in the daily working culture of an agile team. The qualitative open questionnaires distributed to the teams after the trial, however, draw another perspective on our findings. While several participants saw the personal use of the exercise, none would continue it in a public setting. As a participant from Team 2 commented: *"For some members, the pause before the standup was useful, because they could focus on their activities done in the previous day. But for the rest of the team, the exercise was considered just not suitable with their own way of working."* Several participants in Team 4, for example, indicated that the fact that they conducted the exercises in an open space, they felt looked at by other teams. Others indicated, they would continue with the breathing exercise on their own rather than in the team setting: *"Yes, I want to do those exercises more often. I have chosen to do this at home and not at work."* (Participant Team 7). So, although the results show statistically significant increases of effectiveness on several entries, the perceived usefulness does not raise to the level that the participants want to keep on using it in a public setting. The teams apparently encountered a barrier to introduction of these practices.

This raises the more general question of what conditions could support the adoption of these type of mental practices in agile teams. From the literature (cf. [21]) we know a few: support of management for these practices, voluntary participation and a safe team climate. Management support for these practices seems obvious: if leaders do not support these practices it will not happen. In that respect these mental practices do not differ from other agile team practices that help teams perform better. As a line of research, this would be interesting to look into.

Voluntary participation is a necessary corollary of these type of practices. It enhances intrinsic motivation, which is an important mediator of success of team practices (cf. [41,42]). Lastly, also a safe team climate is important. If, as the qualitative data examples showed, people feel exposed, the practices will not function very well. That is a general factor for well-functioning teams: psychological safety is a crucial characteristic of successful teams. If such a climate is absent, social defense mechanisms will come into play and diminish team performance. Safety has both an environmental side (what space is the team working of meeting in, open or closed) and a communicative side: do people feel safe to utter difficulties, ask questions, disagree, praise each other, etc. In general it means that within the team culture or the organization, it is recognized that emotions play a role and are not subdued. It is generally known from psychological research into emotional agility that if this happens, they will play out in a different but uncontrolled way with mostly negative effects on team climate and effectiveness.

5.3   Mindfulness in Agile Project Teams: A Preliminary Research Agenda

Having studied the results of a mindfulness intervention in agile teams and discussed its relation to existing literature, we now continue to discuss a potential future research agenda. The following is a thematic list of questions, not aiming to be exhaustive, but as possible entry points for an exploration of mindfulness in agile teams:

Effects on leadership competencies and team development. From Porthouse and Dulewicz [38] we know that emotional leadership competencies are more important in agile project teams compared to traditional project teams. Also shared leadership is an integral aspect of agile teams and can be difficult to acquire [28]. *How does mindfulness influence the development of leadership competencies and emotional intelligence? What role do mindfulness practices play in team development?*

Effects on decisions. From Hafenbrack et al. [23] we know that meditation practices are reducing sunk-cost bias. *What types of decisions do mindfulness practices have an impact on?*

Lengths of training and lengths of effect. In this trial we worked with a brief mindfulness exercise at the beginning of a short agile meeting. We did not, however, measure the impact of this short exercise on a longer type of meeting. It could be that the enhancing effect wears off quickly and that for longer meetings the exercise needs to be repeated several times in order to gain its lasting effect. Also, in clinical research, experiments have been more intense in nature. It would be interesting to see if a whole team that volunteers to submit to a whole intensive program will see even better results. *Do longer, more intense mindfulness exercises have greater impact on agile teams? Do short mindfulness exercises also have an impact on longer agile meetings? Do short mindfulness practices become increasingly more effective over time?*

Implementation. Although teams indicated that they benefited from the mindfulness exercise they also communicated that they did not want to continue the exercise once the experiment ended. This is an interesting observation which has a contradicting tension. It would be interesting to find out why we were confronted with this tension. *What is the best possible organizational culture in which mindfulness will thrive? What is the correlation between the effectiveness of a mindfulness exercise and the maturity of a team? If the teams are to sustain such a practice on their own, how would they teach to new team members? And if they have to teach the practice to new members, will it be as good as they have learned is form a mindfulness teacher?*

Interaction with other practices and routines. In this paper, we have only focused on stand-up meetings during this experiment. Future research can broaden the scope and could determine if there is a correlation between the trait mindfulness and the effectiveness of other types of Agile meetings like retrospectives, sprint planning, sprint review or refinements. It would be interesting to find the effect of other types of mindfulness exercises on the effectiveness of team meetings in Agile teams. *What is the effect of other expressions of mindfulness exercises on the effectiveness of meetings in agile project organisations? What is the effect of a mindfulness exercise on other type of meetings in an Agile project organisation?*

Types of teams and domains of practice. Our research has focused on software development teams, it would be interesting to expand our understanding towards other domains of practice. We have seen that the trait mindfulness helps make better decisions and is an enabler for the handling of stress. Some types of teams might benefit even more from exercises in the mindfulness spectrum. Teams that are dealing with higher stress levels than software teams or teams that have an acute need for clear and effective decisions would potentially be better candidates in this regards. Portfolio management teams, innovation teams or board room teams would be suitable candidates to consider. *What type of teams benefits most from the trait mindfulness?*

Costs vs. Benefits. Understanding the costs of a potential implementation is important for management. Hales et al. [43] discuss the costs of implementing mindfulness in a health care context. *What are the costs of implementing mindfulness in project organizations compared to their benefits?*

5.4 Threats to Validity

A controlled trial executed within eight teams in three organizations can be more of a challenge to set up in the operational phase than when designed on paper. To avoid potential sources of bias, we followed the recommendations of Pannucci et al. [44] to prevent bias in clinical trials across stages of research in the planning, data collection, analysis, and publication.

In the pre-trail phase study design and in recruitment selecting a favourable population could impact study results. We addressed selection bias by masking the study purpose. During trail execution, the facilitators educated mindfulness trainers, could have consciously or subconsciously influenced the responses of the team members which could result in higher scores for the treatment teams. We used standardized protocols for execution, data collection and carefully instructed the facilitators, reiterating that masking the study purpose is important for its outcomes. Further, participants might be prone to please the experiment leader and give him the answers he needs for his experiment to be successful. Due to masking the purpose, the participants were not aware of the actual study purpose. Another potential source of bias could be the concept of the breathing exercise, which could polarize some of the participant. Potential skepticism could influence the answers of the participants, provoking interest and random answers. We have tried to notice this within the data set but did not find statistically relevant outliers or noise in the data. In the post-trial phase, bias can occur during data analysis and publication. To address external validity, we compared our findings to existing evidence in the fields of clinical psychology [14] and in professional organizations [21]. To further improve construct validity we applied a mixed methods approach in collecting and data analysis using qualitative and quantitative sources.

6   Conclusions

The goal of this study was to explore the impact of a short mindfulness exercise on the quality and effectiveness of meetings in agile project teams. A controlled trial was designed to observe effects associated with mindfulness in the context of eight Scrum teams in three organizations.

The participants perceived the practice as useful, and statistically significant improvement was reported on some of the dimensions in the groups performing the exercise (listening, decision-making, meeting effectiveness, interaction, emotional responses). The teams in our case organizations will not continue with the exercise in their particular setting. Nonetheless, the result is quite remarkable as the trial shows an instant effect while other studies had a preparation phase of several weeks or more. Further research needs to be done in order to understand the circumstances under which its effects are perceived more or less. If there is more collaboration and more pressure in future business settings to keep our organizations healthy, sustainable and effective, the use of mindfulness might be more essential. To do so we provide concrete ideas for a research agenda to explore the effects further.

The conclusion that we can draw is that mindfulness in the form of breathing exercises indeed enhances the quality of meetings in an agile team. Research indicates the increasing importance of emotional intelligence and empathy to be for future workforce next to analytical skills. Practices such as the here discussed exercise could help build up some of those skills in the future.

Acknowledgments. We thank all the participating organizations, teams and facilitators for generously contributing to this study.

References

1. Inge, J.: Safe data: Recognising the issue. Safety Syst. **21**(1), 4–7 (2011)
2. Bodensteiner, W.D., Gerloff, E.A., Quick, J.C.: Uncertainty and stress in an r&d project environment. R&D Manag. **19**(4), 309–322 (1989)
3. Ashford, S.J.: Individual strategies for coping with stress during organizational transitions. J. Appl. Behav. Sci. **24**(1), 19–36 (1988)
4. Brown, K.W., Ryan, R.M.: The benefits of being present: mindfulness and its role in psychological well-being. J. Pers. Soc. Psychol. **84**(4), 822 (2003)
5. Shapiro, S.L., Schwartz, G.E., Bonner, G.: Effects of mindfulness-based stress reduction on medical and premedical students. J. Behav. Med. **21**(6), 581–599 (1998)
6. Kohls, N., Sauer, S., Walach, H.: Facets of mindfulness-results of an online study investigating the freiburg mindfulness inventory. Pers. Individ. Differ. **46**(2), 224–230 (2009)
7. Kabat-Zinn, J.: An outpatient program in behavioral medicine for chronic pain patients based on the practice of mindfulness meditation: Theoretical considerations and preliminary results. Gen. Hosp. Psychiatry **4**(1), 33–47 (1982)
8. Kabat-Zinn, J.: Full catastrophe living: using the wisdom of your body and mind to face stress, pain, and illness. Dell Pub. A division of Bantam Doubleday Dell Pub. Group, New York (1991)
9. Hyland, T.: Mindfulness and the therapeutic function of education. J. Philos. Educ. **43**(1), 119–131 (2009)
10. Rogers, S.L.: Mindfulness for Law Students: Using the Power of Mindful Awareness to Achieve Balance and Success in Law School. Mindful Living Press, Miami Beach (2009)
11. Vengapally, M.: Preparing to Leave Prison: A Mindfulness-based Intervention to Reduce Recidivism (2014)
12. Bernárdez, B., Durán, A., Parejo, J.A., et al.: A controlled experiment to evaluate the effects of mindfulness in software engineering. In: Proceedings of the 8th ACM/IEEE International Symposium on Empirical Software Engineering and Measurement, p. 17. ACM (2014)

13. Reb, J., Atkins, P.W.: Mindfulness in Organizations: Foundations, Research, and Applications. Cambridge University Press, Cambridge (2015)
14. Keng, S.L., Smoski, M.J., Robins, C.J.: Effects of mindfulness on psychological health: a review of empirical studies. Clin. Psychol. Rev. **31**(6), 1041–1056 (2011)
15. Ward, D.: Overcoming Low Self-Esteem with Mindfulness. SPCK Publishing, London (2015)
16. Shapiro, S.L.: The integration of mindfulness and psychology. J. Clin. Psychol. **65**(6), 555–560 (2009)
17. Moffitt, P.: Emotional Chaos to Clarity: Move from the Chaos of the Reactive Mind to the Clarity of the Responsive Mind. Penguin Publishing Group (2012)
18. Kingsbury, E.: The Relationship Between Empathy and Mindfulness: Understanding the Role of Self-compassion. Alliant International University, San Diego (2009)
19. Segal, Z.V., Williams, J.M.G., Teasdale, J.D.: Mindfulness-Based Cognitive Therapy for Depression. Guilford Press, New York (2012)
20. Stahl, B., Goldstein, E.: A Mindfulness-Based Stress Reduction Workbook. New Harbinger Publications, Oakland (2010)
21. Good, D.J., Lyddy, C.J., Glomb, T.M., Bono, J.E., Brown, K.W., Duffy, M.K., Baer, R.A., Brewer, J.A., Lazar, S.W.: Contemplating mindfulness at work an integrative review. J. Manag. **42**(1), 114–142 (2015). 0149206315617003
22. Reb, J., Narayanan, J., Chaturvedi, S.: Leading mindfully: two studies on the influence of supervisor trait mindfulness on employee well-being and performance. Mindfulness **5**(1), 36–45 (2014)
23. Hafenbrack, A.C., Kinias, Z., Barsade, S.G.: Debiasing the mind through meditation mindfulness and the sunk-cost bias. Psychol. Sci. **25**(2), 369–376 (2014)
24. Arch, J.J., Craske, M.G.: Mechanisms of mindfulness: emotion regulation following a focused breathing induction. Behav. Res. Ther. **44**(12), 1849–1858 (2006)
25. Loewenstein, G., Lerner, J.S.: The role of affect in decision making (2003)
26. Laanti, M.: Agile and wellbeing-stress, empowerment, and performance in scrum and kanban teams. In: 2013 46th Hawaii International Conference on System Sciences (HICSS), pp. 4761–4770. IEEE (2013)
27. Moe, N.B., Dingsøyr, T., Dybå, T.: A teamwork model for understanding an agile team: a case study of a scrum project. Inf. Softw. Technol. **52**(5), 480–491 (2010)
28. Stettina, C.J., Heijstek, W.: Five agile factors: helping self-management to self-reflect. In: O'Connor, R.V., Pries-Heje, J., Messnarz, R. (eds.) EuroSPI 2011. CCIS, vol. 172, pp. 84–96. Springer, Heidelberg (2011). doi:10.1007/978-3-642-22206-1_8
29. Stettina, C.J., Smit, M.N.W.: Team portfolio scrum: an action research on multitasking in multi-project scrum teams. In: Sharp, H., Hall, T. (eds.) XP 2016. LNBIP, vol. 251, pp. 79–91. Springer, Cham (2016). doi:10.1007/978-3-319-33515-5_7
30. McAvoy, J., Nagle, T., Sammon, D.: Using mindfulness to examine ISD agility. Inf. Syst. J. **23**(2), 155–172 (2013)
31. Nagle, T., McAvoy, J., Sammon, D.: Utilising mindfulness to analyse agile global software development. In: ECIS (2011)
32. Stray, V.G., Moe, N.B., Aurum, A.: Investigating daily team meetings in agile software projects. In: 2012 38th Euromicro Conference on Software Engineering and Advanced Applications, pp. 274–281. IEEE (2012)
33. Jordan, S., Messner, M., Becker, A.: Reflection and mindfulness in organizations: rationales and possibilities for integration. Manag. Learn. **40**(4), 465–473 (2009)
34. Koole, W.: Mindful Leadership: Effective Tools to Help you Focus and Succeed. Warden Press, Amsterdam (2014)

35. Pocock, S.J.: Clinical Trials: A Practical Approach. Wiley, Hoboken (2013)
36. Leff, J.: Clinical and methodological problems in interaction studies. In: Epidemi-ological Impact of Psychotropic Drugs. Elsevier, Amsterdam (1981)
37. Miles, M., Huberman, A.: Qualitative Data Analysis: An Expanded Sourcebook, 2nd edn. Sage, Thousand Oaks (1994)
38. Porthouse, M., Dulewicz, V.: Agile Project Managers' Leadership Competencies. Henley Management College (2007)
39. Giluk, T.L.: Mindfulness, big five personality, and affect: a meta-analysis. Person. Individ. Differ. **47**(8), 805–811 (2009)
40. Salas, E., Sims, D.E., Burke, C.S.: Is there a big "five" in teamwork? Small Group Res. **36**(5), 555–599 (2005)
41. Bain, A.: Social defenses against organizational learning. Hum. Relat. **51**(3), 413–429 (1998)
42. Goto-Jones, C.: Zombie apocalypse as mindfulness manifesto (after žižek). Post-modern Cult. **24**(1) (2013)
43. Hales, D.N., Kroes, J., Chen, Y., Kang, K.W.D.: The cost of mindfulness: A case study. J. Bus. Res. **65**(4), 570–578 (2012)
44. Pannucci, C.J., Wilkins, E.G.: Identifying and avoiding bias in research. Plast. Reconstr. Surg. **126**(2), 619 (2010)

Enhancing Agile Team Collaboration Through the Use of Large Digital Multi-touch Cardwalls

Martin Kropp[1]([⊠]), Craig Anslow[2], Magdalena Mateescu[1], Roger Burkhard[1], Dario Vischi[1], and Carmen Zahn[1]

[1] University of Applied Sciences Northwestern Switzerland, Windisch, Switzerland
{martin.kropp,magdalena.mateescu}@fhnw.ch
[2] School of Engineering and Computer Science,
Victoria University of Wellington, Wellington, New Zealand
craig@ecs.vuw.ac.nz

Abstract. Agile software development has become mainstream, and with it many tools have been developed to support Agile software development. Nonetheless, studies show, that most Agile software teams still also use physical cardboards for their daily work. This is error prone and causes a lot of extra effort to keep both in sync. In our research project we conducted an interview study about the reasons for this media break. Based on the findings we developed visualization and interaction concepts for an Agile cardwall using an extra-large multi-touch wall display which provides Agile teams the lightweight collaboration workspace for their Agile meetings. We implemented the concepts in the software prototype *aWall*, and evaluated the usability of aWall in a user study. The evaluation indicates that aWall enables and encourages team work due to the large size of the wall, the easy accessibility and visibility of the needed information, and the integration with existing issue tracking tools. This suggests that augmenting digital cardwalls with large interactive touch technology and integration with task tracking systems is a useful way to support effective collaborative Agile software development processes.

Keywords: Agile software development · Cardwalls · Large wall displays · Multi-touch · Tool · Software processes · Collaboration

1 Introduction

In Agile software development, physical cardwalls continue to be an essential part of the Agile processes despite the relative large number of available digital tools. Although many commercial and open source digital Agile tools like JIRA [3], CA Agile Central (formerly Rally) [16] and VersionOne [12] are available and have been adopted by a large number of Agile companies, studies show that physical cardwalls are still widely used [4,7]. Azizyan et al. conducted interviews with software practitioners and found that 31% of companies used both project management tools and physical cardwalls, where the usage of cardwalls was not restricted to co-located teams [4]. Despite their prevalence, physical cardwalls

© The Author(s) 2017
H. Baumeister et al. (Eds.): XP 2017, LNBIP 283, pp. 119–134, 2017.
DOI: 10.1007/978-3-319-57633-6_8

still have issues as content is not digitalized and not integrated with issue tracking systems. To address the issue with physical cardwalls, we aim to bridge the gap by creating a large digital cardwall that supports elements of the physical nature, integration with existing tracking systems, while also preserving the Agile collaborative work style.

In this paper we present *aWall*, a large digital cardwall, providing a collaborative workspace for Agile teams. While the main focus of aWall is for use by co-located teams, aWall is designed to be used also by distributed teams which is one of the main driver for digital Agile tools (see Fig. 1). aWall has the size of classical physical cardwalls by using large multi-touch high resolution displays and so provides enough space for the whole team to interactively collaborate. We first give an overview of related work, followed by an evaluation of an interview study about the usage of Agile tools in software teams. We then present the design consideration for a large scale Agile cardwall and the user interface design of aWall. The following section presents the evaluation of aWall in a user study which we conducted with software practitioners to evaluate the usability and effectiveness of the chosen approach. The paper concludes with a final summary and outlook for future work.

Fig. 1. aWall – digital Agile cardwall displayed on a large high resolution multi-touch wall (2 × 2 46 Inch 4 K displays) for planning and Agile team meetings.

2   Related Work

Sharp et al. [15] reports that physical artifacts like pin boards, sticky cards, flip charts or whiteboards are used as a means of communication and collaboration by Agile teams. However they also report that there are some disadvantages of physical artifacts such as cards may get lost and they cannot be searched or shared easily. Any attempt to overcome these disadvantages by digitalizing cards and cardwalls should retain the advantages of the physical form while also benefiting from translation to the digital medium [15].

Gossage et al. [7] report in their study that the physical nature of artifacts is important to the collaborative process. For example being able to manipulate the cards easily (writing and posting) and their permanent availability on the card-wall helps support effective communication at least in co-located teams. Physical cardwalls are valued for their flexibility, light-weight and easy usage, providing a big picture, and permanent and instant availability of information. Physical cardwalls are not well suited for distributed environments and displaying large amounts of information is difficult. On the other side, they report that digital tools were not necessarily easy to use, hard to personalize, or to adapt to the teams' needs. They come up with suggestions on the design of digital cardwalls and with critical features: always provide an overview, offer easy zoom-and-pan, to hide details, assign annotations to any object on the board, automatic synchronization, for example.

Paredes et al. conducted a survey of existing literature on information visualization techniques used by Agile software development teams and found that information radiators and cardwalls are most frequently used for Agile teams in communication and progress tracking [13].

Azizyan et al. [4] report that digital Agile tools like JIRA and VersionOne account for less than 10% of tools used to support Agile processes, while physical walls, paper, and spreadsheets account for almost 50%. They also report that it is important to find the right balance between enough features and usability is critical.

A number of research digital tools have been developed for use on large interactive surfaces (e.g. horizontal and vertical). DAP [10] and subsequently AgilePlanner [18] were early prototypes developed to support Agile planning on horizontal tabletops for co-located teams. SmellTagger supports collaborative code reviews for co-located teams using multi-touch tabletops [11].

CodeSpace [5] does not focus on any particular Agile process but uses shared touch screens, mobile touch devices, and Kinect sensors to share information during developer meetings. They report that professional developers were positive with this approach and felt that pointing with hands or devices and forming hand postures are socially acceptable. Anslow et al. [2] evaluated large display walls for collaborative software visualization. SourceVis used large multi-touch tabletops to support code reviews using collaborative visualization techniques [1]. They show in their paper that large displays have the potential to provide a good overview about complex situations and thus can help to get a better understanding of it. Rubart developed a basic prototype for multi-touch tabletops to support Scrum meetings [14] and evaluated the prototype in a study with student groups. They report positive feedbacks with respect to team collaboration, but also difficulties with editing data. Though support of distributed teams is currently not in the focus of our work, dBoard [6] is a very interesting approach in which a Scrum board on a vertical touch screen has been enabled with in-screen video capabilities for distributed development. This might be a possible approach for aWall to support distributed teams.

Based on our review we conclude that most digital Agile tools only partially support collaborative Agile processes and meetings. Digital Agile tools especially seems to lack support for social interaction and team cognitive activities compared with physical tools. Neither existing physical nor digital cardwall tools seem to sufficiently support the collaborative Agile process for Agile teams effectively. With aWall we present an approach to overcome these limitations. aWall tries to combine the advantages of physical and digital cardwalls, by making use of the large screen size and the touch functionality, and serve as an Agile collaborative workspace and information radiator for Agile teams.

3   Pre-study Tool Usage

3.1   Study Method

As a first step in our project we conducted a qualitative interview study among eleven IT companies that have adopted agile methods in their software development. The interviews focused on collaborative processes in agile teams and the tools they use for communication.

We conducted ten semi-structured group interviews and three individual interviews with eleven IT companies. The interviews were conducted with a total of 44 participants (7 female, mean age of all participants was 38.5 years). The participants mostly worked in multiple Agile teams and had different roles in those teams (e.g. Scrum Master, Product Owner, Team Member). The participants had at least one year experience with Agile software development, most between 2–5 years. Each group interview took about two hours and the individual interviews one hour. All interviews were conducted in German. The focus of the interviews was on the employment of agile methods and practices, team and collaborative processes, meetings and tools used. All interviews were audio recorded and transcribed. The transcribed interviews were segmented into small units of analysis and coded using MAXQDA [17]. A category system for the analysis was developed and continuously refined [9].

3.2   Findings

We found that 10 out of 11 teams still use physical cardwalls typically in combination with digital tools, like Jira/Confluence, TFS, Trello. Only one team was working exclusively with digital tools. When using physical cardwalls we found that it is a common practice to put a lot of extra information around the task board as shown in Fig. 2. The extra information includes for example, the Definition-of-Done, team members' periods of absence, burn-down charts, but also private pictures, post cards from holidays or other greeting cards from team members.

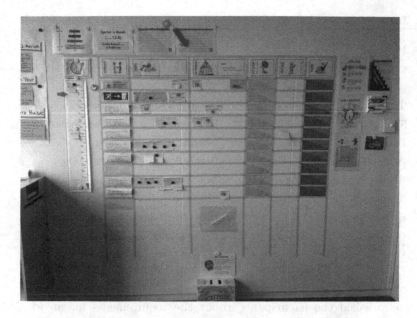

Fig. 2. A physical task board with extra information

When asking for the advantages of physical cardwalls compared to digital Agile boards the most often named reasons were ease of use, always-on visibility, flexibility, good overview, and the focused view on the information. On the disadvantage side the interviewees mainly named that the board is only locally available, the missing traceability and documentation, and the missing integration into digital tools. Table 1 lists the most often named advantages and disadvantages of digital tools by the participants.

The following statements restates opinions from some participants about various aspects about digital tools[1]:

> "Yes, it is all well integrated. If I have it electronically, I have it in the database. I have to capture it only once. That's what I like about the digital tools (I8, 305)[2]."

> "The digital board looks quite nice, is always well ordered (I11, 364)."

> "You have so many options in JIRA, so many input fields. And if you are looking for information, you always have to do a lot of navigation.(I1, 235)."

> "It takes so long to start up the tool. And after five seconds passed, I have to fill out this template. And then I just want to add a picture. I have to take a photo and somehow add it to the system. That's very cumbersome. (I10, 396)."

---

[1] All statements have been translated from German.

[2] The numbers refer to the interview and the line number of the transcription.

Table 1. Pros and Cons of digital agile tools compared to physical tools

Pros	Cons
Changes are stored automatically	Feeling of having no control
A lot of extra features	Too many features
Traceability	Missing visibility for others
Transparency in who did what	High effort for usage/administration
Provide some overview	Missing good overview
Adaptability of tools	High effort for customization
Access from everywhere	Not always on (have to start up)
Teams can meet in virtual rooms	Must be customized before usage
-	Have to navigate to information
-	Performance not always good
-	Displays are too small

We also asked the participants about the requirements for an ideal digital Agile cardwall. The interviewees stressed the importance of non-functional requirements. These included the need for a large size display, configurable views, instant availability of information, overview of information, at all time visible information, easy to reach context dependent information, increased readability of information, simultaneous multi-user touch interaction, direct interaction with data, and no need for navigation.

3.3   Summary

In summary the study results seem to show that available digital tools do not sufficiently well support the required flexible collaborative Agile workstyle. Users value the traceability of information in digital tools, linking possibilities of artifacts, and the flexibility to adapt the tools to the users' needs. The main disadvantages of digital cardwall tools seem to be that they are often too complicated to use, the need to navigate to extra information not shown on the main board, no direct and concurrent interaction by all team members, and small displays, missing overview, missing instant availability.

4   aWall - Digital Agile Collaboration Wall

Based on our study we developed *aWall* to support Agile teams (co-located or distributed) more effectively than existing physical and digital tools. aWall is designed for various Agile team meetings (e.g. daily stand up, sprint planning, and retrospectives) by providing information dashboards, maintaining user stories and tasks, enables customization of Agile processes, and integrates with issue tracking systems. aWall was developed by an interdisciplinary project team of computer scientists and psychologists (from the School of Engineering, and the School of Applied Psychology). We now outline the design and user interface of aWall, followed by a user study to evaluate the prototype.

4.1 Design

Based on the requirements elicited during the interviews, we identified a number of design considerations.

Physical Size. A digital cardwall needs to satisfy not only the needs for interacting with the digital content, but also provide enough physical space to display information to effectively support team collaboration. Therefore, the size of a digital cardwall needs to be at least comparable to that of physical cardwalls. aWall consists of four 46 in. displays (2×2), for a wall size of 2.05 m width and 1.25 m height (see Fig. 1).

High Resolution. Each display in aWall is 3840×2160 pixels, for a total resolution of 15360×8640 pixels. The high resolution display wall provides enough real estate to display large amounts of information at once while still ensuring the readability of text elements, widgets, and views.

Multi-user and Multi-Touch. The display wall consists of a 12 point multi-touch infrared optical overlay (PQ Labs frame[3]) which is attached to the display wall. The multi-touch capabilities allows multiple users to work simultaneously with artifacts and provides an accurate and effective touch experience.

Integration with Issue Tracking Systems. aWall is designed to run on top of existing third party issue tracking systems such as JIRA. Therefore, infrastructure functionality can be reused and already defined Agile processes utilized.

Availability of Information. aWall can replace physical cardwalls and act as the team's external memory of the project. For that, aWall should be installed in a team's open office area, always being switched on, and have a permanent view of the task board.

Web Technologies. In order to have a ubiquitous and easily deployable design, aWall was developed as a web application based on HTML5 and JavaScript technology. For multi-touch support we used the interact.js framework[4].

4.2 User Interface

The aWall user interface contains a number of different views, widgets, and interaction techniques designed to support different types of Agile meetings.

Action and Information View. The results of the interviews showed that most interaction with the cardwall takes place during Agile meetings. Each meeting

---

[3] http://multitouch.com/.
[4] http://interactjs.io/.

has specific goals, operates on different data, and requires different supporting tools and information. To support these different types of information handling, we divide the display into an *action view* and an *information view*. Figure 3 shows the view for a daily standup meeting highlighting the separation into information view and action view. The action view is the main work area, which is dedicated to the core artifacts of a specific meeting. The main interactions during a meeting are performed by users on the action view. The information view provides supporting information and tools needed for the meeting. The information view represents the dynamic memory of the team and as any dynamic system they need to allow for change. For example, the information view for the daily standup meeting contains additional information, like a timer widget showing the meeting moderator and a countdown, a team widget showing the team members, a definition-of-done widget, an impediment list widget, and a burn-down chart for an iteration. When necessary, new widgets can be added and removed from the information view.

Dedicated Views. aWall provides dedicated views that are tailored to the specific needs of Agile meetings. For the sprint planning meeting shown in Fig. 4, the action view is divided into three columns. The left column shows the top priority user stories of the product backlog. The centre column shows the so far selected user stories for the next iteration. The right column shows a detailed view of the currently selected user story. This column can be used by the product owner to discuss and clarify open issues during the meeting with the development team. Relevant documents can be easily attached and opened in the application. Figure 5 shows the retrospective meeting view after team members have sent their iteration feedback where the notes have been ordered on the right side. Users can navigate between the different meeting views by means of a navigation bar displayed at the bottom of the view.

Information Widgets. The information view consists of a set of widgets (e.g. team widget, timer widget, fun widget, avatar widget – see Figs. 3, 4, 5) and can be independently configured for each Agile meeting. Each widget is designed to support distinct aspects of the collaborative Agile process. The team widget shows the team members and can be used to assign people to tasks during a daily standup meeting. The timer widget supports time boxing during the meeting and furthermore, allows to choose a meeting moderator. The moderators' names are stored in the application and future moderators can be suggested based on previous selections. The fun widget allows users to post personal or fun images to the information view to help bring emotion to the cardwall and foster team thinking. The avatar widget can be used to drag avatars to any position on the wall or attach it to tasks or user stories. Both the fun and avatar widgets are designed to help with the interpersonal process in Agile teams (emotion management, team spirit). All widgets can be detached from the information view and moved around the cardwall to facilitate user interaction.

Availability of Information. Any information needed for a meeting is visible and accessible; either on the action view or on the information view. If the team

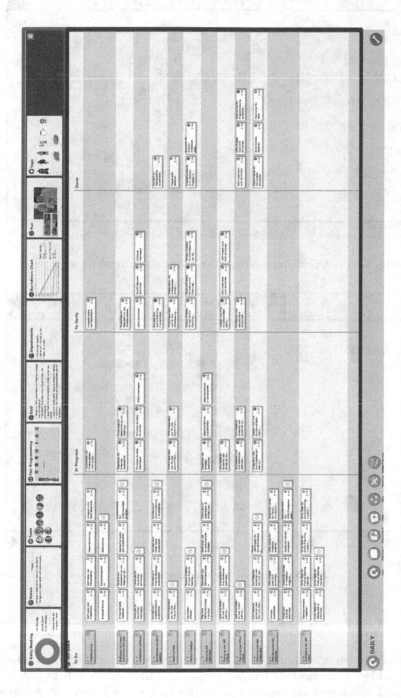

Fig. 3. Daily Standup with the following views: Information View (top section with red border) and Action View (middle section with blue border). (Color figure online)

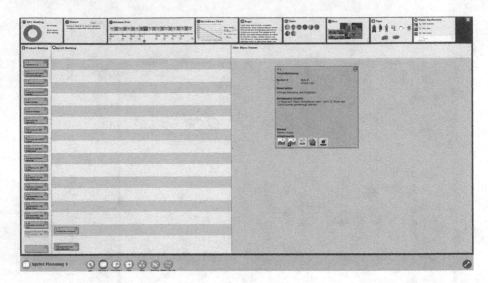

Fig. 4. Sprint planning meeting with a user story detail view.

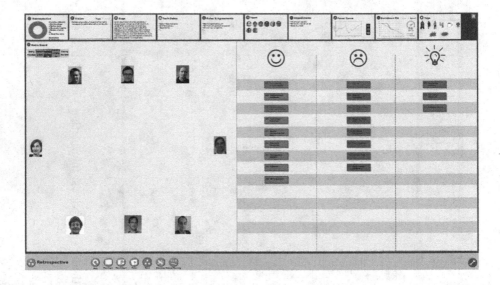

Fig. 5. Retrospective meeting view.

needs different supporting information, additional widgets can be switched on or off in the configuration button on the right side of the information view.

Interaction. aWall supports multi-touch and multi-user interaction. Fluid interaction with widgets and cards is enabled by gestures like tap, double tap, drag-and-drop, and pinch-to-zoom supporting changing task and user story cards position, moving widgets around the cardwall, and changing the size of a widget.

Data can be either entered on the cardwall with a virtual or physical keyboard or via the underlying issue tracker system and mobile devices such as tablets.

Scalability of Information. By default, user story cards and task cards show only a few details (e.g. title). By increasing the card size with a pinch-to-zoom gesture more information is displayed. The text size increases concomitantly with the widening of the cards so that information can be more easily read depending on the distance from the cardwall. When all information is shown the widget automatically switches into edit mode, so that data can be added or modified.

5   User Study

To evaluate the usability of the aWall prototype we conducted a qualitative user study with professional Agile practitioners. The goals were:

1. evaluate the availability of context specific information
2. evaluate reachability and discoverability of functionality and information
3. evaluate the support of Agile workstyle and Agile culture,
4. evaluate the applicability to real life situations in Agile teams.

The user study was conducted with an early prototype of aWall. The participants worked in teams and had to complete various tasks.

5.1   Participants

We recruited 11 employees (nine men and two women – see Table 2) from the same companies that participated in our interview study [8]. Most participants had many years of experience in IT, and several of them in Agile development. They came from different fields and covered a wide spectrum of Agile team roles. Among the participants were four Scrum Masters, two Agile coaches, two senior developers, one Agile grandmaster, one UX consultant and one head of a software development department. Two of the companies were from the assurance domain, one manufacturing, two service providers, one engineering, and one enterprise software development company. Four companies sent two employees, and three companies sent one employee each. All companies had been applying Agile processes for at least one year, and all employees to executed the given tasks in their companies before.

5.2   Procedure

We divided the eleven participants randomly into two groups by five and six people. Both groups completed the same tasks with aWall in two separate workshop sessions. Each workshop session lasted one hour.

Upon signing an informed consent statement, the participants were asked to act as a team during the workshop. Prior to the user study, the participants received a presentation on the interview study results, but did not receive any

Table 2. Demographics of workshop participants: gender, IT experience, Agile experience, job title, company (anonymized), and workshop group.

Gender	IT Exp.	Agile Exp.	Job title	Company	Group
Male	23	3	Head SW dev	D	1
Male	5	1.5	Senior dev	E	1
Male	13	2	Grandmaster	C	1
Male	10	3	Agile coach	F	1
Male	19	4	Senior dev	G	1
Male	10	3	UX consultant	B	1
Female	8	3	Agile coach	C	2
Female	15	5	Scrum master	A	2
Male	15	3	Scrum master	A	2
Male	1	1	Scrum master	E	2
Male	6	2	Scrum master	F	2

information about the aWall application. Each member of the team received three tasks to be solved together in groups using aWall. The tasks involved a daily standup meeting and a sprint planning meeting. After receiving the task, each participant read the task out aloud to the other participants and completed it with their help.

The daily standup tasks included to start the daily standup meeting (task 1), choose a moderator for the meeting (task 2), and update the task board during the meeting (task3), assign team members to a task card (task 4). For example: "*In this team you play the role of team member M. Please find a way to carry out a daily standup. The application suggests a moderator. Please ask the team member suggested by the application to play the moderator. Please act as a team accordingly to the received instructions.*". The sprint planning tasks included to show and discuss a user story during the meeting (task 1) and move the story to the sprint backlog (task 2). Other tasks were to switch on and off different widgets in the information view.

After completing the tasks for each type of meeting we asked the participants about the benefits and difficulties of aWall in an open discussion. The discussions were recorded and the results written down. Both team workshops were conducted by two moderators.

5.3   Findings

The overall feedback for the prototype was very positive, with the participants considering aWall to be usable, capable to support Agile processes in general and especially the collaborative working style in teams.

Size Aspects. The participants especially valued the large size and high resolution of aWall. The large size supports real team collaboration capabilities, similar to physical cardwalls. Displaying a large amount of information at once was deemed positive. As one participant stated[5]:

"With the large size you can display many user stories and tasks."

Readability of Information. Most participants considered the displayed information to be legible, especially since the card titles are relatively large. Some participants considered the actual cards to be too small. Therefore, it is very important to be able to display the whole content of a card and enlarge the font size so that the whole team can read it from a distance. One participant stated:

"That's really a nice feature, that cards can be enlarged and font size increases to improve readability."

Availability of Information. The participants especially valued the availability of additional information and functionality for the different meetings. The separation of the display into action view and information view was easily understood. Some participants mentioned that elements placed on the upper side of the display wall might be out of reach for smaller people. Another participant liked the extra features:

"I like the extra features around the main view and the additional information."

Discoverability of Functionality. The participants discovered most functionality of aWall by themselves and could easily interact with the display wall. There were some issues with discoverability of those functions that were not a straight-forward transfer of the pin-boards into the digital world. For example, the timer widget has no corresponding artifact in the practice of Agile teams. Whereas, direct implementations of the pin-boards functionality (e.g. the task-board shown in the daily standup meeting) were instantly understood and deemed as valuable by the participants. That was also the case for the widgets inspired from Agile practices such as the team widget which is based on the observation that Agile teams sometimes write the team members' names on the cards or even hang their pictures on the pin-boards.

Third-Party System Integration. The integration with third-party tools was positively rated. Tasks modified during the daily standup meeting, are immediately synchronized in the Agile project management tool (JIRA). There is no extra effort to update the tasks manually from the physical cardwall after the meeting. One participant stated:

"The link to JIRA with automatic update of data is important."

Flexibility and Customization. Increased flexibility with respect to both the manner of conducting the meetings and displaying information was considered important by the participants. For example, the timer widget solicited choosing a moderator at the beginning of a meeting. The flexibility provided by aWall was also

---

[5] All quotes have been translated from German.

positively rated, especially with respect to conducting retrospective meetings that sometimes might prove strenuous. The participants considered that it is important to create a proper environment especially for this type of meeting as sometimes they tend to transmute into a drill. Most participants were in favour of a greater flexibility of the time boxing, with only optionally choosing a moderator and not showing the elapsed time, but the time of day during the daily meeting. The participants valued the team widget, but requested to have more information being displayed (e.g. absences, vacation days) and allow for more customization. Furthermore, the participants remarked that they should be able to add functionality to aWall on their own and not be dependent on standard functionality as often is the case with other Agile tools.

Agile Collaborative Workspace. Offering tags and avatars as well as the fun view was positively seen as bringing emotions onto the board. One participant mentioned the positive effect of avoiding media disruption, by being able to do all interaction with only one medium:

> "With such a board we could probably avoid media discontinuity."

Filtering and Representation of Information. The participants requested especially to have filter functions, to highlight and show the desired information. As an example, participants requested to highlight all tasks of a team member, when touching that person in the team view. The usage of colors for different types of user stories was suggested to increase readability (e.g. to distinguish between technical tasks, bug reports, or user requirements).

Task Time Recording. Some participants suggested automatically capturing the time spent on a task combined with computing of the work hours on the task would help provide further metric details of performance.

Provenance of Information. Some participants suggested to have automatic recordings of meetings with voice recognition and transcriptions of the discussions form the interactions in front of the display wall for later recollection and analysis of the meetings.

6   Conclusions

Current Agile cardwalls don't fulfil today's requirements for effective software development. We aim to bridge that gap with aWall, a digital cardwall tool to support co-located and distributed Agile teams. aWall provides a collaborative workspace using large multi-touch displays, information transparency, direct information interaction without the need for navigation, support for the whole Agile process, and dedicated views for different types meetings. We conducted a user study with 11 Agile practitioners and found that they especially valued the large-size of the wall due to the physical space affordances, the dedicated views with context specific information, and the always visible and direct information access. Our future work involves deploying aWall within companies.

Acknowledgments. Many thanks goes to the University of Applied Sciences Northwestern Switzerland for funding this project as part of their strategic initiative to fostering interdisciplinary work, and to the companies and people for participating in this project. Thanks to Robert Biddle for feedback on early drafts of this paper.

References

1. Anslow, C., Marshall, S., Noble, J., Biddle, R.: Sourcevis: collaborative software visualization for co-located environments. In VISSOFT, pp. 1–10. IEEE (2013)
2. Anslow, C., Marshall, S., Noble, J., Tempero, E., Biddle, R.: User evaluation of polymetric views using a large visualization wall. In: SoftVis, pp. 25–34. ACM (2010)
3. Atlassian: JIRA (2015). https://www.atlassian.com/software/jira
4. Azizyan, G., Magarian, M.K., Kajko-Matsson, M.: Survey of agile tool usage and needs. In AGILE, pp. 29–30. IEEE (2011)
5. Bragdon, A., DeLine, R., Hinckley, K., Morris, M.: Code space: touch + air gesture hybrid interactions for supporting developer meetings. In: ITS, pp. 212–221. ACM (2011)
6. Esbensen, M., Tell, P., Cholewa, J.B., Pedersen, M.K., Bardram, J.: The dBoard: a digital scrum board for distributed software development. In ITS, pages 161–170. ACM, 2015
7. Gossage, S., Brown, J., Biddle, R.: Understanding digital cardwall usage. In AGILE, pp. 21–30. IEEE (2015)
8. Mateescu, M., Kropp, M., Greiwe, S., Burkhard, R., Vischi, D., Zahn, C.: Erfolgreiche zusammenarbeit in agilen teams: Eine schweizer interview-studie ber kommunikation, 22 December 2015. http://www.swissagilestudy.ch/studies
9. Mayring, P.: Einfhrung in die qualitative Sozialforschung. Beltz-UTB, Weinheim (2003)
10. Morgan, R., Walny, J., Kolenda, H., Ginez, E., Maurer, F.: Using horizontal displays for distributed and collocated agile planning. In: Concas, G., Damiani, E., Scotto, M., Succi, G. (eds.) XP 2007. LNCS, vol. 4536, pp. 38–45. Springer, Heidelberg (2007). doi:10.1007/978-3-540-73101-6_6
11. Muller, M., Wursch, M., Fritz, T., Gall, H.: An approach for collaborative code reviews using multi-touch technology. In: CHASE Workshop. ACM (2012)
12. Version One. Enterprise agile platform. (2015). http://www.versionone.com. Accessed 6 Jan 2017
13. Paredes, J., Anslow, C., Maurer, F.: Information visualization for agile software development teams. In: VISSOFT, pp. 157–166. IEEE (2014)
14. Rubart, J.: A cooperative multitouch scrum task board for synchronous face-to-face collaboration. In: ITS, pp. 387–392. ACM (2014)
15. Sharp, H., Robinson, H., Petre, M.: The role of physical artefacts in agile software development: two complementary perspectives. Interact. Comput. 21(1–2), 108–116 (2009)
16. CA Technologies. CA agile central (2016). https://www.ca.com/. Accessed 6 Jan 2017
17. Research GmbH VERBI Software, Consult. Maxqda data analysis software (2015). http://www.maxqda.com. Accessed 6 Jan 2017
18. Wang, X., Maurer, F.: Tabletop agileplanner: a tabletop-based project planning tool for agile software development teams. In: TABLETOP, pp. 121–128. IEEE (2008)

Knowledge Sharing in a Large Agile Organisation: A Survey Study

Kati Kuusinen[1]([✉]), Peggy Gregory[1], Helen Sharp[2], Leonor Barroca[2], Katie Taylor[1], and Laurence Wood[3]

[1] University of Central Lancashire, Preston, UK
{KKuusinen,AJGregory,KJTaylor}@uclan.ac.uk
[2] The Open University, Walton Hall, Milton Keynes, UK
{Helen.Sharp,Leonor.Barroca}@open.ac.uk
[3] IndigoBlue, London, UK
laurence.wood@indigoblue.co.uk

Abstract. Knowledge is a core resource for agile organisations that is transformed into products and services during the development process. Sharing of knowledge is essential across any organisation, and it has been claimed that the software industry requires more knowledge management than any other sector. Agile methodologies concentrate on team level collaboration, and some techniques for inter-team knowledge sharing have also proved to be successful. But these techniques focus on within-team and between-team knowledge sharing rather than knowledge sharing across the organisation. This paper presents the results of a survey with 81 responses on organisational knowledge sharing in a multinational agile company. The survey focuses on three aspects of knowledge sharing: within agile teams, beyond the team with company colleagues, and with customers. It concentrates on knowledge sharing practices, ease of knowledge sharing and motivation for knowledge sharing. Summary statistics, regression, and test of equity are used as analysis techniques. Results show that knowledge sharing with team members is significantly easier than with customers or company colleagues beyond their team. In addition, using agile practices improves ease of knowledge sharing within teams but not with customers or colleagues. Extrinsic motivators need to be in place to encourage knowledge sharing across the organisation, especially where such knowledge sharing is not an automatic consequence of completing the work.

Keywords: Knowledge sharing · Agile software development · Organisational knowledge sharing · Learning organisation

1 Introduction

Knowledge is awareness or understanding of something such as information or skills [4]. Knowledge creates most of the value in today's economy and the value of knowledge often increases when shared [23]. Organisational knowledge sharing

© The Author(s) 2017
H. Baumeister et al. (Eds.): XP 2017, LNBIP 283, pp. 135–150, 2017.
DOI: 10.1007/978-3-319-57633-6_9

aims at transferring to the organisation the information, skills and experience a person or team has [10]. This is essential for sustaining the development of quality in software intensive companies [10]. For agile development companies, knowledge is the core resource that is transformed to products and services in the development process [2]. Moreover, Biao-wen [2] claims that the software industry requires more knowledge management than any other sector.

Agile methods focus heavily on the delivery of product and customer value. Moreover, an agile team focuses on applying knowledge instead of sharing it [10]. Agile methods facilitate knowledge sharing in the team but offer limited support for knowledge sharing outside the team [6,17,18]. Agile methods favour tacit knowledge shared informally using face-to-face communication (*personalisation strategy*) in contrast to traditional knowledge management practices [9]. Although attention has been paid to inter-team knowledge sharing [27], and techniques for distributed agile teams have proved to be successful, the focus here is on knowledge sharing across the organisation and not just between teams. The lack of knowledge sharing practices beyond the team can hinder sharing and sustaining knowledge in agile organisations [17].

This paper presents results of a baseline survey organised in a multinational agile software intensive company as part of their effort to improve organisational knowledge sharing. The results show that knowledge sharing with team members is significantly easier than with company colleagues or with customers. In addition, using more agile techniques is associated with increased ease of knowledge sharing with team members but not with colleagues outside the team and not with customers.

The rest of the paper is structured as follows: Sect. 2 introduces related research, Sect. 3 describes the research method, Sect. 4 presents the results, Sect. 5 considers limitations, Sect. 6 discusses the findings and Sect. 7 presents some conclusions and future work.

2   Related Work

Software engineering is a knowledge-intensive activity [25]. Software development teams are made up of knowledgeable individuals who need to be able to use, share, and communicate their knowledge in ways that foster problem solving and creativity. Whereas traditional software project approaches rely heavily on documentation and role-based working as ways of capturing and managing knowledge, agile approaches focus more on informal communication mechanisms within cross-functional teams [6,10].

Agile approaches employ intensive team work, face-to-face knowledge sharing, and trust as vital elements of working practice [1]. Research evidence shows that good team work is crucial for project success, with important facets including communication, coordination, balance of member contributions, mutual support, effort and cohesion [15]. Studies of agile teams have found that agile practices improve both informal and formal communication, and facilitate team and organisational communication [22]. Information visibility and sharing are characteristics of agile approaches, especially when documentation is used. Sharp and Robinson [29] discuss how story cards and the Wall play an important part in the collaboration, co-ordination and communication processes of agile teams. Collaborative online tools are used to keep track of decisions and facilitate communication within collocated and distributed teams [8].

Knowledge management and learning theories have been used to explain the distinctiveness of the agile approach. Nonaka and Takeuchi's [21] distinction between explicit and tacit knowledge has been used to characterise the difference between traditional and agile approaches [6]. Explicit knowledge is objective, rational, and is easier to externalise in documents. In contrast, tacit knowledge is subjective, experience-based, and more likely to be context-specific and therefore easier to discuss than to document. Similarly, Hanssen et al. [14] identify two strategies for knowledge management: codification and personalisation. The codification strategy systematises and stores organisational knowledge, whereas the personalisation strategy supports the flow of information through the organisation through fostering connections between people and supporting a culture of communication. Traditional approaches tend towards codification whereas agile approaches tend towards personalisation.

Agile knowledge sharing practices can be roughly divided into practices among peers (e.g. communities of practice, pairing, coding dojos), among different specialists (shared specialists, interdisciplinary pairing, marathons), and among stakeholders and managers (scrum of scrums, review meetings). As agile becomes more widely adopted within companies and across industry, approaches for facilitating inter-team knowledge sharing and cross-organisational knowledge sharing need to be considered [3]. Inter-team personalisation strategies include Scrum of Scrums, project member rotation, communities of practice and open fishbowl sessions [27]. When viewed at an organisational level, knowledge is a significant competitive asset for a company. However, it is also challenging because of the scale and complexity of organisational environments and because the inter-team strategies do not address the needs of knowledge sharing across an organisation beyond teams collaborating in the same project.

Several authors identify that agile methods supply less advice for how to do this [6,17]. Santos et al. [27] propose a model showing how knowledge sharing between agile teams requires three elements: the adoption of practices, organisational support and appropriate stimuli. Recommended practices include face-to-face conversations, an informative workspace, rotation among teams and projects, collective meetings, pair programming between teams and projects, technical presentations, marathons, and coding dojos. Organisational support includes strategy, structure, culture, environment, top management and leadership support, communication flow and channels, integration among teams and projects, and deeper agile adoption. Appropriate stimuli include problems, common goals, incentives and sustainable pace.

3   Method

The research goal for the study was to identify areas that require improvement in organisational knowledge sharing in an agile company and to provide a baseline for assessing the progress and effectiveness of future actions. The study was initiated by the company who approached the authors[1] with a request to investigate their challenge. A survey[2] was used to reach a wide audience, it was sent to company employees (not customers), and concentrated on knowledge sharing between three groups: team members, company colleagues, and customers. The research questions are as follows.

RQ 1 How is knowledge shared in the organisation?
RQ 2 What motivates knowledge sharing in the organisation?
RQ 3 Is there a relation between agility and ease of knowledge sharing?
RQ 4 Is there a relation between frequency of knowledge sharing activities and ease of knowledge sharing?

3.1   Collaborator Company

The company in which the survey was conducted is a large IT service provider that primarily develops software for UK customers but has staff distributed over three continents. The majority of their workforce is based in India, and are sent to work in development teams at customer sites on a temporary basis in several countries worldwide. Development teams are assigned to a specific customer account and thus have a strong customer focus in their job and day-to-day responsibilities; many teams are embedded in the customer organisation and hence distant from each other. While some cross-organisational knowledge sharing tools and practices have been put in place such as wikis, Yammer, and profession-specific groups for training, these are limited.

3.2   Procedure

The survey was developed iteratively in collaboration with our company contacts and piloted first with students and then with a few company representatives. A link to the online survey was then distributed via a contact person in the company and it was advertised on the company intranet. The survey was open from May to July 2016 and there were altogether 113 responses from company employees of which 81 were completed. Of the 81 complete responses, 36 responded to the open-ended question on how to improve knowledge sharing in the company. No incentives were offered and two reminders were sent. The survey was anonymous. Mean completion time was 11 min (SD 19 min).

---

[1] The authors are members of the Agile Research Network (agileresearchnetwork.org) which is funded by the Agile Business Consortium Ltd. (ABC) Board, The Open University and University of Central Lancashire. Our research approach is explained here: Barroca, L., Sharp, H., Salah, D., Taylor, K., & Gregory, P. (2015). Bridging the gap between research and agile practice: an evolutionary model. IJSA, 1–12.
[2] The survey can be found from here: http://agileresearchnetwork.org/kss

3.3 Survey

The survey addressed practices, motivators and ease of knowledge sharing with team members, company colleagues and with the customer. The survey had three sections, on (1) agile methods and agile techniques employed, (2) knowledge sharing and (3) background information. Questions on knowledge sharing were related to frequency of use of knowledge sharing practices, motivation towards sharing and experienced ease of sharing. Survey themes were as follows

1. Agile methods employed (question 1, multiple choice)
2. Agile techniques employed (question 2, multiple choice)
3. Frequency of use of knowledge sharing practices with team members (question 3, pre-defined list of practices assessed on four-point frequency scale)
4. Frequency of use of knowledge sharing practices with company colleagues outside the team (question 4, pre-defined list of practices assessed on four-point frequency scale)
5. Frequency of use of knowledge sharing practices with customer (question 5, pre-defined list of practices assessed on four-point frequency scale)
6. Motivation for knowledge sharing with team members, company colleagues and customer (question 6, multiple choice)
7. Ease of knowledge sharing with team members, with company colleagues outside the team and with customer (question 7, five-point Likert scale)
8. Suggestions for how to improve knowledge sharing in the company (question 8, open-ended)

In addition we asked for background information including job role, years of experience in the company, the number of customer accounts and the number of people led if any.

The survey was designed to address the needs of the collaborator company and drew on existing literature. The first two questions on agile methods and techniques were adopted from the annual state of agile survey by Version One [31]. Question six on motivation was adapted from [19] and consisted of six statements measuring intrinsic and extrinsic motivation.

3.4 Analysis

We used basic descriptive statistics such as means to summarise responses on the structured questions. Since the data complied with the assumptions [5] of linear regression (F), a commonly used predictive analysis, we used it to study the relation between experienced ease of knowledge sharing and agility or frequency of knowledge sharing activities. We assumed that agility increases with the number of agile techniques employed. Gandomani et al. [11] propose a model and formula for calculating agility based on practices used. They use a list of 44 practices, of which ours is a sub-set. Thus, we use linear regression analysis to test whether experienced ease of knowledge sharing can be predicted from

1. number of specific agile techniques employed (RQ 3)
2. reported frequency of use of knowledge sharing practices (RQ 4)

Based on Shapiro-Wilk test, the data was non-normal and thus we used a non-parametric hypothesis test. The selected Wilcoxon's signed rank test (Z) is a non-parametric statistical hypothesis test for comparing two related samples, e.g. two responses given by one single individual in a survey. We used the Wilcoxon test for equity to measure if there is a statistically significant difference between the experienced ease of knowledge sharing with team members, company colleagues and customers (RQ3, RQ4) and if there is a difference in the frequency of reporting motivation sources for sharing between those three groups (RQ2).

When sharing with either element of each of the partner pairs (team members and company colleagues, team members and customer, company colleagues and customer) the hypotheses are as follows:

1. *there is no difference between the ease of knowledge sharing;*
2. *there is no difference between the frequency of intrinsic motivation sources;*
3. *there is no difference between the frequency of extrinsic motivation sources.*

The hypotheses are a combination of the interests of the studied company and literature. For the open-ended question the data was collated and thematically analysed using an inductive, qualitative, data-driven content analysis with the aim of generating thematic groupings from the data [26], with no preconceived ideas about what would emerge.

3.5   Respondents

The response rate was 9%. The main job responsibility of the 81 respondents was as follows: software development 42%, architecture 16%, project management 15%, software testing or quality 7%, business or system analyst 6%, design or UX design 4%, configuration/support 1% and other roles 9% (coaching or training or a mixture of development and design roles). Of the 81 respondents, 43% did not lead a team or function, 35% led 1 to 9 persons, 14% led 10 to 19 persons and 9% led over 19 persons. Almost all the respondents worked for customer accounts: 4% had not worked for a customer account, 30% had worked for one customer account, 40% for 2 to 4 customer accounts and 27% had worked for five or more customer accounts. On average, respondents had worked for the company for 7 years, standard deviation 6 years.

4   Results

For answers about agile methods and techniques multiple responses were possible. Scrum was the most used agile method reported by 83% of respondents. Kanban and Scrumban were also often used, reported respectively by 32% and 22% of the respondents. The most often employed agile techniques were daily standups, prioritised backlogs, iteration or sprint planning, retrospectives and short iterations or sprints (Fig. 1).

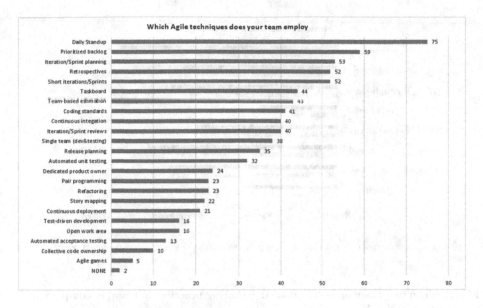

Fig. 1. Employed Agile techniques [31]

4.1 Knowledge Sharing Practices

The most common techniques for knowledge sharing in general were informally, in meetings, and by email (Fig. 2). In general, knowledge sharing was more frequent within teams than with customers or company colleagues outside the team. This is an expected result as teams are often the fundamental social units of an organisation's knowledge creation [16] and Scrum - the most widely used agile method in the company - emphasises the role of collaborative teams. Sharing knowledge with colleagues was most often done informally, whereas when sharing knowledge with customers, meetings were the most frequent technique. Both represent a personalisation knowledge sharing strategy (person-to-person) which is the favoured strategy in agile. The next most commonly used knowledge sharing techniques with customers were email and through the team lead or a senior member of the team.

4.2 Motivation for Knowledge Sharing

The mean number of reported motivation sources per respondent was higher for sharing knowledge with team members than with either company colleagues or customers (Fig. 3). There was a difference between the frequency of intrinsic and extrinsic motivators when sharing with customers compared to when sharing with either team members or company colleagues. When sharing knowledge with team members or company colleagues, a greater number of respondents reported intrinsic sources of motivation than extrinsic sources whereas when sharing with

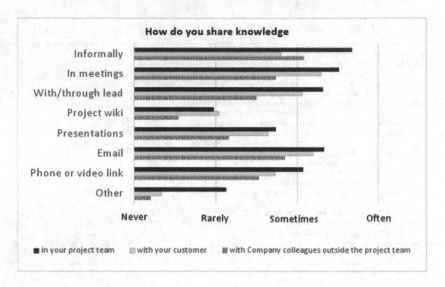

Fig. 2. Mean frequency of use of knowledge sharing practices in team, in company and with customer. N = 81

Table 1. Percentage of respondents reporting motivation source types per sharing partner. N = 81.

Motivation source	Team	Colleague	Customer
Both extrinsic and intrinsic	85%	63%	59%
Intrinsic only	14%	16%	10%
Extrinsic only	1%	10%	21%
None	0%	11%	10%

customers a greater number of respondents reported extrinsic sources of motivation than intrinsic sources (Table 1).

Enjoyment was the most common motivator for knowledge sharing with team members (90% of respondents mentioned it) and with company colleagues (67%) whereas with customer it was strengthening ties (64%) (Fig. 3). Enjoyment is an intrinsic motivator whereas strengthening ties is an extrinsic motivator [16,19].

The Wilcoxon signed rank test was applied to the data. Based on the results, all hypotheses considering motivation sources were rejected apart from the following: *there is no difference between the frequency of intrinsic motivation sources* (1) *when sharing with company colleagues* and (2) *when sharing with customers* (Table 2). However there is a significant difference in the frequency of reporting *extrinsic* motivation sources between sharing knowledge with company colleagues and customers. The most obvious difference is that strengthening ties was an especially frequent source of motivation for sharing knowledge with customers, which is important for maintaining the relationship with the customer.

Table 2. Wilcoxon signed rank test on the frequency of motivation sources for sharing knowledge with team members, company colleagues and customer. N = 81.

Compared sharing partner pair	Test outcome (Z)	Level of significance (p)
Intrinsic: Team members - Colleagues	Z = −3.98	p <.001
Intrinsic: Team members - Customer	Z − −4.94	p <.001
Intrinsic: Colleagues - Customer	Z = −1.53	n.s.
Extrinsic: Team members - Colleagues	Z = −4.12	p <.001
Extrinsic: Team members - Customer	Z = −2.33	p <.05
Extrinsic: Colleagues - Customer	Z = −2.00	p <.05

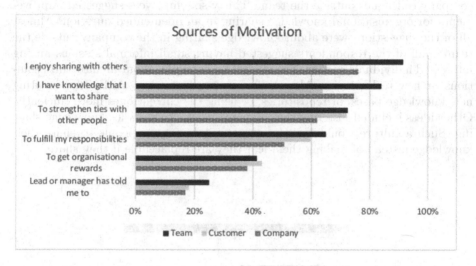

Fig. 3. Frequency of motivation sources for knowledge sharing with team members, customer and company colleagues outside the team. N = 81.

In summary, this test showed differences between the frequencies of *extrinsic* motivation sources for sharing with *all* the sharing partners and between the frequencies of *intrinsic* sources between all the sharing partners except *company colleagues* and *the customer*.

4.3 Ease of Knowledge Sharing

Knowledge sharing within teams was reported to be easy whereas knowledge sharing beyond the team with company colleagues and with customers was less easy (Fig. 4). A Wilcoxon signed rank test was applied to the findings. This revealed that knowledge sharing with team members was significantly easier than with customers ($Z = -4.51$, $p <.001$). It also revealed that knowledge sharing with team members was significantly easier than with company colleagues outside the team ($Z = -4.52$, $p <.001$). Based on the test, the hypotheses *there is no difference between the ease of knowledge sharing with team members and customers* and *there is no difference between the ease of knowledge sharing with team members and company colleagues* were rejected while the hypothesis *there is no difference between the ease of knowledge sharing with company colleagues and customers* was accepted. Of the respondents, 62% strongly agreed that knowledge sharing with team members is easy whereas 28% and 27% strongly agreed that knowledge sharing with customers or with company colleagues, respectively, is easy. Knowledge sharing with customers was considered slightly easier than with company colleagues (Fig. 4). Only 9% did not agree that knowledge sharing is easy with team members whereas 30% did not agree that knowledge sharing is easy with customers and 33% did not agree that knowledge sharing is easy with company colleagues outside the team. Thirty-six employees suggested improvements for organisational knowledge sharing in an open-ended question. Almost all of the suggestions were about knowledge sharing in the company outside the team. Half of the respondents suggested having small informal sessions among interested individuals to share knowledge, for example, about architectural solutions or new technologies. Also, half of respondents suggested either creating new knowledge bases, or repositories, or using the current ones more efficiently. Other ideas included fostering the company culture to embrace knowledge sharing. Such a culture would build on trust and encourage people to share their knowledge instead of making them fear they are replaceable if they share.

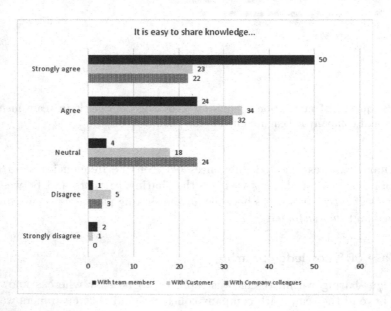

Fig. 4. Perceived ease of knowledge sharing with team members, customer and colleagues. $N = 81$.

4.4   Relation of Agility and Ease of Knowledge Sharing

Experienced ease of knowledge sharing with team members could be predicted from the number of agile techniques employed using linear regression $F(80,1) = 10.7$, $p < .01$. Thus, the greater the number of agile techniques employed, the easier knowledge sharing with team members was experienced.

There is no direct association between the number of agile techniques employed and experienced ease of knowledge sharing with company colleagues, $F(80,1) = 0.0$, n.s, nor between the number of agile techniques employed and experienced ease of knowledge sharing with customers, $F(80,1) = 2.7$, n.s.

4.5   Relation of Frequency and Ease of Knowledge Sharing

There is a direct association between the frequency of use of knowledge sharing practices and experienced ease of knowledge sharing with team members: the more frequently knowledge sharing practices are used, the easier knowledge sharing is, $F(78,12) = 3.6$, $p < .001$. When ease of knowledge sharing with team members was calculated from knowledge sharing practices, using the whiteboard $(t = 3.8, p < .001)$ and doing it informally $(t = 2.8, p < .01)$ are significant positive predictors whereas using Yammer $(t = -2.0, p < .05)$ was a significant negative predictor. Thus, the more frequently whiteboards are used for knowledge sharing or the more frequently knowledge is shared informally with team members, the easier knowledge sharing with team members is experienced. On the contrary, the more often knowledge is shared via Yammer with team members, the less easy knowledge sharing with team members is experienced.

Using a whiteboard requires face-to-face contact whereas Yammer moves people away from physical presence, which may explain the negative association. These results indicate that knowledge sharing is easier where frequent, informal sharing takes place, including using whiteboards as a knowledge sharing tool.

Experienced ease of knowledge sharing with company colleagues can be predicted from the frequency of use of knowledge sharing practices using multiple linear regression, $F(80,11) = 1.9$, $p < .05$. When ease of knowledge sharing with colleagues was calculated from knowledge sharing practices, giving presentations $(t = -2.0, p < .05)$ was a significant negative predictor.

In general, the more frequently knowledge sharing practices are used, the easier knowledge sharing appears to be. However, giving presentations is a negative predictor. A possible explanation for this negative association is that presentations are often one-directional: the presenter shares their information with the audience. Furthermore, the company also shares presentations via email. Using one-directional practices for knowledge sharing may decrease the experienced ease of knowledge sharing.

There is a direct association between the frequency of use of knowledge sharing practices and the experienced ease of knowledge sharing with customers. Experienced ease of knowledge sharing with customers can be predicted from the frequency of use of knowledge sharing practices using multiple linear regression, $F(80, 7) = 5.8$, $p < .001$. When ease of knowledge sharing with customers was calculated from knowledge sharing practices, using a wiki *(t = 3.6, p <.01)* and having meetings *(t = 2.6, p <.05)* were significant predictors. Thus, knowledge sharing is easier when a collaborative exchange of information is frequently used and meetings with the customer are frequent.

5 Limitations

Construct validity relates to the appropriateness of the survey as a measure. Several techniques were used to mitigate this threat. Questions 1, 2 and 6 in the survey were based on questions found in existing literature, to ensure that terminology used was in common use. The survey was developed iteratively and piloted with practitioners. Some of the questions contained repetition asking respondents to consider knowledge sharing from three perspectives, with team members, company colleagues and customers. Factors such as boredom and practice could have impacted the results. Question randomisation or counterbalancing were not used because of limitations of the surveying tool. Multiple response was controlled by allowing only one response per device. **Internal validity** relates to causal conclusions drawn. We used the number of specific agile techniques employed as a measure of agility in the survey, an approach used by [11, 24]. This is not sophisticated, however in the context of this survey it provides a useful indication of how agility varies within the company. The strength of motivators was not asked for and therefore it is unknown if some of them are more powerful than the others. The measures of agility and motivation were both used in the linear regression analysis. Moreover, statistical tests are always prone to incorrect rejection or retaining of the null hypothesis and multiple hypothesis testing increases the risk. We did not use adjustments for these error types since correction of one of the types increases the risk to the other type. **External validity** relates to generalizability of the findings. As only one company was surveyed, the results are specific to that company. Moreover, only a number of employees responded to the survey which makes it prone to non-response bias.

6 Discussion

The summary answers to our research questions are as follows:

RQ 1 *How is knowledge shared in the organisation?* The top three knowledge sharing practices are: sharing informally, in meetings, and through email. Sharing knowledge with colleagues is most often done informally whereas with customers the most common means is in meetings.

RQ 2 *What motivates knowledge sharing in the organisation?* Respondents cited more motivators for sharing with team members than with company colleagues or customers. Motivators for knowledge sharing with team members and with company colleagues are more frequently intrinsic than extrinsic; motivators for knowledge sharing with customers are more frequently extrinsic.

RQ 3 *Is there a relation between agility and ease of knowledge sharing?* Sharing knowledge within teams is statistically significantly easier than with customers or company colleagues. The regression analysis shows that using agile techniques improves ease of knowledge sharing within agile teams but not with company colleagues or with customer.

RQ 4 *Is there a relation between the frequency of knowledge sharing activities and ease of knowledge sharing?* In general the more frequently knowledge sharing practices are used, the easier knowledge sharing is. However, there are nuances in the data with some practices improving knowledge sharing and some hindering it. Our findings suggest that knowledge sharing is easier if face-to-face and informal contact is used, whereas one-way presentations decrease the perceived ease of knowledge sharing.

Our findings indicate that specific agile techniques improve ease of knowledge sharing within teams. This confirms findings from Pikkarainen et al. [22] who found that agile practices improved both informal and formal communication, and [20], who suggest that the "knowledge-as-relationship" focus of agile teams facilitates team knowledge sharing. It also confirms common-sense expectations that agility improves knowledge sharing and communication within the team.

Our findings also suggest that a high level of agility helps knowledge sharing to some extent with customers, but has little impact on knowledge sharing with company colleagues. This finding confirms the view that simply using agile techniques does not help much with inter-team knowledge sharing [6,17].

Software engineers are outcome-oriented and motivated by technically interesting content and the work itself [28]. One of the characteristics of agile working is that all of the team's effort is focused on producing code that provides business value, and that plays directly into this motivation profile. In this context, sharing experiences with company colleagues who are not directly involved in the same project or with the same customer, requires compelling extrinsic motivators. Yet motivators for knowledge sharing with company colleagues were intrinsic rather than extrinsic. Therefore, it seems clear that this organisation does not have sufficient extrinsic motivators in place to encourage knowledge sharing with company colleagues.

These results are influenced by the collaborator's specific cicumstances, and these require further investigation. For example they are mostly based in India and the Indian agile community faces a range of challenges [30], are embedded in customer sites around the world, and hence at a distance from each other.

7   Conclusions and Future Work

Our survey study contributes to an understanding of how knowledge is shared in agile organisations. We provide evidence to support claims that knowledge sharing is easier within agile teams. In this instance, we find that these benefits do not apply to knowledge sharing across the organisation. Extrinsic motivators need to be in place to encourage knowledge sharing across the organisation, especially where such knowledge sharing is not an automatic consequence of completing the work.

Further research is required to investigate how knowledge sharing may be improved across this organisation, to compare their situation with other companies, and to understand better how the organisation's specific situation influences knowledge sharing behaviour. Suggestions from literature will be used to guide the next stage, for example ecosystems, communities of practice, shared specialists, coding marathons and project members' rotation [6,7,27,32]. Santos et al's [27] model of inter-team knowledge sharing suggests that three elements are important in inter-team knowledge sharing: the adoption of specific practices, organisational support and appropriate stimuli. Some of their suggestions for practices, such as job rotation, role pairing between projects and informal cross-organisational networks are not currently in place, but could be introduced. Han and Anantatmula's [13] model for knowledge sharing in large IT organisations identifies organisation, technology, learning and leadership as important components. Their suggestions for leadership highlight the importance of aspects such as a management help with knowledge sharing, verbal praise, encouragement, and career promotion. These observations could be characterised as cultural issues, such as those identified in [12].

References

1. Beck, K., Beedle, M., van Bennekum, A., Cockburn, A., Cunningham, W., Fowler, M., et al.: The Agile Manifesto (2001)
2. Biao-wen, L.: The analysis of obstacles and solutions for software enterprises to implement knowledge management. In: 2010 The 2nd IEEE International Conference on Information Management and Engineering (ICIME), pp. 211–214. IEEE (2010)
3. Bjørnson, F.O., Dingsøyr, T.: Knowledge management in software engineering: a systematic review of studied concepts, findings and research methods used. Inf. Softw. Technol. **50**(11), 1055–1068 (2008)
4. Charband, Y., Navimipour, N.J.: Online knowledge sharing mechanisms: a systematic review of the state of the art literature and recommendations for future research. Inf. Syst. Front., pp. 1–21 (2016)
5. Chatterjee, S., Simonoff, J.S.: Handbook of Regression Analysis, vol. 5. Wiley, New York (2013)
6. Chau, T., Maurer, F., Melnik, G.: Knowledge sharing: Agile methods vs. Tayloristic methods. In: WETICE, vol. 3, pp. 302–307 (2003)
7. Cockburn, A., Highsmith, J.: Agile software development, the people factor. Computer **34**(11), 131–133 (2001)
8. Deshpande, A., Sharp, H., Barroca, L., Gregory, P.: Remote working and collaboration in agile teams. In: International Conference on Information Systems, ICIS 2016. AIS Electronical Library (2016)
9. Dybå, T., Dingsøyr, T.: Empirical studies of agile software development: a systematic review. Inf. Softw. Technol. **50**(9), 833–859 (2008)
10. Ersoy, I.B., Mahdy, A.M.: Agile knowledge sharing. Int. J. Softw. Eng. (IJSE) **6**(1), 1–15 (2015)

11. Gandomani, T.J., Nafchi, M.Z.: An empirically-developed framework for agile transition and adoption: a grounded theory approach. J. Syst. Softw. **107**, 204–219 (2015)
12. Gregory, P., Barroca, L., Sharp, H., Deshpande, A., Taylor, K.: The challenges that challenge: engaging with agile practitioners concerns. Inf. Softw. Technol. **77**, 92–104 (2016)
13. Han, B.M., Anantatmula, V.S.: Knowledge sharing in large it organizations: a case study. Vine **37**(4), 421–439 (2007)
14. Hansen, M.T., Nohria, N., Tierney, T.: Whats your strategy for managing knowledge? In: The Knowledge Management Yearbook 2000–2001, pp. 55–69 (1999)
15. Hoegl, M., Gemuenden, H.G.: Teamwork quality and the success of innovative projects: a theoretical concept and empirical evidence. Organ. Sci. **12**(4), 435–449 (2001)
16. Hung, S.Y., Durcikova, A., Lai, H.M., Lin, W.M.: The influence of intrinsic and extrinsic motivation on individuals' knowledge sharing behavior. Int. J. Hum. Comput. Stud. **69**(6), 415–427 (2011)
17. Karlsen, T.J., Hagman, L., Pedersen, T.: Intra-project transfer of knowledge in information systems development firms. J. Syst. Inf. Technol. **13**(1), 66–80 (2011)
18. Kettunen, P., Laanti, M.: Combining agile software projects and large-scale organizational agility. Softw. Process Improv. Pract. **13**(2), 183–193 (2008)
19. Lin, H.F.: Effects of extrinsic and intrinsic motivation on employee knowledge sharing intentions. J. Inf. Sci. **33**(3), 340–359 (2007)
20. Melnik, G., Maurer, F.: Direct verbal communication as a catalyst of agile knowledge sharing. In: Agile Development Conference 2004, pp. 21–31. IEEE (2004)
21. Nonaka, I., Takeuchi, H.: The Knowledge-Creating Company: How Japanese Companies Create the Dynamics of Innovation. Oxford University Press, New York (1995)
22. Pikkarainen, M., Haikara, J., Salo, O., Abrahamsson, P., Still, J.: The impact of agile practices on communication in software development. Empirical Softw. Eng. **13**(3), 303–337 (2008)
23. Quinn, J.B., Anderson, P., Finkelstein, S.: Managing professional intellect: making the most of the best. In: Strategic Management of Intellectual Capital, pp. 87–100 (1998)
24. Qumer, A., Henderson-Sellers, B.: An evaluation of the degree of agility in six agile methods and its applicability for method engineering. Inf. Softw. Technol. **50**(4), 280–295 (2008)
25. Qumer, A., Henderson-Sellers, B.: A framework to support the evaluation, adoption and improvement of agile methods in practice. J. Syst. Softw. **81**(11), 1899–1919 (2008)
26. Ritchie, J., Lewis, J., Nicholls, C.M., Ormston, R., et al.: Qualitative Research Practice: A Guide for Social Science Students and Researchers. Sage (2013)
27. Santos, V., Goldman, A., De Souza, C.R.: Fostering effective inter-team knowledge sharing in agile software development. Empirical Softw. Eng. **20**(4), 1006–1051 (2015)
28. Sharp, H., Baddoo, N., Beecham, S., Hall, T., Robinson, H.: Models of motivation in software engineering. IST **51**(1), 219–233 (2009)
29. Sharp, H., Robinson, H.: Three 'C's of Agile Practice: Collaboration, Co-ordination and Communication. In: Dingsøyr, T., Dybå, T., Moe, N.B. (eds.) Agile Software Development, pp. 61–85. Springer, Heidelberg (2010)

30. Srinivasan, J., Lundqvist, K.: Agile in India: challenges and lessons learned. In: Proceedings of ISEC 2010 the 3rd India Software Engineering Conference, pp. 125–130. ACM, New York (2010)
31. VersionOne: Annual State of Agile Survey (2016). http://stateofagile.versionone.com. Accessed 29 Nov 2016
32. Wenger, E., McDermott, R.A., Snyder, W.: Cultivating Communities of Practice: A Guide to Managing Knowledge. Harvard Business Press (2002)

Teaching Agile Methods to Software Engineering Professionals: 10 Years, 1000 Release Plans

Angela Martin[1], Craig Anslow[2(✉)], and David Johnson[3]

[1] Xero, Wellington, New Zealand
angela.m.martin@gmail.com
[2] School of Engineering and Computer Science,
Victoria University of Wellington, Wellington, New Zealand
craig@ecs.vuw.ac.nz
[3] Oxford E-Research Centre, University of Oxford, Oxford, UK
david.johnson@oerc.ox.ac.uk

Abstract. Agile methods are an essential resource for software engineers. The Agile movement evolved out of industry and is the common approach to software development today. Teaching Agile methods challenges students' working attitudes, where putting Agile into practice is not possible through simply applying methods prescriptively, but by having an Agile mindset. In this paper we present and discuss our experiences over the last decade of teaching a novel intensive Agile methods week long course as part of a professional Masters of Software Engineering degree programme at the University of Oxford. We describe the typical shape of the course, discuss how students experience Agile values and management practices to foster an Agile mindset, and provide student feedback indicating a consistently positive response to our approach at teaching Agile methods to software engineering professionals. Our reported experiences and material can help other educators who want to run similar courses and adapt where required.

Keywords: Agile software development · Experience report · Group work · Graduate programs · Software engineering professionals

1 Introduction

Since the introduction of the Agile Manifesto, Agile methods in software engineering have gained popularity year on year, and today Agile is not just commonplace, but often expected as a standard industry practice in software development teams. Agile methods were evolved by and are applied by industry [6]. This growth in applying Agile principles in the software industry went hand-in-hand with a growth in Agile training being offered to software engineering professionals in the work place, as well as more recently in undergraduate and some graduate computer science and software engineering degrees.

The University of Oxford Software Engineering Programme (SEP) was established in 1993 and exists to create strong connections between theory and practice in software engineering and to make the expertise of the university available

H. Baumeister et al. (Eds.): XP 2017, LNBIP 283, pp. 151–166, 2017.
DOI: 10.1007/978-3-319-57633-6_10

to those who wish to study part-time while continuing in full-time employment. Most students on SEP are practicing software engineering professionals who often already have university degrees or extensive industry experience. Week-long intensive courses in a variety of subjects are offered, with up to 16 students per class. Each student must take 10 courses in any order over a four year period and are used as credit towards a Masters' degree (MSc) in Software Engineering awarded by the University of Oxford. In 2007 the Agile Methods (AGM) course[1] was introduced in response to the growing needs for software engineering professionals to understand and introduce Agile in their work places.

Teaching Agile methodologies often focuses on learning a particular method [6], such as Scrum [14] or XP [2]. It was recognized that the intensive nature of the week long part-time courses at Oxford made it difficult for an in-depth dive into the variety of Agile methods and practices to fit into the short time span of an individual course. To this end, the Agile Methods course is devised to bring students into an Agile mindset – through a combination of (1) coupling lectures with simulated exercises of Agile management practices, (2) critical analysis and debate around case studies on Agile adoption, and (3) hands-on approach of Agile practices within the classroom.

In this paper, we present an approach to teaching Agile to software engineering professionals and discuss our experiences over the last 10 years of delivering the course. We give a course outline describing the pre-course assignment, case studies, lecture content, group exercises, post-course assignment, and finally discuss lessons learned from teaching the course over a long period of time. Other educators who wish to run similar courses can learn from our experiences and material reported in this paper and adapt where required.

2   Course Outline

The Agile Methods course aims to give an overview of Agile to software engineering professionals and help them understand and adopt an Agile mindset. The learning objectives of the course are as follows: (1) compare and contrast the different agile methods, (2) determine the suitability of agile methods for a particular project and organization, (3) evaluate how well a project is following agile principles, and assist the project to become more agile (where appropriate), (4) understand the relationship between the customer and the development team in agile projects and the responsibilities of both communities, and (5) how to foster organizational change to build better software.

The course is scheduled for a week and spans five consecutive days (Monday to Friday), where each day is timetabled from 0900 to 1730, except for Friday where the class concludes at lunch time (see Table 1 for an example Agile Methods course schedule). The week long class is split into discrete time boxes, with three sessions in the mornings, and three in the afternoons, concluding each day with a learning stand up. Each time box consists of a lecture, an exercise, or a case study discussion, with breaks in between each session.

---

[1] https://www.cs.ox.ac.uk/softeng/subjects/AGM.html.

Table 1. An example University of Oxford Agile Methods (AGM) course schedule. Encoding: Lectures – yellow, Group Exercises – blue, Case Study – green. Three sessions in the morning and three in the afternoon followed by a learning stand-up. Small coffee and tea breaks happen between each session.

Time	Monday	Tuesday	Wednesday	Thursday	Friday
0900-1000	Introduction	Case Study	Case Study	Case Study	Case Study
1015-1115	Agile Manifesto	XP	Empirical Research	Personas	Retrospectives
1130-1230	Communication	Release Planning & User Stories	Lean & Kanban	User Stories	Retrospective Q&A, Survey
1230-1330	*Lunch*	*Lunch*	*Lunch*	*Lunch*	*Lunch*
1330-1430	Case Study	Case Study	Case Study	Estimation	
1445-1545	Scrum	Iteration Planning & Estimation	Kanban Game	Release Planning	
1600-1700	Marshmallow Challenge	Coffee Machine Game	Kanban Game Cont'd	Iteration Planning	
1700-1730	Learning stand-up	Learning stand-up	Learning stand-up	Learning stand-up	

The only prerequisite is that a student must be already enrolled in the SEP. To cover enough Agile background material and different methods we use Agile Software Development Ecosystems [8] as the text book. A pre-study assignment is given to each student to help them prepare in advance of the teaching week and a post-course assignment as the student's assessment.

2.1 Pre-study Assignment: Case Study

It is important for students to begin their study about Agile in advance of the teaching week, and we cater for this by sending them an assignment four weeks in advance of the course. One of the main themes that the course explores is that of Agile adoption; and not just the idealized version of Agile adoption, but the in-the-trenches realities of Agile adoption. We incorporate a case-based learning approach which is common in MBA programs [7].

Students are assigned a case study on Agile adoption and prepare a short presentation to be delivered during the class, followed by a mediated class discussion. Table 1 highlights the case study presentations schedule in green and Sect. 6 lists the case studies for the 2016 course editions. The case study papers are Agile adoption experience reports from past XP and Agile conferences. The case studies involves students actively discussing different industry-based case studies that focus on different organizations that go through an Agile adoption process. No single case study describes an easy Agile adoption story; each highlights a different discussion point around adoption or organizational change.

Each student presents their case study once throughout the week for up to 30 mins. The student summarizes the paper and leads a discussion. The students are asked to first present on who the organization is, who the author is and what their role is within the organization, and what they are trying to achieve or improve in the organization. The class then discusses what should the organization do based on this information. The presenter then describes what the authors actually did and what the outcome of the case study was. Finally, the class discusses if what the authors did made sense, if something different should be recommended, and compares this study with other case studies that have already been presented.

This case-based learning approach enables students to gain an appreciation of how difficult Agile adoption is at an organizational level. By discussing a range of case studies we aim to equip students with knowledge of a broad range of situations that may arise and be able to think critically about where Agile methods can and should be applied in practice.

2.2   Lectures

During the week lectures are delivered that fit into one hour time boxes and consist of presentations and class exercises. Throughout the week we disperse the lectures among case study sessions and group exercises, to keep class activity varied and to ensure the theory is backed up with practical exercises. Table 1 highlights the lectures in yellow.

Agile Manifesto. After an introductory lecture, we present the Agile manifesto and the 12 underlying principles. We focus on the main idea of the manifesto that is: *We are uncovering better ways of developing software by doing it and helping others do it.* We emphasize the importance of the main items of the manifesto, discuss the principles of the manifesto and give some examples to illustrate these principles and values. Finally, we finish the lecture with some of the common misconceptions about Agile methodologies and from our own experience such as *If you're going to adopt Agile development, you should do it 100%* and *Switching to Agile development offers excellent immediate benefits.*

Agile Methods. We present lectures on time-boxed methods in Agile, where we give an overview of both Scrum and XP. For each method we give an overview of the main features, the different practices and roles that team members have, and explain the core values and contributions. In both methodologies we focus on explaining delivering business value with regular steps, monitoring features delivered, and adjusting plans according to results. Then we discuss balancing allowing the business to change their mind while the development team continues to get work done on a stable scope. We present the different team roles, different practices such as sprints/iterations, maintaining a product backlog, planning, daily meetings, and iteration reviews. We emphasize the values of Agile teams: commitment, focus, openness, respect, and courage. Scrum and XP have similar and overlapping structures, roles, and values. There are however some subtle differences that we highlight in the Scrum and XP lectures, for example where XP has a greater emphasis on engineering practices such as pair programming and Test-Driven Development (TDD). We feel it is important to cover both of these time boxed methodologies, as Agile training frequently champions one method over the other. Our approach is to give students an understanding of what Agile methodologies are available to them, with a view to helping them to think in an Agile mindset and not focus on just the methods. We additionally give overviews of other methods including: Kanban, Lean, Crystal, DSDM, and CRISP-DM.

Release and Iteration Planning. Understanding user stories is a an important aspect to software release planning in Agile. Not only are they used to elicit requirements from customers and communicate ideas among a team, they are used as units of customer value. In Agile, delivering customer value is a priority, and by creating user stories teams can plan releases, as well as iterations, around maximizing value for their customers. We present lectures on how to generate personas (fictional end-users as a focus for delivering value to somebody) and use them in-turn to generate candidate user stories. We then show how to estimate the amount of work a user story might require to be implemented. One of the key things we try and get across is that user stories are not all equal, and that an estimation of the amount of work required to implement one varies from team to team. Estimation is difficult, and requires team discussion and agreement, and we illustrate this idea with students playing Planning Poker[2], among other methods, to estimate animal points (see Fig. 1(a)). We then show how user stories with estimates can be used to plan releases (e.g. a release after 4 week sprints) by selecting a series of user stories that delivers minimum demonstrable value for customers (in order to receive feedback in as short a time as possible). At the same time iteration planning (e.g. weekly) is discussed to show how an Agile team should aim to have working software as early as possible and often. Coupled with the team release planning exercise, our aim is to put students through the motions of becoming customer-focused and in the mindset of team collaboration to achieve goals in an iterative manner. We also discuss how to effectively track progress during release and iteration planning using various techniques such as information radiators (e.g. burn down/up charts).

Guest Lectures. We typically invite expert guest lecturers (industry practitioners or other academics) to deliver specialist content. In particular we have had lectures on Example Driven Development (xDD) (e.g. TDD, ATDD, BDD), Lean & Kanban, change management, and empirical research on how Agile methods are used in practice.

Retrospectives. The final lecture is on retrospectives, where we typically have a guest lecture present and then perform a retrospective exercise with the class. This lecture focuses on the ideas from Derby and Larsen [5] and Kerth [9]. Once the retrospective has completed, the post-course assignment (Sect. 2.4) is explained and handed out and then finally students conduct a course survey which is used for course evaluation purposes.

---

[2] http://www.planningpoker.com/.

2.3   Group Exercises

One of the key approaches we take with teaching our Agile Methods course is to encourage peer learning and learning-by-doing. To reinforce the lectures students participate in a number of exercises, working as pairs and groups. Table 1 highlights the group exercises in blue.

Communication. We explain to the students how important it is to communicate effectively with customers on Agile projects by illustrating the customer design cartoon[3]. To reinforce this message the students complete a communication exercise – Offing the Off-Site Customer [4]. This exercise involves pairs of students where one acts as a "customer" and the other as a "programmer". The aim of the exercise is for the programmer to elicit requirements from the customer in order to draw a diagram of the product vision on paper (see Fig. 1(b)). The customers are given a drawing that they need to communicate to the programmers to recreate, without visually communicating the drawing. The exercise is played out over two rounds. In the first round the customers must only communicate with the programmer via handwritten text messages on index cards. In the second round, the customers and programmers are allowed to use verbal communication. After each round, the students reflect on the experiences of trying to communicate the drawings between them. The point of this exercise is to suggest that people in close proximity to each other with minimal physical barriers have a better chance of communicating effectively. We encourage the students to think about their own work place and to find a way to set up environments to encourage regular and meaningful collaboration.

Prototyping. To get a feel of prototyping with time-boxed methods, students complete the Marshmallow Challenge[5] and are asked to prototype a fully functioning coffee machine out of cardboard based on ideas from Cockburn [4] (see Fig. 1(c)). The goal of the coffee machine exercise is to try Scrum for an iteration and then walk a mile in a product owner's shoes as part of a second iteration. The students are divided into teams (up to four). During the first iteration the teams have 7 min to write stories about how the machine will work and prepare materials (e.g. boxes, tape, scissors, cups, water). For each iteration they have 5 min to plan what stories they will implement, followed by 10 min to design and implement the stories, and finally a group presentation to the class. The purpose of this exercise is to get the students to work in a simulated environment as a team in a time-boxed manner, and to understand that prototyping and early releases only need to demonstrate a concept to a customer to deliver value.

Agile Debate. To help students gain a better understanding of the differences between the Scrum and XP methodologies we ask them to perform a debate. The class is separated into two sides: Scrum and XP. We give them two well-known,

---

[3] http://projectcartoon.com.
[4] http://www.jamesshore.com/Presentations/OffingTheOffsiteCustomer.html.
[5] http://www.tomwujec.com/design-projects/marshmallow-challenge/.

and highly contrasting, quotes, from Martin Fowler[6] and Ken Schwaber[7] as the basis for their arguments. The students use the session to come up with their own arguments and perform the debate with the lecturer as the adjudicator. The aim of the debate is for the students to understand that there is no silver-bullet when it comes to applying and adopting Agile methods.

Kanban Game. To help students gain an appreciation of the Kanban method we get them to play the getKanban[8] board game (see Fig. 1(d)). getKanban is a physical board game designed to teach the concepts and mechanics of Kanban for software development in a classroom setting. Each team can have up to six people. Each team has a playing board representing a Kanban task board, and a collection of story cards representing work to be done. Teams compete to maximise profit by optimizing the flow of work. We simulate the game for up to 21 days. During the game the teams construct charts based on data from the game including a Cumulative Flow Diagram, a Run Chart, and a Lead Time Distribution Chart. To help make the game more realistic there are a number of simulated events that occur throughout the game that challenge the teams (e.g. a developer needs to attend a training course) and require them to make various system design, prioritization, and resource allocation decisions. We allow a couple of hours to play the game and have a debrief session at the end to help students understand the intricacies of the method.

Team Release Planning. Building on the accompanying lecture sessions, students carry out a team release planning exercise which covers most of Thursday. This puts into practice everything they have been taught about Agile. In this exercise, we split the students into groups of no more than four per team. In this exercise, we do not mandate any team structure – we allow the students to self-organize, much like a real Agile team would be expected to do. The lecturer sets a particular domain area (e.g. solve London's transport issues) in which each team can then pick their own idea for a small product or service. They create a release plan (including personas and user stories) over four weeks and four time-boxes on a card wall, with the aim of being able to release a first version of their product to a customer after the four weeks. At the end of the exercise, each team presents their release plan to the rest of the class (see Fig. 1(e)).

Retrospective. A retrospective on the course is performed on the last day where an external guest lecturer usually facilitates. Students record their thoughts about the course on post-it notes into three categories: positive, could be better, and aspects that were a surprise. Students place the ideas into different days of the course on a card wall based on the timetable (see Fig. 1(f)). The facilitator walks through the card wall and identifies and discusses key themes. The aim of this exercise is for students to reflect upon what they have learned.

Learning Stand-up Meeting. At the end of each day the students perform a learning stand-up meeting similar to a daily stand-up meeting (see Fig. 1(g)).

---

[6] http://martinfowler.com/bliki/FlaccidScrum.html.
[7] http://kenschwaber.wordpress.com/2010/06/10/waterfall-leankanban-and-scrum-2/.
[8] https://getkanban.com/.

(a) Estimation: plan- (b) Communication: customers & (c) Prototyping: cardboard
ning poker with ani- programmers diagrams.   coffee machine.
mal cards.

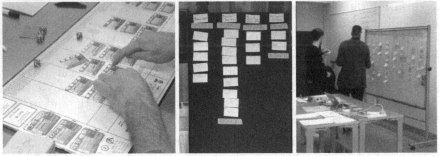

(d) getKanban board game.   (e) Team   Release (f) Retrospective on the
                              Planning Exercise.   class.

(g) Learning Standup that happens at the end of each day.

Fig. 1. Agile methods course – some sample class exercises that simulate some key
points about different Agile practices including: estimation, communication, prototyping with cardboard, Kanban, release planning, class retrospectives, and daily learning
stand up meetings.

The stand-up meeting is for each student to address the questions like they would
in a daily stand-up, hence fostering Agile team values of openness, respect, and
courage. The questions focus on what have they learned during the day and
what they would like to learn. Students write answers on post-it notes, present
them to the group, and then put them on a learning card wall.

2.4   Course Assignment: Essay and Release Plan

The course is assessed with an assignment where students are given six weeks to develop a mock four-week release plan and complete an essay. The *release plan* is based on a fictitious product idea (e.g. develop an application for a hospital to help support children who suffer from a medical condition like autism). The release plan is documented as a report, outlining the different personas, user stories (based on one persona), and the release plan itself, similar to the team planning exercise performed in class. They need to include the rationale for deciding the team's capacity for each sprint, and why they think that this release plan makes the most sense for the customer. Developing the release plan in the assignment aims to assess what the students learned in class, and we ask them to reflect on this aspect comparing with their experience on the team release planning exercise. The *essay* involves comparing and contrasting different Agile adoption paths from two of the case studies (Sects. 2.1 and 6). One question that students are asked to address is, "is there a one-size fits all Agile adoption strategy?" The assignments are assessed following a marking guide[9] where all submissions are awarded a numerical grade between 0 and 100, interpreted as follows: 0 and 49 denotes a fail, 50 and 69 denotes a pass, and 70 and 100 denotes excellence. Most students are awarded a pass, some with excellence, and few with fail; and grades are released approximately six weeks from submission. Students can defer submitting the assignment and wait for a later edition, but this is rare.

3   Discussion

Teaching the AGM course over the last decade has given us in-depth experiences from which to draw upon, that we would like to share. Throughout the duration of this course, we have gathered student feedback to help inform and evolve the course along the way, as well as having gathered formal feedback from students, some of which we now discuss.

Lectures. One of the biggest challenges in designing this course is catering for the intensive nature of the course delivery. While there are just over 30 h of face-to-face time allocated to the course, we were conscious not to overwhelm students with only lectures. To this end, about a third of the class time was allocated for lectures, broken up with exercises and case study discussion sessions. While lectures are useful for delivering information to students, our key aim was to enable the Agile mindset. In this case, we put further emphasis on learning-by-doing with hands-on exercises and class discussion. For each lecture, we ensured that a relevant exercise or case study followed. Keeping the lectures to a planned limit of only one hour per session we felt also deferred any feelings of fatigue or boredom, which is vitally important in a short but intensive learning environment. The students found the theory was important to learn and appreciated the lecture content on empirical studies of Agile project teams which showed evidence about the use of different practices within industry.

---

[9] http://www.cs.ox.ac.uk/softeng/handbook/examinations.html.

Group Exercises. The exercises were carefully chosen to help the students put into practice, or to help them quickly understand, the lecture material. As discussed above, the lectures were normally paired with relevant exercises or case studies. For example, to take the learning from the release planning lecture and put it into practice, we would follow the lecture with an exercise on story estimation. Each of the exercises aimed to teach important aspects about the different Agile methods. The communication exercise highlights the importance of fast and frequent customer feedback. The prototyping exercise looks at how Agile teams are formed and how to respond to change. The estimation exercise put the use of abstract story points into practice on non-software artifacts to help understand that estimation is a team effort and not a formula that is uniformly applied. The Kanban board game exercise aims to demonstrate the Kanban method and allows students to put the method in action to understand workflow.

Team Release Planning Exercise. The team release planning exercise involves putting into practice the learning from all the previous lectures and exercises. We encouraged the students to self-organize and gave them reminders and guidance on the course material. We mainly left them to make their own decisions on how to plan their product releases. This exercise always proves to be the most challenging for the students, as it was designed to simulate the real planning of a hypothetical product or service, where the exercise often took many hours or a whole day. The task also requires a level of creativity that many students were uncomfortable with, but it was essential to move them away from their comfort zone in order to get into an Agile mindset where all members of a team should be able to feel they can contribute.

Assignments. The assignment tasks mirrored much of what was taught during the class, where students are asked to write a short essay comparing and contrasting two case studies, and then to create a release plan similar to their team release planning exercise. The essay question was generally straight forward as the case study presentations and debates prepared students well for this part of the assignment. The release planning exercise, however, proved challenging for many. The main difficulty in this task was that in class it was done as a group exercise, while in the assignment the students were asked to do a similar plan but on their own. Some students took the initiative to simulate the group environment by asking work colleagues to carry out the collaborative parts of the exercise, such as estimation. Others on occasions, however, fell back into old habits or forgot the learning in class and strayed on a tangent to what was expected. The creativity aspect of the release planning exercise, on occasions, proved problematic, where students either could not come up with an idea for a product that was suitable to generate a good number of personas and user stories, or that sometimes a student would get carried away and produce an assignment submission that was all about their great idea, but little in substance for demonstrating what they learned in class. What we learned is that setting such an assignment, care should be taken to ensure the students remember they need to focus and demonstrate their learning in their submissions.

Practical Approach to Teaching Agile. The design of the class delivery gives students a practical approach to an Agile environment. The time-boxed class sessions planned throughout the week reflects how sprints or iterations are planned in time-boxed Agile methods such as Scrum and XP. We used pair-stairs[10] to encourage students to pair with their colleagues during the week, much like when applying the XP practice of pair programming. The daily learning stand-up reflects the practice of daily stand-up meetings in a Scrum or XP team. The use of visual cues around the classroom to learning material, but also to the collective class experiences such as in the prototyping and the release planning exercises, provides the tactile experience that Agile working environments give. Finally, getting the students to perform the retrospective exercise gives them the experience of participating in a realistic retrospective.

Evolving Agile Teaching Content. One of the things we have observed that is changing in the students over the last few years is that more students attending the course identify themselves as already having Agile training, or as being Agile practitioners in their organizations. This reflects what we see today in the software industry – that Agile is no longer a niche, and is an expected workplace practice in software engineering teams. To this end we have taken the opportunity, through the retrospectives, to be Agile in our planning of the course itself, and to take on board "customer feedback" from our students and make continual changes based on this feedback. For example we have introduced new games and techniques into the course such as the getKanban board game and used more recent and up to date Agile adoption case studies over time.

Student Feedback. Over each iteration of the Agile Methods course, as discussed earlier, feedback is gained by putting students through a retrospective exercise at the end of the teaching week to help inform any changes to the next instance of the class. Alongside this, students have been returning student feedback questionnaires since 2010, where overwhelmingly the feedback has been positive. The students were asked to rate between 1 (strongly disagree) and 5 (strongly agree) their level of agreement on 12 statements, for example:

- The lectures added significant value to the course material
- The lectures included valuable contributions from other students in class
- The exercises helped me to understand the topics covered in the lectures

The aggregate and average score over the time period for which we have data is 4.32 out of 5 based on 132 completed questionnaires[11] (see Fig. 2). The last three editions of the course feedback scored the most highly and were above the SEP all courses average of 4.55, at 4.6, 4.73, and 4.66 respectively. This feedback shows some perceived evidence that the course structure and content has matured where students are generally satisfied with what is being delivered.

While the feedback was generally positive, there were however some negative comments on the course content in the feedback questionnaires. Many of these

---

[10] http://pairstair.com.
[11] Statements and raw data located in https://tinyurl.com/AGM-Student-Feedback.

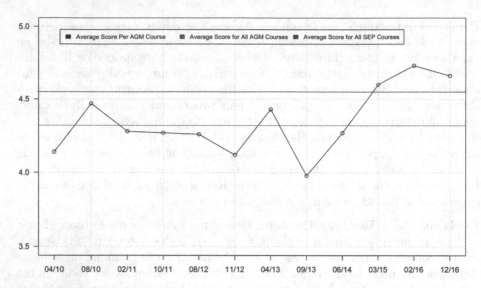

Fig. 2. AGM course evaluation as perceived feedback by students since 2010. Black – average score for each AGM course by the students. Red – average score for all AGM courses. Blue – average score for all SEP courses. Last three editions scored the highest. (Color figure online)

focused on the fact that given such a short space of time allocated in class, there was far too broad material in the Agile space to impart in further depth onto the students. In particular, we received comments such as:

"The course content is not enough to stretch 5 days."

"The large amounts of material made timing difficult."

This is a clear acknowledgment that the amount of material around Agile methods makes teaching the subject very difficult, especially in an intensive teaching environment. There was some skepticism about the game-like exercises, however, on further reflection with students several weeks after the course had completed even those students acknowledged that they had taken on board the learning from the exercises when they returned to their own organizations to share their new-found knowledge around Agile. Some of the positive comments we received included:

"Excellent way of teaching! You have expanded my horizon and gave me an excellent introduction to Agile."

"One of the best courses I have studied at Oxford. The lecturer and their use of guests made the course better and maybe of benefit to other courses! Initially I had doubts about the lecturer coming from industry but for this course it works better as they can draw on experience."

"A useful course with a timeliness of current industry trends."

"Good and helpful lecturers. The idea of students studying and presenting a case study is brilliant and helped a lot with understanding and discussing."

We have kept the Agile Methods course content timely by consciously putting Agile into practice in how we prepare and deliver the Agile Methods course itself. Feedback, in particular via the retrospective exercise, has allowed us to keep the course up to date with student and industry needs.

4   Related Work

Related work has mainly focused on teaching Agile to undergraduate and graduate students as part of computer science and software engineering curriculum's. The majority of these courses are typically group based projects, last 10–16 weeks, and teach Scrum and or XP. Our work reports on teaching a novel Agile methods course to *software engineering professionals* that are already working within industry and likely already have a degree, potentially in a computing subject, or have extensive software industry experience.

Lu and DeClue [12] discuss how Agile skills improve the marketability of new graduates. They also highlight the challenges posed in teaching Agile to undergraduates that stem from prerequisite experience and maturity. These challenges include fostering Agile approaches to skills such as communication, self-organization, and teamwork, where students who have less experience in a workplace may find mastery of these skills more difficult.

A panel at SIGCSE 2016 [3] raised a number of issues for teaching Agile methods in software engineering courses at a variety of computer science programs. The panel focused only on undergraduate university teaching (100 to 400 levels), hence novices to Agile with limited development experience.

Anslow et al. [1] reported their experience of teaching Agile methods to undergraduate and graduate students and presented a course outline along with associated teaching materials. They recommended not to teach the course to different levels simultaneously due to the nature of different levels of assessment required, abilities of the students, and additional administrative overheads.

Steghöfer et al. [16] reported on their efforts to improve teaching Agile, and Scrum in particular. They aimed to teach in a realistic manner but without encountering the technical difficulties of creating a real product by introducing exercises decoupled from software, such as LEGO Scrum.

Kropp et al. [10,11,13] looked at the status of Agile in education and industry and proposed a competency model on which to base integration of Agile into undergraduate teaching at two different universities. They found the most difficult competencies to teach are Agile values and management practices which they put significant emphasis on. Our AGM course also focuses on values and management practices and we have a complimentary course that focuses on Agile engineering practices[12] such as TDD and continuous integration.

Soundararajan, et al. [15] developed an advanced graduate-level course (to non-software professionals) in Agile software engineering at Virginia Tech. Their

---

[12] http://www.cs.ox.ac.uk/softeng/subjects/APE.html.

course has similarities to our approach where they focus on Agile product development, host guest talks from industry experts, and encourage students to present and debate Agile case studies within the class.

5   Conclusions

For today's computer science students who look towards entering a career in software engineering, skills beyond programming and technical excellence are essential. For any new graduate entering the tech industry, knowledge of Agile is essential. We hope that by sharing our extensive experiences in teaching Agile we can help foster excellence in Agile methods education in formal educational settings, such as in high school, university degree programs, and perhaps also in industrial training. From our experiences in teaching the Agile Methods course at the University of Oxford, we can extract many aspects of what we taught to graduate students that could be applied in any Agile teaching course. We believe that putting Agile theory into practice with a hands-on approach will lead to more effective learning. Based on the material reported in this paper other academics who wish to run similar courses can learn from our experiences.

6   Agile Methods: Case Study Papers for 2016

P1. M. Albisetti. Launchpad's quest for a better and agile user interface. In *XP*, pages 244–250. Springer, 2010.
P2. K. Boekhout. Mob programming: find fun faster. In *XP*, pages 185–192. Springer, 2016.
P3. C. Fry and S. Greene. Large scale agile transformation in an on-demand world. In *AGILE*, pages 136–142. IEEE, 2007.
P4. S. Hublikar and S. Hampiholi. Pause, reflect and act, the pursuit of continuous transformation. In *XP*, pages 201–208. Springer, 2016.
P5. M. Keeling. Put it to the test: Using lightweight experiments to improve team processes. In *XP*, pages 287–296. Springer, 2010.
P6. T. Little, F. Greene, T. Phillips, R. Pilger, and R. Poldervaart. Adaptive agility. In *AGILE*, pages 63–70. IEEE, 2004.
P7. S. McCalden, M. Tumilty, and D. Bustard. Smoothing the transition from agile software development to agile software maintenance. In *XP*, pages 209–216. Springer, 2016.
P8. B. Pieber, K. Ohler, and M. Ehegötz. University of Vienna's u:space turning around a failed large project by becoming agile. In *XP*, pages 217–225. Springer, 2016.
P9. D. Poon. A self funding agile transformation. In *AGILE*, pages 342–350. IEEE, 2006.
P10. M. Rajpal. Lessons learned from a failed attempt at distributed agile. In *XP*, pages 235–243. Springer, 2016.
P11. N. Robinson. A technical story. In *AGILE*, pages 339–343. IEEE, 2007.

P12. K.H. Rolland, V. Mikkelsen, and A. Næss. Tailoring agile in the large: Experience and reflections from a large-scale agile software development project. In *XP*, pages 244–251. Springer, 2016.

P13. C. Sudbery. How XP can improve the experiences of female software developers. In *XP*, pages 261–269. Springer, 2016.

P14. A. Takats and N. Brewer. Improving communication between customers and developers. In *AGILE*, pages 243–252. IEEE, 2005.

P15. I. Tsyganok. Pair-programming from a beginner's perspective. In *XP*, pages 270–277. Springer, 2016.

P16. B. Victor and N. Jacobson. We didn't quite get it. In *AGILE*, pages 271–274. IEEE, 2009.

Acknowledgments. Thanks to Jeremy Gibbons and Jim Davies from the Software Engineering Programme at the University of Oxford for their support. Thanks to guest lectures by Antony Marcano, Duncan Pierce, Lazaro Wolf, and Robert Biddle. Thanks to Rob Chatley for expert advice. Thanks to Clint Sieunarine and Ross Gales for being teaching assistants.

References

1. Anslow, C., Maurer, F.: An experience report at teaching a group based agile software development project course. In: SIGCSE, pp. 500–505. ACM (2015)

2. Beck, K., Andres, C.: Extreme Programming Explained: Embrace Change. Addison Wesley, Reading (2004)

3. Campbell, J., Kurkovsky, S., Liew, C.W., Tafliovich, A.: Scrum and agile methods in software engineering courses. In: SIGCSE, pp. 319–320. ACM (2016)

4. Cockburn, A.: Agile Software Development: The Cooperative Game. Addison Wesley, Boston (2006)

5. Derby, E., Larsen, D.: Agile Retrospectives: Making Good Teams Great. Pragmatic Bookshelf, Raleigh (2006)

6. Hazzan, O., Dubinsky, Y.: Why software engineering programs should teach agile software development. SIGSOFT Softw. Eng. Notes **32**(2), 1–3 (2007)

7. Lee, S.H., Lee, J., Liu, X., Bonk, C.J., Magjuka, R.J.: A review of case-based learning practices in an online MBA program: a program-level case study. Educ. Technol. Soc. **12**(3), 178–190 (2009)

8. Highsmith, J.: Agile Software Development Ecosystems. Addison Wesley, Boston (2002)

9. Kerth, N.L.: Project Retrospectives: A Handbook for Team Reviews. Dorset House Publishing Co., New York (2001)

10. Kropp, M., Meier, A.: Teaching agile software development at university level: Values, management, and craftsmanship. In: International Conference on Software Engineering Education and Training (CSEET), pp. 179–188. IEEE (2013)

11. Kropp, M., Meier, A.: New sustainable teaching approaches in software engineering education. In: EDUCON, pp. 1019–1022. IEEE (2014)

12. Lu, B., DeClue, T.: Teaching agile methodology in a software engineering capstone course. J. Comput. Sci. Coll. **26**(5), 293–299 (2011)

13. Meier, A., Kropp, M., Perellano, G.: Experience report of teaching agile collaboration and values: agile software development in large student teams. In: International Conference on Software Engineering Education and Training (CSEET), pp. 76–80. IEEE (2016)
14. Schwaber, K., Beedle, M.: Agile Software Development with Scrum. Pearson, Upper Saddle River (2001)
15. Soundararajan, S., Chigani, A., Arthur, J.D.: Understanding the tenets of agile software engineering: Lecturing, exploration and critical thinking. In: SIGCSE, pp. 313–318. ACM (2012)
16. Vogel, B., Kilamo, T., Kurti, A.: Teaching distributed agile development to software professionals: a flexible approach. In: European Conference on Software Architecture Workshops, ECSAW, pp. 31:1–31:8. ACM (2015)

Are Software Startups Applying Agile Practices? The State of the Practice from a Large Survey

Jevgenija Pantiuchina[1], Marco Mondini[1], Dron Khanna[1], Xiaofeng Wang[1(✉)], and Pekka Abrahamsson[2]

[1] Free University of Bozen-Bolzano, Piazza Domenicani 3, 39100 Bolzano, Italy
{Jevgenija.Pantiuchina,marco.mondini,dron.khanna,xiaofeng.wang}@unibz.it
[2] Norwegian University of Science Technology, 7491 Trondheim, Norway
pekkaa@ntnu.no

Abstract. Software startups operate under various uncertainties and the demand on their ability to deal with change is high. Agile methods are considered a suitable and viable development approach for them. However, the competing needs for speed and quality may render certain agile practices less suitable than others in the startup context. The adoption of agile practices can be further complicated in software startups that adopt the Lean Startup approach. To make the best of agile practices, it is necessary to first understand whether and how they are used in software startups. This study targets at a better understanding of the use of agile practices in software startups, with a particular focus on lean startups. Based on a large survey of 1526 software startups, we examined the use of five agile practices, including quality related (regular refactoring and test first), speed related (frequent release and agile planning) and communication practice (daily standup meeting). The findings show that speed related agile practices are used to a greater extent in comparison to quality practices. Daily standup meeting is least used. Software startups who adopt the Lean Startup approach do not sacrifice quality for speed more than other startups do.

Keywords: Software startups · Agile practice · Lean startup · Minimum viable product · Pivot · Quality vs Speed

1 Introduction

Startups are organizations designed to create new products or services under the conditions of extreme uncertainty, which constantly seek repeatable, profitable and scalable business models and aim at rapid growth [1,2]. Software startups are startups that have a primary focus on developing new and innovative software-intensive products or services from which business value is created. Even though sharing common characteristics with other types of startups, such as resource scarcity and a lack of operational history [3], software startups are often caught up in the wave of technological change frequently happening in software industry, such as new computing and network technologies and devices [4].

H. Baumeister et al. (Eds.): XP 2017, LNBIP 283, pp. 167–183, 2017.
DOI: 10.1007/978-3-319-57633-6_11

As the ability to accommodate frequent change is essential in the startup context, agile methods have been considered the most suitable process model since they enable software startups to embrace change, and allow development to adapt to business strategies [5]. Fast release with an iterative and incremental approach shortens the lead time from idea conception to production to market, which is especially important for software startups as "done is better than perfect" and "move fast and break things" are the slogans or mantras that they follow in order to respond to the challenges they are confronted with [6].

However, since software startups are constantly under the huge pressure of time-to-market and need to move really fast, product quality may be treated with a low priority and technical debt is accumulated to gain the speed to market [7]. As a result, certain agile practices that ensure the quality of software, such as refactoring and test-driven development, may not be considered viable practices for software startups, especially at the early stages [8]. But the accumulated technical debt, if not paid back in time, will eventually slow down the development speed [7], which means software startups cannot afford to ignore quality and related engineering practices as they progress through the stages of development.

The adoption of agile practices can be further complicated when software startups follow the Lean Startup approach to develop their business, which puts even more emphasis on quick prototyping [9], testing prototypes with potential customers, and getting early feedback. The use of Lean Startup approach may intensify the so-called "developers dilemma"—the balancing act between quality and speed to achieve fast product iteration [10], and render the agile practices related to quality even less viable to software startups.

To understand how software startups can better use and benefit from different agile practices for their needs for quality and speed, it is important to understand firstly if and how software startups are currently using agile practices. The existing software engineering literature has accumulated a growing body of knowledge on the application of agile methods in established companies, large or small. However it casts very few lights on the use of agile practices in software startups, let alone in the startups who adopt the Lean Startup approach. Based on this observation, the study presented in this paper targets at understanding the state of the practice of agile practices in software startups, and the potential influence of the Lean Startup approach on the use of agile practices. The overall research questions that guide our study are:

RQ1: *Are software startups applying agile practices?*
RQ2: *Are software startups that adopt Lean Startup applying agile practices?*

To depict the state of the practice, we utilize the data collected in a large online survey conducted from September 2013 to September 2014. Based on the responses from 1526 surveyed software startups worldwide, we could obtain a good understanding of the state of the practice of agile practices applied in software startups.

The rest of the paper is organized as follows. Section 2 reviews the related work that has been conducted so far to understand the use of agile practices in software startups. In Sect. 3, we explain how the online survey is utilized to answer the research questions. The findings are presented in Sect. 4 and further discussed in Sect. 5, together with the reflection on the limitations of and validity threats to the study. The paper ends with Sect. 6 in which potential future work is outlined.

2 Related Work

2.1 Agile Methods in Software Startups

The emergence of agile methods was a response to the inability of heavy-weight, waterfall-like development methodologies to allow software organizations to respond to change. Popular agile methods, such as Scrum and XP, have been adopted by both small and large companies worldwide over the years, rendering agile a mainstream software development approach [11]. At their core, agile methods focus on incremental and iterative development. The nimbleness and flexibility allowed by different agile practices, such as short iterations, continuous integration, etc., enable software organizations to address change effectively [12,13]. The effective adoption and use of agile methods in established companies have been manifested in a growing body of agile research [14–16].

When the context is switched to software startups, the picture is less clear-cut. Some studies suggest in a general manner that agile methods are viable and suitable for software startups (e.g., [17,18]). For example, Duc and Abrahamsson [9] find that four out of five startups they studied have adopted agile development processes. However, these studies do not specify clearly which particular agile method or agile practices have been used in software startups.

Other studies suggest a different picture. Coleman and O'Connor [5] argue that startups are creative and flexible in nature and are reluctant to introduce process which may hinder their natural attributes. They have very limited resources and typically wish to use these resources to support product development. Giardino et al. [18] observe that, to quickly validate the product in the market, software startups tend to use agile methods, but in an ad-hoc manner. Yau and Murphy [8] go further and contend that, given that the communication and cooperation dynamics in startups are very different from more established companies and the fact that the initial focus of a startup might be significantly different from its final objective, even the agile approach seems to impose too much rigidity and process on them. Without denying that agile methods offer clear benefits to startups over some of the more traditional methods, the authors question whether they are appropriate in tackling the problems faced by startups. Doubts are cast on the usefulness of agile practices including test-driven development, pair programming, user stories, velocity and backlogs [8].

2.2 Lean Startup and Agile Practices

The Lean startup approach is considered a variant to agile methods in software engineering literature [18]. It advocates the identification of the most risky parts of a software business and the use of Minimum Viable Products (MVPs) to systematically test them and change the course of the development if needed. According to Ries [1], a MVP is "[the] version of a new product which allows a team to collect the maximum amount of validated learning about customers with the least effort." MVPs should be the main focus of both business and product development activities in software startups [9]. The strategic change is termed *pivot* in Lean Startup.

Even though the Lean Startup approach is seen as a recent advancement in agile community, and regarded by some as a more "extreme" agile approach than extreme programming (XP) or Scrum [19], difference between the two has been argued. Agile methods seem to be able to prescribe on how to develop a working software faster, but are unable to provide the answer to what product should be developed in the first place [20]. Although agile methods advocate to build software iteratively, they only work when problems are known to the stakeholders. Instead, startups typically are looking for right problems to solve and need to figure out who are their customers [2]. Lean Startup advocates startups to build products iteratively and get early feedback to test riskiest assumptions about their business models. The combined use of agile and Lean Startup seems a sensible approach for software startups.

The research conducted by Duc and Abrahamsson [9] is focused on different types of MVPs that software startups utilize and what are their main purposes. They argue that the adoption of MVP might be influenced by many contextual factors, and one most relevant factor is the product development methodology. They further suggest that the continuous integration—one of the agile practices—might be the impetus for the popular adoption of evolutionary prototypes and single-feature MVP in four of the five cases they studied.

However, Yau and Murphy [8] contend that certain agile practices may not be in consistency with the primary focus of software startups that adopt the Lean Startup approach. Quality is important for a software startup but cost and time may be larger deciding factors. A small scale startup that has not obtained much funding will probably have a short runway, and thus a limited amount of time and money. The priority in this case should be to create an MVP, which may lack in quality but is functional enough to show to investors. Terho et al. [10] also argue the need of balancing between quality and speed in creating MVPs, the intensified "developers dilemma" faced by software startups. As a consequence, the agile practices that are focused on quality of software, such as test-driven development and refactoring, may be compromised or even not taken on board.

3   Research Method

3.1   Survey Questions

This study utilizes a large online survey that was conducted between 2013 and 2014. The original survey explored various aspects of startups and covered a large set of questions. The authors had the opportunity to access the survey data and select the questions that were pertinent to the purpose of this study.

Table 1 shows the list of questions used in this study, as the result of the selection process. The questions are mainly divided into three categories:

- questions related to the demographic information of the respondents and the background information of the surveyed software startups;
- questions related to agile practices, which form the core category. We used the list of agile practices reported in the 10th annual agile report from VersionOne [11] as the commonly accepted agile practices. The original survey includes five questions relevant to agile practices: regular refactoring, test first, frequent release, agile planning, and daily standup meeting. All are close-ended questions. Four are ordinal and the one about daily stand-up meeting is binary. All of them require a single answer and are not mandatory.
- questions related to the Lean Startup approach, which allow us a more focused examination of the use of agile practices in software startups that adopted the Lean Startup approach. We identified three questions from the original survey which indicate whether a startup is following the Lean Startup approach or not. These questions reflect the key Lean Startup concepts: hypothesis-driven, MVP and pivot.

Table 1. Survey questions used in the study

Background questions	
About respondent	Select your gender
	How old are you?
	What is your motivation with this startup?
About startup	What kind of startup are you a part of?
	What is the total size of your team?
	How many founders are there on your team that own a significant piece of equity?
	What's the stage of your primary product?
	How many core features does your product have?
Agile practice related questions	
Regular Refactoring	How often do you refactor code?
Test First	When do you start writing tests?
Frequent Release	What is the frequency of your product release cycle?
Agile Planning	How far ahead do you plan your product development pipeline?
Daily Standup	Do you do daily stand up meetings?
Lean Startup related questions	
Hypothesis-driven	We identified the riskiest hypotheses about our business in order to test them first
MVP	We built minimally viable products to test our hypotheses
Pivot	How many pivots have you had?

3.2   Data Cleaning and Validation

To ensure the quality and validity of the survey data, we went through a careful data cleaning and validation process on the original dataset, which is described in detail in this section. The process was mainly automatized using R software package. Additionally, we have removed suspicious data entries manually.

To start with the data cleaning process, we set the threshold of 50 (out of a total of 278 original survey questions) as the minimum number of answered questions that a data entry should contain. All the rows with less than 50 answers were removed from the dataset. Afterwards, we merged rows if they were answered by the same person and for the same startup, because the survey collection application saved the data as a separate entry if the survey was interrupted and then restarted again. We also removed duplicate columns that might have been introduced during the data exporting process. We also fixed various obvious errors that may be attributed to the original survey design or data exporting process.

After this rudimentary step, we started automatized and manual data cleaning column by column (question by question). We removed all the rows where startup names were missing, to ensure that respondents have answered the questions by referring to specific startups. We also removed the rows with empty emails. We have decided to exclude from the sample the answers referring to the same startup but answered by different respondents because there was not a convincing rationale as to which answer to keep: the CEO's or the developer's. Each of them has its pros and cons. Fortunately there were not many duplicated startups. We also checked startup names, emails and websites and further removed the rows with suspicious values, for example, the answers that containing "none", "not", "test", "xyz", "untitled", etc. We then applied the regular expressions to all the columns that had a fixed set of values to further remove invalid answers. For example, if a question was Boolean, we ensured that only "0"s and "1"s were in the corresponding column. In the last step, we printed all the possible values for each closed question and ensured that only the valid answers were present in the dataset.

After the initial cleaning, we checked the validity of the data using a set of validation cases that we discovered based on a close inspection of all the survey questions. The validation cases detected a set of unrealistic, impossible, invalid combinations of answers which rendered certain data entries invalid, which in turn were removed from the dataset. All the validation cases we used are described in an online document that can be accessed at https://figshare.com/s/08c35ec98fd85e827594

The original dataset had 10171 entries. After applying the data cleaning and validation process, the final cleaned dataset has a sample size of 1526. By performing such strict data cleaning and validation steps, we may have removed some valid entries unintentionally. But removing some valid entries is a trade off that is worth making in order to obtain a clean dataset to conduct the data analysis.

3.3   Data Analysis

To answer the research questions posed in Sect. 1, we analyzed the data in two steps:

Step 1: To answer RQ1, firstly the structure of the five questions related to agile practices was analyzed using exploratory factor analysis. Two factors fit the model and the practices group in pairs: regular refactoring with test first, and frequent release with agile planning. Instead daily standup meeting does not show a significant correlation with any of the two factors. Therefore three dimensions can be defined to group the five agile practices: quality (regular refactoring and test first), speed (frequent release and agile planning), and communication (daily standup meeting). Next the internal consistency between the two items in the quality and speed dimensions was analyzed using Cronbach's alpha. However a low level of reliability estimates ($\alpha = 0.41$ and $\alpha = 0.50$ respectively) was obtained, which meant that the two items within each dimension were not suitable to aggregate. Therefore, the further analysis was conducted on each individual agile practice, rather than at the group level. To allow a sharper comparison, for each agile practice, we divided the startups into using the practice vs. not using it based on their answers to the question. In this way we converted the four agile questions that were categorical (ordinal) into binary. We examined the frequency of the use of five agile practices in the surveyed startups. Since software startups at different product development stages may adopt agile practices differently, we further investigated the difference using Chi-square. The hypothesis for each of the agile practices can be formulated as the following:

H_{a1}: There is significant difference in the use of [the agile practice] among software startups at different product development stages.

Step 2: The focus of this step was to analyze the use of agile practices in the software startups that adopted the Lean Startup approach, in order to answer RQ2. To identify lean software startups in the sample, we used the three questions related to the Lean Startup approach, as explained in Sect. 3.1. The software startups that answered "yes" to the first two questions and have pivoted at least once were considered adopting the Lean Startup approach therefore lean software startups. 229 out of 1526 are lean startups. The use of the five agile practices in these lean startups was compared to that in the rest of the whole sample, to understand if there was difference in agile practice use between the two sub samples. For this purpose again Chi-square tests were used. The hypothesis under the test regarding each agile practices can be formulated as the following:

H_{a2}: There is significant difference in the use of [the agile practice] between lean software startups and non lean software startups.

   Since pivot is an important aspect of software startups, we also examined the number of pivots the surveyed startups made as part of Step 2 analysis.

   The data analysis process was conducted using R software environment.

4   Results

The cleaned dataset contains information about 1526 software startups, provided by 1526 respondents who either founded or worked for these startups. Not surprisingly only a very small percentage (8%) are females in comparison to the much larger percent of males (76%, the remaining 16% didn't reveal gender information). The age of these respondents spread from 18 to 72 (based on 1219 cases that contain age information), with a mean of 34 and a median of 32 (sd = 9.58). A slight majority of the respondents (52.3%) have the age between 25 and 35. It is intriguing to understand what motivated the respondents to found or work for these startups. As expected the majority of answers reflect an entrepreneurial mindset: "Build a Great Product" covers the 52% of the motivations, followed by "Change the world" (29%). "Make a Good Living", "Get Rich" and "Create a quick flip" are motivations for only less than 20% of the respondents.

Regarding the types of these software startups, more than half of them (877) are working on web-based products. 264 software startups provide both web and mobile solutions. Mobile applications are the focus of 171 startups. Only 65 startups provide non web-based software solutions. The remaining 149 startups either work on products where software plays a less significant role or did not provide specific information regarding the types of their startups.

1461 software startups answered the question "What is the total size of your team?" with meaningful values. The distribution of the sample is skewed right significantly, with 81.2% of the software startup teams with less than 9 members. The mean of the team size is 7.23 and the median is 4 (sd = 19.15). When the number of founders is concerned, even though we could not obtain the direct data from the survey, we could infer from the question "how many founders are there on your team that own a significant piece of equity?" that most often an entrepreneurial team has two co-founders that have significant equity of the company, followed by 1-significant-founder and trio co-founder teams.

The distribution of the software startups across product development stages is shown in Fig. 1. It can be seen that it follows a normal distribution, with software startups that have functional products with limited users as most common, and those with mature products as the minority. A closer look at the number of core features that these products have reveals that the average number of the core features of a product is 5 ($mean = 5.2, median = 4$, sd = 4.07). 72% of the startups work on products that have 5 core features or less.

Product stage	Number of startups	
Concept	121	
In development	230	
Working prototype	267	
Functional product with limited users	721	
Functional product with high grow	123	
Mature product	60	

Fig. 1. Startup distribution with respect to product stages

4.1   Agile Practices in Software Startups

Two agile practices, regular refactoring and test first, allow software startups to focus on the quality of their products. 1240 startups responded to the question related to regular refactoring, and 1273 to test first. As shown in Fig. 2, regarding refactoring, slightly less than 45% of the startups do care about the quality and refactor the code every few weeks or even once a week. However, a bit more than one fourth of those rarely or never do refactoring. If refactoring "once a week" and "every few weeks" are considered regular therefore an agile practice (blue bars in Fig. 2), the other options indicate that regular refactoring is not practiced in the startups. It can be concluded that a slight majority of the startups surveyed are not doing regular refactoring.

Regular refactoring	Percentage of startups
Once a week	15.2%
Every few weeks	29.6%
Every few months	18.7%
A few times a year	11.2%
Rarely/never	25.3%

Fig. 2. Startup distribution with respect to the frequency of code refactoring (Color figure online)

Similar results are shown in the test first practice. It is evident from Fig. 3 that around 32% of them are writing tests as soon as they write features, therefore practicing test first (blue bar). However, again one fourth of the startups never write tests. Among the other options, "as soon as we know we're going to keep a feature" indicates clearly the test first practice is not used. Even though we could not interpret properly the options "as soon as we reach a legal agreement with a customer" and "other" due to a lack of access to the original survey design, we could still conclude that the majority of the startups surveyed do not adopt the test first practice.

Test first	Percentage of startups
As soon as we write a feature	32.3%
As soon as we reach legal agreement with a customer	3.7%
As soon as we know we are going to keep a feature	26.2%
Never	25.1%
Other	12.7%

Fig. 3. Startup distribution with respect to the frequency of code testing (Color figure online)

Agile planning and frequent release are the two practices that allow software teams to be able to collect feedback on their products and adjust their development speed accordingly. 1391 startups responded with their release frequencies and 1290 indicated how far ahead they planned their product development

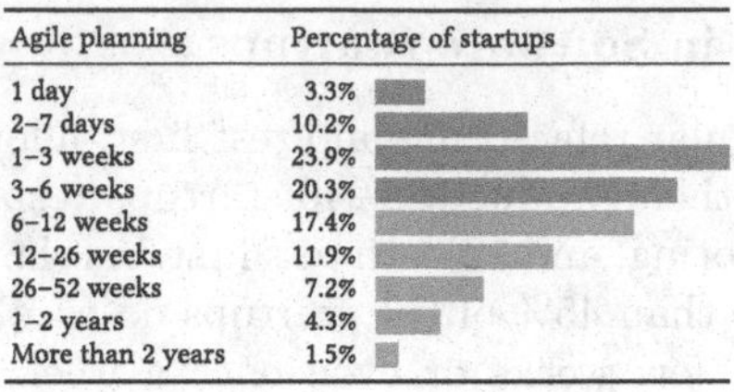

Agile planning	Percentage of startups	
1 day	3.3%	
2–7 days	10.2%	
1–3 weeks	23.9%	
3–6 weeks	20.3%	
6–12 weeks	17.4%	
12–26 weeks	11.9%	
26–52 weeks	7.2%	
1–2 years	4.3%	
More than 2 years	1.5%	

Fig. 4. Startup distribution with respect to agile planning (Color figure online)

pipelines. Regarding planning, Fig. 4 shows that most often the software startups plan ahead for 1 to 3 weeks (about 24%), more than 10% plan for 2 to 7 days, and about 3% are doing daily planning. Only less than 6% put up a yearly or longer-term plan. In total, more than 57% of the startups plan in an agile manner in terms of the time frame covered by the planning (shown by the blue bars. We used 30-day sprint to draw the division). Agile planning should be for 3 to 6 weeks (30 working days) or shorter.

As shown in Fig. 5, the most common (about 21%) release frequency used by these software startups is every 2 to 3 weeks, followed by every 1–3 months (about 19%). It is interesting to see that more than 13% of the startups are practicing continuous delivery and release product once per day or even multiple times per day. However, more than 15% other startups have really low release frequency (every 3–6 months or even more than 6 months), which is worrying given the fact that they are software startups and moving fast is not an option but a must for many of them. The bars in Fig. 5 are divided into two groups: those with release frequency of 2–3 weeks or less (blue bars) therefore indicating frequent release (again the 30-day sprint length was used as the division line), and those indicating low release frequency (taking more than one sprint to release a new version). It can be seen that more than 64% of the startups do frequently release their products.

Daily standup meeting is an agile ceremony used to facilitate communication among software development teams and organizations. Among the 1286 software startups that answered the question, more than 70% are not using the practice, in contrast to about 30% that said "yes" to the question.

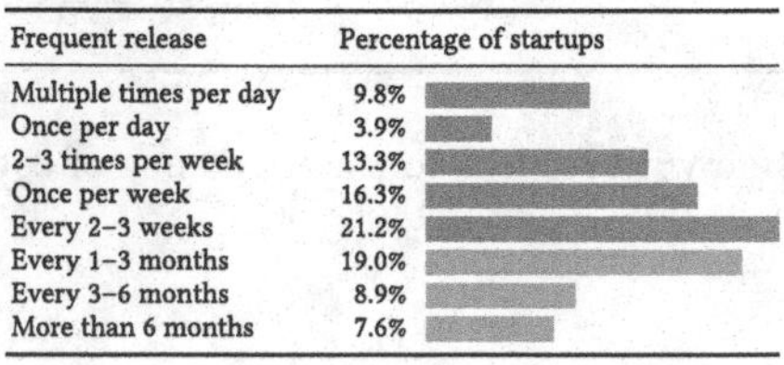

Frequent release	Percentage of startups	
Multiple times per day	9.8%	
Once per day	3.9%	
2–3 times per week	13.3%	
Once per week	16.3%	
Every 2–3 weeks	21.2%	
Every 1–3 months	19.0%	
Every 3–6 months	8.9%	
More than 6 months	7.6%	

Fig. 5. Startup distribution with respect to frequency of product releases (Color figure online)

Table 2. The use of agile practices in software startups across product stages

Product development stage	Regular refactoring		Test first		Frequent release		Agile planning		Daily standup meeting	
	Yes	No	Yes	No	Yes	No	Yes	No	Yes	No
Concept	49	47	41	41	2	0	63	36	23	76
In development	93	93	74	97	144	80	118	78	53	146
Working prototype	111	107	87	119	158	108	138	91	59	170
Functional product with limited users	246	337	190	323	483	230	350	257	198	403
Functional product with high growth	40	63	42	51	79	44	53	51	32	72
Mature product	16	35	24	19	29	31	20	32	16	35

Table 2 shows the use of the five agile practices by the software startups across different product development stages. As explained in Sect. 3.3, the use of the agile practices are simplified into "yes"/"no" Boolean options, to allow a sharper comparison. Table 2 does show that for each agile practice, the percentage of software startups using it varies across the product development stages. However, there is no discernible pattern in the variance of the percentages.

To test H_{a1}, Chi-square tests were applied. A pre-examination excluded frequent release from the test since the assumptions requested to run Chi-square test were not met. We run the tests on the cleaned sample ($n = 1526$). Since the data entries that have empty answers to each agile practice and/or product development stage were removed, each test has a different sample size (as shown in Table 3, Column 2). The test results show that regular refactoring and agile planning are linked to the development stages (the respective H_{a1} is supported). Instead, H_{a1} regarding test first and daily standup meeting cannot be supported.

4.2   Agile Practices in Lean Software Startups

Regarding the individual responses to the three Lean Startup questions from the whole sample, 489 out of the 1526 replied with a definitive "yes" to the statement

Table 3. Agile practices across product stages—Chi-square test results

Practice	n	Chi-square	Degrees of freedom	p-value	Result
Regular refactoring	1237	13.638	5	0.01808	H_{a1} supported
Test first	1108	11.06	5	0.05021	H_{a1} rejected
Agile planning	1287	12.365	5	0.030121	H_{a1} supported
Daily standup meeting	1283	7.736	5	0.1714	H_{a1} rejected

Table 4. Pivoting in lean startups across product stages

Product stage	No. of lean startups	Mean of number of pivots
Concept	3	2.0
In development	40	2.1
Working prototype	57	2.4
Functional product with limited users	107	2.0
Functional product with high growth	17	2.4
Mature product	5	2.6

"We identified the riskiest hypotheses about our business in order to test them first", and 55% claimed that "We built minimally viable products to test our hypotheses". It is interesting to explore the pivoting behavior of these startups in terms of the number of pivots they have made. 1440 out of 1526 gave valid answers to the number of pivots. The mean is 1.528 and median is 1 (sd = 2.06), in a range from 0 to 30 pivots.

229 out of the 1526 software startups are considered following the Lean Startup approach based on the selection criteria specified in Sect. 3.3. When looking closely at the pivoting in this subset, the number of total pivots the surveyed startups experienced ranges from 1 to 15, with the mean equal to 2.153 and the median to 2 (sd = 1.73). From the perspective of product development stages, we can see that, as shown in Table 4, the mean of the number of total pivots of startups at different stages ranges from 2 to 2.6. The lean startups that progressed to the stages of having functional or mature products in total have not pivoted more than those at the early product development stages.

Table 5 shows the use of the five agile practices in lean startups in comparison to that in the rest of the sample. It can be seen that there is a higher percentage of lean startups using each of the agile practices for all the five agile practices.

To test H_{a2}, we used the Chi-square test on the two groups: lean startups vs. non-lean startups. The results are shown in Table 6. The difference between

Table 5. The use of agile practices in lean startups vs. non lean startups

Agile practice	Lean startup subset		Non lean startup subset	
	Yes	No	Yes	No
Regular refactoring	99	99	456	586
Test first	86	86	372	567
Frequent release	164	61	733	433
Agile planning	119	83	626	462
Daily standup meeting	76	124	306	780

Table 6. Agile practices in lean vs. non-lean startups—Chi-square test results

Practice	n	Chi-square	Degrees of freedom	p-value	Result
Regular refactoring	1240	2.3723	1	0.1235	H_{a2} rejected
Test first	1111	6.0471	1	0.0139	H_{a2} supported
Agile planning	1290	0.0815	1	0.7752	H_{a2} rejected
Frequent release	1391	7.8438	1	0.0051	H_{a2} supported
Daily standup meeting	1286	7.3417	1	0.0067	H_{a2} supported

the two groups is not significant in terms of the use of regular refactoring and agile planning. Instead, the percentage of lean startups using test first, frequent release or daily standup meeting is significantly higher than that of non-lean startups.

5 Discussion

So are software startups using agile practices? The results of our study reveal that a majority of software startups do not use quality related agile practices, such as regular refactoring and test first. It reflects the major concern expressed in the literature that quality has a low priority and technical debt is accumulated in software startups, especially at their early stages. When the agile practices regarding the speed of development are concerned, our study shows that a large majority of software startups do move fast by adopting frequent releases and short-term agile planning. This is in line with the literature that emphasizes that speed matters significantly to software startups [7]. However, the under use of quality related agile practices in comparison to speed related practices is not unique to software startups. The same pattern has been manifested in the surveys of agile and lean adoption in software organizations in general. For example, in the 10th annual agile survey conducted by VersionOne (based on 3,880 completed responses) [11], it is shown that speed related practices (e.g., short iterations, iteration planning, release planning) are employed more often in the surveyed organizations than quality related practices (such as unit testing, refactoring, test-driven development). A smaller scale academic survey on agile and lean usage in Finnish software industry with 408 responses demonstrates the same tendency [21]. It seems that, in terms of balancing speed and quality concerns, software startups are not so different from the general population of software organizations. Agile practices related to speed are more often used by both software startups and established companies alike.

In contrast, our findings regarding daily standup meeting indicate that this well-known agile practice is not used in software startups to the same extent as in established software organizations. According to the VersionOne survey [11], daily standup meeting is the most popular agile practice among the surveyed organizations, with an adoption rate of 83%. Its popularity is echoed in the academic survey too [21]. In our survey instead, daily standup meeting is the least frequently used practice among the five agile practices studied. Only about 30% of the software startups use this practice. One explanation of such different could be that daily standup meeting is a typical agile ceremony used by software development teams and organizations to facilitate communication. Because most startup teams have very small sizes (as described in Sect. 4), informal communication happens frequently, which renders formal communication practices less necessary. Yau and Murphy [8] offer similar arguments. They contend that, in small scale startups with only a few members, many problems that agile methods set out to solve do not exist, e.g., the communication issue.

In this study we further examined the use of agile practices by software startups at different stages of product development. The results of the hypothesis testing (H_{a1}) show that the use of agile practices including regular refactoring and agile planning does vary across the product development stages. Instead, the use of test first and daily standup meeting is not significantly associated with the stages. We cannot draw any conclusion regarding frequent release. This finding provides partial support to the claim in the literature that not all software engineering practices are usable or beneficial in different stages of startups [22]. It is an interesting direction to investigate which software engineering practices are most useful and beneficial to which stages of startups.

Another specific angle investigated in our study is the use of agile practices by software startups that adopted the Lean Startup approach. Some studies have expressed the concerns that startups adopting the Lean Startup approach have to sacrifice certain agile practices or product quality due to limited funding and short runway in order to move fast and test business hypotheses with MVPs [8,10]. However, the findings reported in Sect. 4.2 do not substantiate these concerns. On the contrary, they reveal that lean software startups tend to use agile practices more than the rest of the startups surveyed. Especially in terms of test first, frequent release and daily standup meeting, significantly higher portions of lean startups practice them. With these practices that address both needs of quality and speed, lean software startups may be in a good position to manage the "developers dilemma" [10], better at balancing between quality and speed to achieve fast product iteration.

Even though not a main focus of this study, it is worth noting the somehow surprising finding regarding the number of pivots made by lean startups across different product development stages. Pivot is considered a key component of the Lean Startup approach, an action that startups are encouraged to take based on the validated learning they obtain through testing risky business assumptions early and often [1]. Therefore, one would expect that the total number of pivots increases as startups progress along the development stages and pivot continuously. However, the result regarding pivoting reported in Sect. 4.2 does not conform to this expectation. Further investigation is needed to understand the pivoting in software startups.

Lastly, the results reported in this paper need to be viewed in the lights of the limitations of and validity threats to the study. The lack of access to the original survey design and no control to the quality of collected data pose the biggest limitation to our study, constraining the types of analysis that can be conducted and consequently the results that can be obtained. For these reasons, we went to great lengths to clean and validate the data to ensure its quality. Another limitation is due to the fact that there are a very limited number of questions in the original survey that can be associated with agile methods and practices with an acceptable level of confidence. At the end only five agile practices were brought into the study. In addition, each agile practice had only one corresponding question (item), so the risk of not obtaining valid data was increased due to the lack of multiple items to probe the same practice. These concerns pose a potential threat to the construct validity of the study. Instead, the external validity is ensured by the size and random nature of the sample. Therefore the findings of this study can be generalized to a general population of software startups.

6   Conclusion

In the past years agile methods have become main-stream software development approaches in established companies, small or large. They are considered natural choices for software startups too, since startups operate under various uncertainties and the demand on their ability to deal with change is high. Meanwhile software startups have to focus on business development as well as product development. Lean Startup is the approach that an increasing number of startups adopt to test the riskiest business assumptions in their business models. This study provided a better understanding of the state of agile practices in software startups, with a particular focus on lean startups. Based on a large survey of 1526 software startups, we found out that different agile practices are used to different extents, depending on the focus of the practices. Speed related agile practices are used to a greater extent in comparison to quality related practices. Communication practices represented by daily standup meeting is least used. In addition, unlike what is speculated in the literature, software startups who adopt the Lean Startup approach do not sacrifice quality for speed more than other startups do. Our study is the first step towards more in-depth understanding of how software startups can better use agile practices and eventually benefit from them.

In our current study we could not identify any questions specific to lean practices, such as kanban, from the original survey questions. Future work can investigate how lean practices are used in software startups. Meanwhile, "doing agile", using agile practices, does not ensure software startups of "being agile", being able to respond to change and uncertainty. This study was focused on "doing agile". Future work can assess the agility of software startups, and establish the link between "doing" and "being" agile to startup success. It would be also effort worth spent to design a new survey that is focused on investigating the adoption of agile and lean methods as well as Lean Startup in software startups.

Acknowledgement. Thanks a lot to Carmine Giardino who shared the original survey data with us.

References

1. Ries, E.: The Lean Startup: How Today's Entrepreneurs Use Continuous Innovation to Create Radically Successful Businesses. Crown Business, New York (2011)
2. Blank, S.G.: The Four Steps to the Epiphany: Successful Strategies for Products that Win. Cafepress.com, Foster City (2005)
3. Sutton, S.M.: The role of process in a software start-up. IEEE Softw. **17**, 33–39 (2000)
4. Unterkalmsteiner, M., Abrahamsson, P., Wang, X., Nguyen-Duc, A., Shah, S., Bajwa, S.S., Baltes, G.H., Conboy, K., Cullina, E., Dennehy, D., et al.: Software startups-a research agenda. e-Informatica Softw. Eng. J. **10**(1), 89–123 (2016)
5. Coleman, G., O'Connor, R.V.: An investigation into software development process formation in software start-ups. J. Enterp. Inf. Manag. **21**(6), 633–648 (2008)
6. Thomas, S.: Done is better than perfect: how to beat perfectionism paralysis (2016). http://engageme.online/done-is-better-than-perfect-how-to-beat-perfectionism-paralysis/
7. Giardino, C., Paternoster, N., Unterkalmsteiner, M., Gorschek, T., Abrahamsson, P.: Software development in startup companies: the greenfield startup model. IEEE Trans. Softw. Eng. **42**(6), 585–604 (2016)
8. Yau, A., Murphy, C.: Is a rigorous agile methodology the best development strategy for small scale tech startups? Technical report (CIS), Paper980, p. 9 (2013)
9. Duc, A.N., Abrahamsson, P.: Minimum viable product or multiple facet product? The role of MVP in software startups. In: Agile Processes, in Software Engineering, and Extreme Programming, vol. 251, pp. 118–130 (2016)
10. Terho, H., Suonsyrjä, S., Systä, K.: The developers dilemma: perfect product development or fast business validation? In: Abrahamsson, P., Jedlitschka, A., Nguyen Duc, A., Felderer, M., Amasaki, S., Mikkonen, T. (eds.) PROFES 2016. LNCS, vol. 10027, pp. 571–579. Springer, Cham (2016). doi:10.1007/978-3-319-49094-6_42
11. VersionOne: The 10th Annual State of Agile Report. Technical report (2016)
12. Highsmith, J., Cockburn, A.: Agile software development: the business of innovation. Computer **34**(9), 120–127 (2001)
13. Beck, K., Andres, C.: Extreme Programming Explained: Embrace Change, 2nd edn. Addison-Wesley Professional, Boston (2004)
14. Dybå, T., Dingsøyr, T.: Empirical studies of agile software development: a systematic review. Inf. Softw. Technol. **50**(9), 833–859 (2008)
15. Abrahamsson, P., Conboy, K., Wang, X.: "lots done, more to do": the current state of agile systems development research. Eur. J. Inf. Syst. **18**, 281–284 (2009)
16. Dingsøyr, T., Nerur, S., Balijepally, V., Moe, N.B.: A decade of agile methodologies: towards explaining agile software development. J. Syst. Softw. **85**(6), 1213–1221 (2012)
17. Paternoster, N., Giardino, C., Unterkalmsteiner, M., Gorschek, T., Abrahamsson, P.: Software development in startup companies: a systematic mapping study. Inf. Softw. Technol. **56**(10), 1200–1218 (2014)
18. Giardino, C., Unterkalmsteiner, M., Paternoster, N., Gorschek, T., Abrahamsson, P.: What do we know about software development in startups? IEEE Softw. **31**(5), 28–32 (2014)

19. Gilb, T., Gilb, K.: "Lean Startup" - the most extreme agile method by far. Agile Rec. (9), 53–54 (2012)
20. Bosch, J., Holmström Olsson, H., Björk, J., Ljungblad, J.: The early stage software startup development model: a framework for operationalizing lean principles in software startups. In: Fitzgerald, B., Conboy, K., Power, K., Valerdi, R., Morgan, L., Stol, K.-J. (eds.) LESS 2013. LNBIP, vol. 167, pp. 1–15. Springer, Heidelberg (2013). doi:10.1007/978-3-642-44930-7_1
21. Rodríguez, P., Markkula, J., Oivo, M., Turula, K.: Survey on agile and lean usage in finish software industry. In: Proceedings of the ACM-IEEE International Symposium on Empirical Software Engineering and Measurement - ESEM 2012, p. 139 (2012)
22. Eloranta, V.P.: Towards a pattern language for software start-ups. In: 19th European Conference on Pattern Languages of Programs, pp. 1–11 (2014)

Adopting Test Automation on Agile Development Projects: A Grounded Theory Study of Indian Software Organizations

Sulabh Tyagi[1(✉)], Ritu Sibal[1], and Bharti Suri[2]

[1] Netaji Subhash Institute of Technology, Delhi University, New Delhi, India
sulabhtyagi2k@yahoo.co.in, ritusib@hotmail.com
[2] Guru Gobind Singh Indraprastha University, New Delhi, India
bhartisuri@gmail.com

Abstract. The role of test automation in Agile Software Development projects is of paramount importance. It is absolutely necessary to automate tests on agile projects as the number of test cases will continue to grow with each successive sprint. Through a Grounded Theory study involving 38 agile practitioners from 18 different software organizations in India, we identified five key challenges faced by agile practitioners and different strategies to overcome those challenges while practicing test automation. Understanding these challenges and strategies would help agile teams in streamlining their test automation practices.

Keywords: Test automation · Test driven development · Agile software development · Grounded theory

1 Introduction

The widespread use and popularity of agile methodologies are primarily due to their ability to produce quality software in less time with limited manpower. Most of the software industries are using scrum and XP methodologies of agile software development. Testing is an integral part of development in agile projects rather than a distinct Software Development Life Cycle (SDLC) phase [1].

Software test automation refers to the activities and efforts that intend to automate engineering tasks in a software test process using well-defined strategies and systematic solution [2]. According to [3] test automation is one of the most effective solution for projects which have strict deadlines as it speeds up the test execution and increases the test coverage.

Automation on a scrum project is not optional, for a team to sprint effectively and deliver value quickly, it needs to rely heavily on test automation [4]. Crispin and Gregory [5] argued that test automation is the key factor for successful agile software development and the core of agile testing. In a study by Puleio's [6] test automation was seen as a key factor in agile testing to keep development and testing in synchronization. It is evident from the above studies that test automation is a crucial ingredient of agile software development projects. Further, a study from Collins [7] reported that test

© The Author(s) 2017
H. Baumeister et al. (Eds.): XP 2017, LNBIP 283, pp. 184–198, 2017.
DOI: 10.1007/978-3-319-57633-6_12

automation works very well if the agile teams find the right way to implement test automation in their projects and presented some strategies to minimize the risk during test automation implementation.

The objective of this study is to create an understanding on different challenges faced by agile practitioners while adopting test automation on agile projects and to present some possible strategies to overcome those challenges. To provide more empirical insight in this area, a grounded theory study has been conducted that involved 38 agile practitioners from 18 different software organizations in India. We hope our research will help in understanding the issues while adopting test automation on agile projects and streamlining it through proper strategies.

The rest of the paper is structured as follows: in the next section a brief overview of the Grounded Theory is presented; the third section describes the findings of this study; the fourth section discusses these findings; the fifth section presents limitations of this study and the last section concludes the paper.

2 Research Method

2.1 Grounded Theory

Grounded Theory (GT) is a systematic research method where prominence is on the generation of theory that derived from systematic and rigorous analysis of data [8, 9]. The emphasis in GT is on new theory generation which means rather than beginning with a pre-conceived theory in mind, the theory evolves during the research process itself and thus the product of continuous interplay between data collection and analysis of that data [10].

Which version of ground theory. Glaser GT states that researchers should start with the general 'area of interest' and beginning a GT study with specific research questions can lead to pre-conceived ideas or hypothesis of the research phenomena [11]. Other two versions of GT are Straussin GT [12] and Charmaz's constructivist GT [13]. This study employed the Glaserian version as our objective was to find out the issues from the real life experience of the agile practitioners related to our general area of interest i.e. Agile Project Management rather than imposing our own pre-conceived ideas and concerns that could influence this study and also due to plenty of resources available on Glaserian GT [8]. GT has been chosen as our research method for many reasons. Firstly, agile software development focuses on people and interactions, and GT, allows us to study social interactions and the behavior of people. Secondly, GT is most suited to areas of research that have not been explored in detail, and according to our knowledge, the research studies on test automation practices in agile software development is also scarce. Thirdly, GT focuses on theory generation rather than extending or verifying existing theories [14]. Finally, GT is being liberally used to study the agile teams [11, 15–18]. Following Glaser's guidelines, the study started with a general area of interest – Agile project management – rather than beginning with a specific research problem. Problems and its key concerns will emerge in the initial stages of data analysis and it did [19].

2.2 Data Collection

Data collection in GT is guided through theoretical sampling whereby researchers iteratively collect and analyze their data to decide what data to collect next and where to find the data [20]. A GT study requires the theoretical sampling to be continued until theoretical saturation is reached that is when no more new concepts or categories emerge from the data, and further data collection would be a waste of time [21].

Recruiting Participants. This study involved 38 agile practitioners from 18 different software organizations in India with size varied from 50 to 200,000 employees located in Bengaluru, Mumbai, Pune, Noida and Gurgaon. The project duration varied from 6 to 36 months and team size varied from 7 to 20 people on different projects with wide range of domains like software consultancy, e-commerce platforms. Due to ethical considerations and to keep our participants identity confidential, we used codes P1 to P38 to identify our participants. Table 1 shows the participants and project details of this research study. We contacted members of Agile Software Community of India [22] and also took part in Agile India 2016 International Conference [23] on Agile that provided us the platform to collaborate with many agile practitioners across India and abroad. Many practitioners agreed to be a part of our research and participated in this study.

Interviews. Face-to-face semi-structured interviews were conducted with agile practitioners using open-ended questions over a period of eighteen months. Normally, each interview lasted for about one hour and was scheduled at the mutually agreed location. The interviews were audio recorded with the consent from the participants on ensuring full confidentiality, so that we could concentrate on the conversation. Ten participants were interviewed from four different software organizations in first phase of our study. Interview began with warm up questions regarding participants experience, their roles, nature of duties and different agile project management practices in their respective projects. Each participant had a 3–4 or more years of hands-on experience on either scrum, XP or both. Initial sample of participants comprised Scrum Masters, Developers, Product Owners (PO's) and Testers. Then we progressed to our second phase of interviews and expanded our sample participants to Senior Management people (Chief Technical Officer, Vice-President), Agile coaches and Devops to gain the well rounded perspective from participants, also the set of questions were gradually modified as per Glaser [20] to achieve theoretical saturation of our core category - Adopting Test Automation. After completion of each interview, it was transcribed and analyzed line by line to identify key points, codes, concepts and categories. Data collection and its analysis were performed iteratively. Constant comparison of interview transcripts helped us in guiding future interviews, and then we continuously fed back the analysis of interviews and observations from our study into the emerging results. All the data was personally collected and analyzed by the primary author so that consistency can be maintained in the application of GT.

Observations. We also performed passive observations in two projects denoted as Sigma and Delta in two different Indian software organizations denoted as X and Y. X

Table 1. Summary of participants and project details. (Agile Position: Agile Coach (AC), Chief Technical Officer (CTO), Developer (DEV), Devops (DO), Product Owner (PO), Scrum Master (SM), Senior Agile Coach (SAC), Senior Developer (SD), Senior Quality Analyst (SQA), Senior Tester (ST), Test Analyst (TA), Tester (TES), Vice-President (VP)

Participant (Code)	Agile Position/ Experience (yrs)	Project distribution location	Agile method	Domain	Team size	Project duration (Mos)	Sprint duration (Wks)
P1, P2	TES/3, SM/10	India-UK	Scrum	Finance	10–12, 16–18	12, 24	2
P3, P4	ST/4, PO/5	India-USA	Scrum & XP	Network Mgmt. Services	10	10 to 12	2–3
P5, P10	SM/6, ST/5	India-South East Asia	Scrum & XP	Insurance	12–14, 12	8–10, 15–16	3–4
P6	TES/4	India-Europe	Scrum & XP	Mobile Retail	18	18–20	3–4
P7, P8	TES/3, SD/5	India-USA	Scrum & XP	E-Commerce	14	12–14	1–2
P9	SD/4	India-Australia	Scrum & XP	Banking & Finance	20	24	3–4
P11, P12	AC/12, CTO/16	India-USA - Australia	Scrum & XP	Software Consultancy & Services	14–15, 18–20	12–14, 15–16	2–4
P13, P14	AC X 2/8, 10	India-New Zealand	Scrum & XP	IT & Agile Training	7–8	36	2–3
P15	DEV/3	India-UK	Scrum & XP	Telecom	12–13	42	3–4
P16, P17	TA/5, VP/12	India-UK	Scrum & XP	Insurance	9–10	12	2–3
P18, P19	SM/7, AC/8	India-Western Europe	Scrum	Health Care	18–19	24	3–4
P20, P21	TES/3.5, DO/4	India-USA	Scrum & XP	Energy Metering Solutions	10–12	36	3–4
P22, P23	TES/4, DEV/4.5	India-Canada	Scrum & XP	Finance	9–10, 12	24, 18–20	3–4
P24, P25	ST/5.5, TA/5	India-Australia	Scrum & XP	E-Commerce	10, 9–10	12, 12–14	1–2, 2–3
P26	SQA/4	India-South East Asia-Australia	Scrum	Information Security	8–9	18	3–4
P27	TES/3.5	India-Western Europe	Scrum	Web Portal	12–13	10–12	1–2
P28	SM/8	India-Western Europe	Scrum & XP	IT & Agile Training	10–12	12–14	2–3
P29, P30	SM/10, VP/12	India-USA	Scrum & XP	IT Infrastructure	12–14	16–18	2–3
P31	SAC/12	India-Europe	Scrum & XP	IT & Agile Training	8–9	24	3
P32	SM/6	India-Europe	Scrum & XP	Agile Training	10–11	12	3–4
P33	PO/3	India-Europe	Scrum & XP	Finance	12–13	15–16	2–3
P34	ST/4.5	India-UAE	Scrum	Banking & Finance	15–18	24	2–3
P35	TES/4	India-USA	Scrum	Telecom	10–11	10–12	3–4
P36, P37	SM/7, DEV/4	India-USA	Scrum & XP	E-Commerce	12–14, 18–19	6–8, 18	2–3 1–2
P38	PO/4.5	India-UK	Scrum & XP	Telecom	20	12–14	2–3

is into smart metering and energy management solutions with presence in over 30 countries and Y is into e-commerce business with presence in over 4 countries.

Observation period in Sigma and Delta was 8 and 6 months respectively. Sigma was practicing agile mainly blend of scrum and XP from past 3 years but Delta was relatively new to agile and practicing scrum from past 1 year. We observed daily stand ups, sprint retrospectives, sprint review meetings, end sprint demos, pair programming practices, daily smoke and regression tests and we had taken field notes along the way about our observations and transcribed them for analysis. Moreover, we compared the codes emerged during observations with the codes from the interviews that helped us in achieving triangulation. The interview data was further strengthened by our observations from these two projects.

2.3 Data Analysis

Coding. Following Glaser's two successive stages of substantive coding: open and selective coding, we began our data analysis with open coding. It helps us in directing our research by identifying a core category and serves as the initial step of the theoretical analysis in GT [14]. Then, selective coding was performed to identify the categories that were related to the core and to ascertain theoretical saturation.

Constant Comparative Method. Here, codes are compared with other codes to produce concepts, codes are compared further with concepts to produce new concepts and finally concepts are compared with other concepts to produce categories [14].

Memoing. Memos are written notes to log reflections between data, codes and their relationships as they occur in researchers mind [20]. In our case, we wrote memos as soon as we had some ideas about emerging codes and their relationships.

Phase 1: Identifying the core category. We commenced phase 1 of our interviews on our general area of interest "Agile Project Management" and performed open coding on data that generated initial codes, which guided us on further data collection as per theoretical sampling process of classic GT [20]. We continued collecting and analyzing our data iteratively that gradually led us to our core category i.e. "Adopting Test Automation" on agile projects.

Open Coding. In open coding interview transcripts are being analyzed in detail and key points are identified from each interview transcript [24]. In the next step, key points are collated and particular code is assigned to each key point [25]. Code is a phrase used to summarize the key point in 2 to 3 words. Using the constant comparative method, the codes from each interview were compared constantly with the codes from the same as well as from other interviews and also with data based on our observations and written memos. The constant comparison and grouping of similar codes lead to the second level of abstraction, called concepts. Further, this method is repeated on concepts to produce the third level of abstraction, called categories.

Open coding was ended on identifying our core category *"Adopting test automation"*. Two potential near core categories were also emerged like "Quality work delivery" and "Manage changing requirements", but we selected "Adopting test automation" as our category as it is related to most other categories in a meaningful way. An example of open coding process is shown in Table 2 that depicts the emergence of our core category from the combined analysis of interviews and observations.

Table 2. Example of Open Coding Process

Open coding	Interview Quotation – P5, Scrum Master	Observation (Org.: Y, Project: Delta)
Statement/Field note	"Most important question…whether or not your project is truly time driven, whether or not you are delivering high quality product, time is speed for us and we can achieve that [speed and quality] by embracing automation."	Acceptance testing was practiced manually till sprint 3, consuming lot of time and effort. UI changes were frequent due to constant new product launches, decision to automate acceptance tests, acceptance tests automation started
Key point	Need for timely delivery of quality products, Achieving speed, Quality through automation	Manual acceptance consumes time and effort, Frequent UI changes, Automating acceptance tests
Code	Timely delivery, Quality products, Embracing automation	Time and effort loss, Constant UI changes, Acceptance tests automation
Concept	Achieving quality and speed by embracing automation	Achieving speed by embracing automation
Category	Adopting test automation	

Phase 2: Refining the core category. As per theoretical sampling process, selecting new interviewees and sites for data collection should come from the results of the coding process [14]. We progressed into phase 2 and continued our data collection process.

Table 3. Example of selective coding process

Selective coding	Interview Quotation – P6, Tester	Observation (Org.: X, Project: Sigma)
Statement/Field note	"Our project…lot of business logic, we handle lot of features additions & changes…has accumulation effect on our tests too…which makes them grow in numbers with every sprint and it is really difficult to maintain [test scripts]"	Frequent change requests received from the customers, constant addition, modification of page elements, effect on test scripts size, making test script maintenance difficult for the team
Key point	Adding new features, Test scripts continue to grow, Difficulty in test script maintenance	Frequent change requests, Constant changes in test scripts, Difficulty in test script maintenance
Code	Grow in test scripts, Difficulty in maintaining test scripts	Constant test script changes, Difficulty in maintaining test scripts
Concept	Difficulty in test script maintenance	Difficulty in test script maintenance
Category	Test script maintenance	

Selective Coding. Here, only those interview transcripts were coded that were related to our core category i.e. "Adopting Test Automation". Constant comparative method was used on interview transcripts and observations to find out codes, concepts and finally the categories related to our core. Table 3 shows an example of selective coding process.

The other concepts and categories emerged in a similar manner which sheds light on the problems faced by agile teams while adopting test automation. Observations gathered from the two projects were also analyzed and compared to the concepts derived from the interviews. It was found that our observations supported the data provided in the interviews, thereby strengthening our interview data. During our data analysis one more set of concepts emerged that formed the strategies used by agile teams in order to overcome those challenges as described in the present study. Figure 1.a shows different levels of data abstraction using GT and Fig. 1.b explains the emergence of category choosing the right tool from underlying concepts.

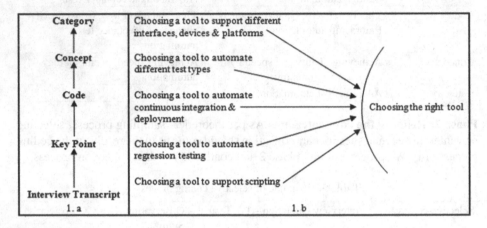

Fig. 1. a. Different levels of data abstraction in GT. **b.** Emergence of category *choosing the right tool* from concepts

Determining Theoretical Saturation. The selective coding continues until the researcher has sufficiently integrated the core category and its connections to other relevant categories [20]. On reaching a stage where further data collection and its analysis were leading us to the same categories with no new data, we found out that our categories have reached saturation. Then we started sorting the theoretical memos conceptually and this process is called sorting that forms the theoretical outline of our study.

The last step in GT is generating a theory also know as Theoretical Coding. It involves the conceptualization of how different categories and their associated properties relate to each other as hypothesis so that can be integrated into a theory [19, 26]. We followed Glaser's guidelines and performed theoretical coding at the later stages of analysis [14].

Table 4 shows different concepts and categories that form the challenges and corresponding concepts that form the adopted strategies while practicing test automation on agile projects. Also, the number within the parenthesis indicates the number of interviewees who referred these challenges/strategies. As the codes, concepts, and categories emerge directly from the data, which is collected from the real world, the resulting theory is grounded within the context of the data [17].

Table 4. Strategies adopted on different agile projects

Challenges	Strategies
Choosing the right tool (26)	• Know your test automation requirements, Know your tool (14) • Cost Benefit Analysis (CBA) (11)
Managing test environment (15)	• Upfront planning for managing test environment (11) • Virtualization (10)
Test script maintenance (18)	• Automation testing framework (12) • Page Object Model (POM) (8)
Mindset toward automation (17)	• Engender automation awareness (12) • ROI evaluation (11)
Effective communication (16)	• One team approach (10)

In the following section, we present the research findings from our study. Selected interview quotations are provided under each category to better explain it in the present context. Our results are grounded further by key points, codes, and concepts from the interviews as well as the observations from two agile projects. It is difficult to describe here in detail due to space reasons.

3   Results: Adopting Test Automation on Agile Projects

In this section, we present our grounded theory: Strategies used by agile practitioners while adopting test automation in their projects. We have selected quotations from our study to explain the challenges faced by agile teams and strategies opted by them.

3.1   Challenge 1: Choosing the Right Tool

Test automation is very important right from the start of any agile project. It is essential to know the project requirements, which tests needs to be automated and what tools are needed. Agile practitioners admitted that while transitioning to scrum and XP, they were still using traditional record and playback tool but results were highly unsatisfactory.

Other associated concerns include choosing a tool for automating continuous integration and deployment, automating acceptance and regression tests and a tool for effective test management.

> "Output of sprint N has to combine with sprint N + 1, daily defect fixes that continuously check in to the code, this whole process is continuous integration (CI), it also takes lot of time, and only by automating our CI process we could survive our project deadlines." – P10, Senior Tester

Choice of test automation tool particularly in agile projects is a very crucial decision as if you would end up choosing a wrong tool with the partial or incomplete evaluation; it may lead to loss of efforts spent in each sprint, loss of licensing fees as well as loss of automation opportunities. In order to prevent these losses, some strategies were used to overcome the problem of choosing the right tool. Two adopted strategies are explained below:

Strategy 1: Know your Test Automation Requirements, Know your Tool. One should be scrupulous while choosing a test automation tool in agile projects. Agile teams should understand their project needs and then decide on test automation tool, it is imperative to first know the exact automation requirements of the projects like test types (unit, acceptance, regression, etc.) needs to be performed, coding languages to be used on the project and suitability of choosing between licensed and open source tools; it is good to choose a tool based upon the compatibility with the application under test (AUT).

> *"A lot of licensed and open source tools are available...You must know that what you want to do with that [Tool] and for what [purpose] as requirements may vary depending on project size, cost and allocated time."*– P16, Test Analyst

Strategy 2: Cost Benefit Analysis (CBA). Cost of the tool is also one of the important deciding factors in most agile projects. Licensed tools have certain benefits over open source tools like good user support, sufficient training material and ease of use but that comes with the cost.

> *"...would be using that [tool], whether it's a licensed or open source it depends on CBA (Cost to benefit analysis) of that tool w.r.t our project."* – P32, Scrum Master

It is always better to know what test types needs to be automated, tools utility with project needs, its ability to integrate with other project and defect management tools.

3.2   Challenge 2: Managing Test Environment

The ultimate aim of any agile project is to deliver quality product and test automation plays an important role in adding that quality to the product in such short sprint durations. Keeping test environment as close as possible to production environment ensures the quality of the test automation. Agile teams were facing difficulties while creating multiple test environments for every different configuration, platforms and workflows.

> *"Why it is worth to have Test Automation in agile projects because it helps you in achieving your quality objectives, test environment should be a replica of your live [production] environment...if you practice this then the code that go into upper [production] environment would meet quality criteria."* – P13, Agile Coach

Strategy 3: Upfront Planning for Managing Test Environment. Testing whether it is automation or manual is only been successful when performed in the proper test environment. In agile, it is very common to have multiple test environments, multiple configurations for the single business application so upfront planning for managing test environment is very important.

"... important to have upfront plan for managing your test environments... by maintaining spreadsheets containing all our test environment related information like different configurations, different test devices and test data used by those devices, any database related information and continuously update it." – P29, Scrum Master

Strategy 4: Virtualization. It serves an important strategy in managing issues related to test environment management. Virtual machine setup provides that additional space to both developers and testers to test their application under test (AUT). It was used to reduce the overhead caused by different OS and hardware configurations.

"...by using virtual machines test environments can be created according to the requirement and the scope of the test... Above all it is scalable and has on demand access which reduces our burden of managing test environment."– P25, Test Analyst

Participants were using a document to gather different test environment requirements to plan for managing their existing environment or building a new. VMware workstations were also used for managing test environments related issues.

3.3 Challenge 3: Test Script Maintenance

For every new addition or modification in feature, test script needs to be modified and maintained for the entire duration of the projects with multiple sprints and this was a challenge for them.

"...The scale of regression testing grows with each sprint and so does the test scripts, so how you would add more test cases to the existing regression test suite? How you maintain those scripts?" – P34, Senior Tester

Maintainability of code was a big issue, many participants worked on web based applications where test script was created by identifying web page elements and their associated properties, so if any page element whether it is a dropdown box or submit button had changed then they needed to track and modify that script.

Strategy 5: Automation Testing Framework. Majority of our participants admitted that having a good automation testing framework solved their test script maintenance problem to the larger extent. Automation testing framework is an engine that runs your automation test scripts with the help of some tool like Selenium or Unified Functional Tester (UFT) to test your application under test. Most commonly used frameworks were: Data driven framework – modular functions are stored in external files and called by test scripts; Keyword driven framework – keyword is assigned to every user action (like button click), stored in a spreadsheet and called by test scripts; Hybrid framework – combination of data and keyword driven frameworks; and Behaviour driven framework – creating examples to describe the user behavior while using the application under test.

Strategy 6: Page Object Model (POM). Another technique used by many agile practitioners to make test script maintenance easier was Page Object Model (POM) approach. Here, each web page element (button, text box) is modeled as an object within the test code and represents as one class.

3.4   Challenge 4: Mindset Toward Automation

Whenever any project is transitioning to agile then it is important to have support from the management so that every team member proactively put up his concern and ask for any assistance that is needed to overcome any constraint regarding implementing test automation. They need to understand that test automation is a long term investment and should support the team by providing enough budget and time.

> *"Transition to agile...need support from your senior management particularly when you embrace test automation in agile...have realistic expectations from the team and...accept initial failures and invest in terms of tools or trainings...only this kind of thinking can encourage use of test automation in any agile project."* – P20, Tester

Strategy 7: Engender Automation Awareness. Agile teams need a shift in their thinking while adopting test automation. They should know the merits and demerits of having test automation in their projects and how to use it [test automation] effectively.

> *"When you wrap test automation around agile...not easy to adapt as your team won't have that thinking that agile demands...to create automation awareness in your team...try to create it by providing coaching, workshops or short trainings on test automation in agile environment."* – P13, Agile Coach

Strategy 8: ROI Evaluation. Senior management should provide the required infrastructure and environment necessary to conduct effective test automation practices. Eleven of our participants used ROI (Return on Investment) evaluation to get their support. ROI calculation is based on evaluating the benefits of test automation with respect to its implementation costs in terms of tool cost, manpower cost, time needed to build required infrastructure for automation.

3.5   Challenge 5: Effective Communication

Many participants admitted that lack of communication in their teams often results in poor automation planning, late feedbacks and wrong automation effort estimates. Test automation is teamwork and should be taken care of by both developers and testers.

> *"...have to consider a lot many things...plan automation, what features to automate in each sprint, when to start automation and one thing is crucial...conversation element - PO talking to developers, testers talking to developers and creating a wonderful coordination with effective communication."* – P38, Product Owner

While implementing test automation, it is very important for developers and testers to collaborate with each other, testers should help developers in designing unit test cases and developers should help testers in automating acceptance tests. The more they communicate more effective test automation would become.

Strategy 9: One Team Approach. One team approach was the key crusader in building effective communication between testers, developers and PO's as mentioned by ten agile practitioners. Many agile teams were giving much emphasis to have proactive communication with each other including both verbal and written communication so that every team member developed this feeling that they are working together as one single team not as separate entities.

"When you automate...expected to not only report defects but also to communicate [defects] effectively to the development team and track it till closure. When you have that [proactive communication] surrounding your team that keeps everyone in one loop then results are more than satisfactory." – P32, Scrum Master.

If there is any defect then it should be properly determined whether it is because of script or actually a test case has failed and it can only be possible when testers proactively talk to developers and also send a mail to team's group mail id for better information flow.

4   Discussion and Related Work

Agile projects have daily rounds of unit tests, integration tests, acceptance tests and continuous deployment. The serious effect of not having perfect test automation in place forms the rationale behind our study.

The choice of the right tool from a plethora of available tools is a decisive step towards successful test automation. This is confirmed by studies of Oliveira [27] and Collins [28]. If one tool is not working well for the project, in the next iteration, agile teams should try something new [28]. Yoder [29] discussed the importance of selecting automation tools and when automated tests should be run under "Automate First" pattern.

The implications of managing test environment and test script maintenance revealed by our findings are also supported by a number of studies. Deak [30] highlights a number of negative factors that influence testing like insufficient number of test environments and weak infrastructure. Karhu [31] contributes test environment, test maintenance and implementation time as key concerns about test automation infrastructure. Fewester et al.'s study [32] mentioned negative impact on test automation cost due to improperly managed test script maintenance cost. Bach [33] advocates the benefits of test automation over maintenance cost of constantly changing test scripts suite.

For successful test automation, management should be open to test automation practices and their financial benefits in spite of time constraints. Late testing mindset need to be changed to early testing mindset in agile environment [34] and management support is also desired in terms of having realistic expectations from the test automation [35].

According to [34] efficient communication and interaction between testers and developers improved both testing and development, eventually improving information flow and efficiency in process. Graham [36] suggested active participation of testers in requirement reviews along with developers for performing test planning in parallel. Yoder [29] also reported whole team approach as one of the pattern for agile quality mindset.

5   Limitations

The inherent limitation with grounded theory research study is that the research findings are grounded in the specific contexts that are explored in the research. Data triangulation was used for reducing researcher bias, as we gathered the data from two sources, namely, interviews and observations that may yield more reliable data than using a single data source. The context in this research was governed by our choice of research destinations and the availability and accessibility of agile practitioners to participate in this study. We do not claim that our findings are universally applicable to all the agile projects practicing test automation, however, they accurately characterize the contexts studied.

6   Conclusion

A Grounded Theory study has been conducted over a period of eighteen months that involved 38 agile practitioners from 18 software development organizations in India. This study investigated the test automation adoption from the specific perspective of agile practitioners through their real life project experiences using GT. Unlike most of the participant organizations, some of them were recently transitioned to agile software development methods. However, all of them were striving to build good test automation infrastructure for their projects. During the study, we discovered the various challenges and strategies adopted thereof by agile teams while establishing good test automation practices in their projects. Main contribution of this paper is towards understanding the key challenges while adopting test automation in agile projects and providing some widely used strategies to overcome those challenges. This study can be utilized by agile software development teams to have a plan of action and streamline the test automation to get maximum benefits. We acknowledge this fact that all challenges and strategies adopted by software development organizations practicing test automation in agile projects may not have emerged in this study. This may also serve as the foundation for conducting future studies in the same area.

Acknowledgments.   Our big thanks to all agile practitioners for participating in this study. This research is supported by our institute's TRF academic grant. Thanks to Prof. Yogesh Singh for his immense support and guidance.

References

1. Sayed, I.N.: The case of agile testing. White Paper, cognizant 20-20 insights (2016). https://www.cognizant.com/InsightsWhitepaper. Last accessed 08 Jan 2016
2. Gao, J., Tsao, J., Wu, Y.: Testing and Quality Assurance for Component-Based Software. Artech House, Boston (2003)
3. Dustin, E., Rashka, J., Paul, J.: Automated Software Testing: Introduction, Management, and Performance. Addison-Wesley, Boston (1999)
4. Cohn, M.: Succeeding with Agile: Software Development Using Scrum, 1st edn. pp. 314–316. Addison-Wesley Professional, Boston (2009)

5. Gregory, J., Lisa, C.: More Agile Testing. Addison-Wesley, Upper Saddle River (2015)
6. Puleio, M.: How not to do Agile testing. In: Proceedings of the Conference on AGILE 2006 (AGILE 2006), pp. 305–314. IEEE Computer Society, Washington, DC (2006). doi:http://dx.doi.org/10.1109/AGILE.2006.34
7. Collins, E., Lucena Jr., F.: Strategies for agile software testing automation: an industrial experience. In: Proceedings of the 2012 IEEE 36th Annual Computer Software and Applications Conference Workshops (COMPSACW 2012), pp. 440–445. IEEE Computer Society, Washington, DC (2012)
8. Glaser, B.: Grounded theory institute: methodology of Barney G Glaser (2010). http://groundedtheory.org/. Last accessed 28 Nov 2015
9. Hoda, R., Noble, J., Marshall, S.: Agile undercover: when customers don't collaborate. In: XP 2010, Norway, pp. 73–87 (2010)
10. Goulding, C.: Grounded Theory: A Practical Guide for Management, Business and Market Researchers. Springer, Berlin (2002)
11. Dorairaj, S., Noble, J., Malik, P.: Understanding team dynamics in distributed agile software development. In: Wohlin, C. (ed.) XP 2012. LNBIP, vol. 111, pp. 47–61. Springer, Heidelberg (2012). doi:10.1007/978-3-642-30350-0_4
12. Corbin, J., Strauss, A.: Basics of Qualitative Research: Techniques and Procedures for Developing Grounded Theory, 4th edn. Sage, London (2015)
13. Charmaz, K.: Constructing Grounded Theory, 2nd edn. Sage (2014)
14. Glaser, B.: Basics of Grounded Theory Analysis: Emergence vs. Forcing. Sociology Press, Mill Valley (1992)
15. Dorairaj, S., Noble, J., Malik, P.: Understanding lack of trust in distributed agile teams: a grounded theory study. In: 16th International Conference on Evaluation & Assessment in Software Engineering (EASE 2012), pp. 81–90. IET (2012)
16. Hoda, R., Noble, J., Marshall, S.: Organizing self-organizing teams. In: ICSE 2010, pp. 285–294. ACM, South Africa (2010)
17. Martin, A., Biddle, R., Noble, J.: The XP customer team: a grounded theory. In: Proceedings of the AGILE Conference, pp. 57–64 (2009)
18. Whitworth, E., Biddle, R.: The social nature of Agile teams. In: Agile 2007, pp. 26–36. IEEE Computer Society, USA (2007)
19. Glaser, B.: Doing Grounded Theory: Issues and Discussions. Sociology Press, Mill Valley (1998)
20. Glaser, B.: Theoretical Sensitivity: Advances in Methodology of Grounded Theory. Sociology Press, Mill Valley (1978)
21. Glaser, B.G., Strauss, A.L.: The Discovery of Grounded Theory: Strategies for Qualitative Research. Sociology Press, Aldine (1967)
22. Agile Software Community of India. http://www.agileindia.org/. Last accessed 12 June 2016
23. Agile India 2016. http://www.2016.agileindia.org/. Last accessed 10 Feb 2016
24. Urquhart, C., Lehmann, H., Myers, M.D.: Putting the 'theory' back into grounded theory: guidelines for grounded theory studies in information systems. Inf. Syst. J. 20(4), 357–381 (2010)
25. Georgieva, S., Allan, G.: Best practices in project management through a grounded theory lens. Electron. J. Bus. Res. Methods 6(1), 43–52 (2008)
26. Glaser, B.: The Grounded Theory Perspective III: Theoretical Coding. Sociology Press, Mill Valley (2005)
27. Oliveira, J.C., Gouveia, C., Filho, R.Q.: A way of improving test automation cost-effectiveness. In: CAST. EUA, Indianapolis (2006)

28. Collins, E., Lucena Jr., F.: Software test automation practices in agile development environment: an industry experience report. In: Proceedings of the 7th International Workshop on Automation of Software Test (AST 2012), pp. 57–63. IEEE Press, Piscataway (2012)

29. Yoder, J.W., Wirfs-Brock, R., Washizaki, H.: QA to AQ part six: being agile at quality "Enabling and Infusing Quality". In: HILLSIDE Proceedings of 23rd Conference on Pattern Languages of Programs, October 2016

30. Deak, A.: A comparative study of testers' motivation in traditional and agile software development. In: Product – Focused Software Process Improvement, pp. 1–16 (2014)

31. Karhu, K., Repo, T., Taipale, O., Smolander, K.: Empirical observations on software testing automation. In: Proceedings of the 2nd International Conference on Software Testing, Verification, and Validation (ICST 2009), Denver, Colo, USA, pp. 201–209 (2009)

32. Fewster, M.: Common Mistakes in Test Automation, Grove Consultants (2001). https://www.stickyminds.com/sites/default/files/presentation/file/2013/01TAU_M5.pdf.   Last accessed 02 Feb 2016

33. Bach, J.: Test automation snake oil. Windows Tech. J., 40–44 (1996)

34. Taipale, O., Smolander, K.: Improving software testing by observing practice. In: Proceedings of the 2006 ACM/IEEE International Symposium on Empirical Software Engineering (ISESE 2006),   pp.   262–271.   ACM,   New   York   (2006).   doi:http://dx.doi.org/10.1145/1159733.1159773

35. Kettunen, V., Kasurinen, J., Taipale, O., Smolander, K.: A study on agility and testing processes in software organizations. In: Proceedings of the 19th International Symposium on Software Testing and Analysis, pp. 231–240 (2010)

36. Graham, D.: Requirements: requirements and testing: seven missing-link myths. IEEE Softw. 19(5), 15–17 (2002). doi:10.1109/MS.2002.1032845

Safety Critical Software

How is Security Testing Done in Agile Teams?
A Cross-Case Analysis of Four Software Teams

Daniela Soares Cruzes[1](✉), Michael Felderer[2], Tosin Daniel Oyetoyan[1],
Matthias Gander[2], and Irdin Pekaric[2]

[1] SINTEF Digital, Trondheim, Norway
{danielac,tosin.oyetoyan}@sintef.no
[2] University of Innsbruck, Innsbruck, Austria
{michael.felderer,matthias.gander,irdin.pekaric}@uibk.ac.at

Abstract. Security testing can broadly be described as (1) the testing of security
requirements that concerns confidentiality, integrity, availability, authentication,
authorization, nonrepudiation and (2) the testing of the software to validate how
much it can withstand an attack. Agile testing involves immediately integrating
changes into the main system, continuously testing all changes and updating test
cases to be able to run a regression test at any time to verify that changes have
not broken existing functionality. Software companies have a challenge to
systematically apply security testing in their processes nowadays. There is a lack
of guidelines in practice as well as empirical studies in real-world projects on
agile security testing; industry in general needs a more systematic approach to
security. The findings of this research are not surprising, but at the same time are
alarming. The lack of knowledge on security by agile teams in general, the large
dependency on incidental pen-testers, and the ignorance in static testing for
security are indicators that security testing is highly under addressed and that more
efforts should be addressed to security testing in agile teams.

Keywords: Security testing · Agile testing · Case study research

1   Introduction

Security testing can broadly be described as (1) the testing of security requirements that
concerns confidentiality, integrity, availability, authentication, authorization, non-repudiation [16] and the testing to validate the ability of the software to withstand attack
(resiliency) [28]. This process can be performed by showing conformance with the
security properties, similar to requirements-based testing; or by trying to address known
vulnerabilities, similar to traditional fault-based testing. It is essential to take testing into
account in all phases of the secure software development lifecycle, i.e., analysis, design,
development, deployment, as well as maintenance. Thus, security testing must be
holistic covering the whole secure software development lifecycle. Proper security
testing requires a mix of techniques as there is no single testing technique that can be
performed to effectively cover all security testing and their application within testing

© The Author(s) 2017
H. Baumeister et al. (Eds.): XP 2017, LNBIP 283, pp. 201–216, 2017.
DOI: 10.1007/978-3-319-57633-6_13

activities at unit, integration, and system level [2]. Nevertheless, many companies adopt only one security testing approach, for instance penetration testing.

Agile testing is one approach that is increasingly being adopted by software companies. This approach does not just mean testing on agile projects, but testing an application with a plan to learn about it and let the product information and customer feedback guide the testing. Agile testing involves immediately integrating changes into the main system, continuously testing all changes and updating test cases to be able to run a regression test at any time to verify that changes have not broken existing functionality [18, 23]. In agile software development, there is a focus on the feature implementation and delivery of value to the customer and, as such, non-functional aspects of a system should also be of attention. Non-functional requirements testing is challenging due its cross-functional aspects and lack of clarity of their needs by business in the most part of projects, therefore, although important, the non-functional requirements are often neglected in agile testing for many reasons, such as experience, culture, awareness, priority, cost and time pressure [5].

There is a lack of guidelines in practice as well as empirical studies in real-world projects on security testing; for agile projects in general needs a more systematic approach to security. The main contribution of this paper is to deepen relevant knowledge and experience on the characterization of security testing in an agile context. Based on the "traditional waterfall testing approaches and techniques", we have analyzed four teams and asked about how they perform these in the agile context. We then provide recommendations of ways to improve it based on lessons learned and good practices from the cases. In addition, we provide an improved understanding on how research and practice are aligned.

The remainder of the paper is organized as follows. In Sect. 2, we provide background on software and security testing. It also forms the backbone of the used interview guide. Section 3 presents the research methodology and describes how the studies were conducted. Section 4 presents the main findings of the case studies. Section 5 discusses the cross-case analysis findings. Finally, Sect. 6 concludes the paper and highlights directions of future work.

2   Background on Software and Security Testing

Software testing consists of all software development lifecycle activities, both static and dynamic, concerned with evaluation of software products and related artifacts to determine that they satisfy specified requirements, to demonstrate that they are fit for purpose and to detect defects. Testing can be classified according to the three dimensions objective, scope, and accessibility shown in Fig. 1.

Test objectives are reason or purpose for designing and executing a test. The reason is either to check the functional behavior of the system or its nonfunctional properties. Functional testing is concerned with assessing the functional behavior of an SUT (System under Testing), whereas nonfunctional testing aims at assessing nonfunctional requirements with regard to quality characteristics like security or performance.

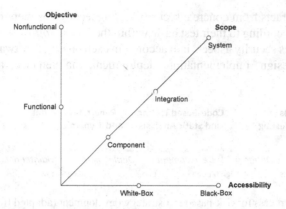

Fig. 1. Software testing dimensions objective, scope and accessibility (adopted from [16]).

The *test scope* describes the granularity of the SUT and can be classified into component, integration and system testing. It also determines the test basis, i.e., the artifacts to derive test cases. Component testing (also referred to as unit testing) checks the smallest testable component in isolation. Integration testing combines components with each other and tests those as a subsystem, that is, not yet a complete system. System testing checks the complete system, including all subsystems. A specific type of system testing is acceptance testing where it is checked whether a solution works for the user of a system. Regression testing is a selective retesting to verify that modifications have not caused side effects and that the SUT still complies with the specified requirements.

In terms of *accessibility* of test design artifacts we can classify testing methods into white-box and black-box testing. In white-box testing, test cases are derived based on information about how the software has been designed or coded. In black-box testing, test cases rely only on the input/output behavior of the software. This classification is especially relevant for security testing, as black-box testing, where no or only basic information about the system under test is provided, enables to mimic external attacks from hackers.

Security testing is testing of security requirements related to security properties like confidentiality, integrity, availability, authentication, authorization, and non-repudiation in addition to testing the resilience of the system against attack. In security testing, there are two principal approaches that can be distinguished, i.e., security functional testing and security vulnerability testing [33]. Security functional testing validates whether the specified security requirements are implemented correctly, both in terms of security properties and security mechanisms. Security vulnerability testing addresses the identification of unintended system vulnerabilities. It uses the simulation of attacks and other kinds of penetration testing attempting to compromise the security of a system by playing the role of a hacker trying to attack the system and exploit its vulnerabilities [1]. Furthermore, security vulnerability testing requires specific expertise, which makes it difficult and hard to automate [21]. By identifying risks in the system and creating tests driven by those risks, security vulnerability testing can focus on specific parts of a system implementation where an attack is likely to succeed.

Figure 2 abstracts from concrete security testing techniques mentioned before, and classifies them according to their test basis within the *secure software development life-cycle*, which takes security aspects into account in each phase of software development, i.e., analysis, design, implementation, deployment, maintenance, and additionally testing.

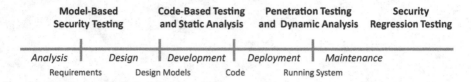

Fig. 2. Process for risk-based test strategy development (adopted from [16]).

Model-based security testing is grounded on requirements and design models created during the analysis and design phase. Examples are misuse cases and threat models. In misuse cases, test cases relating to an attacker's perspective are captured and used to exercise the system [31]. During the design, a threat model can be used to capture security issues and translated into test cases that can be used for security testing [20].

Code-based testing and static analysis is based on source, bytecode, or binary created during development. This testing approach in many cases uses static analysis tools to find code-based defects [6]. There is a range of issues that could be focused by a static analysis tool such as duplications, coding rules, code complexity, unit test coverage, and structural complexity. As regards security testing, specific frameworks exist that provide platform for common enumeration of security defects in the implementation and design. The Common Weakness Enumeration (CWE) [8] provides a formal list of software weaknesses. The OWASP Top-10 provides the list of the most common web application vulnerabilities [26]. The SANS Top-25 list shows the most widespread and critical errors that are applicable to all types of applications [11].

Penetration testing and dynamic analysis are based on running systems, either in a test or production environment. It is referred to as a black-box testing approach because the tester has no access to the source code of the system under test. Penetration testing seeks to break into running software but from ethical point of view. As a result, the rule of engagement must always be defined before such a test is carried out [28].

Refactoring and feature implementation may break existing security controls, increase the attack surface, and introduce new vulnerabilities into the system. In the agile context, it would be an activity that would need to be continuously performed to validate that the security properties of the system is not compromised.

2.1 Four Quadrants of Agile Testing

Crispin and Gregory [9] discuss the Agile Testing quadrants that are widely adopted in practice. Each quadrant in Fig. 3 reflects different reasons to test. Traditionally, software testing is involved late in the development process to detect failures, but typically not to prevent them. Companies focus almost exclusively on the right hand side (Q3 and

Q4), criticizing the product, but not playing a productive part in supporting the creation and guidance of the product (Q1 and Q2). In agile testing, the testers are not only involved in identifying, but also in preventing failures by continuous interaction with developers and customers. Automation is an important enabler for agile testing. Automation of the tests in Q1 is usually easiest to implement, and at the same time has a big impact on the process effectiveness. Tests in Q3 are usually performed manually. Tests in Q4 are heavily dependent on tools and specialized skill sets. But, manual exploratory testing by a knowledgeable security tester is indispensable to detect issues that automated tests can miss.

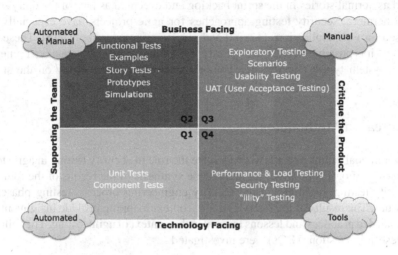

Fig. 3. Agile test quadrants [9]

Agile testing increases the need for improved communication and coordination between testers and developers, in addition to a new mind-set at the personal and organizational levels. In the rush to deliver functionality, most agile teams lack to think about security [5]. Authorization is often the only aspect of security testing that the agile teams consider as part of business functionality.

During the last years there have been several efforts to reconcile software security with the conflicting premises imposed by agile methodologies [4, 19, 24]. In a systematic review of agile challenges for secure software development Queslati et al. [24] conclude that the reported security assurance challenges are as follows: security assessment favors detailed documentation; tests are, in general, insufficient to ensure the implementation of security requirements; tests do not cover in general, all vulnerability cases; security tests are in general difficult to automate; and continuous changing of the development processes conflicts with audit needs of uniform stable processes.

Probably, the most widely known software security methodology is Microsoft's framework, which is integrated into the Microsoft Agile Security Development Lifecycle [22]. Other approaches also exist. Recently, Baca et al. [3] demonstrate how security features can be integrated into an agile software development method process at Ericsson AB. The approach focuses on risk management. Chólis et al. [7] describe a case study of a software security testing process based on the Microsoft Software Development Lifecycle for Agile. The case company moves their software engineering teams from waterfall to agile. The case shows that a synchronization between the tasks of agile software engineering teams and the independent security team is possible. Türpe et al. [34] report on a one-year study of penetration testing and its aftermath at a major software vendor, and show how an agile development team managed to incorporate the test findings. Rindel et al. [30] describes a case of building a secure identity management system and its management processes. The project's steering group required the use of Scrum. In the implementations of this model the security testing, reviews and audits are viewed as normal stories in the sprint backlog and executed as part of the daily scrum.

Furthermore, security testing approaches for agile projects have especially been proposed for web applications [12, 32] and service-oriented systems [15]. These cases show how it is possible to integrate security testing into agile software development for specific system types. Our research comprises an independent study on the state of practice in security testing in agile teams.

3   Research Methodology

The overall goal of this paper is to investigate the role of security testing in agile teams, process-wise. For this purpose, we present the synthesis of the results of the four cases in security testing, highlighting the security engineering process, testing phases and techniques. The results of the interviews and context mapping provide insights into the recommended practices and lessons learned in the context of agile testing. The following three research questions (RQs) were investigated:

(RQ 1)   How is the traditional security engineering process managed/organized in the agile teams?
(RQ 2)   How does the agile teams perform security testing in each testing phase?
(RQ 3)   How are traditional security testing techniques generally used in the agile software development lifecycle?

This study is carried out in four teams in two countries, i.e., Austria and Norway, within three organizations and denoted as 1, 2, 3-Team1, and 3-Team2, as shown in Table 2. Organizations 1 and 2 are located in the same country while organization 3 is located in another country. Organization 3 is a company with roughly 90 engineers. The team setup are both co-located and distributed. 3-Team1 has teams distributed in separate locations while 3-Team2 has the core development teams (frontend and backend) in the same location and interacts with a QA team that sits in a separate location. 3-team1 develops identity management APIs that are mainly consumed by other teams within the organization. They do not interact with external users. 3-Team2 on the other hand, develops solution for storage and processing of end user images and videos.

We prepared semi-structured interview guide (see Table 1) using a qualitative data collection approach that is based on in-depth literature review of the state-of-the-art in security testing. The interviews were compared with the collected information about the organizational contexts and interactions with the companies. The resulting interview audios were then analyzed using the thematic analysis approach [10] to crosscheck and compare the answers in order to find behavioral confirmation and disconfirmation as well. The transcripts and recordings of the interviews were categorized, tabulated, and also analyzed by coding of the interviews. All the transcriptions and coding were validated with other researchers before analysis. By doing so, another researcher independently double-checked the codes and data to tag the key words, phrases and paragraphs. It is important to note that basic information on each context was considered (see Table 2). This information served as a context to better understand the points of view of each participant connected to the results. In this analysis, we considered in which areas the cases suggest the same points, where they differ, and where the cases conflict.

Table 1. Semi-structured interview guide

#	Questions
1	Can you briefly describe the kind of system you develop? Back-end or Front-End?
2	Can you give us a brief introduction of how your development team is organized? (Developers, Testers, Architects, CSOs, etc.), (Distributed, Co-located, etc.)
3	How is your agile software development process? Which practices do you adopt? (Fill in the table with agile and lean practices)
4	How is your security engineering process (for example, security requirements, secure design, secure coding, security testing) organized/managed in your team? Can you describe how you organize your security testing along these axes of the Fig. 1?
5	Can you describe the kind of security testing that you perform in each testing phase listed below? **Phases of testing** / **Components** Unit Testing / Classes, functions, statements, data Integration Testing / Modules, packages, etc. System Testing / System Regression Testing / Classes, Modules, System UAT Testing / System Production/Configuration Testing / System
6	Figure 2 shows the security testing techniques generally used in secure software development lifecycle. Could you talk about how you perform these activities in your agile software development? How often are security testing or security related activities done in your agile cycles? How do you decide when to perform them? How do you decide when not to perform them?
7	Do you see benefits of performing security testing?
8	On the test automation and continuous integration. Do you automate your testing activities? To what extent? How do you incorporate security testing in this process?
9	Anything you would like to add?

Table 2. Teams under study

Team	Team Size	Type of software	Other context information
1	20 Frontend and backend developers divided in teams of 5	Medical Information System	Applies a Scrum-based agile process; the software is certified according to medical standards
2	6 developers	Security service tools	Scrum-based agile process
3–A	21 developers (UI, Backend, Mobile, and Infrastructure)	Identity Management APIs that are consumed by other business units and teams	A mix of Agile Practices. Not specifically scrum by the book. DevOps approach is also spread used
3–B	22 developers (Frontend (web/mobile) and backend teams)	Mobile client and backend system for close storage and processing of images and videos	A mix of Agile Practices. Not specifically scrum by the book. DevOps approach is also spread used

4   Results

We collected our main findings in a mind map shown in Figs. 4, 5 and 6. These results are then discussed in more detail in the next subsections.

4.1   RQ 1: How Is the Traditional Security Engineering Process Managed/ Organized in the Agile Teams?

We found three main themes from the interviews in relation to the roles and responsibility (Fig. 4). The first observation is that larger companies have their own chief security officer, who is not part of the teams to not interfere with any daily team activities. Sometimes the responsibility of the chief security officer overlaps with the project owner in order to ensure that the applications being developed do not impose security risks. One team mentioned that their project owner (PO) or project manager (PM) has domain-specific security knowledge, which is not the case for the other teams. In fact, for the smaller companies, there is no such chief security officer role. One problem that the teams experienced with involving the security officer is that it is hard to identify when to include him in the activities.

The second observation is that external experts are normally hired for penetration testing. However, a problem experienced by one of the companies is that external consultants do not have sufficient domain knowledge needed for security testing. Therefore, some domain-specific vulnerabilities are left undiscovered. The periodicity of the

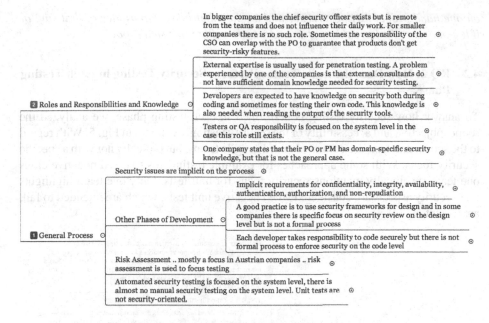

Fig. 4. Mind map: security software engineering process.

execution of these tests is quite ad-hoc, sometimes linked to big deliveries or when there are too many changes in the source code. The results of the tests are not completely integrated in the development process and almost never get into the planning of the activities of the sprint.

The third observation is that testers or QA personnel focus on the system level in the case this role still exists and the developers take care of the daily activities and developers are expected to have knowledge on security both during coding and sometimes for testing their own code. This knowledge is also needed when reading the output of the security tools. One interviewee said: "*We generally organize mainly as software developers, we generally have a software engineering role and we are expected to be with a broad knowledge, and skill set, computer science engineering and security and safe programming*". But there is no specific validation of this stated 'broad knowledge and skill set'. Another interviewee stated on some tool output: "*Normally, the errors are quite readable. From technician level, the developer that develops component should also understand the message of the tool. For instance, if the tool says, open API C# token found, hopefully developers also know what it says. The tools check very huge part, but they cannot check all. This is the responsibility that developer has while developing.*" It was clear that this knowledge was not something systematically evaluated or externalized, just assumed, as the agile mindset brings the focus to people instead of process and tools the teams are not completely sure of how much knowledge on secure coding was in the teams.

Automated unit testing is not security-oriented at all. Risk assessment is performed mostly by the Austrian teams (Team 1 and Team 2), and is applied to focus testing. One interviewer said: "*Yes, we are using risk assessment, it is a kind of matrix where we have on one hand probability occurrence and on the other hand importance of that stuff or if it can occur. We have this matrix and we are using it for small tools".*

4.2   RQ 2: How Does the Agile Teams Perform Security Testing in Each Testing Phase?

To answer how security testing is performed in each testing phase, we analyzed the scope, objective and accessibility of the security testing, as shown in Fig. 5. With regard to the scope, unit tests are commonly used in agile teams, but typically not with a specific security focus. With some approaches for example testing positive and negative cases one team specifically mentions security focus for unit tests. Only one team highlights that security aspects are considered when negative unit tests, which are intended to fail, are executed.

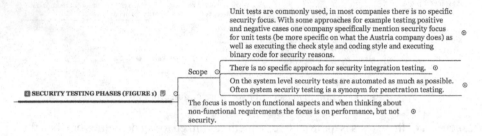

Fig. 5.   Mind map security phases.

Static source and binary code analysis is performed for security reasons on the unit level. All teams stated that no specific security aspects are considered during integration testing. Security testing is most prominent on the system level. On this level security tests are typically a synonym for penetration testing, typically performed as black box testing. Security tests on the system level are to a large extent automated and there is almost no manual security testing on this level. White-box aspects are typically only considered during static source or binary code analysis.

When testing non-functional requirements, the focus in the interviewed teams is typically on performance. One interviewee said: *"We usually have unit test. And those are trying to exercise the happy path, which should already catch a many of basic the problems. We don't have much integration tests. We have also some performance tests. And that may go to the non-functional category, but we do not have much. We worry mostly on if the code works as it is supposed to work".*

4.3   RQ 3: How Are Traditional Security Testing Techniques Generally Used in the Agile Software Development Lifecycle?

For this question, the interviewees were asked to analyze Fig. 2. It shows the security testing techniques generally used in traditional secure software development lifecycle, i.e., model-based security testing, code-based testing and static analysis, penetration testing and dynamic analysis as well as security regression testing. The interviewees were asked to talk about how they perform these activities in their agile software development and how often security testing or security related activities are done in their agile cycles. An overview of the results is shown in Fig. 6.

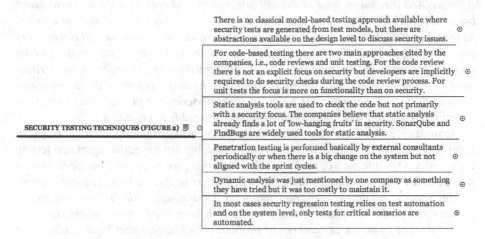

Fig. 6. Mind map security testing techniques findings.

In general, there is no classical model-based testing approach available where security tests are generated from test models, but there are abstractions available on the design level to discuss security issues. One interviewee said: *"We don't do any model-based testing. We consider security aspects as part of design and we don't try to buy a formal model around that. During development as we said we do code-based testing and static analysis. And that is probably on where most of our focus is. We have done some dynamic security tests in the past. As I said, those took a lot of manual effort and it was very unstable, it broke up often with some UI changes and it was hard to keep up"*.

For code-based testing there are two main approaches referred to by the companies, i.e., code reviews and unit testing. When it comes to code review, there is no explicit emphasis on security, but developers are implicitly required to do security checks during the code review process. As for unit tests the focus is more on functionality than on security.

Static analysis tools are used to check the code but not primarily with a security focus. The interviewed teams believe that static analysis already finds the most important 'low-hanging fruits' in security. SonarQube and FindBugs are widely used tools for static analysis for the teams interviewed.

Penetration testing is performed basically by external consultants periodically or when there is a big change on the system but not aligned with the sprint cycles. One interviewee stated: *"We do penetration testing from external testers from the company, this was done together with the University of Innsbruck and plus our customers are doing against software. They are completely independent and we are not informed, we offer our aid only if there is a problem, and if we take Austrian medical network for example, it is not allowed to go live without testing from external company and that does not only involve our software but the whole system."*

Dynamic analysis was only mentioned by one interviewee as something they have tried but it was too costly to maintain it. He said: *"It was taking too much time to keep it for us. And it requires a lot of manual integration and once that the scenario broke because of an UI change or something and then we would have again manual effort to fix that. For me, what makes code review and static analysis to work so well is that every time you compile the code you can see the feedback on it. On the dynamic tests, you cant do that very easily at that point you have to wait, and there is a lag between you writing your code and you receiving some feedback on it. Even if it is part of the development process, it doesn't happen right away. In my experience the further away from your commit, it less likely that you will either notice or be able to change it".*

In most cases security regression testing relies on test automation and on the system level only tests for critical scenarios are automated, but not a specific regression testing for security. One interviewee said: *"So what is working well is, I think our development processes are well structured and the biggest problem is, that we have frequent changes of user stories and that is very challenging on the one hand side on the development process and on the other side testing process. You have to adopt everything. The user stories are not from our customers, the problem the changing part is more about our c-level changes, on time this and one time that. So this is very big problem which also is very big problem for agile software development because it is very big problem".*

5   Discussion

Based on the results, we discuss recommendations for practice and research as well as limitations of this work.

5.1   Recommendations for Practice

With regard to the security engineering process, it is evident that the teams assume that developers have some security knowledge, but the issue is that they did not state how they conduct security engineering processes as well as what they need. For this reason, there is a demand for better use of guidelines for secure coding and testing practices like the OWASP guidelines [25]. Moreover, there should be a more systematic approach of spreading knowledge in security inside the teams. In a recent survey, Oyetoyan et al. [27] found that the developers' confidence in their software security knowledge is low, and therefore more efforts should be spend on getting the level of security knowledge higher at the companies. This is stronger in agile setting context because there is a strong dependency on people and not on process and tools. In addition code review and static analysis are used more and more in software projects, but without specific focus on security [27]. For this reason, processes of code reviews and static analysis should be more focused on security.

Even though the teams rely on penetration testing performed by externals, there is a danger of external penetration testers not having domain knowledge to catch important vulnerabilities. While independent penetration testing is possible, there is a need that the penetration testing feedback is well integrated with the whole development process lifecycle [7, 34]. Chóliz et al. [7] have focused their study on the security testing activities, with the clear objective of synchronizing the tests from the independent security team with the agile rhythm of sprints, with frequent deliveries, of the software engineering teams, showing that the rate of found security vulnerabilities increased gradually. The results of Türpe et al. [34] suggest that penetration tests improve developers' security awareness, but long-lasting change of development practices is hampered if security is not properly reflected in the communicative and collaborative structures of the organization, e.g. by a dedicated stakeholder.

POs should have more security awareness because they are the only one responsible for maximizing the return on investment (ROI) of the development effort. In addition, the PO is responsible for product vision and constantly re-prioritizes the Product Backlog, thereby adjusting any long-term expectations such as release plans and making sure the team considers the stakeholders interests. The main issue with the explicit functional security requirements is that, most of the time stakeholders do not explicitly state them as requirements, and neither do the product owners. On the other hand, the non-functional security requirements are not features, which mean they never become a user story. In other words, they are not inserted into the product backlog. From the performed study, we see that security issues are implicitly handled on the process, but there is need for a more systematic approach to handle security issues in the development process. As shown by Rindel et al. [30] it is possible to have the security user stories as part of the product backlog.

5.2 Recommendations for Research

Research can help to increase knowledge and application of security testing in several respects. First, knowledge can be increased by the development of suitable courses and guidelines based on empirical evidence showing which approaches work in which context. Good efforts have been done in the last years [3, 7, 30, 34]. Therefore more empirical studies are needed which investigate challenges of security testing and derive respective evidence-based guidelines to address them.

With regard to model-based security testing, lightweight approaches are needed, which support the model creation, for instance, by learning of domain language concepts, based on design-level abstracts that are available also in agile teams. Also, a general understanding of the return of investment of model-based security testing approaches, which has already been highlighted as a challenge in [17], would help to apply such approaches efficiently. The issue of efficiently applying model-based testing approaches becomes even more critical when agile teams develop systems where the connection between safety and security is essential as in modern Internet-of-Things applications.

As seen in the results, system testing is often limited to penetration testing and testing of functional security requirements is often neglected. As automation is difficult to achieve fully, but at the same time, important for successful application in agile teams, suitable automation support and innovative techniques are required [29].

So far, security testing in agile teams makes little use of security risk assessments, which typically exist in an implicit or explicit for in other organization units. Risk assessment can be used to develop risk-based testing approaches [14], which can guide decisions during testing, and for instance help to select and prioritize security regression tests [13]. Baca et al. [3] shows that using a risk analysis approach, it s possible to find more severe risks, besides, more advanced skills and a deeper awareness of the problems become available. More research needs to be done in order to understand the best way to apply risk management in agile projects and especially on security.

5.3 Work Limitations

Common criticisms to a case study also apply to this study, among them one may list: uniqueness, difficulty to generalize the results, and the introduction of bias by participants and researchers. In our study, we generalized the findings from empirical statements to theoretical statements, which involved generalizing data from interviews and perceptions by discussing them in accordance with the literature. Interview data were though our primary source of information.

Qualitative findings are highly context and case-dependent. Our findings apply to software projects teams within four participating teams. However, all the participants were professionals using typical development technologies in a typical working environment, e.g., the natural setting demanded by the case study approach. We described the main characteristics of each case and company, including context and settings, data collection, analysis, and analysis process, as well as quotations with our major findings. This makes the results easier to generalize.

As commonly done in in-depth qualitative studies, we also had to do a trade-off between the number of participants, the duration and the cost of this study. The number of subjects interviewed in this context is not quantitatively significant, but gives deeper insights on the issues investigated in this work.

6 Conclusion

In this paper, we investigated by a cross-case analysis of four teams, two from Austria and two from Norway, how security testing is performed in agile teams. We investigated how the security engineering process is managed/organized in agile teams, how security testing is performed in each testing phase, and how security testing techniques are generally used in the secure software development lifecycle.

Although the study is based only on the results of a limited amount of agile teams, i.e., four, agile teams, we could derive recommendations for research and practice. The findings of this research are not surprising, but at the same time are alarming. The lack of knowledge on security by agile teams in general, the large dependency on incidental penetration testers, and the ignorance in static testing for security are indicators that security testing is highly under addressed and that more efforts should be addressed to security testing in agile teams.

In the future, we plan to replicate this study and to develop and evaluate suitable security testing approaches to support the adoption of security testing in agile teams through action research studies with industry.

Acknowledgments. This work was partially supported by the SoS-Agile (247678/070) project funded by the Research Council of Norway, and by MOBSTECO (FWF P 26194-N15) funded by the Austrian Science Fund. The authors are grateful to all involved in this study, specially the interviewees for their insights and cooperation and to the software companies for supporting this work.

References

1. Arkin, B., Stender, S., McGraw, G.: Software penetration testing. IEEE Secur. Priv. **3**(1), 84–87 (2005)
2. Austin, A., Williams, L.: One technique is not enough: a comparison of vulnerability discovery techniques. In: ESEM 2011, pp. 97–106 (2011)
3. Baca, D., Boldt, M., Carlsson B., Jacobsson, A.: A novel security-enhanced agile software development process applied in an industrial setting. In: ARES 2015, pp. 11–19 (2015)
4. Beznosov, K., Kruchten, P.: Towards agile security assurance. In: NSPW 2004, pp. 47–54 (2004)
5. Camacho, C.R., Marczak, S., Cruzes, D.S.: Agile team members perceptions on non-functional testing: influencing factors from an empirical study. In: ARES 2016, pp. 582–589 (2016)
6. Chess, B., McGraw, G.: Static analysis for security. IEEE Secur. Priv. **2**(6), 76–79 (2004)
7. Choliz, J., Vilas, J., Moreira, J.: Independent security testing on agile software development: a case study in a software company. In: ARES 2015, pp. 522–531 (2015)
8. Common Weakness Enumeration (CWE), 5 March, 2017. https://cwe.mitre.org/index.html
9. Crispin, L., Gregory, J.: Agile Testing: A Practical Guide for Testers and Agile Teams. Addison-Wesley Professional, Boston (2009)
10. Cruzes, D., Dybå, T.: Recommended steps for thematic synthesis in software engineering. In: ESEM 2011, pp. 275–284 (2011)
11. CWE/SANS TOP 25 Most Dangerous Software Errors, 5 March 2017. https://www.sans.org/top25-software-errors/
12. Erdogan, G., Meland, P.H., Mathieson, D.: Security testing in agile web application development - a case study using the EAST methodology. In: Sillitti, A., Martin, A., Wang, X., Whitworth, E. (eds.) XP 2010. LNBIP, vol. 48, pp. 14–27. Springer, Heidelberg (2010). doi:10.1007/978-3-642-13054-0_2
13. Felderer, M., Fourneret, E.: A systematic classification of security regression testing approaches. Int. J. Soft Tools Technol. Transf. **17**(3), 305–319 (2015)
14. Felderer, M., Schieferdecker, I.: A taxonomy of risk-based testing. Int. J. Softw. Tools Technol. Transf. **16**(5), 559–568 (2014)
15. Felderer, M., Agreiter, B., Breu, R., Armenteros, A.: Security Testing by Telling Test Stories. Modellierung **161**, 195–202 (2011)
16. Felderer, M., Büchler, M., Johns, M., Brucker, A.D., Breu, R., Pretschner, A.: Chapter one-security testing: a survey. Adv. Comput. **101**, 1–51 (2016)
17. Felderer, M., Zech, P., Breu, R., Büchler, M., Pretschner, A.: Model-based security testing: a taxonomy and systematic classification. Softw. Test. Verification Reliab. **26**(2), 119–148 (2016)

18. Fitzgerald, B., Stol, K.-J.: Continuous software engineering: a roadmap and agenda. JSS **123**, 176–189 (2017)
19. Keramati, H., Mirian-Hosseinabadi, S.: Integrating software development security activities with agile methodologies. In: AICCSA 2008 (2008)
20. Marback, A., Do, H., He, K., Kondamarri, S., Xu, D.: A threat model-based approach to security testing. Softw. Pract. Experience **43**(2), 241–258 (2013)
21. McGraw, G., Potter, B.: Software security testing. IEEE Secur. Priv. **2**(5), 81–85 (2004)
22. Microsoft, Agile Development Using Microsoft Security Development Lifecycle 5 March 2017. http://www.microsoft.com/en-us/sdl/discover/sdlagile.aspx
23. Moe, N.B., Cruzes, D., Dybå, T., Mikkelsen, E.M.: Continuous software testing in a globally distributed project. In: ICGSE 2015, pp. 130–134 (2015)
24. Oueslati, H., Rahman, M.M., Othmane, L., Ghani, I., Arbain, A.F.: Evaluation of the challenges of developing secure software using the agile approach. Int. J. Secure Softw. Eng. **7**, 17 (2016)
25. OWASP Foundation: OWASP Testing Guide v4. 5 March, 2017. https://www.owasp.org/index.php/OWASP_Testing_Project
26. OWASP Top 10. 5 March 2017. https://www.owasp.org/index.php/Top_10_2013-Top_10
27. Oyetoyan, T.D., Cruzes, D.S., Jaatun, M.G.: An empirical study on the relationship between software security skills, usage and training needs in agile settings. In: ARES 2016, pp. 548–555 (2016)
28. Paul, M.: Official (ISC)2 Guide to the CSSLP CBK, 2nd edn. (ISC)2 Press (2014)
29. Peischl, B., Felderer, M., Beer, A.: Testing security requirements with non-experts: approaches and empirical investigations. In: QRS 2016, pp. 254–261 (2016)
30. Rindell, K., Hyrynsalmi, S., Leppänen, V.: Case study of security development in an agile environment: building identity management for a government agency. In: ARES 2016, pp. 556–563 (2016)
31. Sindre, G., Opdahl, A.L.: Eliciting security requirements with misuse cases. Requirements Eng. **10**(1), 34–44 (2005)
32. Tappenden, A., et al.: Agile security testing of web-based systems via HTTP unit. In: Proceedings of Agile Conference. IEEE (2005)
33. Tian-yang, G., Yin-sheng, S., You-yuan, F.: Research on software security testing. World Acad. Sci. Eng. Technol. **70**, 647–651 (2010)
34. Türpe, S., Kocksch, L., Poller, A.: Penetration tests a turning point in security practices? In: Organizational Challenges and Implications in a Software Development Team, WSIW@SOUPS 2016 (2016)

An Assessment of Avionics Software Development Practice: Justifications for an Agile Development Process

Geir K. Hanssen[1]([✉]), Gosse Wedzinga[2], and Martijn Stuip[2]

[1] SINTEF, Trondheim, Norway
geir.k.hanssen@sintef.no
[2] NLR, Amsterdam, The Netherlands
{gosse.wedzinga,martijn.stuip}@nlr.nl

Abstract. Avionic systems for communication, navigation, and flight control, and many other functions are complex and crucial components of any modern aircraft. Present day avionic systems are increasingly based on computers and a growing percentage of system complexity can be attributed to software. An error in the software of a safety-critical avionic system could lead to a catastrophic event, such as multiple deaths and loss of the aircraft. To demonstrate compliance with airworthiness requirements, certification agencies accept the use of RTCA document DO-178 for the software development. Avionics software development is typically complex and is traditionally reliant on a strict plan-driven development process, characterized by early fixture of detailed requirements and late production of working software. In this process, requirement changes and solving software errors can lead to much rework, and create a risk of budget and schedule overruns. This raises the question whether avionics software development could benefit from the application of agile approaches. Based on the results of three activities: (1) a literature study on industrial experience with the use of agile methods in a DO-178 context, (2) an expert assessment of the DO-178 objectives, and (3) a survey conducted among European avionics industry, an outline is presented of an agile development process, where Scrum is extended to achieve the DO-178 objectives. The application of agile methods is expected to support frequent delivery of working software and ability to respond to changes, resulting in reduced risk of budget and schedule overruns.

Keywords: Avionics · Certification · Safety critical software · DO-178 · Software Life-Cycle · Agile · Scrum

1 Introduction

Avionic systems play a crucial role aboard modern aircraft. These systems offer pilots operational support in areas such as communications, navigation, and control of the aircraft during all phases of flight and in all weather conditions. A system is safety-critical when its failure could result in loss of life, significant property damage, or damage to the environment [11]. An example of a safety-critical avionic system is the flight control system, which governs the attitude of an aircraft and, as a result, the flight path it follows. Safety-critical systems are not limited to the avionics domain only,

© The Author(s) 2017
H. Baumeister et al. (Eds.): XP 2017, LNBIP 283, pp. 217–231, 2017.
DOI: 10.1007/978-3-319-57633-6_14

examples of other important domains include, process control [20], medical equipment [17], and automotive [9].

Present day avionic systems are increasingly based on computers and more functions are implemented as software. Certification agencies, like the European Aviation Safety Agency (EASA), accept the use of RTCA document DO-178 [18] for the development of avionics software to provide assurance of compliance with airworthiness requirements. Document DO-178 requires the achievement of many safety objectives, which is generally costly and time consuming [4, 10].

The avionics industry traditionally uses the V-model, or a variant thereof, as life-cycle model for software development. This matches DO-178 well when looking at the life-cycle data items that have to be produced. There are, however, also disadvantages. For example, no working software is produced until late in the development life-cycle. Errors detected in this stage can lead to much rework of earlier performed activities, and increase the risk of budget and schedule overruns [4]. In the same way, changes in requirements in a late stage can also lead to much rework with similar consequences.

The application of agile methods could be a solution for these problems. The difficulty lies, however, in the fact that the looseness of an agile process does not seem to be reconcilable with the rigour imposed by DO-178. For example, agile development considers responding to change more important than following a plan, while DO-178 is strictly plan driven. The main question addressed by this research is how agile methods can be adapted to be usable in an avionics development process that is governed by DO-178.

The following of the paper describes our research method (Sect. 2), an analysis of DO-178C (Sect. 3), an overview of research and industry experience (Sect. 4), a survey of present practice (Sect. 5), and an outline of an agile process aligned with DO-178 (Sect. 6). Conclusions and further work are presented in Sect. 7.

2 Research Method

In order to answer our research question, three complimentary activities have been carried out and used to propose a DO-178-aligned agile process.

(1) An assessment of DO-178 has been performed to indicate how an agile strategy for meeting the objectives could look like and whether there are potential conflicts by using an agile method (Sect. 3.2). Annex A of DO-178 contains 10 summary tables with 71 objectives. The information provided for each objective includes: (a) a brief description, (b) its applicability for each software criticality level, (c) the requirement for independent achievement, and (d) the data items in which the results are collected. Each objective has been assessed to determine how the objective can be met using an agile approach like Scrum and whether there is a need for extensions beyond what can be considered a plain agile approach. The work performed by K. Coetzee[1] was taken as a starting point.

---

[1] http://www.embeddedfool.net/blog/2015/04/08/a-more-agile-do-178/ (last accessed, Dec. 5, 2016).

(2) Relevant literature addressing the application of agile methods in the avionics domain has been reviewed and main findings about opportunities and limitations of using agile methods for development of avionics software were summarized (Sect. 4). In order to build an understanding of the status of research and reported industrial experience on the use and effects of agile methods in development of safety-critical avionics software, a search for relevant literature has been conducted with Google Scholar. We applied search phrases based on relevant terms such as 'agile', 'avionic', and 'DO-178'. To strengthen the search, we applied snowballing, meaning that relevant work referenced in identified publications was checked for relevance and potentially included if the focus and quality was found sufficient. From this search, 11 publications were found that potentially could offer insight into industrial experience.

(3) A survey was done as an online questionnaire to establish a better overview of the state–including challenges and potential points of improvement–of software development and certification in the avionics industry, and to map the current status of using or plans to use agile methods. As part of the ASHLEY[2] EU-project, we selected professionals believed to have sufficient knowledge about their own organization and about how software is developed and certified. 29 contact persons were selected, each representing a unique ASHLEY partner organization. 10 contact persons completed the questionnaire fully or partially.

Our study has some limitations. Firstly, the literature review identified a relatively low number of relevant studies providing industrial experience. This is however a valuable insight as it nevertheless summarizes the present state of research within this specific domain. Secondly, the survey has a relatively low number of respondents. This is due to resource priorities, but is somewhat compensated by selecting qualified respondents, each representing a major avionic system provider in Europe. The results present the most comprehensive overview of this industry so far.

3 Certification Aspects of Avionics Software Development

3.1 Overview of Document DO-178C

Document DO-178C, "Software considerations in airborne systems and equipment certification" [18] governs the approval of software for avionic systems by certification authorities, such as EASA. In this paper, we simply write DO-178 when referring to revision C of the document.

DO-178 distinguishes five software levels (A–E) based upon the failure condition that may result from erroneous behaviour of the software. Software is classified as (the highest) level A, if erroneous software behaviour can cause or contribute to a catastrophic failure condition of the aircraft, which would result in multiple fatalities, usually

---

[2] Avionics Systems Hosted on a distributed modular electronics Large scale dEmonstrator for multiple tYpe of aircraft, http://www.ashleyproject.eu (last accessed, Dec. 9 2016).

with loss of aircraft. For lower software levels, the consequence of erroneous software behaviour gradually reduces to no effect on safety (level E).

DO-178 is a process-based standard relying on evidence that the various activities associated with software development have been performed successfully. DO-178 categorizes processes into three types: (1) the software planning process, which defines and coordinates the activities of all processes (2) the software development processes, which produce the software product, and (3) the integral processes, which ensure the correctness of the software product and confidence in the software development processes and their outputs. DO-178 does not address system life-cycle processes, but it does describe the interaction with system processes, including system safety assessment.

Table 1. Assessment of objectives for the software development processes.

DO-178 Objective	Agile Strategy	Remarks
1. High-Level Requirements (HLRs) are developed	A system is divided into features. Features are divided into stories. Stories consist of HLRs (and their test cases)	Features are client-valued functions. At the end of each Sprint, the implemented user stories are used to update the HLRs
2. Derived HLRs are defined and provided to the system processes, including system safety assessment process	Derived HLRs are not directly traceable to system requirements. They are developed in the same way as HLRs (see objective 1)	Derived HLRs are provided to the system processes to determine if there is any impact on the system safety assessment and system requirements
3. Software architecture is developed	Start with a high-level architecture and update/refine it at each software release	Closure activities include a review of the software architecture to make sure it is consistent with the source code
4. Low-Level Requirements (LLRs) are developed	Develop LLRs by defining conditions and associated actions [13]	LLRs can be contained in the source code or the unit tests (embedded in the source code)
5. Derived LLRs are defined and provided to the system processes, including system safety assessment process	Derived LLRs are not directly traceable to HLRs. They are developed in the same way as LLRs (see objective 4)	Derived LLRs are provided to the system processes to determine if there is any impact on the system safety assessment and system requirements
6. Source Code is developed	Develop source code by applying Test-Driven Development (TDD)	Stories are implemented during Sprints
7. Executable Object Code and Parameter Data Item Files, if any, are produced and loaded in the target computer	Develop object code by applying Continuous Integration (CI) and Continuous Delivery (CD)	When a defined set of features is completed, a release will follow

DO-178 provides guidance by (1) stating objectives for software life-cycle processes, (2) describing activities that provide a means for satisfying the objectives, and (3) describing evidence in the form of data items to demonstrate that the objectives have been satisfied. DO-178 does not prescribe a particular software life-cycle or methodology. A software development project defines its software life-cycle by specifying a set of processes and their sequence. The usual sequence through the software development processes is requirements, design, coding, and integration.

3.2   Assessment of Document DO-178C

The assessment revealed that objectives for the software development processes (DO-178, Table A-2) and testing (DO-178, Table A-6) can be achieved by applying agile techniques. The remaining objectives are either outside the agile process or there are no suitable agile techniques to achieve them. These objectives can be achieved using traditional methods (inspections, reviews, analyses, management records).

Table 1 presents the assessment of the 7 objectives for the software development processes (DO-178, Table A-2).

In conclusion, agile methods can be used to achieve a subset of the DO-178 objectives. No prohibitive conflicts have been identified.

4   Overview of Existing Research and Industry Experience

Most of the 11 reviewed publications provide discussions at a conceptual level without any empirical data, indicating that this is a relatively new and immature–but growing– concept within the avionics domain. Some empirical data is presented in only three of the papers. Wils et al. [22] provide some minor insights from the Barco company, Paige et al. [16] present a very small-scale experiment, and Carlson and Turner [1] make a review of five case studies.

This lack of empirical data from industry is in contrast to non-safety-critical domains where the use of agile methods has become common, with correspondingly more empirical research available [6]. One comparable domain, the process control domain, where the IEC 61508 standard applies, is a bit more advanced, but in general it seems that the application of agile methods and techniques to safety-critical software is in its early stages [8]. However, the emergence of literature presenting ideas over the past few years means that the industry is seeking new opportunities for improving their software development processes inspired by other domains.

4.1   Why This Interest in Agile Methods?

The common background and motivation for nearly all reviewed publications is the need for improving the software development process, including certification based on DO-178B/C. The trend seems to be that avionic system complexity is increasing [5]. Requirements tend to be more volatile (even late in the development process), calling for better approaches to manage requirements and their changes in more flexible ways

[5, 15, 16]. We also see an increased customer orientation where industry wants to listen more closely to customers [1, 3, 16, 21, 22], opening up for a more flexible development process with less emphasis on complete and detailed up-front design. Experience also indicates that cost and schedule overruns are happening too frequently [1, 4].

4.2   Evidence and Documentation

Regardless of the process framework, e.g., V-model or an agile process, there is a set of formal data items that has to be produced [5], but an agile process may allow for doing this more efficiently as well as data items may be updated more often. However, if an agile approach is to be used, it calls for some extensions [16], as agile methods, such as Scrum, do not specify such documentation at all. Examples of such data items that are required by certification authorities are the Plan for Software Aspects of Certification (PSAC) and the Software Accomplishment Summary (SAS) [18]. These documents, together with the plans that concern the definition of the life-cycle processes may best be kept outside the agile process.

4.3   More Flexible Management of Requirements and Change

One of the main characteristics of the established practice and application of the V-model is that development of avionics software may be characterized as document driven and sequential [16]. This may become challenging in cases where requirements change throughout a development project, even despite there have been made very detailed plans and design up-front. Change may come from several sources, like design revisions, review of safety analysis, and verification [16]. Recent figures indicate that requirements change can be quite extensive, from 25% in typical projects to 35% in large and complex projects [21], and discovering problems and dealing with changes late in the process may become very costly [4]. According to Wils et al., agile methods may lower the change effort as compared to traditional development [22]. This does not mean that up-front plans are to be avoided, as that would conflict seriously with the process objectives in DO-178. However, the role of agile requirements management is to detail high-level requirements per iteration, not to create new high-level requirements [5]. New high-level requirements could be added after the Sprint, as part of the Sprint review. Up-front requirements may not be complete or even in conflict (and need to be refined) [5].

However, there is a potential conflict here–that flexible requirements management negatively affects the software verification process. If previously verified components of a system are changed, the verification results need to be updated. This requires strict configuration management and relentless testing of the software under development [2].

4.4   Applicability and Obstacles

In general, the consensus seems to be that there is no conflict per se for using agile methods in development of avionics software [2, 3, 13, 21, 22]. In fact XP/Agile is claimed to be particularly suitable [3] to deal with the increasing complexity and requirements volatility in safety-critical software projects. As changes inevitably do happen, we could make use of better strategies to manage changes.

However, agile methods, such as Scrum, were not designed to support development of large and complex systems like safety-critical avionic systems and there is a lack of techniques and practices to meet the objectives of DO-178. E.g., the requirements for data items and traceability have to be met by setting up a well-functioning framework of tools to support and automate the process to a large extent [3, 22]. An agile process, with short iterations of work, frequent feedback, and evaluation of status and incremental development of the software supports the production of some of the needed data items as part of the development itself. Instead of explicitly producing separate documents, some of the information may be extracted from tools and logs. One of the core objectives of agile methods is to minimize the effort for producing documentation [16, 21]. There is work going on to extend Scrum to make it applicable to regulated domains, for example the SafeScrum framework [14] and R-Scrum [7], which seek to meet requirements mentioned above.

Besides practical aspects of setting up an agile process and a chain of supporting tools, we also need to clarify such a change with the certification authority. A more or less radical change in process will affect the work to be done by this stakeholder and it is of course important that the certification authority representative gets all requested information and eventually gets confidence that the applied approach has led to a safe product without extra problems and in an efficient way.

Besides the core principle of incremental and iterative development, agile methods may also be seen as a collection of practices and techniques. From Chenu [3] and Paige et al. [16], we extracted the following set that may be particularly relevant to safety-critical systems development:

- Test-driven development (need some adaptation, see also [12]).
- Coding standards (already mandatory for DO-178 levels A–C).
- Design improvement/refactoring (creates some challenges with respect to safety analysis [5]).
- The planning game (from XP).
- Emphasis on communication (other than through extensive documentation).

4.5 Team Efficiency and Motivation

One of the main aspects of agile methods is how people work together. As a contrast to plan-based methods where developers take on specialized roles, following detailed plans, agile methods rely on multi-disciplinary teams, with the idea that this better enforces learning and motivation [3]. Furthermore co-located teams are also believed to improve design flexibility and a shared vision of the system under development [1]. A team may also have Designated Engineering Representatives (DERs), who are embedded representatives of the certification authorities within the development team [5].[3]

---

[3] Under EASA regulation, Certification Verification Engineers (CVEs) perform equivalent tasks as DERs.

4.6 Testing

Extensive testing and full traceability is fundamental in development of avionics software and implementation of all requirements has to be verified by tests [3]. Testing is also strongly emphasized in agile methods, which focus on test-driven development and high test-coverage. However, for avionics software development purposes, agile methods need to extend testing activities–e.g. by having more thorough acceptance testing (not (only) relying on customer feedback) [2, 16]. Carlson and Turner argue that incremental testing increases iteration pace and enables issues to be revealed and dispatched [1]; they also argue that testers should be part of the development team (provided that any independency requirements are guaranteed).

4.7 Adoption of New Software Process Models

Experience (e.g. from object-oriented development) shows that uptake and acceptance of a new practice takes time–we should expect the same for agile methods as well [21, 22]. The avionics domain relies on well-established and well-proven practices and processes and it is natural to be careful with new ideas, like agile methods, as they may seem to impose more challenges than benefits. However, as this literature in sum shows, there seems to be a growing interest at least.

4.8 Relating Findings to Other Domains

The literature review done here has focused explicitly on the avionics domain. However, we find that the main challenges and approaches clearly coincide with other domains where safety-critical software is essential. Other studies show that the same type of challenges are being addressed, e.g., for process control systems [20], medical equipment [17], and automotive [9], and that agile methods may be applicable to other safety standards and frameworks like IEC 61508, SPICE, and IEC 62304.

5 Survey to Assess Present Practice

A questionnaire was used to gain insights into the organizations' profiles, their maturity, their relationship to safety standards and authorities, various life-cycle aspects, and perceived challenges and problems.

5.1 Respondents' and Organizations' Profiles

Respondents have a great variety in profiles, from developers and testers to managers. Their organizations also have a wide range of business models, target markets (civil passenger aircrafts on the top), and type of software applications (real-time embedded systems being the most common).

5.2 Maturity

The avionics domain/industry is mature and professional with established system providers having decades of experience. There is a wide range of methods for requirements analysis and architectural and detailed design in use. There is also a wide range of testing approaches in use (white/black-box–unit/module/system/hardware-in-the-loop). All practice extensive testing and inspection. Customer involvement is extensive. There is extensive use of DOORS® from IBM Rational for requirements analysis and management, but half of the respondents also use typical office tools.

5.3 Relationship to Safety Standards and Authorities

DO-178 is clearly the most relevant standard for all organizations. Applications are developed at all levels of DO-178, where level C is the most common (60% of the respondents). Consequently, there is a very high coverage of data items. When asked about the level of interaction with the external assessor, 50% report that they collaborate with the assessor in all phases of the project. The rest report a lower level. The average estimate of costs related to verification and certification (including all reviews and testing) is 40% of the total project budget.

5.4 Life-Cycle Aspects

There are a wide variety of software life-cycle models in use. The V-model is in use in some form by all organizations, while 25% use incremental/iterative methods in some form. Customers are involved to a very high degree. Testing (in general) and code inspection/analysis are used by all respondents. Formal methods are applied by about a third of the respondents.

5.5 Perceived Challenges and Problems

The top challenges with respect to verification and certification include: (1) having sufficient resources, infrastructure, and competency/staff, (2) having sufficient quality of customer communication, including requirements specification and feedback, and (3) demonstrating compliance with DO-178 requirements to certification authority. The top-rated problems with the software development process are requirements management (frequent changes, insufficient requirements, ambiguous requirements, and addition of new requirements), late discovery of problems/defects, and project cost overruns.

6 Towards an DO-178-Aligned Agile Approach

As mentioned in Sect. 3.1, document DO-178 [18] does not prescribe a particular software life-cycle model. This makes it possible to define software life-cycles, such as, waterfall, V-model, incremental, and spiral, but also to apply agile methods. Scrum is considered to be a suitable (non-safety) agile framework that could be used as a baseline.

It is the most commonly used agile framework in the software industry, in general, with a large number of training resources, industrial experience, and available research literature. Scrum will have to be extended for the development of avionics software to enable delivery of all required data items in compliance with DO-178.

6.1 Scrum Phases

In his seminal paper [19] on the Scrum development process, K. Schwaber made a distinction into the phases Pregame, Game, and Postgame. In this paper, we use the terms Preparation, Development, and Closure, which are also frequently used, e.g., [13]. Applying the Scrum phases to the software development and software verification processes of DO-178, as depicted in Fig. 1, allows the mapping of agile methods to these processes.[4]

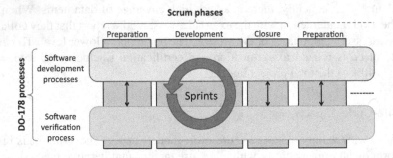

Fig. 1. Application of Scrum phases to DO-178 processes.

During the Preparation phase, planning and architecture activities are performed. Scrum's concept of planning is somewhat broader than that of DO-178. Scrum includes the definition of the next software release based on the currently known backlog, analysis of system requirements, and development of user stories. The architecture activities establish (or update) the software structure. During the Development phase, the functionality of a new release is developed as well as tests for new or changed code. The software is designed, and source code is implemented, integrated, and tested during a sequence of Sprints. In the Closure phase, the software release is prepared, including system testing, final documentation, and release. The sequence of Preparation, Development, and Closure is repeated until the final software release has been completed. In the next sections, the activities in each phase are described in more detail.

6.2 Preparation Phase Activities

During the Preparation phase, the allocated system requirements, or a subset thereof, are taken and high-level requirements (HLRs) are produced in the form of features that

---

[4] For simplicity, the DO-178 planning process and integral processes other than software verification are not shown in Fig. 1.

are further divided into user stories. A software architecture is established (or refined), which, together with the prioritized HLRs, as part of the product backlog, is provided to the Development phase. As required by DO-178, outputs of all processes are verified, e.g., by means of review or analysis. Further details are presented in Table 2.

Table 2. Activities during Preparation phase.

DO-178 Process	Inputs	Activities	Outputs
Software requirements	Allocated system requirements, software level	Define system features and prepare user stories. A story consists of HLRs	HLRs, trace data
Software design	HLRs	Establish or refine software architecture, including partitioning concept	Software architecture, trace data
Software verification	HLRs, software architecture, trace data	Define test cases for HLRs. Verify all outputs	HLR test cases, verification results

The planning process of DO-178 is kept outside the agile process. It is responsible for establishing and updating all plans, including the Software Development Plan, the Configuration Management Plan, and the Plan for Software Aspects of Certification. The latter document is used for communication with the authorities.

6.3 Development Phase Activities

The Development phase consists of a sequence of Sprints, all with preferably the same fixed duration (from 1 to 4 weeks). The number of Sprints is not fixed. The result of a Sprint is a set of implemented and tested user stories that are integrated into a working application. In addition, a Sprint produces information for the assessor (the data items). The application can be demonstrated to stakeholders, but not all features may be complete and hence it is not releasable. Further details are presented in Table 3.

Agile development promotes the Test-Driven Development (TDD) technique. A cyclic process is performed whereby first LLRs are established together with their test cases. Next, test code is produced and all tests are executed to verify that they fail. Then, source code is produced that just passes the tests. Finally, the code is refactored and tests are re-executed. This cycle repeats until all LLRs have been implemented. In practise, the TDD technique implies that software development activities will be performed in conjunction with software verification activities.

6.4 Closure Phase Activities

Upon start of the Closure phase, a sufficient number of features should be completed to warrant release of the application. During Closure, all data items that already exist in some form (see outputs in Tables 2 and 3) are brought up to date. The remaining data

Table 3. Activities during Development phase.

DO-178 Process	Inputs	Activities	**Outputs**
Software design	HLRs, software architecture, trace data	Define Low-level requirements (LLRs) by conditions and associated actions [13]	LLRs, trace data
Software coding	LLRs	Produce code for the LLRs	Source code
Integration	Source code	Perform continuous integration	Executable object code
Software verification	HLRs, HLR test cases, software architecture, LLRs, source code, executable object code, trace data	Establish test cases for LLRs. Produce test code for HLRs and LLRs. Execute (automated) tests. Verify all outputs	HLR test procedures, HLR test results, LLR test cases, LLR test procedures, LLR test results, verification results

items required for compliance with DO-178 are produced by other processes than software development and software verification. For example, the software configuration process produces the Software Configuration Index and the certification liaison process produces the Software Accomplishment Summary.

6.5 Remarks and Potential Issues

The proposed process aims to address some of the key challenges we identified in the survey, in particular challenges related to requirements management. Breaking work down in shorter iterations, including planning (Preparation) and evaluation (Closure) means that planning may be done using updated information from previous Sprints, and that each Sprint provides information needed to meet the requirements of DO-178 (in the form of data items). From related research we know that such a process needs to be supported by tools to automate test-driven development and documentation creation as much as possible in order to save time and to ensure quality and consistency [8].

Including agile approaches in the development process for avionics software promises the usually cited benefits such as frequent delivery of working software, including all data items required by DO-178, and the ability to deal with frequent changes in requirements. There are, however, also a number of potential issues.

Contrary to the waterfall model, or the V-model, HLRs are defined in batches; each time that the Preparation phase is entered, a sufficient number of HLRs are defined for the subsequent sequence of Sprints. Having no overview of the complete set of HLRs in an early phase of the development could lead to an inadequate software architecture that may need drastic (and therefore costly) revision during subsequent Preparation phases. This means that also agile projects needs to invest in a sufficient level of detail of HLRs and overall system architecture early. An agile process though may create better opportunities to manage changes when they occur.

Another issue is that the definition of derived HLRs late in the development, e.g., after several cycles of Preparation, Development, and Closure have taken place, may have consequences for the safety analysis [21]. For example, if derived HLRs imply new interfaces that falsify earlier independence claims, a higher software level could be required, creating additional (verification) work that could have been done more efficiently when known beforehand.

7 Conclusions and Further Work

The development of safety-critical software by the avionics industry is governed by RTCA document DO-178. The document places much emphasis on documented and traceable verification to achieve an acceptable level of confidence that the software development activities have been performed successfully. Indeed, our survey, among major players in the European avionics industry, confirmed that verification and certification constitutes a large portion of the total costs of development (estimated 40%). The survey also revealed other challenges perceived by this industry, including requirements volatility, late discovery of problems/defects, and project cost overruns.

The adoption of an agile framework could be a solution for these challenges; this is in line with other related safety-industry oriented research [7, 8]. At present, the lifecycle model mostly used by the avionics industry to organize software development is the V-model, or variants thereof. DO-178, however, does not preclude the use of any particular model, and in general, there seem to be no obstacles for adopting an agile framework. It is clear that agile methods, like Scrum, need to be adapted to fit in the development and certification of avionics software. In particular, such methods need to be extended to fulfil requirements of traceability and documentation. Some of these may be enabled by use of proper tools that provide a high level of automation.

Using Scrum as a basis, an approach has been outlined that benefits from agile methods and can also satisfy the objectives of DO-178. Some DO-178 objectives are achieved in an agile way, while others, in particular a subset of the verification objectives, are achieved by traditional means (management plans, reviews, and analyses). Benefits expected from the agile approach include reduction of risks, adaptability to changing requirements, and overall a reduction of development cost.

There are, however, issues that need further investigation. One of these is that software requirements are defined in batches; each time, sufficient software requirements are defined for the subsequent sequence of Sprints. Having no overview of the complete set of software requirements in an early phase of the development could lead to an inadequate software architecture that would need thorough revision later on.

To conclude, agile methods may promise to resolve some of the specific challenges in the avionics domain, but there is still a clear need for more research and industrial experimentation to verify applicability and to demonstrate improvement effects.

Acknowledgments. The authors would like to thank the anonymous contributors to the survey and Rob Udo from NLR for his contributions to this research. Also the insightful comments from the reviewers are much appreciated. The research leading to these results has received funding from the European Community's Seventh Framework Programme FP7/2012-2016 under grant agreement no. ACP2-GA-2013-605442.

References

1. Carlson, R., Turner, R.: Review of agile case studies for applicability to aircraft systems integration. Procedia Comput. Sci. **16**, 469–474 (2013)
2. Cawley, O., Wang, X., Richardson, I.: Lean/Agile software development methodologies in regulated environments – state of the art. In: Abrahamsson, P., Oza, N. (eds.) LESS 2010. LNBIP, vol. 65, pp. 31–36. Springer, Heidelberg (2010). doi:10.1007/978-3-642-16416-3_4
3. Chenu, E.: Agility and lean for avionics. In: Lean, Agile Approach to High-Integrity Software Conference, Paris (2009)
4. Chenu, E.: Agile and Lean software development for avionic software. Whitepaper, Thales Avionics (2011)
5. Coe, D.J., Kulick, J.H.: A model-based agile process for DO-178C certification. In: Proceedings of 2013 World Congress in Computer Science, Computer Engineering, and Applied Computing, Las Vegas (2013)
6. Dingsøyr, T., Nerur, S., Balijepally, V., Moe, N.B.: A decade of agile methodologies: towards explaining agile software development. J. Syst. Softw. **85**(6), 1213–1221 (2012)
7. Fitzgerald, B., Stol, K.-J., O'Sullivan, R., O'Brien, D.: Scaling agile methods to regulated environments: an industry case study. In: Proceedings of the 2013 International Conference on Software Engineering. IEEE Press (2013)
8. Hanssen, Geir K., Haugset, B., Stålhane, T., Myklebust, T., Kulbrandstad, I.: Quality assurance in scrum applied to safety critical software. In: Sharp, H., Hall, T. (eds.) XP 2016. LNBIP, vol. 251, pp. 92–103. Springer, Cham (2016). doi:10.1007/978-3-319-33515-5_8
9. Hantke, D.: An approach for combining spice and scrum in software development projects. In: Rout, T., O'Connor, R.V., Dorling, A. (eds.) SPICE 2015. CCIS, vol. 526, pp. 233–238. Springer, Cham (2015). doi:10.1007/978-3-319-19860-6_18
10. Hilderman, V.: DO-178B Costs Versus Benefits. HighRely Inc., HighRely Whitepaper (2009)
11. Knight, J.C.: Safety critical systems: challenges and directions. In: Proceedings of the 24rd International Conference on Software Engineering, ICSE 2002. IEEE (2002)
12. Lambourg, J., Comar, C.: Methodology: agile development of safety critical systems. OpenCoss Framework 7 project (2012)
13. Meunier, V., Destouesse, M., Cros, T.: How to "take credit" of agile principles within a certification context? (2008) (Presentation)
14. Myklebust, T., Stålhane, T., Hanssen, G., Wien, T., Haugset, B.: Scrum, documentation and the IEC 61508-3: 2010 software standard. In: International Conference on Probabilistic Safety Assesment and Management (PSAM). PSAM, Hawaii (2014)
15. Paige, Richard F., Charalambous, R., Ge, X., Brooke, Phillip J.: Towards agile engineering of high-integrity systems. In: Harrison, Michael D., Sujan, M.-A. (eds.) SAFECOMP 2008. LNCS, vol. 5219, pp. 30–43. Springer, Heidelberg (2008). doi:10.1007/978-3-540-87698-4_6
16. Paige, R.F., Galloway, A., Charalambous, R., Ge, X.: High-integrity agile processes for the development of safety critical software. Int. J. Crit. Comput.-Based Syst. **2**(2), 181–216 (2011)
17. Rottier, P.A., Rodrigues, V: Agile development in a medical device company. In: AGILE 2008 Conference (2008)
18. RTCA, DO-178C: Software considerations in airborne systems and equipment certification (2011)

19. Schwaber K.: SCRUM development process. In: Sutherland, J., Casanave, C., Miller, J., Patel, P., Hollowell, G. (eds.) Business Object Design and Implementation, pp. 117–134. Springer, London (1997). ISBN 978-3-540-76096-2
20. Stålhane, T., Myklebust, T., Hanssen, G.K.: The application of Scrum IEC 61508 certifiable software. In Proceedings of ESREL, Helsinki, Finland
21. VanderLeest, S.H., Buter, A.: Escape the waterfall: agile for aerospace. In: Proceedings of IEEE/AIAA 28th Digital Avionics Systems Conference, DASC 2009, p. 6, (6D3). IEEE (2009). doi:10.1109/DASC.2009.5347438
22. Wils, A., Baelen, S., Holvoet, T., Vlaminck, K.: Agility in the avionics software world. In: Abrahamsson, P., Marchesi, M., Succi, G. (eds.) XP 2006. LNCS, vol. 4044, pp. 123–132. Springer, Heidelberg (2006). doi:10.1007/11774129_13

Short Research Papers

Inoculating an Agile Company with User-Centred Design: An Empirical Study

Silvia Bordin[1(✉)] and Antonella De Angeli[1,2]

[1] Department of Information Engineering and Computer Science, University of Trento,
via Sommarive 9, 38123 Trento, Italy
{Silvia.bordin,antonella.deangeli}@unitn.it
[2] School of Computer Science, University of Lincoln, Brayford Pool, Lincoln, LN6 7TS, UK

Abstract. We present an empirical study on facilitating the adoption of user-centred design (UCD) in small Agile companies. To this end, we introduced a curated set of qualitative design practices in an Agile organisation, engaging developers in a lightweight series of workshops. Our results suggest that the approach followed enhanced internal communication and promoted a concrete shift towards a more user-centred perspective. However, the presence of a predominant non-Agile customer seems to have limited potential benefits.

Keywords: Qualitative research · Training developers · User-centred mindset

1 Introduction

Still in 2013, Moreno et al. stated that "the integration of usability engineering methods into software development life cycles is seldom realized in industrial settings" [11]. One reason for this is the "sheer lack of usability specialists in the industry" [5], which results in insufficient knowledge about the work of the end user [8] and in the so-called "developer mindset" [1], overly focused on technological aspects. Another issue relates to the limited suitability of most usability and UX methods for the Agile setting [15], with several authors [2, 4, 7] reporting a particular scarcity of lightweight practices for user involvement in development projects despite the benefits induced by the ability to perform usability and UX work in an agile context [4, 15]. In addition, even companies realising a need to increase the usability of their products may be unable to invest in the resources needed to achieve this [5], and this is particularly true in the case of small enterprises [1, 5].

To facilitate the adoption of user-centred design (UCD) in small Agile companies, we curated the identification of a small set of design techniques; we then planned an action research intervention for presenting them to developers and assessing the impact of these techniques on their working practices. A first iteration has been reported in [3], while a second iteration is reported here. Our results suggest that even such a lightweight approach may support the enactment of a user-centred mindset. However, the impact of the intervention has been limited by the relationship with a dominant customer resistant both to Agile and UCD: we conclude by pointing out the need both for researchers and

H. Baumeister et al. (Eds.): XP 2017, LNBIP 283, pp. 235–242, 2017.
DOI: 10.1007/978-3-319-57633-6_15

practitioners to investigate more effective ways to communicate the business benefits that the two approaches may bring.

2   Related Work

The term "user-centred design" denotes a broad set of techniques, methods, procedures and processes that places the user at the centre of an iterative design process [17]. The acknowledged benefits of involving users in systems design [e.g. 1] include improved quality and acceptance of the system, and cost saving [12]. Although promising to support "the execution of software development projects targeting the delivery of useful *and* usable software" [4], the integration of UCD and Agile development is however not trivial to achieve [e.g. 2] and limited empirical research exists on the topic [4, 7]. One of the ways to enact this integration, particularly in the limited-resource context of small enterprises, is "to use the software developers as a UX work resource by enhancing their qualifications within the field of usability and UX" [14], or in other words to train developers on usability techniques. Advantages include "the potential of easing problems regarding the lack of usability specialists in the industry" [5]; the chance for small companies to lessen "the need to staff usability specialists, which cannot be funded" [5]; a good fit with the Agile feature of team members being able to perform every given work task [13]. This is where we place our contribution.

We also point out, however, that also the customer needs to be supportive of the integration of UCD and Agile, allowing for a suitable design to be researched [2] and for adequate access to users. Scepticism is more frequent in large customers [10] and may result in a lack of customer engagement, which can be a big challenge for development teams [10] especially given the relevance placed on the customer by the Agile philosophy. The solution may require the capability of demonstrating business value, management support, and nurturing a change of mindset and culture in the customer [9]: how to effectively communicate this has however remained largely an open point to date.

3   Action Research Intervention

The activities described here were carried out in "the Company", a branch of a large Italian IT group providing cyber security and network configuration services to the largest telecommunication operators of the country. The Company had long adopted Agile successfully, and had one main customer, a large telecommunication provider that we will call "the Telco". Being the Telco a much larger venture, the power relationship between the two parties was naturally asymmetrical, although generally warm. However, the Telco is also a highly structured corporate, whose constrained workflow prevents a full implementation of Agile in the projects followed by the Company, and where some representatives seem to oppose contacts between the Company and final users of their software. While trying to reduce their dependency from the Telco, the Company realised that they were lacking sufficient skills in usability and interface design, and that this could be an issue in proposing their products to fresh customers; therefore, they asked for our help.

3.1   Method

We followed the Cooperative Method Development approach, a "domain specific adaptation of action research" that moves from an ethnographically-inspired understanding of the "existing practice of software development in concrete industrial settings" and aims at improving such practice by cooperating with practitioners [6].

Design techniques presented to developers were chosen to overcome potential communication breakdowns in the integration of UCD and Agile [2], and to reflect surveys on the usability techniques most used in industry [e.g. 14], particularly accounting for their feasibility of integration into an Agile environment and of teaching non-UX professionals. These methods include low-fidelity prototyping, usability testing, personas, expert evaluations, and user task analyses. We remark that this intervention is meant for "supporting developers during ongoing day-to-day product development" [13] and that "we do not discard the need for a usability expert" [8].

3.2   Preliminary Understanding

The first author interviewed developers in June 2016 about their perception of the working environment, their current working practices, and their attitude towards UCD-related themes. The interview study lasted two days and involved 7 people. For what concerns the organisational setting, the Company employs about 20 people, mostly young graduate developers, and exhibits a pretty flat hierarchy. The environment is predominantly technical, yet with a positive and rather curious attitude towards UCD-related themes, to the point that employees explicitly argued in favour of the collaboration with our University in front of the group managers, who tend to adopt a more "command and control" approach instead.

The Company proposed to focus on what we will call the Software (a desktop application used to configure and monitor networking devices for corporate customers of Telco) as a running example during the intervention, for a variety of reasons: it is entirely developed within the Company for Telco; it has evolved over several years as the juxtaposition of different parts, and would now need a refactoring; being one of the main projects of the Company, it is sufficiently well known to all employees.

3.3   Implementation

In August 2016 a series of four workshops, each lasting a whole day, was carried out at the Company site. The agenda of workshops is outlined in Fig. 1 and was grounded on different elements: on a practical level, we accounted for the results of preliminary interviews and for the feedback from our previous iteration of a similar series of workshops [3]; on a more theoretical level, we accounted for the stages of the traditional UCD lifecycle, and the set of focal points to consider in the integration of UCD and Agile development [2], namely the extent of user and customer involvement, the role of documentation, the synchronisation of design and development iterations, and ownership over UX tasks.

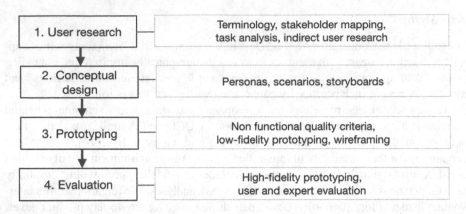

Fig. 1. Workshops overview.

Three developers (who will be referenced as D1 to D3) were appointed to attend the whole workshop cycle, led by the first author in the role of a facilitator. All of them expressed great interest in user-related themes: D1 was self-taught on UCD techniques, while D2 and D3 were not familiar at all with them.

"One doesn't even know where to start from, without knowing any basics" (D3)
"More than once [design choices] have been a stab in the dark" (D1)
"If there's one skill in the Company we are really lacking it is interface design … we try to do what we can" (D2)

Workshops started by motivating more formally the advantages of adopting UCD, that is by presenting well-known reports from industry [e.g. 18] highlighting user involvement as a key factor for project success, and in contrast the lack of it as one of the most common reasons for failure. We then considered the workflow supported by the Software, illustrated in a very technology-centred way in its user manual, and guided participants in re-elaborating it focusing on the perspective of users. In collaboration with the facilitator, participants then outlined the stakeholder network related to the Software, which confirmed how the needs of actual users were generally mediated when reported to the Company, if collected at all. A task analysis was then performed for actors most likely to interact significantly with the Software, and was represented through use-case diagrams. The project manager was chosen as the reference user: information on the characteristics of Software users in this role was retrieved indirectly, i.e. through LinkedIn and narratives of other Company employees, and then expressed through a couple of personas representing different levels of expertise; these in turn inspired scenarios and storyboards.

Once a reference persona was chosen, participants rated the dimensions of usability listed in [12] through poker planning, regarding them as non-functional quality criteria for the Software. Participants then elaborated different low-fidelity prototypes for a specific interface of the Software; however, a later inspection revealed that these alternatives could not support the same workflow articulation as the existing interface. Hence, since the latter was anyway rather complex, participants asked for support in wireframing a more logical re-grouping of its functionalities.

Finally, the different purposes of low- and high-fidelity prototypes and how to communicate them were illustrated, since D1 repeatedly pointed out that Telco would not accept discussing over a "non serious" low-fidelity prototype and that previous attempts at doing this had failed. In addition, a session of user testing was simulated on the ERP system in use at the Company for demonstrative purposes. After the end of the intervention, participants organised a wrap-up session and, a few weeks later, a dissemination seminar for their colleagues.

3.4   Evaluation

In December 2016, an external researcher interviewed participants about what they remembered of proposed techniques after a few months and whether they felt that their approach to design and development had changed. Interviews were loosely transcribed and thematically analysed. Overall, participants positively welcomed our intervention, regarding it as a chance of professional growth. They appreciated having learnt concrete techniques, and remembered them correctly:

"I enjoyed wireframing a lot. It really gave me a different point of view" (D1)
"We should organise the info with wireframes, the poor user will be scared" (D3)

In addition, they expressed appreciation also for the presence of a trainer, reiterating the effectiveness of scaffolding [19]:

"In terms of common sense, this is what every developer should do. Yet having someone explaining you the steps to follow is something different" (D2)
"Now I have a method"(D3)

The training seems in fact to have contributed to enacting a shift from a technology-focused mindset to a more user-centred one:

"Before we used to say – [the user] will have to get over it" "The interface as the means to achieve an objective from the user's point of view" "The goal is to remove the need for a manual – even for us as developers!" (D3)
"We'll surely follow this approach rather than – bah, let's just do something" "I have been assigned to a project where the interface is set in stone [by Telco], BUT [developers and management] all agree that we are going to apply UCD techniques at the first suitable occasion" (D2)

D2 and D3 in fact claimed to have applied proposed techniques as much as possible to the improvement of minor parts of the Software interface that had been assigned to them, and to have used them to support communication with colleagues:

"Prototypes and scenarios can be used internally to understand how to design something [...] I proposed some prototypes to my colleagues and this simplified the discussion" "In my opinion personas should be shared by the whole team... to raise awareness among colleagues" (D3)

Participants also commented on the positive attitude shown by the rest of the Company at the end of the dissemination seminar they led:

"We reported to the rest of the Company and the reaction was – let's hope we will soon have projects where to apply this approach" (D2)

Despite the satisfaction and interest shown, participants did not believe the approach would prove fully applicable in the interaction with their customer due to the strong "developer mindset" [1] of Telco's representatives, even harder to overcome due to the unbalanced power relationship with the Company:

> *"Personas cannot be used with Telco: our customer is very much feature-oriented and in a dominant position [...] it does not want to see the prototype, it wants to see the product" "Some techniques will be more applicable than others, because it is impossible to access users [...] We have no [user] feedback. Clearly we miss it"* (D1)
>
> *"I guess the customer would be disappointed by storyboards on paper [...] it may think we did not put too much effort into such a proposal"* (D3)

4   Discussion

In terms of the applicability of the presented approach to other small enterprises, we suggest that, together with the Company's "culture receptive to UCD" [2], developers' consolidated familiarity with Agile (including being used to change and flexibility, iteration, and frequent interaction with the customer) may have allowed a deeper appropriation of UX techniques, resulting in a potentially sustained impact over working practices. Furthermore, participants demonstrated an accurate recall of techniques and of their rationale, and reported a spontaneous sharing of their learning with colleagues, applying proposed techniques whenever possible to support interface design and internal discussion. This reflects claims in [16], where Agile and UCD-inspired practices are considered to have a positive impact on mutual understanding and communication; moreover, these factors suggest that even a lightweight intervention such as the one described in this paper may support the enactment of a more user-centred mindset. This can constitute a first step for the organisation towards the awareness of the benefits of integrating UCD, providing elements to decide whether to proceed in developers' UX training or to hire a specialist designer.

The impact of proposed techniques seems however to have been limited by the Company doing Agile in a non-Agile environment, where this label includes both the culture of the parent group and of the Telco. We argue that the same challenges encountered in this setting [9, 10] can be found when introducing UCD in an environment not accustomed to it. We envision as future work the evaluation of the set of UCD techniques in an Agile company whose customer is also Agile: this would be the most favourable context. In conclusion, we point out to the research and practitioners' community that there is still a lack of suitable ways to clearly communicate to reluctant customers the potential benefits of Agile and UCD [10].

Acknowledgments. We thank Angela Di Fiore for collaborating in the evaluation interviews, and our participants and the whole Company for their welcoming and kind support. This work has been possible thanks to the funding granted by the Italian Ministry of Education, University and Research (MIUR) through the project "Città Educante", project code CTN01_00034_393801.

References

1. Ardito, C., Buono, P., Caivano, D., Costabile, M.F., Lanzilotti, R.: Investigating and promoting UX practice in industry: an experimental study. Int. J. Hum. Comput. Stud. **72**(6), 542–551 (2014)
2. Bordin, S., De Angeli, A.: Focal points for a more user-centred agile development. In: Sharp, H., Hall, T. (eds.) XP 2016. LNBIP, vol. 251, pp. 3–15. Springer, Cham (2016). doi: 10.1007/978-3-319-33515-5_1
3. Bordin, S., De Angeli, A.: Supporting cooperative work by integrating user-centred design and agile development. Submitted at the European Conference on Computer-Supported Cooperative Work (2016)
4. Brhel, M., Meth, H., Maedche, A., Werder, K.: Exploring principles of user-centered agile software development: a literature review. Inf. Softw. Technol. **61**, 163–181 (2015)
5. Bruun, A.: Training software developers in usability engineering: a literature review. In: Proceedings of the 6th Nordic Conference on Human-Computer Interaction: Extending Boundaries. ACM (2010)
6. Dittrich, Y., Rönkkö, K., Eriksson, J., Hansson, C., Lindeberg, O.: Cooperative method development. Empirical Softw. Eng. **13**(3), 231–260 (2008)
7. Dybå, T., Dingsøyr, T.: Empirical studies of agile software development: a systematic review. Inf. Softw. Technol. **50**(9), 833–859 (2008)
8. Eriksson, E., Cajander, Å., Gulliksen, J.: Hello world! – experiencing usability methods without usability expertise. In: Gross, T., Gulliksen, J., Kotzé, P., Oestreicher, L., Palanque, P., Prates, R.O., Winckler, M. (eds.) INTERACT 2009. LNCS, vol. 5727, pp. 550–565. Springer, Heidelberg (2009). doi:10.1007/978-3-642-03658-3_60
9. Gregory, P., Barroca, L., Sharp, H., Deshpande, A., Taylor, K.: The challenges that challenge: engaging with agile practitioners' concerns. Inf. Softw. Technol. **77**, 92–104 (2016)
10. Hoda, R., Noble, J., Marshall, S.: The impact of inadequate customer collaboration on self-organizing agile teams. Inf. Softw. Technol. **53**(5), 521–534 (2011)
11. Moreno, A.M., Seffah, A., Capilla, R., Sanchez-Segura, M.-I.: HCI practices for building usable software. Computer **46**(4), 100–102 (2013)
12. Nielsen, J.: Usability Engineering. Morgan Kaufmann, San Francisco (1994)
13. Øvad, T., Bornoe, N., Larsen, L.B., Stage, J.: Teaching software developers to perform UX tasks. In: Proceedings of the Annual Meeting of the Australian Special Interest Group for Computer Human Interaction, pp. 397–406. ACM (2015)
14. Øvad, T., Larsen, L.B.: The prevalence of UX design in agile development processes in industry. In: Agile Conference (AGILE), pp. 40–49. IEEE (2015)
15. Øvad, T., Larsen, L.B.: How to reduce the UX bottleneck–train your software developers. Behav. Inf. Technol. **35**(12), 1080–1090 (2016)
16. Pikkarainen, M., Haikara, J., Salo, O., Abrahamsson, P., Still, J.: The impact of agile practices on communication in software development. Empirical Softw. Eng. **13**(3), 303–337 (2008)
17. Rogers, Y., Sharp, H., Preece, J.: Interaction Design: Beyond Human-Computer Interaction. John Wiley & Sons, Hoboken (2011)
18. The Standish Group CHAOS Report (2014). https://www.projectsmart.co.uk/white-papers/chaos-report.pdf
19. Vygotsky, L.S.: Mind in Society: The Development of Higher Psychological Processes. Harvard University Press, Cambridge (1980)

242   S. Bordin and A. De Angeli

On the Usage and Benefits of Agile Methods & Practices

A Case Study at Bosch Chassis Systems Control

Philipp Diebold[1(✉)] and Udo Mayer[2]

[1] Fraunhofer Institute for Experimental Software Engineering, Fraunhofer-Platz 1,
67663 Kaiserslautern, Germany
philipp.diebold@iese.fraunhofer.de
[2] Bosch Chassis Systems Control, Robert-Bosch-Allee 1, 74232 Abstatt, Germany
udo.mayer@de.bosch.com

Abstract. Since software became a major part of the car, we were interested in identifying which agile practices are used and adapted at Bosch automotive. Therefore, we conducted a multi-case study with nine interviews from five Bosch projects. Our results showed a strong focus on Scrum. Most of the Scrum practices are adapted due to the specific project context. Practices from other agile methods, e.g. XP, are used and adapted as well. We further collected the benefits of the practices, most often resulting in improved transparency and planning. The results are used to support automotive projects in selecting and applying agile practices according to their specific process improvement goals.

Keywords: Automotive · Agile practices · Scrum deviations · Case study

1 Introduction

Within software engineering, agile development has shown to be a commonly used approach [8, 9, 12]. Since embedded domains struggle with the integration of different disciplines, e.g. hardware and electronics, there is a lot more communication necessary [11]. These domains are currently using agile only to some extent in order to profit from the benefits of agile development, e.g. shorter time-to-market. This was one of the major reasons for Bosch Chassis Systems Control (CC) to become more agile. Thus, the state of agile in projects is interesting. Knowledge about usage, adaptations of Agile Methods and Practices, and their benefits should help spreading of agile.

2 Chassis Systems Control of the Bosch Group

The division CC is part of the business sector Mobility Solutions of the Bosch Group. The business sector Mobility Solution generated sales of 41.7 billion euros in 2015 (Bosch Group in total: 70.6 billion euros) which makes the Bosch Group to one of the world's largest automotive suppliers. The division CC develops and manufactures innovative components, functions and systems that are designed to make driving a safe and

H. Baumeister et al. (Eds.): XP 2017, LNBIP 283, pp. 243–250, 2017.
DOI: 10.1007/978-3-319-57633-6_16

comfortable experience. The projects of this study are developing systems for (highly) automated driving, e.g. a highway pilot.

3   Study Design

Research Questions. Our objective is to better understand the usage, reasons and adaptions as well as benefits of agile methods and practices within Bosch CC. Thus, we ended up with the following research questions: RQ1 - Which agile elements (incl. agile methods and agile practices [3]) are used? RQ2 - How is the usage of the agile practice deviating from the textbooks? RQ3 - What are the benefits of the agile practices?

Case and Subject Selection. Possible cases (Bosch CC projects) and subjects (interviewees) were identified by Bosch based on the organizational scope and their usage of agility. The latter was mandatory for participation. We identified 15 candidates representing five projects. Nine of the 15 candidates participated, covering all five projects.

Data Collection Procedure. We conducted structured interviews with the participants, seven face-to-face and two via phone. The questions were categorized into (1) introduction, (2) usage and (3) benefits of agile elements (first methods, then practices), and (4) project context. The principal author conducted all interviews as follows: He explained the idea and reason behind this study, the data collection, and the guaranteed anonymity. He asked for used agile methods and agile practices. He discussed about the experienced impacts, mainly benefits of the different elements. During the gathering of the benefits, we were open to any mentioned benefits. If they had no idea, we named potential benefits as triggers. For not biasing them, the interviewees had to give examples for these benefit triggers. We ended up in a coded list of the benefits (cf. Table 2).

Analysis Procedure. We analyzed the notes of the interviews qualitatively. First, we extracted the data from each interview (usage of agile elements, where and how, and their benefits). Second, we compared and aggregated information from interviews related to the same project. Third, we compared the project-aggregated results among each other and with our experience and literature.

4   Results

We covered different team sizes and developed functions and considered different roles of the interviewees: group leaders, department leaders, project leaders/managers (cf. Table 1). Two participants performed the Scrum Master role.

4.1   RQ1: Usage of Agile Methods and Practices

Four Agile Methods were used by the projects: Scrum (n = 4 projects), Flow (n = 2), iPeP (n = 1), and SAFe (n = 1). The practices that were used in **all five projects** belong to Scrum, namely Sprint, Backlog, Sprint Planning, and Daily Stand-Ups, although one

Table 1. Project characteristics

Project	Size	Locations	Project phase [6]	Participating roles
P1	60 persons, 7 sub-teams	2 in Germany	Pre-development	system project lead
P2	8 teams	1 in Germany, Europe, Asia each	Pre-development	technical project lead & project lead
P3	33 persons	2 in Germany	Series development	project lead & team lead
P4	8 persons	1 in Germany	Pre-development	Group lead
P5	70 persons	1 in Germany, Europe, Asia each	Pre-development	project lead, SW project lead & department lead

project reported that it is not using Scrum. The practices that were used in **most projects** were Sprint Review, Sprint Retrospective, Burndown-charts, Definition of Done, Scrum Master, and Product Owner (PO) (all Scrum), and User Stories and Epics (both XP). Continuous Integration, Release Planning and Scrum-of-Scrums completed the set. The practices that were used in **few projects** were: Planning Poker and Pair Programming (both XP), 80%-rule and Pull-system (both Lean/Flow), and Backlog Grooming (Scrum). In Table 2, we show the use of agile practices.

Table 2. Benefits of used agile practices on goals (numbers indicate how many projects mentioned a benefit)

(numbers indicate how many projects mentioned a benefit)

Agile Practice	understandability	knowledge transfer	communication	transparency	feedback	satisfaction	team empowerment	focusing	structuredness	planning	time-to-market	risk management	# adressed benefits	# using projects
Daily Stand-Up			3	5					2				3	4
Sprint				2			1	2	1			1	5	5
Sprint Review	1		2	1					1				4	4
Retrospective		1			1	1							3	4
Sprint Planning						1				4		1	3	5
Backlog	1		2					1	1				4	5
Burndown-Charts			3										1	4
Scrum Master							1	1					2	4
Product Owner			1					1	1				3	4
80%-Rule								1		2		2	3	2
Planning Poker							1			2			2	1
User Stories								1					1	4
Epics										3			1	3
Cont. Integration			2								1		2	3
Scrum-of-Scrums			4	1				1	1				4	3
# practices	**2**	**1**	**3**	**8**	**1**	**3**	**3**	**2**	**4**	**10**	**1**	**3**		

4.2   RQ2: Deviations of Agile Practices

The used practices are now discussed regarding their deviations from existing guidelines, e.g. the Scrum Guide:

The major issue of the **Scrum Master** was the manifestation as "caretaker", e.g. in one team the Scrum Master was only inviting for the different Scrum meetings. Further, often the Scrum Master was not the only role. Being a project leader or a PO in combination might result in a conflict of interests. The **PO** also deals with the aspect of several roles by one person without problems. But some teams defined an additional "feature responsible", which covered POs tasks, e.g. breaking down the features into Stories. Finally, within one project, they struggled with the issue of having a Chief-PO communicating with the customer high-level, but not knowing the requirements in detail.

The most deviating aspect of **sprints** was their length. For one project (needing four weeks) more than two weeks were necessary for the integration of hardware aspects. Another one worked with varying lengths over time.

The **Scrum-of-Scrums** meetings conducted weekly by the larger teams or projects was in one case a team-meeting in which all project members participated. In another case, it was conducted by the project lead to keep the offshore team on track.

The **Daily Stand-Ups** deviated in three different aspects: (1) Usage only for status-tracking purpose, (2) Meetings lasting up to one hour, (3) Frequency of the meeting: Instead of every day, teams conducted it every other day, every three days, once a week, or unregularly. An extended duration of the meeting (one hour) was the consequence.

Sprint Planning: Within the sprint shift (Review, Retrospective, and upcoming Planning), most of the teams performed all three meetings en-block in about three days. In one of the larger teams, they found a solution to break down the Backlog to the teams by the PO. The planning itself was conducted within the single teams without the PO.

Sprint Review: The composition of meeting participants ranged from meetings without the customer and only with the team leaders and functional owners up to an "open event". Some meetings were unstructured without agenda or open topic list. Others were not conducted as an "acceptance meeting" with stakeholders or PO.

Sprint Retrospective: This meeting varied within the timing: One team performed it every other sprint, because two weeks were too short to resolve impediments. Another team directly resolved smaller impediments during the meetings. One interviewee mentioned that the retrospective was only weakly defined and valued within their team.

Within the **Backlog**, two major variations existed: Some included prioritization, whereas other did not. Different backlogs were used, from team-, project- or overall backlogs up to release backlogs. These kinds also contained various backlog items, e.g. User Stories vs. Epics. Two teams did not use **User Stories** as prescribed by the given templates, since they were not used to it and needed more information.

Planning Poker: One team used this practice for estimating the granularity-level to refine the story or not. Furthermore, not all teams used "story points" as values, but e.g. person hours or days. Finally, one deviation was that in one team just the "key player" (a senior developer or feature responsible) decided on the estimation value.

Within the **80%-Rule**, one interviewee mentioned that they are not considering it for the workload, but on their throughput. In the only case using the **pull-principle**, the responsibility regarding the different functions was clear such that it was "obvious who is going to pull what". Thus, sometimes one team member just "assigned" the tasks.

4.3 RQ3: Benefits of Agile Practices

Most of the considered agile practices are beneficial for *planning* (10 practices) and *transparency* (8), followed by *structuredness* (4), *communication, risk management, satisfaction,* and *team empowerment* (each 3). Checking the overall number of addressed benefits per practice (cf. Table 2), e.g. the highest with five is the sprint, three yield four benefits, and five yield three benefits.

Except for the Definition of Done and the Backlog Grooming, we could gather at least one impact for each of the Scrum practices. Considering the Scrum meetings, except the retrospective, all impact *planning*. Sprint Review as well as the Stand-Ups also influence *communication* and *transparency*. The Sprint Retrospective was the only practice dealing with *feedback* and *knowledge transfer*. The Burndown-Chart is a quite good mechanism for *transparency*. Both Scrum roles impact the *team empowerment*. The improved *satisfaction* resulting from the Scrum Master correspond with that. The PO provides *transparency* as well as *planning* aspects. Considering the Non-Scrum practices, there is information about the impact of six practices: *Risk management, planning* and *structuredness* were impacted by the 80%-Rule. Planning Poker increases *planning* and *team empowerment*. User Stories and Epics influence *planning* (Epics) or *focusing* (User Stories). Continuous Integration improves *transparency* and *time-to-market*. Finally, Scrum-of-Scrums was quite good for *communication* and it affects *transparency, structuredness,* and *planning*.

5   Related Works and Discussion

Distribution/Frequency of Agile Practices. Within VersionOne [12], the most used agile practices were Daily Stand-Ups, prioritized Backlogs, short Iterations (=Sprints), Retrospective, Iteration Planning, and Release Planning. All of them were used by at least one project, except for the Release Planning. For the other practices mentioned by [12], there are some differences: The Sprint Reviews are used less often than in our study, whereas, Continuous Integration is more common. Focusing on agile practices, Kumos [9] reports that almost all of the top six used agile practices are Scrum practices, all used by the Bosch projects. Scrum is also the prevalent agile method in automotive [8]. Similar to our results, the Planning, Daily Stand-Ups, Review, and Retrospective are used. We cannot confirm that the Sprint Review is used less often. In our study it was the Retrospective.

Deviations of Agile Practices. A prior study on Scrum variations [1] showed similar patterns, with the Scrum Master and PO given to people already owing a role, e.g. developer or team lead. However, within our cases most of the Scrum roles were staffed. Considering the 15–30 min of the Daily Stand-Ups, this timeframe is exceeded by some cases and extended up to one hour. The frequency deviation of the Stand-Up is also common [1]. For the sprint length variance from two to four weeks could be confirmed. Only one project reasonably decided to have four weeks due to synchronizations of teams and disciplines such as hardware and software.

Benefits of Agile Practices. Considering the benefits reported by [12], we see some similarities: The benefits *increased team productivity, improved project visibility, increased team moral/motivation, better delivery predictability*, and *reduced project risk* can directly be mapped to the ones reported to us. In contrast, the benefits dealing with engineering and quality, such as *enhancing software quality, software maintainability*, or *improving engineering discipline*, were not mentioned within our interviews. Compared to [9], five of nine benefits were also mentioned by our participants: *transparency, customer orientation, timing, teamwork*, and *employee motivation*. The results of [9] (similar to [12]) additionally showed *quality* as highly impacted, not indicated by our results.

Besides these studies, there are some practices studied in detail with their different impacts, e.g. User Stories [4], Planning Poker [5] or Pair Programming [7]. Furthermore, some studies analyzed which agile practice influence one specific benefit, e.g. [10] dealing with communication: Daily Stand-Ups improve *communication* and *transparency*, due to keeping developers, project leaders, and customers aware of the status. Iteration Planning created awareness of the *project plan* and iteration goals, whereas the Retrospective was a good way for working on *process improvement*. Even if we consider the benefits on a more fine-granular level, the results confirm each other.

6   Validity of the Results

An interview guideline and data collection sheet eased aggregation and comparisons. The guideline reduced the risk of misinterpretation and increased the objectivity. We could not recognize any misunderstanding, since all interview participants were aware of the common concepts, methods and practices. Additionally, we experienced that assuring anonymity led the interviewees to answer openly. Regarding the interviewed people within a project, we selected independent ones (not from the same team). Thus, our data is a representative sample of agile development in the area of autonomous driving. Within the data analysis, the aggregation of interview data within one project was the most difficult and error-prone, because of considering different project roles and teams with their viewpoints into one data set. The IESE and Bosch team discussed the aggregated results involving colleagues for an external point of view. We provided a summary report of the results via e-mail and gathered the feedback. We also performed a presentation and discussion session with all participants. That our qualitative results from Bosch CC are in line with most of the related work is another strong indicator for their validity.

7   Conclusions and Future Work

Within this paper, we present the results of an interview series covering five different automotive projects at Bosch CC with overall nine interviews on the topic of usage, deviation, and benefits of single agile practices.

The usage of agile methods as well as the underlying agile practices shows a similar picture as common studies. The most commonly used method is Scrum, which is adapted and extended by other practices. There seem to be similar variations of agile practices in the automotive domain as in information systems. Our study could confirm some of the benefits mentioned by other agile surveys, and could provide further answers to the question, which agile practice provides what specific benefits, and furthermore, that agile practices overall are most beneficial for *transparency* and *planning*.

Within future work, we intend to use the elicited data to instantiate the Agile Capability Analysis [2] for Bosch CC, a goal-oriented SPI approach using agile practices. The next step will be the integration of A-SPICE® and connection to the agile practices.

Acknowledgements.   We thank all interviewees for their time, participation, and openness. We also thank A. Schmitt, T. Zehler, S. Theobald and Dr. P. Fröhlich for providing feedback.

References

1. Diebold, P., Ostberg, J.-P., Wagner, S., Zendler, U.: What do practitioners vary in using scrum? In: Lassenius, C., Dingsøyr, T., Paasivaara, M. (eds.) XP 2015. LNBIP, vol. 212, pp. 40–51. Springer, Cham (2015). doi:10.1007/978-3-319-18612-2_4
2. Diebold, P., Zehler. T.: The agile practice impact model. In: Proceedings of ICSSP 2015. ACM (2015)
3. Diebold, P., Zehler, T.: The right degree of agility in rich processes. In: Kuhrmann, M., Münch, J., Richardson, I., Rausch, A., Zhang, H. (eds.) Managing Software Process Evolution, pp. 15–37. Springer, Cham (2016). doi:10.1007/978-3-319-31545-4_2
4. O'hEocha, C., Conboy, K.: The role of the user story agile practice in innovation. In: Abrahamsson, P., Oza, N. (eds.) LESS 2010. LNBIP, vol. 65, pp. 20–30. Springer, Heidelberg (2010). doi:10.1007/978-3-642-16416-3_3
5. Haugen, N.: An empirical study of using planning poker for user story estimation. In: Proceedings of AGILE 2006, pp. 23–34. IEEE (2006)
6. Hirz, M., Dietrich, W., Gfrerrer, A., Lang, J.: Overview of virtual product development. In: Hirz, M., Dietrich, W., Gfrerrer, A., Lang, J. (eds.) Integrated Computer-Aided Design in Automotive Development, pp. 25–50. Springer, Heidelberg (2013)
7. Hulkko, H., Abrahamsson, P.: A multiple case study on the impact of pair programming on product quality. In: Proceedings of ICSE 2005, pp 495–504. ACM (2005)
8. Kugler Maag CIE. Agile in Automotive – State of the Practice (2015)
9. Kumos, A.: Status Quo Agile 2014. University of Applied Science Koblenz (2014)
10. Pikkarainen, M., Haikara, J., Salo, O., Abrahamson, P., Still, J.: The impact of agile practices on communication in SW development. ESEJ **13**(3), 303–337 (2008). Springer
11. Shen, M., Yang, W., Rong, G., Shao, D.: Applying agile methods to embedded software development: a systematic review. In: Proceedings of SEES 2012, pp. 30–36. IEEE (2012)
12. VersionOne: The 10th annual State of Agile Report (2016)

Checklists to Support Test Charter Design in Exploratory Testing

Ahmad Nauman Ghazi[✉], Ratna Pranathi Garigapati, and Kai Petersen

Blekinge Institute of Technology, Karlskrona, Sweden
{nauman.ghazi,kai.petersen}@bth.se, pranathi.r8@gmail.com

Abstract. During exploratory testing sessions the tester simultaneously learns, designs and executes tests. The activity is iterative and utilizes the skills of the tester and provides flexibility and creativity. Test charters are used as a vehicle to support the testers during the testing. The aim of this study is to support practitioners in the design of test charters through checklists. We aimed to identify factors allowing practitioners to critically reflect on their designs and contents of test charters to support practitioners in making informed decisions of what to include in test charters. The factors and contents have been elicited through interviews. Overall, 30 factors and 35 content elements have been elicited.

Keywords: Exploratory testing · Session-based test management · Test charter · Test mission

1 Introduction

James Bach defines exploratory testing as simultaneous learning, test design and test execution [3]. Existing literature reflects that ET is widely used for testing complex systems as well and is perceived to be flexible in all types of test levels, activities and phases [7,13]. In the context of quality, ET has amassed a good amount of evidence on overall defect detection effectiveness, cost effectiveness and high performance for detecting critical defects [1,9–11,13]. Session-based test management (SBTM) is an enhancement to ET. SBTM incorporates planning, structuring, guiding and tracking the test effort with good tool support when conducting ET [4].

A test charter is a clear mission for the test session and a high level plan that determines what should be tested, how it should be tested and the associated limitations. A tester interacts with the product to accomplish a test mission or charter and further reports the results [3]. The charter does not pre-specify the detailed test cases which are executed in each session. But, a total set of charters for an entire project generally include everything that is reasonably testable. The metrics gathered during the session are used to track down the testing process more closely and to make instant reports to management [11]. Specific charters demand more effort in their design whilst providing better focus. A test session often begins with a charter which forms the first part of the scannable session

H. Baumeister et al. (Eds.): XP 2017, LNBIP 283, pp. 251–258, 2017.
DOI: 10.1007/978-3-319-57633-6_17

sheet or the reviewable result. Normally, a test charter includes the mission statement and the areas to be tested in its design.

Overall, the empirical evidence of how test charters are designed and how to achieve high quality test charters are designed are scarce. High quality test charters are useful, accurate, efficient, adaptable, clear, usable, compliant, and feasible [4]. In this study we make a first step towards understanding test charter design by exploring the factors influencing the design choices, and the elements that could be included in a test charter. This provides the foundation for further studies investigating which elements actually lead to the quality criteria described by Bach [4]. We make the following contributions:

C1: Identify and categorize the influential factors that practitioners consider when designing test charters.

C2: Identify and categorize the possible elements of a test charter.

The remainder of the paper is structured as follows: Sect. 2 presents the related work. Section 3 outlines the research method, followed by the results in Sect. 4. Finally, in Sect. 5, we present the conclusions of this study.

2   Related Work

Test charters, which are an SBTM element plays a major role in guiding inexperienced testers. The charter is a test plan which is usually generated from a test strategy. The charters include ideas that guide the testers as they test. These ideas are partially documented and are subject to change as the project evolves [4]. SBTM echoes the actions of testers who are well experienced in testing and charters play a key role in guiding the inexperienced testers by providing them with details regarding the aspects and actions involved in the particular test session [2].

The context of the test session plays a great role in determining the design of test plan or the charter [4]. Key steps to achieve context awareness are, for example, understanding the project members and the way they are affected by the charter, and understanding work constraints and resources. When designing charters Bach [4] formulated specific goals, in particular finding significant tests quicker, improving quality, and increasing testing efficiency.

The sources that inspire the design of test charters are manifold (cf. [4,8,12]), such as risks, product analysis, requirements, and questions raised by stakeholders. Mission statements, test priorities, risk areas, test logistics, and how to test are example elements of a test charter design identified from the literature review and their description [1,4,6]. Our study will further complement the contents of test charters as they are used in practice.

3   Research Method

Study Purpose and Research Questions: The goal of this study is to investigate the design of test charters and the factors influencing the design of these charters and their contents.

RQ1: What are the factors influencing the design of test charters? The factors provide the contextual information that is important to consider when designing test charters, and complements the research on context aware testing [4].

RQ2: What do practitioners include in their test charters? The checklist of contents supports practitioners to make informed decisions about which contents to include without overlooking relevant ones.

Interviews: Interviews (three face-to-face and six through Skype) were conducted with a total of nine industry practitioners through convenience sampling combined with choosing experienced subjects who are visible in the communities discussing ET (see Table 1).

Table 1. Profile of the Interviewees

Interview ID	Role	Experience in testing	Organizational size
1	Senior systems test engineer	4 years	More than 500
2	Test quality architect	10 years	50–500
3	Test specialist	10 years	50–500
4	Test consultant	12 years	More than 500
5	Test strategist	3 years	Less than 50
6	CEO, Test consultant	30 years	More than 500
7	Test manager	20 years	More than 500
8	CEO, Test lead	4 years	50–500
9	Test quality manager	13 years	50–500

The interviews were semi-structured, following the structure outlined below:

1. *Introduction to research and researcher:* The researchers provide a brief introduction about themselves, followed by a brief description on the research objectives.
2. *Collection of general information:* In this stage, the information related to the interviewee is collected.
3. *Collection of research related information:* This is the last stage where the factors and contents of test charters have been elicited.

Data analysis: All the interviews were recorded by consent of the interviewees and later transcribed manually. The qualitative data collected using literature review and interviews was later analyzed using thematic analysis [5]. After thoroughly studying the coded data, similar codes have been grouped to converge their meaning to form a single definite code.

Validity: The potential bias introduced by interviewing thought leaders and experienced people in the area who are favorable towards exploratory testing may bias the results, and hence may not be fully generalizable. Though, we have not put any value on the factors and contents elicited, and they may be utilized differently depending on context. That is, identifying the potential elements to

254 A.N. Ghazi et al.

include in test charters is the first step needed. To reduce the threat multiple interviews have been used. Using a systematic approach to data analysis (thematic analysis) also aids in reducing this threat.

4 Results

RQ1: What are the factors influencing the design of test charters? Based on interviews with test practitioners, 30 different factors have been identified (see Table 2). The table provides the name of the factors as well as a short description of what the factor means.

We categorized the factors and identified the following emerging categories, namely:

- *Customer and requirements factors:* These factors characterize the customer and their requirements. They include: F01: Client Requirements, F10: Business Usecase, F15: Quality requirements, F27: Client location, and F30: User Journey Map.
- *Process factors:* Process factors characterize the context of the testing in regard to the development process. They include: F21: Process Maturity Level and F25: SDLC Phase.
- *Product factors:* Product factors describe the attributes of the product under test, they include: "F08: Functional flows, F09: Product Purpose, F14: Product Characteristics, F19: General Software design, F20: System Architecture, F22: Product Design Effects, and F28: Heterogeneous Dimensions.
- *Project management factors:* These factors concern the planning and leadership aspects of the project in which the testing takes place. They include: F05: Timeframe, F06: Project Purpose, F12: Effort estimation, F17: Test Team Communication, F18: Project Plan, and F29: Project Revenue.
- *Testing:* Testing factors include contextual information relevant for the planning, design and execution of the tests. They include: F02: Test Strategy, F03: Knowledge of Previous Bugs, F04: Risk Areas, F07: Test Function Complexity, F11: Test Equipment Availability, F13: Test Planning Checklist, F16: Test coverage areas, F23: Feedback and Consolidation, F24: Session Notes, and F26: Tester.

RQ2: What do practitioners include in their test charters? The interviews revealed 35 different contents that may be included in a test charter. Table 3 states the content types and their descriptions.

Similar to the factors we categorized the contents as well. Seven categories have been identified, namely testing scope, testing goals, test management, infrastructure, historical information, product-related information, and constraints, risks and issues.

- *Testing scope:* The testing scope describes what to focus the testing on, be it the parts of the system or the level of the testing. It may also describe what not to focus on and set the priorities. It includes: C02: Test Focus, C03: Test Level, C04: Test Techniques, C10: Exit Criteria, C14: Specific Areas of Interest, C19: Priorities, C28: Coverage, and C33: Omitted Things.

Table 2. Factors influencing test charter design

Charter influence factors	Description
F01: Client requirements	Requirements elicited from clients
F02: Test strategy	Set of ideas that guide the test plan
F03: Knowledge of previous bugs	Knowledge regarding system related bugs that occurred in the past
F04: Risk areas	Results of product risk analysis
F05: Time-frame	Time needed for test mission execution, time constraints
F06: Project purpose	Purpose of the project
F07: Test function complexity	Complexity of the tested functions
F08: Functional flows	Flow of data and functions
F09: Product purpose	Principle goal(s) of the product
F10: Business use-case	Business use-case for the system
F11: Test equipment availability	Accessibility to tools and equipment needed for the software tests
F12: Effort estimation	Effort needed to carry out the test mission
F13: Test planning checklist	Testing heuristics appointed for the particular test charter
F14: Product characteristics	Features of the product
F15: Quality requirements	Quality requirements of the product
F16: Test coverage areas	Parts of the system to be tested
F17: Test team communication	Means of communication between the testing team members
F18: Project plan	Plan for the project prior to its execution
F19: General software design	Design of the system software
F20: System architecture	Structure, interfaces and platforms of the system
F21: Process maturity level	Maturity of the process (e.g. CMMI levels)
F22: Product design effects	Impact of product design and features on other modules
F23: Feedback and consolidation	Feedback and consolidation of the test plan based on the comments of previous testers and clients
F24: Session notes	Notes filled during previous test sessions
F25: SDLC phase	Phase involved in the system development life-cycle
F26: Tester	Testers and their experience level
F27: Client location	Location of the client, local or global
F28: System heterogeneity	Differences between interacting systems (different programming languages, platforms, system configuration)
F29: Project revenue	Business returns for project
F30: User journey map	User interaction with the product over time

Table 3. Contents of test charters

Content type	Description
C01: Test setup	Description of the test environment
C02: Test focus	Part of the system to be tested
C03: Test level	Unit, Function, System test, etc.
C04: Test techniques	Test techniques used to carry out the tests
C05: Risks	Product risk analysis
C06: Bugs found	Bugs found previously
C07: Purpose	Motivation why the test is being carried out
C08: System definition	Type of system (e.g. simple/ complex)
C09: Client requirements	Requirements specification of the client
C10: Exit criteria	Defines the "done" criteria for the test
C11: Limitations	It tells of what the product must never do, e.g. data sent as plain text is strictly forbidden
C12: Test logs	Test logs to record the session results
C13: Data and functional flows	Data and work flow among components
C14: Specific areas of interest	Where to put extra focus on during the testing
C15: Issues	Charter specific issues or concerns to be investigated
C16: Compatibility issues	Hardware and software compatibility and interoperability issues
C17: Current open questions	Existing questions that refer to the known unknowns
C18: Information sources	Documents and guidelines that hold information regarding the features, functions and systems being tested
C19: Priorities	Determines what the tester spends most and least time on
C20: Quality characteristics	Quality objectives for the project
C21: Test results location	Test results location for developers to verify
C22: Mission statement	One liner describing the mission of the test charter
C23: Existing tools	Existing software testing tools that would aid the tests
C24: Target	What is to be achieved by each test
C25: Reporting	Test session notes
C26: Models and visualizations	People, mind maps, pictures related to the function to be tested
C27: General fault	Test related failure patterns of the past
C28: Coverage	Charter's boundary in relation to what it is supposed to cover
C29: Engineering standards	Regulations, rules and standards used, if any
C30: Oracles	Expected behavior of the system (either based on requirements or a person)
C31: Logistics	How and when resources are used to execute the test strategy, e.g. how people in projects are coordinated and assigned to testing tasks.
C32: Stakeholders	Stakeholders of the project and how their conflicting interests would be handled
C33: Omitted things	Specifies what will not be tested
C34: Difficulties	The biggest challenges for the test project
C35: System architecture	Structure, interfaces and platforms concerning the system, and its impact on system integration

- *Testing goals:* The testing goals set the mission and purpose of the test session. They include: C07: Purpose, C22: Mission Statement, and C24: Target.
- *Test management:* Test management is concerned with the planning, resource management, and the definition of how to record the tests. Test management includes: C12: Test Logs, C18: Information Sources, C21: Test Results Location, C25: Reporting, C26: Models and Visualizations, C31: Logistics, C32: Stakeholders, and C34: Difficulties.
- *Infrastructure:* Infrastructure comprises of tools and setups needed to conduct the testing. It includes: C01: Test Setup and C23: Existing Tools.
- *Historical information:* As exploratory testing focuses on learning, past information may be of importance. Thus, the historical information includes: C06: Bugs Found, C16: Compatibility Issues, C17: Current Open Questions, and C27: General Fault.
- *Product-related information:* Here contextual product information is captured, including: C08: System Definition, C13: Data and Functional Flows, and C35: System Architecture.
- *Constraints, risks and issues:* Constraints, risks and issues to testing comprise of the items: C05: Risks, C15: Issues, and C29: Engineering Standards.

5   Conclusion

In this study two checklists for test charter design were developed. The checklists were based on nine interviews. The interviews were utilized to gather a checklist for factors influencing test charter design and one to describe the possible contents of test charters. Overall, 30 factors and 35 content types have been identified and categorized.

The factors may be used in a similar manner and should be used to question the design choices of the test charter. For example:

- Should the test focus of the charter be influenced by previous bugs (F03)? How/why?
- Are the product's goals (F09) reflected in the charter?
- Is it possible to achieve the test charter mission in the given time for the test session (F12)?
- etc.

With regard to the content a wide range of possible contents to be included have been presented. For example, only stating the testing goals (C22) provides much room for exploration, while adding the techniques to be used (C04) may constrain the tester. Thus, the more information is included in the test charter the exploration space is reduced. Thus, when deciding what to include from the checklist (Table 3) the possibility to explore should be taken into consideration.

In future work we need to empirically understand (a) which are the most influential factors and how they affect the test charter design, and (b) which of the identified contents should be included to make exploratory testing effective and efficient.

References

1. Afzal, W., Ghazi, A.N., Itkonen, J., Torkar, R., Andrews, A., Bhatti, K.: An experiment on the effectiveness and efficiency of exploratory testing. Empirical Softw. Eng. **20**(3), 844–878 (2015)
2. Bach, J.: Session-based test management. Softw. Testing Qual. Eng. Mag. **2**(6) (2000)
3. Bach, J.: Exploratory testing explained (2003)
4. Bach, J., Bolton, M.: Rapid software testing. Version (1.3. 2) (2007). www.satisficc.com
5. Christ, R.E.: Review and analysis of color coding research for visual displays. Hum. Factors J. Hum. Factors Ergonomics Soc. **17**(6), 542–570 (1975)
6. Ghazi, A.N.: Testing of heterogeneous systems. Blekinge Inst. Technol. Licentiate Dissertion Ser. **2014**(03), 1–153 (2014)
7. Ghazi, A.N., Petersen, K., Börstler, J.: Heterogeneous systems testing techniques: an exploratory survey. In: Winkler, D., Biffl, S., Bergsmann, J. (eds.) SWQD 2015. LNBIP, vol. 200, pp. 67–85. Springer, Cham (2015). doi:10.1007/978-3-319-13251-8_5
8. Hendrickson, E.: Explore it! The Pragmatic Programmers (2014)
9. Itkonen, J., et al.: Empirical studies on exploratory software testing (2011)
10. Itkonen, J., Mäntylä, M.V.: Are test cases needed? Replicated comparison between exploratory and test-case-based software testing. Empirical Softw. Eng. **19**(2), 303–342 (2014)
11. Itkonen, J., Rautiainen, K.: Exploratory testing: a multiple case study. In: 2005 International Symposium on Empirical Software Engineering, p. 10. IEEE (2005)
12. Kaner, C., Bach, J., Pettichord, B.: Lessons Learned in Software Testing. Wiley, New York (2008)
13. Pfahl, D., Yin, H., Mäntylä, M.V., Münch, J., et al.: How is exploratory testing used? In: Proceedings of the 8th ACM/IEEE International Symposium on Empirical Software Engineering and Measurement, ESEM 2014 (2014)

Discovering Software Process Deviations Using Visualizations

Anna-Liisa Mattila[1]([⊠]), Kari Systä[1], Outi Sievi-Korte[1], Marko Leppänen[1], and Tommi Mikkonen[2]

[1] Tampere University of Technology, Tampere, Finland
{anna-liisa.mattila,kari.systa,outi.sievi-korte,marko.leppanen}@tut.fi
[2] University of Helsinki, Helsinki, Finland
tommi.mikkonen@helsinki.fi

Abstract. Modern software development is supported by a rich set of tools that accumulate data from the software process automatically. That data can be used for understanding and improving software processes without any manual data collection. In this paper we introduce an industrial case where data visualization of issue management system was used to investigate software projects. The results of the study show that visualization of issue management system data can really reveal deviations between planned process and executed process.

Keywords: Software visualization · Mining software repositories

1 Introduction

Various business information systems are focal for corporate management, and often companies utilize metrics as critical success indicators for their business [1]. So, in management of any process, both access to valid process data and the ability to understand the meaning of the data are essential.

Building automated data collection frameworks requires time and effort and is an investment for the company [2], but collecting data manually from the employees is a tedious and error prone effort. Fortunately in software development the effort required to access the data can be reduced significantly as many tools, such as version control and issue management systems, already automatically collect some data [3]. Thus, utilization of this ready-at-hand data could make process analysis more feasible for software companies.

Raw data items or numbers can rarely illuminate the analyst. Therefore, visualization methods are used to get a better overall picture of the organization and its business. When visualizations are available, various stakeholders can enjoy improved transparency to the actual status and react to possible issues faster. The usefulness of these visualizations is not limited to managers only, as everybody can benefit from good visualizations of the progress and properties of the project. This follows the spirit of Andon boards that are used to notify

© The Author(s) 2017
H. Baumeister et al. (Eds.): XP 2017, LNBIP 283, pp. 259–266, 2017.
DOI: 10.1007/978-3-319-57633-6_18

management, maintenance, and other workers of a quality or process problems in the Toyota Production System [4].

Many kinds of visualizations are used to show different aspects of software engineering process. Standard visualisation methods in project planning, such as *Gantt charts* [5] and Scrum *burndown charts* [6] can be used as well as workflow visualizations such as *Kanban board* [7,8]. The current state of the project can be communicated to the developer team using *radiators* and *dashboards* [8,9]. When in software process management and improvement, it is important to know what happened in the past and for this purpose various timeline based visualizations have been developed [10,11]. The idea in these methods is to show what happened in the past based on data. This kind of visualizations can be used as a tool in retrospective meetings [10], and during the development to spot abnormalities in the process [11].

In this paper we present experiences on visualizing data from software repositories. We explore the software process in two industrial projects. The paramount goal of our work is to help stakeholders, especially project managers, to observe the execution of software process to find deviations from the planned process, and to detect possible problems in the projects.

2   Research Process

The main research questions of the study are: (1) *Can we show deviations from the assumed software process by visualizing data gathered from software repositories?* (2) *Is the visualization of project data helpful for keeping track of the projects?* To answer these questions, we decided to study software projects where we could access the data starting from the beginning of the project. Issue management system was chosen as our data source as it is used for managing and reporting the software projects. The research process is presented in detail in Fig. 1.

Selected Cases. The cases studied are two industrial projects of a Finland-based multinational large-sized company involved in software R&D. We selected the company based on their interest towards the research. The company representatives selected the studied projects with the following constraints: suitable

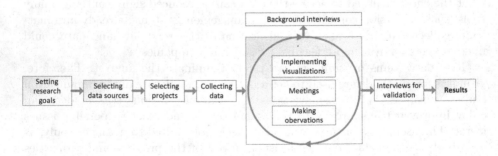

Fig. 1. The research process.

data are available from the beginning of the project, the project is currently in the development phase, and selected projects are comparable with each other.

Both of the studied projects are sub-projects of a larger software entity. In this paper, we refer to the projects as project A and project B. In project A, a software platform is developed whereas in project B a user interface for the software is developed. Both projects have 5–10 team members; the team composition varies based on the current need. Most of the team members are developers, but in team B there are also dedicated persons for testing and user experience design.

The projects use JIRA[1] for issue tracking. The guidelines for using JIRA are the same in both projects. The projects follow the same software development process, namely Scrumban [12], which is a hybrid of Scrum and Kanban. As the projects have uniform practices and processes, we assume that the project data are comparable between the projects.

The data collection period was from the start of the projects till the beginning of January 2015. The projects had started in 2013 – project A in May and B in August. The data sets we used were anonymized by the company representatives. The data were delivered in text format and contained only the information necessary for visualization and analysis – for example person names, JIRA comments or issue names were not visible to us.

Participants. We had eight participants from the case company. A manager of the larger project entity which the studied projects are part of (P1), a person responsible of the realization of agile ways of working in both projects and who was also a former developer in project B (P2), three developers from project A (P3, P4, P5), and three developers from project B (P6, P7, P8).

Four researchers participated to the research by studying the project data, developing the visualization tool, and participating the meetings with the case company.

The visualization tool. To empirically examine the relationship between project data and the perceived state of the project we built a software visualization tool. We chose to utilize timeline as the visualization format because it enables us to easily explore how projects evolved over time and it is used for similar purposes in other studies as well [11,13]. We held several meetings with participants P1, P2, and P3 from the case company to receive feedback from the visualization. The visualization was developed in an iterative manner where we fine-tuned the visualizations based on the received feedback.

The main element of the visualization is to show lifespans and state changes of issues reported in JIRA. Through the lifespan visualization we can observe which issues have been open for a long time and through which states the issue is finally resolved. Detailed figures of the visualization are provided with other additional material on https://github.com/pervcomp/DSPDUV.

Interviews. We held two interview sessions for developers in the projects studied. The first interviews were held at the beginning of the research process to

---

[1] JIRA – Project management system, https://www.atlassian.com/software/jira.

gain feedback from the initial version of the visualization and get deeper knowledge of the case projects. In the first interview we had three participants: P2, P3, and P6. The second interviews were held four months later to validate our observations made from the visualizations and to gather feedback from the visualization. In the second interview we had seven participants: all the three people interviewed in the first round (P2, P3, and P6) were interviewed again along with two more developers from both projects (P4, P5, P7, and P8). We selected the themes in a fashion that allowed us to (i) validate the assumptions considering the visual observations, and to (ii) reveal the ways of working in the projects as well as possible problems in the team and project.

The interviewing sessions were conducted as follows. Each interview began by discussing the background of the interviewee and continued to the discussion about ways of working, challenging issues in the team work and the project's current status. We showed the visualization to the interviewee during the last part of the interviewing session and asked the interviewee to observe and interpret the visualization. Finally, we discussed the observations made by researchers together with the interviewee to identify potential misinterpretations and to determine causes of the observed issues. Interviewees were also asked to give feedback from the visualization and tell if they thought the visualization is a useful tool for managing projects. The duration of the interviews varied from 30 to 60 min. All interviews were recorded and written notes were made. The interviews were conducted by one researcher.

3   Results

The results are based on studying the visualizations of project data and interviews. The data visualized from the projects were *bug reports*, *epics*, and *stories*. We made assumptions of status and ways of working from the visualizations. The table of assumptions made is available on https://github.com/pervcomp/ DSPDUV with the visualizations and other additional material.

Bugs. When comparing the views that show the lifespans and resolution rate of bug reports we noticed that the resolution rate of bug reports was higher in project A than in project B. When interviewing the participants, we found out that in project A bug fixes were prioritized over implementing new features. Prioritizing the bug fixes over new features was not an actual policy of the software process but an agreement within the team thus in project B similar convention was not applied.

The long life spans and increasing amounts of bug reports in project B could be a sign of technical debt or bad architectural decisions but also relate to problems in organizing and reporting work. Based on the interviews we learned that in project B there was technical debt as they had built the project directly on top of their initial prototype, which should have been just a throw away prototype. In project A the initial prototype was discarded. There were also problems in organizing and reporting work in project B.

Epics. The projects differed in how they used epics to plan greater entities. In project B only three epics were closed during the data collection period and all open epics were in their initial state. In project A epics were closed and opened in a more regular pattern. Based on this we could assume that in project B the role of epics in planning was not clear and they were not used systematically, which was also proven to be the case based on the interviews. Based on the process and instructions given to the teams they were supposed to use epics similarly when planning work.

Stories. When looking at the projects individually we assumed that both projects had problems in organizing and reporting work. The assumption was made based on long lifespans and increasing amounts of open stories that were visible in the visualizations. Also the long lifespans and high amount of open bug reports in project B supported this assumption for project B. Based on the interviews there were problems in organizing work. In both projects the product owner's role was not clear. In project A the product owner was not committed to organize the backlog, and in project B there was no product owner.

Usefulness of the visualization. To get feedback on use of the visualization for tracking the projects, we asked if the interviewees considered the visualization useful. All of the interviewees agreed that the visualization we presented is practical in tracking the projects as it shows clearly the issues which have been open for a long time. Most of the interviewees mentioned that the visualization would be especially useful for the project managers but also for them selfs.

4   Threats to Validity

Wohlin et al. [14] state four different categories when considering threats to validity - conclusion validity, internal validity, construct validity and external validity. We will deal with those that are particularly relevant to our study.

Threats to conclusion validity are concerned with issues that affect the ability to draw the correct conclusion about relations between the treatment and the outcome of an experiment. The threats most concerning our study have to do with "fishing" for a particular result and reliability of measures. In the start of the research process we did not expect any results, but were simply curious about what could be learned by visualizing software project data. Thus, all the observations made are purely drawn from what could be seen and without prejudice. Furthermore, the visualizations were interpreted together with company representatives, who would correct false assumptions. Additionally, the interviews were designed to reveal possible overlooked information from the visualizations.

Reliability of measures, in turn, involves the measured data (from the repositories) and verbal information (interviews). The data itself is visualized *"as is"*, without any human involvement required in between, so it is valid. The interview questions, in turn, were designed in a way that would allow as open answers as possible and for the interviewer to also perform follow-up questions. Naturally, the wording of the questions is still always critical, and for example a pilot study of the interviews could have been beneficial.

Threats to internal validity concern causality and threats to conclusions about relationships between treatment and outcome. In our experiment the most relevant threat regards *selection*, i.e., selecting the subjects, in our case the interviewees from the company, and how volunteering might affect the results. The interviewees were selected so that we had at least one developer and one person in charge of the process for both projects, who answered questions on both interview rounds, thus ensuring a versatile perspective of the project. For the second round the subjects were selected among developers based on who had the time. Thus there was no direct volunteering, which might affect results, and also selection was not made on any other criteria than having different roles, which should ensure a true view of the project. However, there was also no means to control the backgrounds of interviewees either.

Finally, construct validity concerns generalizing the result of the experiment. The most relevant threat to this study are *hypothesis guessing* and *evaluation apprehension*, both having to do with whether the interviews can be trusted. We argue that evaluation apprehension is not a concern, as all interviewees were willing to discuss the problems in their projects, and did not attempt to hide them from the researcher. As for guessing the hypothesis, we did not show the visualization to the interviewees until in the end of the interview, so all answers were purely given based on the questions.

The final category of threats given by [14] relates to external validity are conditions that limit the ability to generalize the results of the experiment to industrial practice. This does not concern us, as our cases were from the industry, and thus we can argue that the results already reflect industrial practice. However, more research need to be done for generalization of results.

5   Discussion and Conclusions

The first research question we addressed in Sect. 2 was *"Can we show deviations from the assumed software process by visualizing data gathered from software repositories?"*. Using the visualization we could note differences in practices between projects that should have had the same practices. We were also able to interpret from the visualization that there were problems in the software process. We learned that problems related to organizing work shows well in the visualization of issue management data. We also learned that different problems show differently. The problems in planning and reporting are visible in long lifespans of issues as well as different kinds of patterns in creating issues where as technical debt may be visible in bug report lifespans and creation rate.

Our second research question was: *"Is the visualization of project data helpful for keeping track of the projects?"*. Based on the feedback we can conclude that the visualization is a useful tool for project managers. Furthermore, we noticed that the visualization raised questions and interest in participants to discuss about the state of the projects. The visualization creates a good common ground for such discussion as it shows empirical evidence.

We have developed the visualization tool further based on the feedback received from the case company. We have also done first experiments using the visualizations in teaching software engineering. As a future work we will investigate the use of the tool for other industrial projects as well as for open source projects to validate our findings and evaluate the tool further.

References

1. Menzies, T., Zimmermann, T.: Software analytics: so what? IEEE Softw. **30**(4), 31–37 (2013)
2. Robbes, R., Vidal, R., Bastarrica, M.: Are software analytics efforts worthwhile for small companies? The case of Amisoft. IEEE Softw. **30**(5), 46–53 (2013)
3. Mäkinen, S., Leppänen, M., Kilamo, T., Mattila, A.L., Laukkanen, E., Pagels, M., Männistö, T.: Improving the delivery cycle: a multiple-case study of the toolchains in Finnish software intensive enterprises. Inf. Softw. Technol. **80**, 175–194 (2016)
4. Liker, J.K.: The Toyota Way. Esensi (2004)
5. Gantt, H.: Work, Wages and Profit. The Engineering Magazine (1910)
6. Schwaber, K., Beedle, M.: Agile Software Development with Scrum, 1st edn. Prentice Hall PTR, Upper Saddle River, NJ (2001)
7. Kerzazi, N., Robillard, P.N.: Kanbanize the Release Engineering Process. In: 2013 1st International Workshop on Release Engineering (RELENG), pp. 9–12. IEEE (2013)
8. Paredes, J., Anslow, C., Maurer, F.: Information visualization for agile software development. In: 2014 Second IEEE Working Conference on Software Visualization (VISSOFT), pp. 157–166. IEEE (2014)
9. Baysal, O., Holmes, R., Godfrey, M.W.: Developer dashboards: the need for qualitative analytics. IEEE Softw. **30**(4), 46–52 (2013)
10. Bjarnason, E., Hess, A., Doerr, J., Regnell, B.: Variations on the evidence-based timeline retrospective method: a comparison of two cases. In: 2013 39th EUROMICRO Conference on Software Engineering and Advanced Applications (SEAA), pp. 37–44. IEEE (2013)
11. Lehtonen, T., Eloranta, V.P., Leppänen, M., Isohanni, E.: Visualizations as a basis for agile software process improvement. In: 2013 20th Asia-Pacific Software Engineering Conference (APSEC), vol. 1, pp. 495–502. IEEE (2013)
12. Ladas, C.: Scrumban - Essays on Kanban Systems for Lean Software Development. Modus Cooperandi Press, USA (2009)
13. Bjarnason, E., Svensson, R.B., Regnell, B.: Evidence-based timelines for project retrospectives - a method for assessing requirements engineering in context. In: 2012 IEEE Second International Workshop on Empirical Requirements Engineering (EmpiRE), pp. 17–24. IEEE (2012)
14. Wohlin, C., Runeson, P., Höst, M., Ohlsson, M.C., Regnell, B., Wesslén, A.: Experimentation in Software Engineering: An Introduction. Kluwer Academic Publishers, Norwell (2000)

Exploring Workflow Mechanisms and Task Allocation Strategies in Agile Software Teams

Zainab Masood[✉], Rashina Hoda, and Kelly Blincoe

SEPTA Research, Department of Electrical and Computer Engineering, The University of Auckland, Auckland, New Zealand
zmas690@aucklanduni.ac.nz, {r.hoda,k.blincoe}@auckland.ac.nz

Abstract. Task allocation is considered an important activity in software project management. However, the process of allocating tasks in agile software development teams has not received much attention in empirical research. Through a pilot study involving mixed open-ended and closed-ended interviews questions with 11 agile software practitioners working within a software development organization in India, we explain the process of task allocation as including three different mechanisms of workflow across teams: team-independent, team-dependent, and hybrid workflow; and five types of task allocation strategies: manager-driven, team-driven, individual-driven, manager-assisted and team-assisted. Knowing these workflow mechanisms and task allocation strategies will help software teams and project managers make more effective decisions around workflow and task allocation.

Keywords: Task allocation · Workflow · Allocation mechanism · Agile software teams · Task allocation strategies

1 Introduction

Successful project completion depends on how well and effectively the project activities are planned and managed throughout [1]. Primary project management activities include managing resources, task allocation, and tracking time and budget in the best possible way [2]. Several studies have researched task allocation in global and distributed software development using traditional or agile methods [3–6]. A limited number of studies have assessed task allocation mechanisms practiced by Free/Libre Open Source Software (FLOSS) development teams; however, they did not cover commercial projects [7]. Overall, task allocation in agile software teams, which are meant to be self-organizing [9, 12], has not be studied.

We conducted a pilot study involving face-to-face interviews with 11 agile practitioners from three teams in a software organization in India. Thematic analysis [8] was performed to derive the different types of workflow mechanisms and task allocation strategies from the interview data. We identified three workflow mechanisms: team-independent, team-dependent, and hybrid workflow. We also identified five types of task allocation strategies: manager-driven, team-driven, individual-driven, manager-assisted and team-assisted. Identifying these mechanisms and strategies helped understand the

H. Baumeister et al. (Eds.): XP 2017, LNBIP 283, pp. 267–273, 2017.
DOI: 10.1007/978-3-319-57633-6_19

flow and forms in which tasks arrives to the team and the basis on which tasks are classified and allocated.

2   Related Work

In traditional software development, the project manager plays a key role in task allocation and management and overall decision making. With the evolution of agile methods, software teams are meant to be self-organizing with high levels of autonomy, teams empowerment and mutual decision making in their everyday work [10, 12] including project management activities such as task allocation [11, 12]. In practice, however, agile teams are seen to display varying levels of autonomy as they gain experience of functioning in a self-organizing way [11]. How the varying levels of autonomy influence task allocation is not well understood. In particular, it is unclear how work flows to and within the team, how tasks are allocated on an individual level, and what are the different types and autonomy levels of task allocation in agile teams.

The research on task allocation in software teams has been largely dominated by distributed contexts in global software development. Imtiaz et al. in their recent survey-based study identified "functional area of expertise and phase-based" task allocation as the most common way of allocating tasks global software development [5]. Other studies, e.g. [4, 6], explored task allocation in distributed agile software development contexts through literature review and proposed models indicating further studies as a promising area of research. Crowston et al. 2007 [7] demonstrated the possible mechanisms of tasks allocation in community-based Free/Libre Open Source Software (FLOSS) development in self-organized volunteer teams. Their findings support self-assignment as one of the common ways of assigning tasks adopted by FLOSS teams. However, not much has been explored in the literature about task allocation mechanisms outside the FLOSS domain and specifically for commercial software development. Overall, much remains to be understood about how work flows to and within agile teams and how they practice task allocation.

3   Research Method

Our pilot study involved mixed open- and closed-ended interview questions with 11 agile practitioners. The overarching research questions were:

RQ1: How does work flow in agile teams?
RQ2: How does task allocation happen in agile teams?

3.1   Participant Selection and Description

An invitation to participate was sent out to members of the Agile software community of India. The company willing to offer a maximum number of teams and participants was selected. Eleven software practitioners from three agile teams working in this digital technology company were included (one additional participant was later dropped since they were the sole representative of a fourth team). Participants were experienced software practitioners and were using agile methods, either Scrum or Kanban, including key agile practices such as Daily Team Meetings, Release and Iteration planning, Pair Programming, Review meetings and Retrospectives. Teams were collaborating with off-shored customers or product teams in the USA through Google Hangout, Skype or Webex. The project management tool used by all teams was Jira. Team, project and participants' details are profiled in Table 1.

Table 1. Team, project contexts and participants demographics (TS: Team Size, SP#: Participants; TX: total experience in years; X: agile experience in years; ATL: Assoc.Tech Lead; TL: Tech Lead; SSE: Senior Software Engineer)

Team	TS	Software method	Project Area/ Context	SP#	Role	Age group	TX	AX
T1	10–15	Scrum	Digital Marketing/ Features & Maintenance	SP1	TL	31–35	10–11	6–7
				SP2	SE	21–25	2–2.5	1
				SP3	ATL	26–30	4–5	4–5
				SP4	SE	21–25	2.5	2.5
T2	5–10	Scrum	Analytics/ Features	SP5	TL	36–40	7	7
				SP6	SSE	26–30	4	2
				SP7	TL	31–35	7.5	7.5
T3	15–20	Kanban	Cloud Services/ Migration & Enhancement	SP8	TL	31–35	5.5	5–6
				SP9	ATL	26–30	4	2
				SP10	SSE	21–25	3.5	1
				SP11	ATL	26–30	4.5	2

3.2 Data Collection and Analysis

We conducted face-to-face interviews lasting 30–40 min with each participant using a combination of open- and close-ended questions about their current projects applying agile methods. Initial questions gathered participants' demographical data, details related to the project, team and the agile methods used. Most other questions focused on task allocation process e.g. how, when and from whom the teams receive the tasks and how the tasks are allocated among the teams and the individuals. These were mostly open-ended questions to allow a range of answers, with some choices being given to facilitate the interviewees during the interview.

All the interviews were recorded with detailed notes taken during the interview. Interview data was transcribed and analyzed manually using thematic analysis [8] to derive the common themes, i.e. patterns of workflow mechanisms and task allocation strategies common across the participants. This was led by one of the authors and supported by the other two through careful reviews and discussions.

4   Findings

In answer to RQ1, we identified three distinct workflow mechanisms (illustrated in Fig. 1) that describe how the teams receive the work from the relevant stakeholders: team-independent, team-dependent, and hybrid workflow. Additionally, in answer to RQ2, we found five different task allocation strategies based on how tasks were allocated within the team: manager-driven, team-driven, individual-driven, manager-assisted and team-assisted.

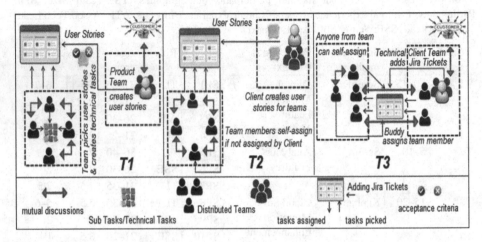

Fig. 1. Teamwise task allocation mechanisms (T1: team independent workflow; T2: team dependent workflow; T3: hybrid workflow)

4.1   Team Workflow Mechanisms

Team Independent Workflow: In this workflow, the tasks are defined irrespective of the team location (US, India). Tasks comes to both teams from Product Owner mostly in form of user stories during sprint planning meeting. Members of all teams individually pick and break user stories into technical tasks. The work allocation is done by volunteering for tasks through mutual discussions. For example, one participant explained:

> "They[Product Team] bring whole description of the ticket[user story]...Everyone is in sprint planning meeting, every developer I should say and then ticket by ticket we volunteer, they do not assign any name." SP1, Tech Lead.

Team Dependent Workflow: Client defines the tasks for respective teams (US, India) separately as user stories during fortnightly iteration planning meeting. Before sprint planning meeting, the team (T2) go through their stories and team members allocate the tasks either individually or through mutual consensus. SP7 described the workflow as follows:

> "Client creates user stories then one day before sprint planning we [T2] go through stories which are meant for India team and we pick whatever we want to do." SP7, Tech Lead

Hybrid Workflow: Team T3 was seen to follow multiple workflow mechanisms, but tasks are typically allocated during a monthly release from the USA technical team, who collaborates with the client. For a few members of the team, the USA team creates Jira tickets with a set priority and complexity level. As specified by SP9:

"Now that teams have been divided so they have to work according to the tasks that are assigned to those particular teams only so it's not like that X team can work on team Y cards." SP9, Associate. Tech Lead

For other team members, work comes as features with a defined priority and release date from the USA team. These features are selected by the Tech Lead in USA, who breaks them into tasks and sub-tasks and allocates them to their 'buddy' programmer in India.

"So the client decides the criticality and to which release these [cards] will belong so once the lead has decided that then pair [buddy] can pick up." SP10, Sr. Software Engineer

4.2 Task Allocation Strategies

In **Manager-driven Task Allocation**, the manager/client/technical-lead allocates tasks to the team members with names against the tasks as stated by a participant, where the 'buddy' was a senior Tech Lead in the USA:

"Nowadays I am given task by my buddy." SP11, Assoc. Tech Lead

In **Team-driven Task Allocation**, the team discusses and mutually decides who will perform which task, for example:

"We are three people [in the team] so mutually decide who will do [what]." SP6, Sr. Software Engineer

In **Individual-driven Task Allocation**, tasks are self-assigned i.e. selected and managed individually without any assistance from others. For example, SP4 quoted practicing self-driven allocation:

"Mostly we volunteer it." SP4, Software Engineer

In **Manager-assisted Task Allocation**, tasks are allocated with some assistance from the manager/client/technical-lead to the team members. As a technical lead, SP1 mentioned assisting team member with picking tasks:

"'Hey [name] you should do this [task]', let say he is new and he doesn't know [so] I help him, 'pick this one because this is lesser complex'." SP1, Tech Lead

In **Team-assisted Task Allocation**, every team member self-assigns tasks with some assistance from fellow team members, for example:

"So any of the pair[s] can pick up [a task]." SP10, Sr. Software Engineer

5   Discussion

We identified five task allocation strategies. Four of these strategies involve either the team as a whole or the manager/client in the task allocation process, making it evident that the task allocation mostly takes place through assistance or mutual discussions. In other words, task allocation strategies rely on collective decision making. A prior study [13] has shown that agile teams make effective decisions collectively compared to individual decisions, benefitting from collective knowledge and experiences.

Another aspect is that for high priority tasks all mechanisms agree on a common allocation method, i.e. tasks are directly allocated to a skilled and experienced person, an aspect supported by previous research [7].

Our study supports the different levels of autonomy evident on agile teams [11] as we found evidence of varying management approaches: manager-driven, manager-assisted and team-driven. Additionally, we also identified a new level: individual-driven task allocation.

With respect to the effectiveness of their current strategy, all the teams reported being satisfied, but some participants shared a few challenges, e.g. vagueness or missing clarity on tasks was the most commonly reported challenge. One participant (SP10) mentioned that with their current task allocation strategy (Team-assisted), work at times is not evenly distributed. Another participant (SP1) revealed drawbacks of picking tasks remotely. Since their client and the USA team are co-located they were perceived to have an advantage in picking tasks over SP1's India team. However, these challenges are not directly related to task allocation, rather, they are also linked to requirements clarity issues and the distributed nature of the team. This illustrates that task allocation is impacted by many factors.

This research study can serve as a basis for exploring other task allocation strategies and internal workflow mechanisms of agile teams. This pilot study included only 11 interviews from the same organization which signifies a limited dataset and context. Our larger study will interview more software teams and individuals representing different roles. Future work can focus on evaluating the effectiveness of the strategies.

6   Conclusion

This study presents a preliminary understanding of workflow mechanisms and task allocation strategies in agile teams. Clients typically provide high-level requirements as features or user stories to the agile teams who then break them down into technical tasks or sub-tasks by themselves or directly allocate them to team members. The team members then select them individually or through mutual discussions within the team. Allocation of tasks usually takes place during iteration or release planning. The findings of this study demonstrate that there are multiple types of task allocation strategies practiced by agile teams based on what suits the completion of the work in the best possible way. A common mechanism found in a majority of the teams is that if the priority of the task is high, then the task is allocated to the most suitable person directly. Also on average, the practice most commonly followed is that the team members collaborate with each other and with their manager/client when assistance is needed.

References

1. Pinto, J.K., Slevin, D.P.: Critical success factors across the project life cycle. Proj. Manag. J. **19**(3), 67–75 (1988)
2. Hoda, R., Noble, J., Marshall, S.: Agile project management. In: New Zealand Computer Science Research Student Conference, vol. 6, pp. 218–221 (2008)
3. Lamersdorf, A., Munch, J., Rombach, D.: A survey on the state of the practice in distributed software development: criteria for task allocation. In: 2009 Fourth IEEE International Conference on Global Software Engineering, ICGSE 2009, pp. 41–50 (2009)
4. Filho, M.S., Pinheiro, P.R., Albuquerque, A.B.: Task allocation approaches in distributed agile software development: a quasi-systematic review. In: Silhavy, R., Senkerik, R., Oplatkova, Z.K., Prokopova, Z., Silhavy, P. (eds.) Software Engineering in Intelligent Systems. AISC, vol. 349, pp. 243–252. Springer, Cham (2015). doi: 10.1007/978-3-319-18473-9_24
5. Imtiaz, S., Ikram, N.: Dynamics of task allocation in global software development. J. Softw. Evol. Process **29**(1) (2016). doi:10.1002/smr.1832
6. Mak, D.K., Kruchten, P.B.: Task coordination in an agile distributed software development environment. In: 2006 Canadian Conference on Electrical and Computer Engineering, CCECE 2006, pp. 606–611. IEEE (2006)
7. Crowston, K., Li, Q., Wei, K., Eseryel, U.Y., Howison, J.: Self-organization of teams for free/ libre open source software development. Inf. Softw. Technol. **49**(6), 564–575 (2007)
8. Clarke, V., Braun, V.: Thematic analysis. In: Encyclopedia of Critical Psychology, pp. 1947–1952. Springer, New York (2014)
9. Moe, N.B., Dingsøyr, T., Dybå, T.: Understanding self-organizing teams in agile software development. In: 2008 19th Australian Conference on Software Engineering, ASWEC 2008, pp. 76–85. IEEE (2008)
10. Highsmith, J.: Agile Project Management: Creating Innovative Products. Pearson Education, Upper Saddle River, NJ (2009)
11. Hoda, R., Noble, J.: Becoming agile: a grounded theory of agile transitions in practice. In: IEEE International Conference on Software Engineering (ICSE2017) (2017)
12. Hoda, R., Murugesan, L.K.: Multi-level agile project management challenges: A self-organizing team perspective. J. Syst. Softw. **117**, 245–257 (2016)
13. Drury, M., Conboy, K., Power, K.: Obstacles to decision making in Agile software development teams. J. Syst. Softw. **85**(6), 1239–1254 (2012)

Are Daily Stand-up Meetings Valuable?
A Survey of Developers in Software Teams

Viktoria Stray[1(✉)], Nils Brede Moe[2], and Gunnar R. Bergersen[1]

[1] University of Oslo, Gaustadalléen 23B, 0374 Oslo, Norway
{stray,gunnab}@ifi.uio.no
[2] SINTEF, Strindveien 4, 7465 Trondheim, Norway
nils.b.moe@sintef.no

Abstract. The daily stand-up meeting is a widely used practice. However, what is more uncertain is how valuable the practice is to team members. We invited professional developers of a programming forum to a survey and obtained 221 responses. Results show that the daily stand-up meeting was used by 87% of those who employ agile methods. We found that even though the respondents on average were neutral towards the practice, the majority were either positive or negative. Junior developers were most positive and senior developers and members of large teams most negative. We argue that the value of the practice should be evaluated according to the team needs. Further, more work is needed to understand why senior developers do not perceive the meetings as valuable and how to apply the practice successfully in large teams.

Keywords: Daily meetings · Stand up meeting · Daily scrum · Communication · Coordination · Teamwork · Team size · Agile adoption · Agile practices

1 Introduction

Agile methods introduced the daily stand-up meeting (DSM) as a practice to improve communication in software development projects. In Scrum, the meeting is mandatory, time-boxed to 15 min and team members address: (1) what they have done the previous work day, (2) what they will do today and (3) what obstacles are preventing them from making progress [1]. Scrum recommends that the DSM should not be used for discussing solutions to obstacles raised. However, empirical studies have found that spending time in the short meeting on discussing and solving problems is valuable [2, 3].

DSMs are task oriented, generally unrecorded, and members gather to focus on a narrow organizational goal. According to Boden [4], such meetings can be characterized as informal. The practice gives team members an overview of what other team members are doing and is therefore an important mechanism to increase information sharing and team awareness [5]. The meeting is often conducted standing up to keep it brief and avoid lengthy discussions, hence the term "stand-up meeting". The practice is also called "frequent short meetings" [6], "morning roll call" [7], and "daily Scrum meeting" [1]. The DSM is an important practice for agile teams because it helps the team in monitoring and managing its performance, which is important for the team to

© The Author(s) 2017
H. Baumeister et al. (Eds.): XP 2017, LNBIP 283, pp. 274–281, 2017.
DOI: 10.1007/978-3-319-57633-6_20

self-manage [8]. Further, such meetings improve access to information that foster employee empowerment [9].

While DSM is a relatively straightforward practice to adopt, it is challenging to implement it successfully. Challenges include finding a suitable time of day, keeping the time limit and whether it should be held daily and standing up [10]. We have previously found DSMs to last 63% longer when team members sit rather than stand during the meeting [5]. Another challenge is members reporting their status to the team leader, resulting in team members not paying attention to each other [8].

Although the DSM is one of the most popular agile practices [11, 12] and the only daily team-based coordination mechanism, the practice has received little research attention. Further, because meeting satisfaction is part of overall job satisfaction [13], it is important to understand what makes this meeting valuable for team members. In a recent, qualitative study of thirteen teams (in Norway, Poland, UK and Malaysia) we found that the attitudes towards DSMs were slightly more positive than negative [5]. However, the level of satisfaction varied within the teams. Therefore, to understand how to implement DSM, it is important to explore satisfaction with the practice on an individual level. This leads to the following research question: *"What are the characteristics of developers perceiving the daily stand-up meeting to be valuable compared to those who do not?"*

Our work also answers a call for more empirical studies on the adoption rate of agile software development methods [14].

2 Method

The target population for this study was professional software developers. Accordingly, we posted the survey on Reddit, which is a social media website that allows scientists to recruit a targeted population [15]. We chose two programming-related subreddits (subforums) that provide news and discussions about computer programming (r/programming, 710 000 subscribers) and web development (r/webdev, 130 000 subscribers). The survey was administered using the Qualtrics software which prevents the survey to be completed more than once by the same respondent. Participation was voluntary. Further, no compensation was offered, which increase the quality of the data because the incentive to cheat is largely reduced [15]. The survey (available from https://figshare.com/s/a10006dd8f5f26141511) took about three minutes to complete.

We received 316 responses, of which 243 contained data that could be analyzed. Because we were interested in the opinions of software professionals currently working in teams, we removed students and those not working or not working in a team. In total, 221 responses were used for the reported results. The majority of responses were from the programming forum (n = 165). Nearly all the respondents were male (96.8%) with a mean age of 31 years (n = 204, sd = 6.86). Among the respondents who answered whether their team was distributed (n = 168), about two-thirds of the respondents (63.1%) reported working in co-located teams, whereas the remaining had team members distributed across sites (36.9%).

All Likert questions used a five-point scale. All nominal-scale questions were presented with a randomized order of categories because the order of response alternatives can influence results [16]. Some questions were not compulsory, which resulted in missing data for the reported variables. Analyses are reported using the R statistical software [17]. To err on the side of caution, we use two-tailed analysis and chose non-parametric statistical tests. The one-sample Wilcoxon test is used to check for statistically significant differences in distributions. When comparing frequencies between two dichotomous variables that contain count data (i.e., frequencies) we used Fisher's exact test which reports the odds ratio (OR) effect size.

3   Results

In our study, the average number of DSMs conducted per week was five, which suggests that it is a daily meeting. Table 1 shows descriptive statistics. We found no difference regarding the frequency of meetings when it comes to being part of a distributed team or not, or to team size. Among all the respondents, one-third reported to work in teams with two to five members, one-third in teams with six to eight members and one-third in teams with nine or more members. We found a difference of 52% points with an odds ratio of 12.3 for agile teams using DSMs over non-agile teams ($p < 0.001$, 95% confidence interval for OR: 5.4–29.5).

Table 1. Descriptive statistics

	Unit	n	Mean (M)	sd	median
Meetings	Frequency per day, DSMs included	166	1.8	1.2	2
Time in meetings	Hours per day; DSMs included	187	1.4	2.0	1
Time programming	Hours per day	196	6.2	2.3	7
Team size	Members including self	168	7.3	3.9	6
DSM valuable	Likert: Negative (1)–Positive (5)	149	3.0	1.2	3
Programming skill self	Likert: Novice (1)–Expert (5)	177	3.7	0.8	4
Programming skill peers	Likert: Novice (1)–Expert (5)	177	3.6	0.8	4

Overall, 70.6% report that they attend DSMs (n = 221). Those who attend and those who do not attend DSMs spend the same amount of hours in meetings (DSMs included) and report similar values for programming skills. However, those who attend DSMs spend almost one hour more each workday on programming ($p = 0.046$, attend: M = 6.5 h, sd = 2.1; not attend: M = 5.6 h, sd = 2.7). Further, those who attend DSMs work in larger teams ($p = 0.03$, attend: M = 6.90 members, sd = 4.7; M = 7.44 members, sd = 3.52); the median difference was 2 team members. Moreover, the practice is regarded as more valuable by those who attend DSMs than those who do not ($p = 0.002$, attend: M = 3.1, n = 123, not attend: M = 2.3, n = 29).

We now report on only those respondents who attend DSMs. While the mean perceived value by these respondents towards the practice was neutral (3.1), only 18.7% chose this middle category on the Likert scale. Most respondents were either positive (44.7%) or negative (36.6%). We coded responses of 4 and 5 as "positive", responses of 1 and 2 as "negative", and removed those who responded neutral to be able to better understand differences between these two groups. We found no relation between working in a co-located or distributed team and the perceived value of DSM. However, those positive were significantly younger (p = 0.008, positive: M = 29.6 years, n = 49; negative: M = 33.5 years, n = 42).

Figure 1 shows the characteristics of the respondents who attend DSMs according to whether they are positive (green, n = 55) or negative (red, n = 45) towards the meetings they attend. The left part of the figure shows that those positive and negative towards their DSMs spent about the same amount of time in meetings: 83 min for those positive versus 77 min for those negative. However, there was a significant difference in meeting frequency; those positive attended fewer meetings per day (DSMs included) than those negative. Those positive towards DSM report somewhat more time spent on programming per day (24 min) than those negative. Being positive towards DSMs was, to some extent, associated with working in smaller teams. As a post hoc analysis, we investigated differences in attitudes further and found that teams with 12 or more members were most strongly associated with negative attitudes towards DSMs.

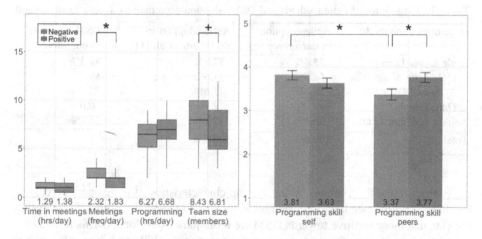

Fig. 1. Characteristics of those positive and negative towards their DSMs being valuable. Significant differences are shown at the top and means are shown at the bottom of the figure (as numbers). Outliers are omitted. Error bars represent the standard errors of the mean. + is p < 0.10 and * is p < 0.05 (two-sided). (Color figure online)

The right part of Fig. 1 shows a minor difference between how those positive and negative towards DSM rated their own programming skills. However, those positive rated the programming skills of their peers as significantly higher compared to how the negative rated their peers. Further, those negative also rated their own skills as significantly higher than that of their peers, whereas it was, to some extent, the opposite for those positive.

4 Discussion

The main explanation of the widespread use of DSM (70,6%) is the high adoption rate of agile development methods among our respondents. Table 2 shows that the agile adoption rate in our survey is higher than what was found by Rodríguez et al. [11]. Rodríguez et al. did not report the adoption rate of DSM but concluded that it was one of the most widely used practices. The last column in Table 2 shows the adoption rate of DSM in both agile and non-agile teams in our study. VersionOne [12] report the DSM to be the most employed agile practice with an adoption rate of 83%. VersionOne's sample mostly consisted of agile practitioners. In comparison, our DSM adoption rate among those using agile or agile in combination with Lean was 87.3%. Our results indicate that the practice has spread to companies not using agile methods because 35.4% of the respondents who work in non-agile teams also report using DSM. Thus, being agile implies that DSMs are used to a large extent which supports that DSM is a practice that distinguishes agile from non-agile teams [17].

Table 2. Usage rates of agile methods and DSM adoption according to development method

Development method	Agile adoption in our survey	Agile adoption in Rodríguez et al. [11]	DSM adoption in our survey
Agile and/or Lean	**73.6%**	**57.8%**	87.3%
Only agile	*54.9%*	*33.6%*	*89.0%*
Agile and Lean	*18.7%*	*21.6%*	*82.4%*
Only Lean	*0.0%*	*2.7%*	*0.0%*
Neither agile nor Lean	**26.4%**	**42.2%**	35.4%
Total	**100.0%**	**100.0%**	

For our research question, "What are the characteristics of developers perceiving the daily stand-up meeting to be valuable compared to those who do not?", our results indicate that those positive towards DSM are more junior developers. This inference is supported by age, how they rate their own programming skills and their self-reported skills compared to the perceived skill of their peers. Those positive towards DSM also participate in fewer meetings than those negative. The same variables also indicate that those negative towards DSM are more senior developers. One explanation for why a senior developer regards DSM as less valuable is because seniors may already know what goes on in the team and does not get any new information in the meeting. The personal gain from the meeting is thus reduced. Moreover, being able to have quick problem-solving discussions in the DSM make developers perceive the DSM as more valuable [5]. Senior developers often work on more complex tasks, and it might be that high complexity problems are seldom discussed at the meeting because they require too much time. It is more likely that the problems a junior developer encounter are more easily solved in a DSM.

A second explanation is that senior developers attend more meetings than junior developers. The DSM then becomes an additional daily interruption, which reduces the satisfaction with such meetings. Perceiving the meeting to have too high frequency negatively affects the attitude towards DSMs [5]. Moreover, meeting load affects employees well-being [18] so companies should be sensitive to the number of meetings the developers have to attend. While it has been claimed that DSMs eliminate the need for other meetings [1], we found no difference between hours spent in meetings for those who attend or do not attend DSMs.

In a self-managing team, the team goal should be more important than the individual goal, and then a developer should rate the DSM value depending on the team needs. One respondent commented: *"I think some people need the daily stand-up format. So even though I personally don't feel like I need it, I feel it benefits us all to do it because of the different personalities."* Because we do not know the perspective of the respondent we do not know if the respondents are considering the value from an individual or team perspective, or a mixture of the two views.

We found that larger teams are more likely to have DSMs. Paradoxically, the larger the team, the less is the satisfaction with DSM. Large teams using DSMs should therefore pay special attention to improving the quality of these meetings. In particular, developers were negative towards DSM when teams consisted of 12 or more team members. Previous research also found a negative correlation between the number of meeting participants and the attitude towards DSM [5].

The main limitation of this study concerns the representativeness. Although the distribution of self-reported programming skill in this study is nearly identical to our earlier study of programming skill of developers [19], the sample and target population may differ. For example, it is possible that only those who knew or had a strong (polarized) opinion of DSMs responded to the survey. This may bias results in favor of more respondents reporting using DSM and more variability in opinions than is actually present in the target population. Another potential concern is that we had subjects from two different programming forums, but the results we report still hold when analyzing the data from the two forums separately.

5 Conclusion and Future Work

The present study investigated the perceived value of daily stand-up meetings (DSMs) and reports the adoption rate of the practice. Among those who use agile methods, the majority conducts DSMs. Although it is a common practice, the perceived value of the meeting varies with junior developers being more positive and senior developers more negative towards the DSMs they attend. A possible explanation is that junior developers receive more relevant information and assistance in solving problems during the meeting. In contrast, senior developers often work with larger, more complex and independent tasks that are more difficult to share with team members on a daily basis. Agile teams are expected to be self-managed, and the need of the team should be more important than that of the individual. The value of the practice should, therefore, be evaluated according to the team needs. Consequently, senior developers should be made more aware that DSMs are beneficial for the junior developers as well as the team as a whole. Another result was that developers in larger teams see the meeting as less valuable than developers in smaller teams. Because the work in large teams is often loosely coupled, the information shared during the meeting may be less relevant for the individuals. Consequently, large teams in particular need to invest resources in improving the practice to make it valuable.

Future work should investigate other criteria of the participants, such as role and domain. Because the perceived value of meetings affects job satisfaction, there is a need to understand why senior developers and large teams do not perceive the meeting as more valuable. The DSM is a widely adopted practice and is an important mechanism for information sharing and team awareness, thus, how to apply the practice successfully in large teams should also be studied.

Acknowledgments. We are grateful to the survey respondents and to the reviewers. This work was supported by the Smiglo project, which is partly funded by the Research Council of Norway under the grant 235359/O30.

References

1. Schwaber, K., Beedle, M.: Agile Software Development with Scrum. Prentice Hall, Upper Saddle River (2002)
2. Stray, V.G., Moe, N.B., Aurum, A.: Investigating daily team meetings in agile software projects. In: The 38th EUROMICRO Conference on Software Engineering and Advanced Applications (SEAA 2012), Cesme, Turkey, 17 August 2012
3. Pikkarainen, M., Haikara, J., Salo, O., Abrahamsson, P., Still, J.: The impact of agile practices on communication in software development. Empirical Softw. Eng. **13**, 303–337 (2008)
4. Boden, D.: The Business of Talk: Organizations in Action. Polity Press, Cambridge (1994)
5. Stray, V., Sjøberg, D., Dybå, T.: The daily stand-up meeting: a grounded theory study. J. Syst. Softw. **114**, 101–124 (2016)
6. Rising, L.: Agile meetings. STQE, pp. 42–46 (2002)
7. Anderson, D.J.: Agile Management for Software Engineering: Applying the Theory of Constraints for Business Results. Prentice Hall, Upper Saddle River (2003)
8. Moe, N.B., Dingsøyr, T., Dybå, T.: A teamwork model for understanding an agile team: a case study of a Scrum project. Inf. Softw. Technol. **52**, 480–491 (2010)
9. Allen, J.A., Lehmann-Willenbrock, N., Sands, S.J.: Meetings as a positive boost? How and when meeting satisfaction impacts employee empowerment. J. Bus. Res. **69**, 1–8 (2016)
10. Stray, V.G., Lindsjørn, Y., Sjøberg, D.: Obstacles to efficient daily meetings in agile development projects: a case study. In: The ACM/IEEE International Symposium on Empirical Software Engineering and Measurement (ESEM 2013), Baltimore, USA, 13 September 2013
11. Rodríguez, P., Markkula, J., Oivo, M., Turula, K.: Survey on Agile and Lean Usage in Finnish Software Industry. ACM, New York (2012)
12. VersionOne: VersionOne 10th Annual State of Agile Report. https://versionone.com/pdf/VersionOne-10th-Annual-State-of-Agile-Report.pdf

13. Rogelberg, S.G., Allen, J.A., Shanock, L., Scott, C., Shuffler, M.: Employee satisfaction with meetings: a contemporary facet of job satisfaction. Hum. Resour. Manag. **49**, 149–172 (2010)
14. Stavru, S.: A critical examination of recent industrial surveys on agile method usage. J. Syst. Softw. **94**, 87–97 (2014)
15. Shatz, I.: Fast, free, and targeted: reddit as a source for recruiting participants online. Soc. Sci. Comput. Rev., pp. 1–13 (2016)
16. Schwarz, N., Hippler, H.J.: Response alternatives: the impact of their choice and presentation order (1991)
17. Murphy, B., Bird, C., Zimmermann, T., Williams, L.: Have agile techniques been the silver bullet for software development at Microsoft? In: The Proceedings of the 2013 ACM/IEEE International Symposium on Empirical Software Engineering and Measurement (ESEM 2013), Baltimore, USA, 7 July 2013
18. Luong, A., Rogelberg, S.G.: Meetings and more meetings: the relationship between meeting load and the daily well-being of employees. Group Dyn. Theor. Res. Pract. **9**, 58–67 (2005)
19. Bergersen, G.R., Sjøberg, D., Dybå, T.: Construction and validation of an instrument for measuring programming skill. IEEE Trans. Softw. Eng. **40**, 1163–1184 (2014)

Doctoral Symposium Papers

Knowledge Management and Reflective Practice in Daily Stand-Up and Retrospective Meetings

Yanti Andriyani[✉]

SEPTA Research, Department of Electrical and Computer Engineering,
The University of Auckland, Building 903, 386 Khyber Pass, New Market Auckland,
Auckland 1023, New Zealand
yand610@aucklanduni.ac.nz

Abstract. Knowledge management and reflection are important aspects in daily stand-up and retrospective meetings, which contribute to agile teams continuous improvement. Research in knowledge management in agile software development has shown knowledge classifications which do not seem closely related with agile practitioners and current research has not treated agile reflective practice in detail. This research, which will focus on daily stand-up and retrospective meetings, addresses two objectives: (i) to investigate specific knowledge types (i.e. product, project and process knowledge) in everyday agile practice and knowledge management strategies applied by agile teams; (ii) to explore the actual knowledge involved in the meetings, which helps agile teams to perform reflection and use that knowledge for reflection. Case studies will be applied for this research to analyse both meeting practices. It is expected that the research results will provide a framework for agile teams to manage knowledge and perform reflection, which would be useful for team and process improvement.

Keywords: Agile software development · Knowledge management · Reflective practice · Agile retrospective meeting · Daily stand-up meeting

1 Introduction

Agile Software Development (ASD) is a group of software methods that use an "inspect and adapt" process as a part of regular reflection for continuous improvement [1]. Daily stand-up and retrospective meetings are practices that are meant to help evaluate team progress, impediments, and plans and find ways to improve [2]. In the daily stand-up meetings, agile teams share progress, discuss the impediments that occur in the team and share their plans daily [3]. The retrospective meeting enables agile teams to inspect the feedback shared and discuss the ways to improve.

Supervisor: Dr. Rashina Hoda, Department of Electrical and Computer Engineering, The University of Auckland, email: r.hoda@auckland.ac.nz.
Co-Supervisor: Prof. Robert Amor, Department of Computer Science, The University of Auckland, email: trebor@cs.auckland.ac.nz.

H. Baumeister et al. (Eds.): XP 2017, LNBIP 283, pp. 285–291, 2017.
DOI: 10.1007/978-3-319-57633-6_21

Knowledge management is an important aspect for agile team creativity, which can lead to improving the agile process [4]. By knowing how to manage knowledge, which is useful for team learning, agile teams would be able to reflect and find ways to improve the process [4]. While the daily stand-up and retrospective meetings are meant to be used to share knowledge and perform reflection, in practice what specific knowledge (e.g. contextual information, understanding, insight, experience), knowledge types (e.g. product, process and project) and knowledge management strategies help agile teams perform reflection are not well understood.

With the motivation to address these research problems of knowledge management and reflective practice in ASD, this paper contains some initial findings of our research, which include a concept of knowledge management in ASD and a reflection framework in retrospective meetings (Sect. 5). However, there are some issues that are still unclear on how to correlate these findings. We hope that the consortium can provide suggestions and feedback on:

1. The content and presentation of our preliminary theoretical models.
2. Best practice in cross-team comparison and analysis of data and combined presentation.
3. Recommendations on known or hypothesized relationship(s) between knowledge management and reflective practice.

2   Relevant Prior Work

2.1   Knowledge Management in ASD

Knowledge is the combination of content from more than one categories of information, which taken from documents, practices and norms [5]. Relevant prior research shows several classifications of knowledge management in ASD. Several reviews focus on knowledge management school classification [6] and knowledge management concept in ASD [7].

There are three categories of knowledge management [8] (i.e. technocratic, economic and behavioural) of which two of categories (technocratic and behavioural) are associated with ASD [6] and the third category (economic) is not related to ASD. The *technocratic* category emphasizes on explicating knowledge and its flows. The technocratic school is further subdivided into three schools: system, engineering and cartographic schools. The system school refers to knowledge management strategies that use technology, such as JIRA, Wiki and GitHub; the engineering school focuses on the business context of software processes; and the cartographic school focuses on experts in a team as a centre of knowledge for the team. The behavioral category is further subdivided into three schools: organizational, spatial and strategic schools. This school focuses on collaboration and communication as knowledge management strategies. Developing the network among teams and using office space to support team communication are included in the behavioural school.

Another research is about knowledge management concept map in ASD [7]. Yanzer et al. [7] present several concepts map, such as ways of communication, human and social factors, tools for knowledge management and knowledge representation forms. The human and social factor concept covers knowledge management adoption in agile projects. Other concepts, which include the ways of communication, tools for knowledge management and knowledge representation forms, focus more on techniques and tools to manage the discussion.

Specific explanation about knowledge classification in software engineering [9] is explained by Ebert & De Man [9], which classifies knowledge types into three types, such as product, project, and process knowledge. Product knowledge is the knowledge that consists of product features, which is related to other product features, protocols, products and standards. Project knowledge is the knowledge about project resources, such as work products, budget, milestones, team performance and targets achieved. Process knowledge is the knowledge about the workflow related to business process, supporting technologies and how teams integrate their work with others.

Referring to the aforementioned knowledge classification, this research intends to investigate the knowledge types (product, project and process knowledge) involved in ASD. By referring to these knowledge types, the explanation of knowledge involved in ASD would be more detailed and closely related with agile practices.

2.2 Reflective Practice in ASD

Most studies in the topic of reflective practice in ASD have only focused on how to perform retrospective meetings with the broad explanation on the reflective practice. One of the techniques introduced to be implemented in retrospective meeting is Post Iteration Workshop (PIW) [10]. PIW is performed in retrospective meeting by collecting obstacles and generating tasks and decisions. Postmortem review is another technique that is applied in retrospective meeting [11]. This review is useful to highlight five important issues during a two-week sprint that need to be focused on.

In addition, reflective practice is also explained in Babb et al. [12]. In their study, they investigate reflection in agile practices by introducing the Reflective Agile Learning Model (REALM). REALM classifies some agile practices based on Argyris and Schön's [13] classification, which embody reflection-in-action and reflection-on-action. Although reflection in each agile practice is captured in REALM, the specific knowledge used by agile teams to perform reflection has not been investigated.

To fill this gap, this research attempts to investigate what knowledge is managed by agile teams in performing reflection and how the reflection occurs in daily stand-up and retrospective meetings. By referring to Bain [14] about level of reflection (i.e. reporting, responding, relating, reasoning and reconstructing), the explanation about reflective practice in those practices would be more specific.

3   Research Objectives

This research attempts to answer the following research questions:

RQ1. What specific knowledge types (i.e. product, project and process knowledge) are involved in daily stand-up and retrospective meetings and how do agile teams manage that knowledge?

RQ2. What actual knowledge helps agile teams perform reflection and how agile teams use that knowledge for reflection in daily stand-up and retrospective meeting?

The aims of this research are to explore knowledge types based on three knowledge types (i.e. product, project and process), the strategies in managing that knowledge in daily stand-up and retrospective meetings for agile team's reflection.

4   Research Design

In order to answer the research questions, this research will apply Yin's case study research methodology [15], which is classified into three phases: (a) Define and design, (b) Collect, prepare and analyse (i.e. data), (c) Analyse (i.e. findings) and conclude. Figure 1 summarises the structure of Yin's case study and shows some phases in this research. The colours indicate the research progress. Green refers to the tasks that are "done", yellow indicates the tasks that are "in progress" and red refers to "to do" tasks. The current research focuses on phase b which is to analyse collected data (interviews and observations).

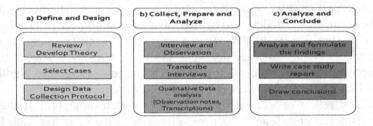

Fig. 1. Case study method [15] (Color figure online)

Firstly, in the define and design phase, a concept about knowledge management in ASD was generated through the Systematic Literature Review (SLR-'review/develop theory'). The next phase in the case study is to collect, prepare and analyze (phase b). Data collection was started by conducting interviews (individual and group) and meeting observations, which aims to gain specific explanation from the participants and understand the situation and actual knowledge managed in the meetings.

The next steps after observations and interviews are transcribing the interviews and analyzing them. The interviews transcripts were analyzed by using a qualitative data analysis technique called thematic analysis [16] by generating initial codes, searching for themes, defining and naming themes and finally producing the report that will be integrated on the next phase. Lastly, in the analyse and conclude (phase c), the analysis results of each team will be compared with those from other teams to formulate the findings and conclude the research. The results will be analysed comprehensively and followed by formulating the findings (phase c).

5   Current Research Progress

This research has two initial findings, which emerged knowledge management and reflection in daily stand-up and retrospective meeting. Initial findings were generated from SLR and case studies are described in the section below.

5.1   Initial Findings on Knowledge Management in ASD

A Systematic Literature Review was performed that reviewed 46 empirical studies focused on knowledge management in ASD selected from an initial pool of 2317 papers from reputed databases such as Springer, Scopus, and IEEE Xplore. Using a combination of thematic analysis [16] to analyse the primary studies and a Grounded Theory [17] approach to synthesise the results, it was discovered that:

1. Agile practices were found to be associated with the three types of software engineering knowledge proposed by Ebert & De Man [9]: timelines, team progress, and plans representing *project knowledge*; requirements and designs representing *product knowledge*; and coding techniques and synchronised teamwork representing *process knowledge*.
2. To manage the knowledge, agile teams use three specific knowledge management strategies: *discussions* (e.g. sharing requirements), *artefacts* (e.g. user stories) and *visualisations* (e.g. burn down charts).

A theoretical model was generated from the results (see Fig. 2), which explains that the three knowledge types are managed by performing agile practices and knowledge management strategies. This result was submitted currently under review.

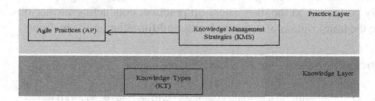

Fig. 2. A theoretical model of knowledge management in ASD

5.2   Initial Findings on Reflection in Agile Retrospective Meeting

A case study was conducted using data collected from interviews of sixteen software practitioners from four agile teams and observations of their retrospective meetings. Collected data was analyzed by applying thematic data analysis [16]. By transcribing data, generating codes, searching for themes, reviewing themes, defining and naming themes, the findings of this case study were formulated in the form of a paper, which has been accepted in XP 2017 conference ("Reflection in Agile Retrospective").

This case study aims to investigate what aspects are focused on during the retrospective meeting and how reflection occurs in the retrospective meeting. By applying thematic analysis to analyze the interviews, it was discovered that identifying and discussing *obstacles, discussing feelings, analyzing previous action points, identifying background reasons, identifying future action points and generating a plan* are important aspects involved in the retrospective meeting, which is useful for agile team reflection. These aspects are associated with five (grouped to three) levels of reflection from education [14]. The levels of reflection from education appear related to the answer of how reflection occurs in the retrospective meeting, which can be classified into three levels of reflection [14], *reporting and responding, relating and reasoning, and reconstructing*.

According to these findings, a reflection framework for agile retrospective meeting was presented on Fig. 3. The framework combines five steps of the standard agile retrospective – set the stage, gather data, generate insight and decide what to do, close the retrospective – and the levels of reflection – reporting and responding, relating and reasoning, and reconstructing [14] include the aspects involved on each step.

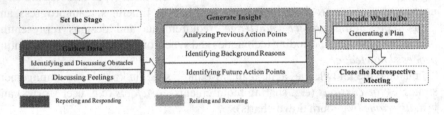

Fig. 3. A reflection framework for agile retrospective meeting

There are some research tasks remains, as can be seen in Fig. 1 (phase b and phase c), in which some tasks are in progress. Next steps include writing up the results of the case study pertaining to the daily stand-up practice, conducting further observations, analysing the transcription of software teams and formulating the findings.

References

1. Fowler, M., Highsmith, J.: The agile manifesto. Softw. Dev. **9**, 29 (2001)
2. Ringstad, M.A., Dingsøyr, T., Brede Moe, N.: Agile process improvement: diagnosis and planning to improve teamwork. In: O'Connor, R.V., Pries-Heje, J., Messnarz, R. (eds.) EuroSPI 2011. CCIS, vol. 172, pp. 167–178. Springer, Heidelberg (2011). doi: 10.1007/978-3-642-22206-1_15
3. Santos, V., Goldman, A., de Souza, C.R.B.: Fostering effective inter-team knowledge sharing in agile software development. Empirical Softw. Eng. **20**(4), 1–46 (2014)
4. Crawford, B., De La Barra, C.L., Soto, R., Misra, S., Monfroy, E.: Knowledge management and creativity practices in software engineering. In: Proceedings of the International Conference on Knowledge Management and Information Sharing, KMIS 2012, pp. 277–280 (2012)
5. Davenport, T.H., Prusak, L.: Working Knowledge-How Organizations Manage What They Know, vol. 5, pp. 193–211. Harvard Business School Press, Boston (1998)

6. Bjørnson, F.O., Dingsøyr, T.: Knowledge management in software engineering: a systematic review of studied concepts, findings and research methods used. Inf. Softw. Technol. **50**, 1055–1068 (2008)
7. Yanzer Cabral, A.R., Ribeiro, M.B., Noll, R.P.: Knowledge management in agile software projects: a systematic review. J. Inf. Knowl. Manage. **13**, 1450010 (2014)
8. Earl, M.: Knowledge management strategies: Toward a taxonomy. J. Manage. Inf. Syst. **18**(1), 215–233 (2001)
9. Ebert, C., De Man, J.: Effectively utilizing project, product and process knowledge. Inf. Softw. Technol. **50**(6), 579–594 (2008)
10. Cockburn, A., Highsmith, J.: Agile software development: the people factor. Computer **34**, 131–133 (2001)
11. Dingsöyr, T., Hanssen, G.: Extending agile methods: postmortem reviews as extended feedback. Adv. Learn. Softw. Organ. **2640**, 4–12 (2003)
12. Babb, J., Hoda, R., Nørbjerg, J.: Embedding reflection and learning into agile software development. IEEE Softw. **31**, 51–57 (2014)
13. Argyris, C., Schon, D.A.: Organisational Learning II: Theory, Method and Practice, Organisation Development Series. Adisson Wesley, Reading (1996)
14. Bain, J.D., Ballantyne, R., Packer, J., Mills, C.: Using journal writing to enhance student teachers' reflectivity during field experience placements. Teach. Teach.: Theo. Pract. **5**, 51–73 (1999)
15. Yin, R.K.: Case Study Research: Design and Methods, vol. 5, p. 11. Sage Publications, Inc, Thousand Oaks (2003)
16. Braun, V., Clarke, V.: Using thematic analysis in psychology. Qual. Res. Psychol. **3**, 77–101 (2006)
17. Glaser, B.G., Strauss, A.L.: The Discovery of Grounded Theory: Strategies for Qualitative Research. Aldine Pub. Co., Chicago (1967)

Self-Assignment: Task Allocation Practice in Agile Software Development

Zainab Masood[(✉)]

Department of Electrical and Computer Engineering, The University of Auckland, Building 903, 386 Khyber Pass, Newmarket Auckland, Auckland 1023, New Zealand
zmas690@aucklanduni.ac.nz

Abstract. Self-assignment is a self-directed way of task allocation commonly practiced by members of agile teams. However, not much is known about different aspects of self-assignment in literature. This research focuses on two objectives with respect to self-assignment. The first objective is to explore what strategies agile practitioners follow to self-assign tasks of different nature (i.e. new feature, enhancement, and bug-fix). The second objective is to identify the challenges associated with self-assignment and investigate how agile practitioners overcome these challenges to achieve project outcomes. Grounded theory is chosen as the research methodology for this study with data collection through interviewing agile practitioners and observing teams practicing self-assignment. Based on the results, we would propose a theory for self-assignment as a task allocation practice and a set of context-driven guidelines. Knowing the proposed theory and guidelines will help the agile practitioners and companies to make self-assignment a valuable practice in their settings.

1 Introduction

Agile development methodology emerged as an alternative to conventional, sequential and phase-based development. It follows an iterative and incremental approach to development and is open to changes throughout the project [1]. In contrast to traditional development processes, agile offers a different approach to managing the software development cycle. Agile software development constitutes a set of methods and practices based on twelve principles formulated in the Agile Manifesto [2]. The leading agile methodologies (Scrum, XP, Kanban) suggest different strategies and practices to ensure smooth development to achieve project outcomes.

An agile team is a cross-functional group of people who brings a different set of skills to the team. The essence to successful agile teams is their capability to self-organize accompanied by ownership. We find many contributions by researchers made

---

Supervisor: Dr. Rashina Hoda, The University of Auckland, email: r.hoda@auckland.ac.nz.
Co-Supervisor: Dr. Kelly Blincoe, The University of Auckland, email: k.blincoe@auckland.ac.nz.

H. Baumeister et al. (Eds.): XP 2017, LNBIP 283, pp. 292–297, 2017.
DOI: 10.1007/978-3-319-57633-6_22

exclusively on self-organization and self- organizing nature of the teams [3]. However, there is a dearth of research on how task allocation is done in self-organizing agile teams and what are the common practices followed by agile practitioners to achieve their goals.

Agile methodology uses self-assignment method for the allocation of tasks among team members [4]. However, we do not have enough studies and evidences regarding how software engineers tend to choose these tasks for themselves. There are certain factors that tend to motivate the engineers and developers to prioritize while self-assignment of tasks. During the process of self-assignment, they also have to face issues that need to be addressed for proper allocation and self-assignment. This study will be focusing on mainly these two aspects of self-assignment i.e. strategies and challenges for self-assignment in agile methodology. The contribution will be twofold. Firstly, it will add theoretical knowledge about self-assignment as a way of task allocation. Secondly, the results of this study will benefit developers and managers to overcome challenges during the process of task allocation.

2 Feedback or Areas Seeking Advice

At this time, we are seeking feedback and advice for the following things:

- What is the best way to compare findings from different sources and present overall findings in a way that data integrity is not compromised?
- Advice on reaching theoretical saturation for different task allocation strategies under different contexts.

3 Related Work

The success of a software development project depends heavily on the way the related project management activities are executed [5]. These activities primarily include managing the resources, organizing the software teams, allocating tasks to relevant stakeholders, monitoring time, budget, and resources [4]. These activities are carried out differently depending on the project management approach followed. In traditional software development, a project manager plays a key role in task allocation. The main duty of a project manager is to assign tasks to the project teams. This work is assigned keeping in mind the knowledge, skills, expertise, experience, proficiency and technical competence of the team member [6].

The benefits of agile methodologies include but are not limited to teams empowerment, collaborative atmosphere, shared decision-making and a transparency with a client [4, 7]. In addition, the concepts of 'light touch' management and self-organizing teams are the essence of agile teams [1]. These benefits have taken many software firms by a storm, as a result adopting many of these practices in their everyday project management activities including task allocation [4, 8]. This has affected the way the tasks allocation takes place in agile teams. Instead of manager directing or assisting the tasks, these teams are meant to practice picking up tasks or volunteering for tasks [7].

Self-directed task allocation or self-assignment is an attribute of agile teams [4, 8]. In theory, every member of the agile team is meant to assign a task or user story to themself [4]. This method of assigning tasks has also been observed in open source software (OSS) development in both commercial and non-commercial projects [9, 10]. Research on industry practices gives some evidence to support this method of task allocation but how this takes place is not very deeply investigated. For this reason, it is potentially a promising area for study leading to both academic and practical implications.

4   Research Basis

In this study, we intend to explore self-assignment of tasks in agile software development teams. The main research questions governing the research are:

RQ1: How agile practitioners practice self-assignment of tasks? What are the best strategies for self-assigning different types of tasks (new feature, enhancement, bug fixation) in agile software teams?

RQ2: What are the challenges associated with self-assignment of tasks? How agile practitioners overcome these challenges?

5   Research Plans

To answer RQ1 and RQ2, we will focus on how task allocation is played out in agile teams. In particular, this will center on the strategies that teams and individuals undergo in practice using different agile methodologies and for different projects including challenges associated with using these practices. We also plan to study self-assignment as task allocation in different scenarios and contexts and the study will not be limited to a single domain.

- Identifying strategies for tasks of different nature(New feature, Bug Fix, Enhancement)
- Classification of common strategies
- Strengths and weaknesses of the common strategies
- Identifying best strategies in their settings
- Factors affecting self-assignment of tasks
- Comparing self-assignment to alternative methods of task allocation
- Challenges faced with different strategies(threats to autonomy and cross-functionality, complexity and dependency dimensions)
- Identifying the areas of improvements with these strategies
- Evaluating the generated theory using GT guidelines
- Proposing a context-driven set of guidelines which agile practitioners may take into account while self-assigning tasks to get the best out of it.
- If time permits, evaluating the effectiveness of these guidelines through survey based feedback.

6 Research Method

We studied few research methodologies [13] and selected Grounded Theory (GT) for our study [11, 12, 14]. Grounded theory was developed in the early 1960's by Glaser and Strauss. It is chosen as the research methodology mainly due to listed reasons.

- Interest of the researcher towards generating theory explaining how self-assignment is practiced by agile practitioners
- GT is suitable for research areas which have not been explored thoroughly before.
- GT is extensively used for studying agile software teams, human and social aspects of software engineering, and many project management issues [3].
- GT *treats everything as data* giving researcher the freedom to use quantitative data, qualitative data, video, diagrams, and existing theories [14].

Initially, literature and related work are explored generally on identifying how and when tasks are allocated using traditional and non-traditional software methods for software projects. As recommended by Glaser, a minor literature review is conducted in the area of research [12] i.e. self-assignment as a practice of agile teams and individuals. Additionally, we went through articles describing grounded theory in other areas which helped to understand the research methodology and the emergence of the theory from the data [15–17].

As the research is mainly qualitative in nature, the intended data source is semi-structured interviews with agile practitioners of the relevant industry. In terms of data collection, we intend interviewing a total of 40–50 agile practitioners with team observations. But for some parts of the study e.g. factors affecting self-assignment, survey-based data collection will be pursued. Ongoing data analysis and synthesis procedures will be employed on collected data leading to findings of the research. In later stages, when the findings will be sufficiently developed latest and previous related literature will be reviewed again. We intend to assess the generated theory on the basis of four criteria: fit, work, relevance, and modifiability as recommended by Glaser [11].

The main components as adopted by some of the researchers are listed below [14]:

- Data Selection and Collection: Theoretical Sampling (Recruiting participants; Interviews; Observations; Surveys; Questionnaires);
- Data Analysis: Open Coding; Selective Coding; Theoretical Coding; Constant Comparison; Memoing; Sorting; Theoretical Saturation; Generating Theory

7 Validity Threats and Control

The most relevant validity threats to the research along with some checks to be taken to minimize them are given below.

- To reduce researcher bias, we intend to collect data from different sources interviews, observed meetings, and questionnaire. Such data triangulation will help us to generate more substantial data.

- Additionally, to collect multiple perspectives we plan to collect data from different contexts so that we do not limit this study to a particular setting, also we will be interviewing different roles belonging to variant sized organizations working on different software types.
- The supervisor and the co-supervisor, have strong expertise in empirical methods, especially GT and will keep a constant check to make sure that the researcher is not inclined to some side at some point during the study.

8 Current Status

- We have completed an initial round of literature review of related work on task allocation from a pool of papers published between 1990 to 2016 and gathered related work on task allocation generally in software projects and explicitly for agile projects.
- We have also explored some research methodologies to analyze and synthesize the data. After studying few research methodologies we decided to use grounded theory.
- Additionally, we conducted a pilot study to explore self-assignment in agile teams and investigated few aspects associated with it on a relatively small number of agile practitioners. During this study, we found self-assignment to be a potential area for further research as it has not been addressed extensively in the literature. The findings of this study are formulated and submitted to XP 2017 conference and accepted as a short paper ("Exploring Workflow Mechanisms and Task Allocation Strategies in Agile Software Teams") and the social aspects of the study are formulated, submitted to CHASE2017 and accepted as notes paper ("Motivation for Self-Assignment: Factors Agile Developers Consider").
- At present, we are collecting data. We have been successful in gaining some agile practitioner participants and continue to approach others.

References

1. Hoda, R., Noble, J., Marshall, S.: Agile project management. In: New Zealand Computer Science Research Student Conference, vol. 6, pp. 218–221 (2008)
2. Manifesto for agile software development (2001). http://agilemanifesto.org. Accessed 7 Jan 2017
3. Hoda, R., Noble, J., Marshall, S.: Developing a grounded theory to explain the practices of self-organizing Agile teams. Empirical Softw. Eng. 17(6), 609–639 (2012)
4. Hoda, R., Murugesan, L.K.: Multi-level agile project management challenges: a self-organizing team perspective. J. Syst. Softw. 117, 245–257 (2016)
5. Pinto, J.K., Slevin, D.P.: Critical success factors across the project life cycle. Proj. Manage. J. 19(3), 67–75 (1988)
6. Acuna, S.T., Juristo, N., Moreno, A.M.: Emphasizing human capabilities in software development. IEEE Softw. 23(2), 94–101 (2006)
7. Deemer, P., Benefield, G., Larman, C., Vodde, B.: A lightweight guide to the theory and practice of scrum. Version 2 (2012)
8. Hoda, R., Noble, J.: Becoming agile: a grounded theory of agile transitions in practice. In: IEEE International Conference on Software Engineering (ICSE 2017) (2017)

9. Crowston, K., Li, Q., Wei, K., Eseryel, U.Y., Howison, J.: Self-organization of teams for free/libre open source software development. Inf. Softw. Technol. **49**(6), 564–575 (2007)
10. Kalliamvakou, E., Damian, D., Blincoe, K., Singer, L., German, D.M.: Open source-style collaborative development practices in commercial projects using github. In: Proceedings of the 37th International Conference on Software Engineering, vol. 1, pp. 574–585. IEEE Press (2015)
11. Glaser, B.G.: Basics of Grounded Theory Analysis: Emergence vs. Forcing. Sociology Press, Mill Valley (1992)
12. Glaser, B.G.: Theoretical Sensitivity: Advances in the Methodology of Grounded Theory. Sociology Pr., Mill Valley (1978)
13. Myers, M.D.: Qualitative research in information systems. Manage. Inf. Syst. Q. **21**(2), 241–242 (1997)
14. Stol, K.J., Ralph, P., Fitzgerald, B.: Grounded theory in software engineering research: a critical review and guidelines. In: Proceedings of the 38th International Conference on Software Engineering, pp. 120–131. ACM (2016)
15. Hoda, R., Noble, J., Marshall, S.: Self-organizing roles on agile software development teams. IEEE Trans. Softw. Eng. **39**(3), 422–444 (2013)
16. Adolph, S., Kruchten, P., Hall, W.: Reconciling perspectives: a grounded theory of how people manage the process of software development. J. Syst. Softw. **85**(6), 1269–1286 (2012)
17. Stray, V., Sjøberg, D.I., Dybå, T.: The daily stand-up meeting: a grounded theory study. J. Syst. Softw. **114**, 101–124 (2016)

Software Development Practices Patterns

Herez Moise Kattan[✉] and Alfredo Goldman

Department of Computer Science, University of São Paulo (IME-USP),
São Paulo, Brazil
{herez,gold}@ime.usp.br

Abstract. Our ultimate goal is to propose a catalog with recommendations on how to organize the work of programmers. In this research we intend to provide experiments to explore the most suitable forms to allow programmers to develop software, either alone, in pair programming or in group. We also explore other approaches like code review. Our goal is not only to reduce the software development cost, but also to improve programmers life quality.

Keywords: Mob Programming · Swarming · Pair programming · Pair and review simultaneous in pairs · Code review · Coding Dojo

1 Introduction

The motivation of our research is to find better ways to organize the programmers work to develop quality software in a productive way suitable to their current context. Our goal is not only to reduce the software development cost, but also to improve the programming experience. Toward to do this a set of unanswered questions related on how many programmers should implement a task emerged:

- When Pair programming should be used?
- When it is interesting to perform Mob programming?
- What are the situations where it is better to do simultaneous work?
- What's the influence of the context and of the team?

2 Description of Points on Which We Would Like to Get the Most Advice on

We would like to have initial hints on when is better to use each one of the techniques and when alternating among them is a good idea. Our research is based upon the process of the Illuminated Arrow (see below).

© The Author(s) 2017
H. Baumeister et al. (Eds.): XP 2017, LNBIP 283, pp. 298–303, 2017.
DOI: 10.1007/978-3-319-57633-6_23

3   Relevant Prior Work

Herez [9] did an extensive work on when to apply pair programming on several teams. The main conclusions were that pair programming should be applied when the task being developed is more complex or when there is a large gap on the programmers experience. On other situations, other more light techniques like code review can be applied without any drawback.

More recently we started to study also the benefits of Mob Programming.

There are points of convergence in the literature about the advantages of the use of Mob Programming over other techniques [9–13]. On a first experiment we figured out that Mob Programming was not very useful when no one in the team knew the language/framework being used [10].

4   Research Objective

Elaborate a catalog with suggestions on how the programmers should organize their work concerning pair programming and related techniques.

5   Research Approach, Study Design and Arrangements

The interpretation made in an interpretive case study is frequently impossible to be auditing posteriorly and, is very difficult to conduct controlled experiments. For this reason, Kattan [2] suggests to conduct application examples to produce raw data. After, to analysis this data, is suggested the use of the Grounded Theory techniques, to looking for one auditable Theory to explain the findings [5].

There are no silver bullets [6], but maybe together we could build illuminated arrows that somehow inspire the correct path to innovators. Figure 1 show the phases of this research method, that reduces the gap between software developers and academic researchers and, thus, produce more ready to use knowledge. The Illuminated Arrow [2] proposed application examples to deepen impartially the initial work of an action research, supported by systematic and tertiary revisions [4].

In Software Engineering it is very difficult to conduct controlled experiments or make convincing Double Blind experiments [3]. Furthermore, human expertise and human subjectivity interfere with the result of experiments. The types of software are very different, each software is unique, it depends on the problem it solves, so is different from medical research, where every human being has blood, lung, heart, brain, etc [2].

The reason to start with an action research is to fix the initial mistakes of the research and to be sure about the benefits and limitations of it. If the result of the initial work, is considered positive, the next step suggest by the Illuminated Arrow is systematically review the literature, making it easier to audit.

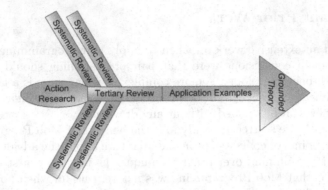

Fig. 1. Phases of illuminated arrow, starting from left and finishing in the right [2].

6 Action Research and Application Examples

The Empirical Study occurs twice. The first is in the beginning of the research as suggested by illuminated arrow, because start with an action research helps to deep the knowledge on this theme. Thus, makes easier the identification of some aspect possible to be improved and will guide the systematics reviews.

The second time, occurs after the literature review and is the empirical study by application examples. Thus, makes easier audits compared with interpretative case studies usely used. The applications examples will be careful design based at the literature reviews and action research.

These application examples will produce raw data about what we observe, toward to confirm and validated some aspects, provide new ideas and these raw data produced we hope that permit emerge one Theory in the way of one recommendation system to software developers about the better set of practices based on a specific context.

7 Data Analysis Methods and Techniques

The use of grounded theory is founded on the premise that the generation of theory at various levels is indispensable for a deep understanding of social phenomena [7,8]. The techniques of data analysis in grounded theory are:

– coding data (that comprises open, axial and selective):

  Open coding, to find categories;

  Axial coding, to find links between the themes/categories;

  Selective coding, to find the core category.

– memo writing;
– theoretical sampling.

8 Summary of the Current Status of the Research and Planned Next Steps

This proposal research is the continuation of Kattan [9] master's thesis. The technique is called Programming and review simultaneous in Pairs, is one extension to the pair programming. It's concluded when the goal is to reduce the time-to-benefit suggest use the Programming and review simultaneous in Pairs, when the pair is compose by professionals with the follows experience levels: intermediate and senior, or senior and senior, or junior and junior. The complexity of these tasks were classified as: low, medium and high.

Kattan reviewed the Mob Programming literature too in his master's dissertation and also applied Mob Programming in one application example.

Figure 2 illustrates the extension to pair programming, was used aspects of Simultaneous Engineering [9] to create one alternative to pair programming. The phases 1, 2, 3, 4, 5 and 6 are illustrated in Fig. 2. Phase 7 is illustrated in the form of the team with the work, because is the reflective rest and conflict resolution, is unformatted due to the miscellaneous possibilities for reflective/productive rest and conflict resolution.

The current status of the research and planned next steps are:

- We are conducting in companies experiments on Mob Programming, Programming and review simultaneous in Pairs, Pair Programming, Code Review and Coding Dojo [1].
- We are continuously reading the live science of this theme in literature in a frequently updating process.
- Beyond the use of questionnaire, we are analysing possible metrics [9].
- Based on feedback of international community we will rock the research and start the data collection.
- After conducting field studies, called here of application examples, we will analyse the data using Grounded Theory techniques.

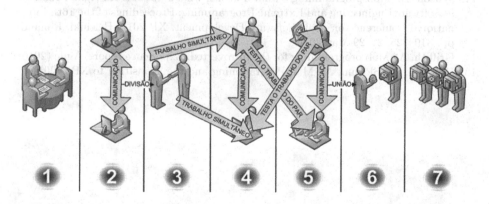

Fig. 2. Programming and review simultaneous in Pairs

References

1. Rooksby, J., Hunt, J., Wang, X.: The theory and practice of randori coding dojos. In: Agile Processes in Software Engineering and Extreme Programming: Proceedings of the 15th International Conference, XP 2014, Rome, Italy, vol. 179, pp. 251–259, 26–30 May 2014
2. Kattan, H.M.: Illuminated Arrow: a research method to software engineering based on action research, systematic review and grounded theory. In: CONTECSI - International Conference on Information Systems and Technology Management 2016, pp. 1971–1978, 21 July 2016
3. Budgen, D., Charters, S., Turner, M., Brereton, P., Kitchenham, B., Linkman, S.: Investigating the applicability of the evidence-based paradigm to software engineering. In: Proceedings of WISER Workshop, ICSE 2006, pp. 7–13. ACM Press, May 2006
4. Kitchenham, B., Charters, S., Budgen, D., Brereton, P., Turner, M., Linkman, S., JØrgensen, M., Mendes, E.: Guidelines for performing systematic literature reviews in software engineering, version 2.3. EBSE Technical Report EBSE-2007-01, Software Engineering Group, School of Computer Science and Mathematics, Keele University Keele, Staffs ST5 5BG, UK and Department of Computer Science, University of Durham, Durham, UK, 9 July 2007
5. Allan, G.: The legitimacy of grounded theory. In: Proceedings of Fifth European Conference on Business Research Methods, pp. 1–8 (2006)
6. Brooks, F.: The Mythical Man-Month: Essays on Software Engineering, 20th Anniversary Edition, 322 pages. Addison-Wesley, Reading (1995)
7. Glaser, E.G.: Advances in the Methodology of Grounded Theory: Theoretical Sensitivity. Sociology Press, Mill Valley (1978)
8. Glaser, E.G., Strauss, A.L.: The Discovery of Grounded Theory: Strategies for Qualitative Research (1967)
9. Kattan, H. M.: Programming and review simultaneous in Pairs: a pair programming extension. Master dissertation, Institute for Technological Research of the State of São Paulo (IPT) (2015). http://aleph.ipt.br/F or http://ipt.br, click on: Online Consultations, then click on: Library
10. Questionnaire. http://ccsl.ime.usp.br/wiki/SwarmQuestionnaire
11. Wilson, A.: Mob programming - what's works, what's doesn't. In: Agile Processes in Software Engineering and Extreme Programming: Proceedings of the 16th International Conference on Agile Software Development, XP 2015, Hclsinki, Finland, pp. 319–325, 25–29 May 2015
12. Griffith, A.: Mob programming for the introverted. Experience report, Agile (2016)
13. Hohman, M., Slocum, A.: Mob Programming and the Transition to XP (2001)

Author Index

Printed in the United States
By Bookmasters